Urban Food Planning

This highly original work examines the rise of the urban food planning movement in the Global North and provides insights into the new relationship between cities and food which has started developing over the past decade. It sheds light on cities as new spaces for food system innovation and on food as a tool for sustainable urban development. Drawing insights from the literature on sociotechnical transitions, the book presents examples of pioneering urban food planning endeavors from North America and Western Europe (especially the Netherlands and the UK). These are integrated into a single mosaic helping to uncover the conceptual, analytical, design, and organizational innovations emerging at the interface of food and urban policy and planning.

The author shows how promising "seeds of transition" to a shared urban food planning agenda are in the making, though the urban food planning niche as a whole still lacks the necessary maturity to lastingly influence mainstream planning practices and the dominant agrifood system regime. Some of the strategic levers to cope with the current instability and limitations of urban food planning and effectively transition it from a marginal novelty to a normalized domain of policy, research, and practice are systematically examined to this end. The conclusions and recommendations put forward have major implications for scholars, activists, and public officials seeking to radically transform the coevolution of food, cities, and the environment.

Rositsa T. Ilieva has a PhD in Spatial Planning and Urban Development and an MSc in Architecture from the Polytechnic University of Milan in Italy. Until 2015, she was a Post-Doctoral Research Fellow in Urban Food Systems at the Tishman Environment and Design Center (TEDC) of The New School, New York City, USA. At present, she is an adjunct lecturer at the Parsons School of Design and the Milano School of International Affairs, Management, and Urban Policy at the same university.

Routledge Studies in Food, Society and the Environment

For further details please visit the series page on the Routledge website:
http://www.routledge.com/books/series/RSFSE/

Urban Food Planning

Seeds of transition in the Global North

Rositsa T. Ilieva

Routledge
Taylor & Francis Group
LONDON AND NEW YORK

from Routledge

First published 2016
by Routledge
2 Park Square, Milton Park, Abingdon, Oxon OX14 4RN

and by Routledge
711 Third Avenue, New York, NY 10017

Routledge is an imprint of the Taylor & Francis Group, an informa business

British Library Cataloguing-in-Publication Data
A catalogue record for this book is available from the British Library

Library of Congress Cataloging-in-Publication Data
Names: Ilieva, Rositsa T., author.
Title: Urban food planning : seeds of transition in the Global North / Rositsa T. Ilieva.
Description: New York : Routledge, 2016. | Series: Routledge studies in food, society and the environment | Includes bibliographical references and index.
Identifiers: LCCN 2016015302 | ISBN 9781138998483 (hbk) | ISBN 9781315658650 (ebk)
Subjects: LCSH: Food supply—Developed countries. | Food security—Developed countries. | City planning—Developed countries.
Classification: LCC HD9000.5 .I446 2016 | DDC 338.1/91732—dc23
LC record available at https://lccn.loc.gov/2016015302

ISBN: 978-1-138-99848-3 (hbk)
ISBN: 978-1-315-65865-0 (ebk)

Typeset in Bembo
by Apex CoVantage, LLC

MIX
Paper from
responsible sources
FSC
www.fsc.org   FSC® C013604

Printed and bound by CPI Group (UK) Ltd, Croydon, CR0 4YY

To my father

'This book offers a systematic reflection on the relation between the emergence of new social practices linked to food and a traditional kind of institutional practice – urban planning. Analysing the growing interest for food and the innovative development of food policies in Europe and North America, Rositsa Ilieva shows how this can be a new lever for making planning more responsible and cities more sustainable and attractive.'

Alessandro Balducci, Professor of Planning and Urban Policies,
Politecnico di Milano, Italy, and former Alderman of City
Planning and Agriculture of the City of Milan, Italy

'This groundbreaking study traces the evolution of urban food planning from marginal to mainstream. It frames diverse food policies and plans as strategic innovations that not only address health, environmental, and social problems, but also position cities to drive broader food system change. It is an essential read for planning scholars and practitioners.'

Nevin Cohen, Associate Professor of Health/Urban
Food Policy, City University of New York, USA

Contents

Foreword

I still recall back in the 1990s having a chat on a sunny Amsterdam terrace with visiting professor Jerry Kaufmann from Madison, Wisconsin. Jerry, who was an expert in the field of planning ethics and my squash buddy, told me that he had embarked upon an exciting new research domain in planning – community food planning. He also informed me that he intended to investigate allotment gardens in the Netherlands. I was flabbergasted because not for a minute had I ever imagined that food could be a relevant topic in planning. We know now, Jerry was right. Food definitely is no longer a stranger to the field of urban and regional planning. Rather, it is acknowledged being a connective tissue in planning. According to Wayne Roberts, the former director of the Toronto Food Policy Council, food is a lever which opens hitherto unknown windows on solutions to issues such as food security, public health, environmental pollution, waste, social cohesion, biodiversity, soil degradation, preservation of agricultural land, keeping intact rural communities, urban storm water management, and the reduction of intraurban car traffic.

The work of Rositsa Ilieva represents a new surge in urban food planning research, a field of expertise which has developed into a full-fledged branch of planning. One important benchmark of emancipation of the field of urban food planning is the application of theories of social change, such as the theories of sociotechnical transition used in this book, to better understand the field's recent past and prospects for future evolution.

Food and planning are really close today. In the US, the number of food-related academic courses in planning is exploding, as is the number of scientific papers. In 2007, the American Planning Association published the first Policy Guide on Community and Regional Food Planning. In 2012, Growing Food Connections identified 299 local governments across the USA that are developing food policy programs. In Europe, the Sustainable Food Planning Group of the Association of European Planning Schools was established in 2009 and is now AESOP's most successful thematic group. Its annual sustainable food planning conference attracts over 200 scholars from all over Europe. The latest milestone is the 2015 Milano Food Charter signed by the mayors of more than a hundred global cities.

This book explores new practical and theoretical dimensions of the emerging field of urban food planning and urban agriculture. As such, it is part of a global transition towards a sustainable future.

Arnold van der Valk
Professor of Land Use Planning at Wageningen
University the Netherlands

Preface

This book is about urban food planning – one of the most dynamic and rapidly expanding city-driven global social movements. It is about an emergent field of theory and practice committed to the design of more equitable, healthy, and environmentally sound agrifood systems by transforming urban and periurban spaces and the social practices that constitute them in cities and metropolitan regions. While the boundaries of the field are still in the making, it is fair to say that it encompasses both efforts to facilitate alternative practices, like urban agriculture and shopping at farmers markets, and efforts to address anomalies in the mainstream food system, such as unequal access to fresh food retail, disproportionate urbanization of prime agricultural land and watersheds, wobbly disaster preparedness of food distribution and transportation networks, and poor or nonexistent organic waste recycling infrastructure.

The focus of the book is on experiences from the Global North, not because food planning innovations do not manifest in developing economies regions – in fact, they greatly do, but because the impact of rich cities on their local and global hinterlands is so extensive and, at the same time, so scarily well concealed, that every effort to address it offers a rare chance to break the myth that we are living in a benign and harmless cornucopia. Only by making visible and by appreciating the critical mass of city-regional food system innovations, taking place in our own backyards, can we debunk the delusion that food is working in the public interest and it is superfluous in urban development projects and sustainability strategies in wealthy states. The goal of integrating local food infrastructures in and around cities has been in urban planning's DNA since its inception, but for over a century it has remained suppressed for cultural, political, and economic reasons. There has hardly ever been a better time to restore it.

The idea for a monograph on the topic was born during my time as a postdoctoral research scholar at the Tishman Environment and Design Center at The New School university in New York City. Most of the seeds for this work and the impetus for researching this topic, however, grew out of my experience as a doctoral student in spatial planning and urban development at the Polytechnic University of Milan in Italy. Being trained as an architect and deeply interested in how objects, spaces, and societies coevolve across multiple scales and how micro-scale interventions can positively influence large-scale urban systems, by the time I embarked on doing my PhD research, the question of how these intricate interrelationships can be unmasked and used to dismantle entrenched unsustainabilities in cities had become central for me.

When I set to map the existing and potential interfaces between food systems and urban planning, I was expecting to focus much of my attention on planning strategies and policy tools geared toward farmland preservation and compact urban growth. Yet, much to my surprise, after reviewing recent scholarship on the topic, I came to the realization that the integration of food – not just agriculture, but food, from seed to table and waste management – as a field of practice in urban planning was already underway in some of the wealthiest countries on the planet, where the concealed inefficiencies of the current food system have become way too big to ignore.

Indeed, I gladly found that the literature on food and planning was already booming, which was a heartening news for a novice doctoral student, but also felt that few comprehensive texts portraying the state of the art of this emerging "movement" in planning existed. This made it hard for me to pinpoint the research areas where major advancements have been already made and where instead new research efforts had to focus the most. Thus, the challenge of creating a roadmap to navigate the amorphous realm of urban food planning novelties quickly became the primary concern of my research. While I did try to take a transversal approach to the exploration of the topic, I was far from the ambition of providing an exhaustive enumeration of all cases and possibilities. The field is extremely dynamic and novelties are continually born, remade, replicated, or disband. My chief intent thus was to take the pulse of urban food planning as an evolving practice *and* a domain of practices – from seeing the city through the food systems lens to crafting new strategies, policies, and alliances to use food as a means to sustainable urban development, while, at the same time, using the socioecological and political levers that cities have to transition the food system to sustainability.

To approach the complexity and mindboggling diversity of initiatives gravitating around the realms of urban food systems and urban planning, I used the conceptual lens of transition theories, which seemed to offer a promising tactic to focus on the coevolution of multiple endeavors and drivers rather than the workings of a single initiative. I tried however to use this lens not as a straitjacket but as an ancillary tool to shed light on an otherwise elusive web of interdependent innovations. While each chapter draws attention to a specific subset of novelties thematically demarcated as conceptual, analytical, design, and organizational, in reality, each contains insights into the elements and research questions defining the others.

I often felt compelled to use the plural pronoun "we," not to deceive the reader – the responsibility for all writing, propositions, interpretations, and possible omissions and impressions is entirely mine – but to underscore that, ultimately, normalizing urban food planning as a concept and as a practice can only happen if it becomes a truly collective endeavor, and if each small step we make to this end is cognizant of its place and potential contribution to the broader community of urban food planning pioneers. As a whole, I hope that the book can usefully expand the conversation about what urban food planning is and what it should become by providing budding food systems minded planners, architects, policymakers, and activists with a snapshot of its multiple achievements and, at the same time, a tool for productively navigating them.

Acknowledgments

This book is the outcome of over six years of doctoral and postdoctoral research during which I have been blessed with the opportunity to meet many of the outstanding frontrunners in the emerging field of urban food planning. The book owes also much to the numerous scholars and practitioners who bravely started charting this new terrain in urban planning research over two decades ago and from whose intuitions and discoveries this book has benefitted enormously. Unfortunately, I did not have the chance to meet in person the late Professor Jerome L. Kaufman – one of the "fathers" of the food systems planning movement in the US – but his work has been an incessant inspiration for my research and this book. The number of those who offered me their invaluable guidance, insights, constructive criticisms, friendship, and selfless support throughout this journey can hardly be overstated and I truly hope that this book is but the beginning of a much larger intellectual expedition in which we can continue to push the envelope of what is normal and possible at the interface of food and planning.

I am eternally grateful to Professor Nevin Cohen, widely known for his leadership in urban food policy scholarship in New York City and my mentor during my time as a postdoctoral research fellow at the Tishman Environment and Design Center (TEDC) at The New School. His academic rigor, innovative research, and contagious passion about the topic have been a stupendous stimulus for my work and central to the development of this manuscript since its early stages of development. Our common interest in the role of cities as drivers of food system innovations and the analytical lens of transition theories provided me with a rare and precious interlocutor and spurred many insightful conversations which significantly aided the maturation of the ideas I had previously investigated during my doctoral research. His impressive knowledge of the food policy milieu in New York City and in the US, as well as the course on urban food systems I had the privilege to teach with him, have been vital in sharpening my understanding of urban food planning innovations and the intricate ways in which they often come about.

I would also like to thank my colleagues and brilliant scholars and educators in environmental studies who made my new appointment at The New School feel like home: Alan McGowan, Timon McPhearson, Robert Buchanan, Zoé

Hamstead, Kristin Reynolds, Biko Koenig, Peleg Kremer, and Katinka Wijman. A big thank you also to Brandon Fischer and Van Lee who seamlessly tackled all administrative tasks during my time at TEDC and helped me with much of the paperwork that enabled me to present and discuss my research at international conferences and at public events at the university. I am extremely grateful also to Professor Fabio Parasecoli, Director of Food Studies Initiatives at the New School, whose guidance and advice have been instrumental to the development of the proposal for this book, the popularization of the concept of urban food planning at several expert panels at the university, and sparked the idea to create a related course.

The lion's share of the research in book owes to the many scholars I had the honor to work with and learn from throughout my doctoral studies at the Polytechnic University of Milan (Politecnico di Milano). First and foremost, I would like to thank Professor Alessandro Balducci, the adviser of my doctoral dissertation, for his vital guidance and support throughout the very early stages of conceiving and developing the research for this book. His mentorship and strategic advice in charting this new terrain in planning theory and practice have been fundamental. I would also like to thank Professor Andrea Calori from the Ecological Spatial Design Lab (LPE) of Politecnico di Milano and Director of Réseau International URGENCI and Professor Stefano Bocchi from the Department of Agricultural and Environmental Sciences, Production, Landscape and Agroenergy (DISAA) of Università degli Studi di Milano for their generous time, encouragement, and precious suggestions since the inception of the idea for this research and the many insightful discussions about urban foodsheds and urban rural linkages.

I am sincerely and heartily grateful to Professor Roberta Sonnino from the Department of City and Regional Planning of Cardiff University for having provided me with an exceptional guidance and mentorship during my visiting research period there, but also in many subsequent moments long after my departure from the UK. I owe sincere thankfulness also to Kevin Morgan for the many insightful comments, support, and advice he gave me during my stay in Cardiff and also in occasion of the several Sustainable Food Planning conferences of AESOP I had the chance to present my work at. I am extremely grateful also to the late Professor Judith Layzer from the Department of Urban Studies and Planning of MIT, whom a cruel illness removed from us in 2015, for having given me the unique opportunity to investigate the North American context of food systems planning research and practice in such a stimulating and inspiring research environment. Her guidance, thought-provoking questions, and encouragement to transform my dissertation into a book have been vital to say the least.

I am truly indebted and endlessly thankful to Professor Arnold van der Valk from the Land Use Planning Group of Wageningen University, who has been an extraordinary mentor during my period as a visiting scholar there and provided me with rare insights into urban food policy and planning in Amsterdam and the value of transition theories in exploring this rapidly evolving domain of practice. Without the many lively conversations, tireless field visits, and strategic connections to leading scholars and professionals advancing urban food planning research, projects, and policies in the Netherlands, some of the key findings of the book would not have emerged.

I would also like to extend my deepest thanks to all the participants at the seminar "Growing Food-Sensitive Cities for Tomorrow," which I organized at Politecnico di Milano to present an earlier version of this research, and who generously came along to help me with constructive advice and offer their own perspective on the topic: Philipp Stierand, Craig Verzone, Viviana Ferrario, Pietro Lembi, Luisa Pedrazzini, and Corinna Morandi. Your contributions have been truly important.

I am also endlessly thankful to the many professionals, experts, and government officials who generously offered their time for interviews and helped me collect relevant information, documents, and images on the cases included in the book and shared their impressions on the idea of urban food planning as a field of practice.

At Routledge, I am especially grateful to senior commissioning editor Tim Hardwick, who believed in the book project since its inception and saw in it a valuable contribution to the Routledge Series on Studies in Food, Society, and the Environment. I would also like to thank Ashley Wright, who provided me with her gracious guidance and advice during the development of the manuscript. It goes without saying that without you this book would have never been possible.

It is hard not to acknowledge my closest friends and colleagues at Politecnico di Milano, among them Michele Buizza, Sara Tommasi, Silvia Villa, and Davide Sironi; they greatly contributed to the initial steps that led to my fascination with food as a matter of sustainability design and, later on, of city planning. I am infinitely grateful for their friendship and leadership by example.

Last but not least, I owe a deep debt of gratitude to my family for their support and understanding and to my husband, Alessandro, for his invaluable encouragement, excitement, and skillful listening and support throughout the entire gestation of the book and its finalization. There are no words to describe my profound appreciation of his wholehearted understanding in all those occasions when my work on the manuscript intruded into our dinners, weekends, and vacations.

1   Why urban food planning?

> Feeding the city in a sustainable fashion . . . is one of the quintessential challenges of
> the twenty-first century and it will not be met without a greater political commit-
> ment to urban food planning and a bolder vision for the city.
>
> –Kevin Morgan, *Feeding the City*

Food is back on the urban policy agenda in the Global North. Local government leaders, legislators, political scientists, architects, and urban planners are
beginning to catch up with over two decades of community food security
activism and grassroots food system innovations. From Vancouver to Amsterdam and from London to Los Angeles, cities are testing the ground for purposefully driving food system transitions to sustainability. Applied research
and education in urban food systems has started germinating across multiple
disciplines, including those whose main focus for long has been the built environment. Thus, some scholars have suggested that food is no more entirely
extraneous to the work of urban policy experts and planners. But how to
construe this nascent interface between urban policy and food? What role
can urban planners and other urban professionals play in fostering sustainability through both globalized and autochthonous food system infrastructures?
What ideas, resources, skills, and partnerships need to be forged to normalize
this new domain of practice?

To demarcate the host of novelties germinating at the interface of food and
planning and other related disciplines, scholars have put forward new conceptual frameworks, such as urban food planning, community and regional food
systems planning, and sustainable food planning. While these have been vastly
successful in recognizing and giving a name to an important social movement
in the making, their breadth and diversity indicate that we are still in a phase
of identity searching, widening of worldviews, exploration, and discovery.
To make the most of this burgeoning phase of experimentation, in this book
it is argued that we need to adopt an evolutionary perspective. After briefly
presenting some of the markers of the growing sensitivity to food systems in
urban policy and planning, this chapter introduces theories of sociotechnical
transitions, which, throughout the rest of the book, will be deployed to piece

together seemingly isolated episodes of urban food planning into a shared mosaic of coevolving innovations.

Cities as drivers of food system transitions

Few of us may be aware of it as yet, but we are living at a time when, for the first time in history, the food system is shaping climate and not merely the other way around. It is one of the markers of what, at the beginning of the twenty-first century, scientists (e.g., Crutzen & Stoermer, 2000) begun to refer to as the "Anthropocene." Extensive deforestation, soaring meat consumption and livestock farming, and the disjoint urban metabolism of post-industrial cities (dumping or burning rather than reusing organic and other recyclable waste) have led, in concert with other anthropic agents, to an unprecedented concentration of greenhouse gases – like carbon dioxide and methane – in the atmosphere and to an impressive spike in fresh water consumption. Cities with their growing populations and globalizing palates have had their fair share in warming up the planet and, from what seems to be the urban-versus-rural population demographics trend for the forthcoming decades (United Nations, 2014), they are just getting started. The ever-shrinking rural population and declining number of farms in business point at an arrangement in which an agrifood system feeding billions is increasingly handled by the hands of few, but it also puts cities in an unprecedented position (Spaargaren et al., 2012) to change something, or just about everything, in that very system. One recent case in point is the boom in sales of organic produce, which, for instance, in the US grew by 83% between 2007 and 2012, and, as of 2014, amounted to $5.5 billion in revenues for US organic farms (USDA, 2015).

Cities are not only the locus of food shopping, consumption, and disposal practices; they are the places where detrimental consequences of the current agrifood system model are experienced by a sheer number of households and where people increasingly mobilize to voice their concerns about the most current, or at least the most visible, of food system flaws. Urban food planning scholars Kevin Morgan and Roberta Sonnino (2010) have termed this bundle of new food system pressures experienced in cities the "new food equation." Part of the equation are the 2007/2008 surge in food prices, the urban food riots which led to the first G8 food summit in 2009, the effects of climate change, land grabbing in Africa and Asia, rapid urbanization, and the obesity "epidemic" in industrialized nations. To these, it would be fair to add the poor geographic and economic access to healthy food options in underprivileged urban and rural communities and their disproportionate affliction by environmental injustices, like heavy food truck traffic and air pollution, to mention a few. As we are moving from the Millennium Development Goals (2000–2015) to the Sustainable Development Goals (2015–2030) crafted by the United Nations' 193 member states, a transition to a just and sustainable food system will continue to be a top priority, with the difference that the onus of taking action at home is now on Global North cities and governments as well.

The term "transition" in this book is used to refer to a profound structural transformation of a system vital to the existence and progress of society, like the food system, via disruptive or incremental changes of the material and nonmaterial components that keep it in place. Such transformation unfolds in a coevolutionary way, in the sense that change in the social and techno-logical dimensions of the system codetermine one another. In the food system domain, exemplary technological breakthroughs are the perennial irrigation system of early Mesopotamian civilizations, the invention of the heavy plough in the Middle Ages, and the twentieth-century "green revolution" marked by the extensive introduction of chemical fertilizers and pesticides in crop production – all novelties that were instrumental to the inception and expan-sion of cities. Examples of influential nonmaterial changes are the institution of the idea that cooking is an oppressive practice and puts women and men in an unequal position, which led to a flourishing market for ready-made meals and processed goods and related dietary and energy consumption anomalies; the dominant negative attitude toward misshapen fruits and vegetables deemed unworthy of selling and eating, which further increased the pile of unjustified food waste; and the urban craze for bottled water, now perceived as a safer and better-tasting option even in cities with excellent tap water.

Historically, the very role of cities in overseeing the food chain that nour-ishes them – from land through grain silos to table – has transitioned from direct control to almost complete delegation of control to the private sector. Since the advent of manmade food production and the formation of the first major centralized urban settlements, cities have indeed worked as command-and-control centers for their supportive food systems (Camagni, 2011). But as the transition of the Italian city of Naples from leaf-based to pasta diet in the seventeenth century shows (La Cecla, 1998), even by means of less direct practices like eating, cities can exert huge influence on their hinterlands; for Naples, the transition to pasta not only saved the population from starvation but led to an urban sprawl comparable to that unleashed by the advent of rail-way food transportation in industrializing London centuries later. In present times, the power of cities to drive food system transitions from the vantage point of consumption has been famously popularized by American journalist and food activist Michael Pollan (2008), exhorting urbanites to "vote with their fork." But, as urban food planners would concede, cities are more than loci of food consumption; as jurisdictions, cities can also influence the food system through the management of human activities in space and reshape local food infrastructures through land use plans, zoning ordinances, building codes, and related regulations.

To the skeptics, who might rightly point at corporate food retail giants or biotech companies literally redesigning food and agriculture today, urban planning powers may be a trifling matter. Yet, when considered in the aggre-gate, together with disruptive household and community practices in cities, they hold the potential to change priorities of higher tier of government and even agribusiness practices. Perhaps, most important, small-scale, city-driven "hacks" of the food system can help normalize the understanding that not all forms of food growing are incompatible with residential and other functional urban areas and not all food growing practices are about producing food per se. Social cohesion, physical and mental health, food literacy, and biodiversity are all important outcomes, which a more diversified urban food system infrastructure can usefully bring about. When considering the relation between cities and food, we tend to think about it as the sole matter of choosing the best way to feed cities and ignore the social, cultural, and environmental opportunities that systems unsuited for ensuring steady and abundant influx of food in cities can yield. If cities are to play a pivotal role in tackling the challenge of sustainable development, this mindset will need to change. The emergent realm of urban food planning is one domain of practices that opens up new spaces to do so.

The time is ripe

What the bulk of urban food system innovations manifesting in cities – across political, research, civic, and professional spheres of social life – goes to show is that the time to talk about urban food planning has come. Over the past decade, more than 90 local food systems strategies have been released by city and regional administrations in the Global North (Figure 1.1), more than 150 food-themed academic articles have been published in English-language architecture and urban planning journals (Figure 1.2), and the number of food policy councils has risen from less than a dozen to more than 280 in North America alone (Center for a Livable Future, 2015); dozens more are in the making across the UK, mainland Western Europe, and Australia. Most important, not only has the sustainability of the food system become a matter of concern for "fast food nations," but countries deemed the frontier of healthy eating and sustainable farming – like Italy, France, and Spain – now have their cities (e.g., Rome, Parma, Milan, Turin, Rennes, Zaragoza) seriously engaged in urban food policymaking. The "Milan Urban Food Policy Pact," signed by more than 100 cities after the closing of the Milan World Expo in October 2015, is one of the corollaries of the ongoing alignment of these globally emerging city-driven efforts.

Further evidence of the political saliency that food, from field to fork, has gained for mayors in the Global North is also the diversity of urban and sustainability planning documents in which it started to appear throughout the past 10 years or so. Stand-alone food system plans (e.g., London Food Strategy [2006], Proeftuin Amsterdam [2007], New York City FoodWorks [2010], Seattle Food Action Plan [2012]), comprehensive urban plans (e.g., The London Plan [2011], The Portland Plan [2012], the Toronto Official Plan [2015]), and thematic food sections in long-term sustainable development plans (e.g., Baltimore Sustainability Plan 2015, Greenest City Vancouver 2020, PlaNYC 2030, Chicago GO TO 2040, Philadelphia 2035) are some of the markers of the growing consideration of food as an urban and a sustainable development matter at the local level.

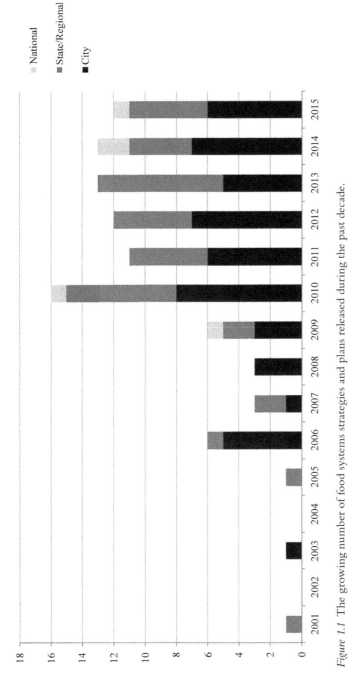

Figure 1.1 The growing number of food systems strategies and plans released during the past decade.

Source: Own elaboration based on bibliographic research conducted using a set of the principle electronic databases for academic records in the respective fields.

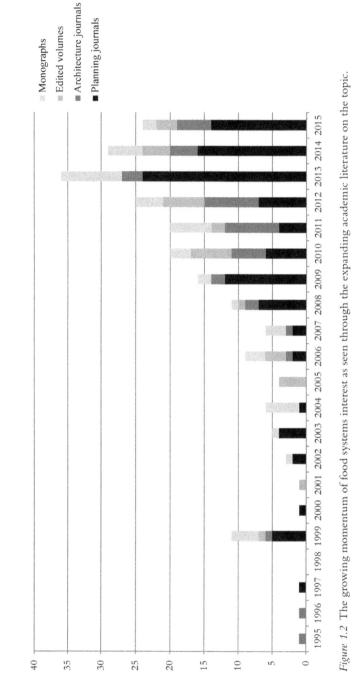

Figure 1.2 The growing momentum of food systems interest as seen through the expanding academic literature on the topic.

Source: Own elaboration based on publicly available documents.

Besides this new generation of food-sensitive urban policy documents, government grants to support the development of new city and regional food infrastructures – with the goal of improving citizens' health, small farmers' ability to stay in business, and cities' climate resilience – are also starting to be made available. Notable examples from the US include the US Department of Agriculture's (USDA) nearly $40 million grants funding available through programs like "Know Your Farmer, Know Your Food" (KYF) for the 2014–2015 fiscal year, the New York State Department of Agriculture and Market's $50 million plan to support environmentally sound farming practices and protect farmland in the Hudson Valley Region announced in 2015, and New York City's over $1.6 million investment for the period 2007–2013 in farmers markets infrastructure to accept federal food purchasing subsidies available for low-income New Yorkers. The nearly $1 million awarded to urban agriculture projects through New York City Department of Environmental Protection's (DEP) 2011 Green Infrastructure Grant Program is one additional example of new forms of municipal support to alternative food spaces and practices in the city.

In addition, over the past decade, nongovernmental organizations have been increasingly advocating for the institutionalization of food systems planning as a formal responsibility of local government and the creation of statutory spaces for long-term capacity building and cross-sectoral collaboration. While the overall number of food policy councils has substantially increased, there is still a great imbalance between those sited inside government agencies, still a tiny fraction, and those working as independent research and advisory bodies. The development of second-order coalitions, such as the Sustainable Food Cities Network (2011) in the UK, bringing together cities that have devised or are in the process of devising a local food system strategy, and the Food Policy Task Force (2012) of the US Conference of Mayors, a nonprofit nonpartisan organization enabling cities to join forces to tackle common policy problems and lobby for higher-tier government assistance, are two instances of alternative ways that cities have been pursuing to build up political leverage, exchange knowledge, and gain credibility in strategizing for food system solutions in the public domain.

As both government officials and civil society leaders are becoming increasingly aware of the power of incumbent land use, building regulations, and land tenure arrangements to facilitate or thwart local food infrastructure projects – from community gardens to fresh food outlets and regional food hubs – the question of how to integrate a food systems perspective into city and regional planning practices has come to the fore of their attention. One indicative example of this is the turn to planning of "Sustain" – a leading UK-based NGO for sustainable food – which, in 2011, with the support of the Royal Town Planning Institute (RTPI), organized a precedent-setting conference entitled "Food and Spatial Planning: How Planning Can Support a Healthy and Sustainable Food System" at the University College London. Since 2004, the organization has been actively committed to the development of advisory reports outlining practical ways in which city planners can use their competencies to advance just and sustainable community food system goals. Among these are "Food and Planning: How London's Planners Can Improve Access to Healthy and Sustainable Food" (2004), "Good Planning for Good Food" (2011), and "Planning Sustainable Cities for Community Food Growing" (2014).

On the other side of the Atlantic, the importance of taking planners on board has also been progressively acknowledged by nongovernmental groups, including specialist urban planning organizations. The American Planning Association (APA), which is the lead organization of professional planners in the US, has released several detailed guidelines highlighting why and how planners can tangibly contribute to the improvement of community and regional food systems. Some of these are the "Policy Guide on Community and Regional Food Planning" (2007), the reports "A Planners Guide to Community and Regional Food Planning" (Raja, Born, & Kozlowski Russell, 2008) and "Urban Agriculture: Growing Healthy, Sustainable Places" (Hodgson, Campbell, & Bailkey, 2011), and the briefing paper on Food Policy Councils (DiLisio & Hodgson, 2011). Documents like these have been essential in providing the building blocks for urban food planning as a distinct statutory practice and clarifying its relation to established planning competencies and routines.

The inception of new working collectives like the Food Systems Planning Steering Committee of APA in 2004, renamed Food Interest Group (FIG) in 2009, and the Sustainable Food Planning Group established within the Association of European Schools of Planning (AESOP) in 2009 – the alter ego of the US Association of Collegiate Schools of Planning (ACSP) – has also marked an important milestone in the recognition of this budding field of research and practice. Being constituted by members of different European countries and scholars of a variety of disciplinary backgrounds, the AESOP food planning group has not embarked on developing any specific guidelines for urban planners as yet.

Nevertheless, the seminal book *Sustainable Food Planning: Evolving Theory and Practice* (Viljoen & Wiskerke, 2012), developed through a collaborative effort between many of the members of the group, has provided a substantial contribution to the popularization of the concept of urban food planning and to the consolidation of an international network of scholars and practitioners eager to advance it. The edited volume comprised more than 40 different contributions, which not only uncovered the great scholarly interest in policy and design strategies for transitioning the urban food system to sustainability, but also the merits of the successful organization of several annual conferences on the topic by the group.

One could tell that the clock of urban food planning has started ticking also by the sheer number of special issues of planning journals (e.g., *Progressive Planning* in 2004, *Journal of Planning Education and Research* in 2004, *International Planning Studies* in 2009 and 2013), master's theses (e.g., Bobbio, 2009; Blum-Evitts, 2009; Morris, 2009; Shumate, 2012; Richardson, 2010; Bidiuc, 2015) and doctoral dissertations (e.g., Mendes, 2006; Schiff, 2007; Stierand, 2008; Ilieva, 2013), research grants (e.g., the "Growing Food Connections" project awarded a $3.96 million grant by USDA in 2013; the "Food Urbanism Initiative" awarded a grant from the Swiss National Science Foundation in 2010; the "Food-Sensitive Planning and Urban Design" awarded a grant by the National Heart Foundation of Australia and VicHealth in 2010; and the "Urban Agriculture Europe" collaborative project awarded a grant by the European Cooperation Network in Science and Technology in 2011), and new university courses (e.g., "Food Systems Planning" at the University of Michigan, Cornell University, University at Buffalo, and New York University; "Planning for Global and Local Food Systems" at the City University of New York; "Urban Planning and the Food System" at the University of Washington; "Community Food Systems" at Simon Fraser University; and "Foodscapes, Urban Lifestyles and Transition" at Wageningen University).

Finally, the time to take stock of the decade-long experimentation in policy, research, and pedagogy in urban food planning is also ripe for the growing number of private architecture and planning firms beginning to offer community and regional food system assessment, design, and construction services. Some examples of these creative firms in the US are Duany Plater-Zyberk & Company, involved in the development of agrarian urbanism projects, Agriburbia LCC (formerly the TSR Group), versed in the integration of intensive agriculture across a wide range of scales from single plots to entire new development schemes, and artist and designer Fritz Haeg, who has been using his expertise in edible landscaping to convert front lawns and rooftops into vegetable gardens on private properties around the world. European architecture and urban design ateliers, like Bohn and Viljoen Architects in the UK and MVRDV in the Netherlands, have also built a robust portfolio in the research and development of local food systems projects, particularly urban agriculture designs, over the last 10 years. An example of a company focused exclusively on the provision of food systems planning services – such as the development of food strategies and policies, farm parks, neighborhood designs, and local food economy assessments – is Urban Food Strategies, which is a Canadian firm recently established by urban planner and agricultural urbanism scholar Janine de la Salle.

The list of urban food planning novelties in each domain is getting longer as this book is being written, and none of the accounts presented above had the aim to be exhaustive. Rather, these offered fragments of emergent government, scholarly, and business practices that served to sketch the backdrop against which the state of the art of urban food planning will be examined throughout the rest of the book. Taken together, they provided a glimpse into the growing momentum of political, professional, and civic enthusiasm about community and regional food systems and provided the inspiration for this book in the first place. In the next chapters, we will return to most of the cases, here only mentioned in the passing, and delve into their specific contributions to the advancement of the urban food planning "movement" (Morgan, 2009; 2013) in the Global North.

An evolutionary perspective

If at the turn of the twenty-first century pioneer food system planners Kameshwari Pothukuchi and the late Jerome L. Kaufman (2000) resolved that the food system was a "stranger" to the urban planning field, 15 years later this no longer seems to be the case. A small but rapidly expanding community of food-system-minded urban planners already exists; they are developing food systems planning guidelines to change the profession, embarking on primary research, designing new university courses to educate the future generation of planners, organizing international conferences, and even setting up new businesses to grow the opportunities for making a real-world impact. Yet, we are still far from a reality in which the food system is an integral part of the formal administrative processes and daily responsibilities of planners in city planning departments, let alone a cross-departmental endeavor (Figure 1.3). Not that cities have not been using their planning powers and competencies to remove barriers for emergent bottom-up initiatives and facilitate the development of new ones, as we will see, they have. It is just that they have hitherto done so in a piecemeal and ad hoc fashion and more as an exception to the rule than as a result of a change in how things are habitually done.

To transition to a planning system whereby urban food planning knowledge is systemically embedded in planning education, research, and practice, we need to inform ongoing and future food systems planning efforts through

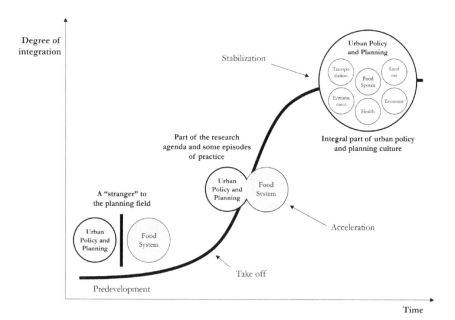

Figure 1.3 The phases of transition toward a food-sensitive urban policy and planning.
Source: The author.

the lessons that this first wave of experiences can teach us. Looking back may seem to slow us down, but it is an essential tactic to move forward better and faster. It would enable us to identify key areas where the contribution of newly enlisted food planners is most needed and to uncover new opportunities to plan for sustainable communities through the lens of food, as well as plan for a more just and sustainable food system through city planning. To make the most of the repository of past and emergent food planning practices, we need a synoptic view that can help us get a sense of how far we have gotten from the 1990s, when only a handful of planners were pointing at the food system as an embarrassing omission in the domain of community and regional planning, and to inquire about how we got here. What worked, what did not work, and why? In short, an evolutionary perspective can help us make sense of what kind of practice urban food planning has evolved into so far and what it would take to stabilize and normalize it in the future. This book is an attempt to approach the development of such perspective.

Theories of sociotechnical transition

One way to appreciate the past decade of budding urban food planning epi-sodes and their promises, flaws, and limitations through an evolutionary per-spective is offered by so-called theories of sociotechnical transition, commonly referred to as transition theories. Transition theories stem from the fields of sci-ence and technology studies and evolutionary economics and were originally used as an explanatory framework in the study of historical instances of radical social and technological change. Frequently recalled examples of past socio-technical transitions in literature are shifts in transportation technology (e.g., from horse-drawn carriages to motor cars, from sailing ships to steamships, see Geels, 2002), information technologies (e.g., from industrial to personal computers, see van den Ende and Kemp, 1999), and urban infrastructure (e.g., from wells to piped water), but also markedly cultural phenomena (e.g., the rise of rock 'n roll as musical genre and recording industry, see Geels, 2006). More recently, in the context of incumbent environmental sustainability chal-lenges, transition scholars have begun to theorize future-oriented conceptual models, like strategic niche management (Kemp, Schot, & Hoogma, 1998; Schot & Geels, 2008), transition management (Rotmans, Kemp, & van Asselt, 2001; Loorbach, 2010), and conceptual niche management (Monaghan, 2009) to help governments purposefully steer transitions to sustainability. Today, sustainability transitions studies are the fastest-growing strand in transition theories literature (Markard, Raven, & Truffer, 2010), and an offshoot, focus-ing specifically on urban transitions, is taking shape (e.g., Bulkeley et al., 2011; Hodson & Marvin, 2010; Bulkeley, Castan Broto, & Maassen, 2014).

However radical, not all sociotechnical transitions entail the complete replacement of existing social practices and technologies; some just add to the options people already have to achieve their daily goals (e.g., to make a phone call we can use a landline telephone, a mobile phone, or a computer with Internet connection). Urban food planning is overwhelmingly about this second kind of sociotechnical transition, whereby the dominant globalized food system is reconfigured rather than entirely replaced by short, fair, and environmentally sound food supply networks. The same goes for the planning domain – urban food planning is not about a wholesale replacement of existing city and regional planning practices, but augmenting them, thereby increasing their effectiveness and even justification (for the "re-justification challenge" of city planning see Sanyal, 2000). The question of whether it is better to transition to a designated department for urban food systems planning or to invest in integrating food systems planning responsibilities across existing sector-specific planning departments, like transportation, housing, economic development, parks, and environmental protection, is a moot point, but the overarching goal of reconfiguring the existing planning system stays the same.

The analytical value of transition theories, compared to frameworks of diffusion of technology and innovation that predate them (e.g., Mansfield 1961; Rogers, 1962), is the emphasis, at least in theory, on transitions as the outcome of the coevolution between changes in social institutions, practices, technologies, and infrastructures, therefore not merely the byproduct of scientific discoveries or the marketing of new objects. This is significant for food system transitions research because, to understand the mechanisms of food system transitions, one needs to appreciate food both as a product and as a multiscale cross-sectoral process. In fact, the transition of the agrifood system to sustainability greatly depends on our ability to grasp it simultaneously as an industrial commodity, an ecological component, and a social construct. Sociotechnical transition theories offer a promising pathway to this end, although scholars caution that they do exhibit some limitations, such as a geographical naïveté (Truffer & Coenen, 2012; Coenen, Benneworth, & Truffer, 2012), poor recognition of scale (Raven, Schot, & Berkhout, 2012), and benign neglect of mundane social practices carried out by nonexpert consumers in everyday life (Shove, 2004). The same scholars, however, have also pointed at possible extensions of the theories and demonstrated that their limitations are not insurmountable.

Urban food planning research requires a concerted intellectual effort by both local food systems and urban studies scholars. Importantly, leading analysts from both fields have recently pleaded in favor of transition theories as a lens through which to advance new knowledge and inform political action. In her presidential address to the readers of the *Agriculture and Human Values* journal – where some of the earliest contributions in the domain of food systems planning were published (e.g., Pothukuchi & Kaufman, 1999) – local food systems scholar and then editor in chief Claire Hinrichs (2014) invited fellow scientists and the journal's community of readers to consider transition theories as a theoretical framework in their research. The same year, in a special issue of *Urban Studies* (Rutherford & Coutard, 2014) on urban energy transitions, urban systems scholars Harriet Bulkeley, Vanesa Castán Broto, and Anne Maassen urged sustainability and urban researchers to consider the role of cities in engendering sociotechnical transitions. Now is the time to fill a further conceptual gap, consider these two lines of research in tandem, and delve into the questions of what role cities can play in food system transitions and how urban food system innovations can bring about more sustainable cities.

The multilevel perspective on transitions

To inquire the state of evolution of the emergent domain of urban food planning through the lens of transition theories, we need to adhere to a particular set of theses about how sociotechnical innovations unfold and to espouse a certain kind of taxonomy of the variables in play. One of the most popular conceptual perspectives on how transitions come about is the multilevel perspective (MLP) (Figure 1.4), whereby sociotechnical transitions result from

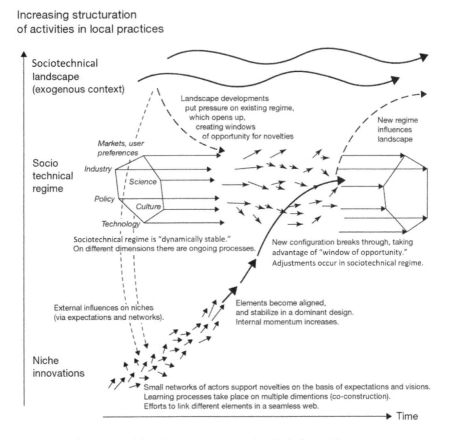

Figure 1.4 A dynamic multilevel perspective on sociotechnical transitions.

Source: Geels (2011).

the interplay of incumbent *landscape* pressures that are impossible to handle by local actors alone (e.g., global warming, peak oil, obesity), disruptive *niches* of innovation (e.g., renewable energy technologies, bike sharing programs, guerrilla gardens), and dominant sociotechnical *regimes* (e.g., transportation, energy, water, agriculture), which, at the same time, deem landscape pressures a priority issue and are farsighted enough to support experimental niche innovations aiming to tackle the issue at stake.

Niches are best defined as "incubation rooms" (Kemp, Schot, & Hoogma, 1998) for emergent innovations that develop out of the networking of isolated novelties (Knickel et al., 2009) or "seeds of transition." The latter are wobbly but "hopeful monstrosities" (Mokyr, 1990 as cited in Geels, 2002) in need of temporary protection (Smith & Raven, 2012) from dominant regimes to properly develop; niches offer them that protection. Regimes, in turn, are the "grammar or rule set . . . embedded in institutions and infrastructures" (Rip & Kemp, 1998) that keep sociotechnical systems stable and in place. The material infrastructure or service *and* the bundle of different social groups (e.g., manufacturers, regulators, intermediaries, sponsors, researchers, end users) collaborating to ensure its provision make up together the sociotechnical system (Geels, 2007). Finally, landscapes are deeply entrenched cultural, political, economic, and geographic phenomena, which are extremely resistant to change, take many generations to form and thus are out of the reach of single individuals or governments (e.g., one cannot change the overall layout of a city or road network overnight); that is, unless they commit to a long-term transformation effort and consistently sustain it across multiple generations (e.g., in the Netherlands, land reclamation from the sea has been carried out since Roman times).

The change of the landscape level of today's carbon-intensive sociotechnical systems is what planning for sustainable development essentially aims at. The landscape pressures of climate change and depletion of fossil fuels may now seem exogenous to these systems, but they are the outcome of their multiyear operation. In fact, one should pay attention to not conflate the three abstract levels – niches, regime, and landscape – of the MLP with geographical scales; they are not. The nested layers of the MLP, which together make up the sociotechnical system, are purely conceptual and help demarcate sociotechnical subsets of different stability and propensity to radical innovation in the system. As Grin (2010) underscores, the three layers also indicate different sources of power for niche, regime, and landscape assemblages of individuals and material objects: niches are the sites where *relational powers* (i.e., ability to network and collaborate) are pivotal, regimes stay in place thanks to their *dispositional powers* (i.e., ability to impose rules of conduct system-wide), and landscapes endure thanks to their *structural powers* (i.e., the ability to shape the physical and ideological environment of multiple generations of sociotechnical regimes).

Transitions unfold in an evolutionary fashion through the progressive coevolution of niche, regime, and landscape level changes. Sociotechnical regimes

in transition, thus, undergo different evolutionary phases along their transformation. In their seminal paper on transition management in public policy,
Rotmans, Kemp, and van Asselt (2001) refer to four major phases of transition,
which can be briefly summarized as a *predevelopment phase*, whereby niches are
still in the making and largely unnoticed by the incumbent regime; a *take-off
phase*, in which actors begin to mobilize around a promising idea or dominant
design and the system begins to change on the margins; a *breakthrough* or *acceleration phase*, when visible structural changes occur thanks to the accumulation of a critical mass of interdependent sociocultural, economic, ecological,
and institutional changes; and a *stabilization phase*, in which the pace of social
change slows down and a new point of temporary dynamic equilibrium is
reached. The shift from one phase to another requires the synchronous alignment of changes at all three levels of system stability – niche, regime, and
landscape (Geels, 2007).

Urban food planning as a niche for social innovation

Observed through this evolutionary lens, urban food planning can be viewed
as a "niche" innovation in the making, able to transform the role of cities and
urban planning in agrifood system change. While niches have typically been
examined in relation to the development of new technological artifacts (e.g.,
computers, cars, steam ships) or infrastructures (e.g., sewages, electricity grids,
bike lanes), transition scholars examining emergent novelties in the urban food
system (Smith, 2006, 2007; Seyfang & Smith, 2007; Hargreaves, Longhurst, &
Seyfang, 2013; Kirwan et al., 2013) and community-based solutions to low-
carbon development more broadly (Bulkeley et al., 2011; Seyfang & Haxeltine,
2012; Hielscher, Seyfang, & Smith, 2013) have called attention to the need to
consider also "social niches" or "grassroots social innovations" in transitions.
Unlike technological niches, which usually develop to target a concrete window of opportunity in the mainstream market, social niches emerge organically
(Bulkeley et al., 2014) and are driven by goals of social and cultural change
rather than mere economic growth (Kirwan et al., 2013, p. 831). Social niche
innovations thus largely pertain to the domain of "new economics" (Boyle and
Simms, 2009; Seyfang, 2009; Gibson-Graham, Cameron, & Healy, 2013).

Being a de facto social innovation (Mulgan et al., 2007), a social niche
develops through the inception of novel social practices, by way of new beliefs,
conventions, and understandings of normality, and results in the creation of
new forms of social organization to solve local inefficiencies or injustices of the
dominant sociotechnical regime. The inception of a social niche has immediate effects on those involved – ideally, satisfying their unmet needs (e.g., lack of
access to healthy food, lack of quality recreational spaces, inability to purchase
basic goods and services), providing them with greater opportunities to partake in problem-solving processes (e.g., through collaborative decision-making
and implementation schemes) and improving their access to strategic resources
(e.g., knowledge, skills, financial means, tools, partnerships) (Moulaert et al.,

2005). The emergent research and practice agenda of food systems planning (APA, 2007, Raja, Born, & Kozlowski Russell, 2008) – asking planners to assess community needs, engage community members in plan-making processes, develop city and regional policies to effectively meet community needs, and forge new partnerships between stakeholders in the system to successfully translate such policies into action – therefore greatly aligns with the overarching goals of social innovation.

As a result, urban food planning is a "hybrid" social niche, encompassing the creative – conceptual, analytical, design, and organizational – responses that urban planners and other expert and community-based social groups in the city have come up with in addressing the fundamental questions of: What is the problem? Why should we care? Who is in charge? How do we solve it? (Figure 1.5). It is, therefore, both a single practice and a bundle of different

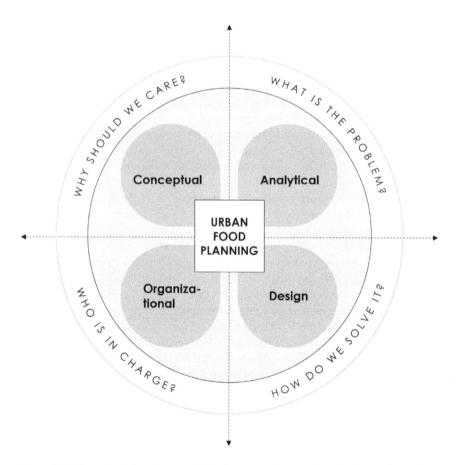

Figure 1.5 Urban food planning as a field of conceptual, analytical, design, and organizational practices.

Source: The author.

practices (e.g., neighborhood food system mapping, design of community gardens and rooftop farms, vacant lots mapping, soil quality mapping, conversion of vacant lots in vegetable gardens, food access assessments, regional foodshed analyses, and many more). Local government provisions, such as zoning and financial incentives for fresh food stores, bans of fast food outlets from school districts, removal of building code barriers for rooftop greenhouses, or reducing restrictions for onsite processing and selling of produce, are also part of the bundle. Thus, differently from other bundled social niches, like the UK-based Transition Towns movement for instance (Seyfang & Haxeltine, 2012), urban food planning novelties stretch beyond the circles of citizens groups and community advocates alone.

Notwithstanding its expert strands, when considered vis-à-vis the dominant sociotechnical regime (that is, the agrifood system), urban food planning still classifies as a grassroots innovation for sustainable development (Seyfang & Smith, 2007). It is city-driven and place-based, hence, evolving at the margins of the mainstream food system and the decision-making processes that govern it. And, it is a distinctly social innovation whereby government planners, architects, designers, researchers, and activists step out of their daily routines and the traditional remits of their professions to engage with food system goals. Truth be told, urban planners have always had a social heart alongside their civil engineering beginnings. As renowned urban planning scholar Klaus R. Kunzmann (2011) puts it, urban planning is essentially about "caring for people in the city," while other prominent planning theorists (e.g., Geddes, 1915; Doglio, 1953) have importantly argued that the purpose of the urban plan is not to provide a technical blueprint, but a canvas for collective social action.

Lastly, if we are to inquire the state of development of urban food planning as an emerging niche for social innovation, two key questions are warranted – what makes a niche innovation successful and how are emerging urban food planning novelties doing compared to such criteria? Strategic niche management (SNM) (Kemp, Schot, & Hoogma, 1998; Schot & Geels, 2008), which is one of the future-oriented conceptual frameworks transition scholars have developed to inform the purposeful design of sociotechnical transitions, offers several useful directions to this end. The ability of niche practitioners to formulate realistic *expectations*, create deep and diverse *social networks* of support, and engage in the generation of new knowledge and second-order *learning* (i.e., change deep-seated cognitive frameworks and ideologies) are three basic prerequisites for budding niches to endure and affect sociotechnical regimes. In his analysis of transitions to renewable energy resources in the Dutch electricity regime, Raven (2006) calls attention also to the importance of the relationship between niches and regimes. Considering their reciprocal stability, he lays out four possible niche-regime scenarios: a *dead-end street* scenario of unstable niches in a stable regime; a *missed opportunities* scenario of unstable niches in an unstable regime; a *problem solver* scenario of stable niches in an unstable regime; and a *promising technology* scenario of stable niches in a stable regime. This ancillary framework usefully bridges the comprehensive multilevel perspective of niches, regimes, and landscape with the strategic niche management approach focused on the internal qualities that make niches succeed or perish.

Throughout the book, we will test the extent to which these theoretical lenses can help us navigate the emergent realm of urban food planning and its "seeds of transition" and identify useful ways to stabilize it as a niche for sustainable development. A more robust bundle of urban food planning practices has the potential to provide a "bolder vision for the city" (Morgan, 2009) and transition urban food planning from an unstable niche in the making to promising social innovation in the position to challenge incumbent planning and food system regimes. Strategic levers for change include opportunities to strengthen present endeavors to represent, understand, and transform the urban food system, as well as to legitimize city-level interventions in the public domain, but also to question its current assumptions and ideologies. As we cruise from one domain of novelties to another, we will have to prudently remember that there is nothing inherently good in a new practice per se as there is nothing inherently sustainable in the scale at which practices are carried out (Born & Purcell, 2006), yet both new ideas and local actions are fundamental in imagining and enacting societal transitions.

Structure of the book

The remaining part of the book is broadly organized in four thematic parts. Chapters 2 and 3 shed light on some of the most compelling arguments that planners, since the inception of the profession in the early twentieth century, have made for the integration of local food infrastructures in the design and development of modern cities. Chapter 3 in particular examines the emergence of a food-sensitive research and practice planning agenda in the domain of planning, over the past decade and a half, in developed-economies cities. Chapter 4 uncovers novelties in the analytical domain of urban food planning and the different tactics that pioneer food planning scholars and practitioners are beginning to adopt to portray the city through a food system lens. The reader will become acquainted with different strategies for the assessment of community and regional food systems and popular concepts in food planning jargon, like urban food deserts and regional foodsheds. Chapters 5 and 6 provide an overview of the burgeoning, but still greatly fragmented, domain of intervention strategies aiming to transform the relationship between cities and food, from seed to fork to landfill. In Chapter 5, food system policies, strategies, and plans devised by municipalities and regional planning agencies are examined, while Chapter 6 delves specifically into the inception of new models for urban development in which community food spaces (e.g., urban farms, edible schoolyards, allotments, local food outlets, composting facilities) are not seen as an accessory but a structuring element in the design of new urban communities. With Chapter 7, we will close the last of the four thematic areas and turn to the organizational domain of urban food planning novelties. We will investigate some of the emergent new political spaces where urban food planning practices are taking place, like municipal food boards and food policy councils, deemed de facto food planning agencies, and learn about the advantages and limitations of different urban food governance arrangements. Finally, Chapter 8 returns to the overarching question – What is the state of evolution of urban food planning? – raised at the beginning of the investigation and offers a synthesis of the findings on the four domains of urban food planning experimentation – conceptual, analytical, design, and organizational – where novel social practices are taking shape.

References

American Planning Association (APA). (2007). *Policy Guide on Community and Regional Food Planning*. Retrieved from https://www.planning.org/policy/guides/adopted/food.htm

Bidiuc, B. (2015). *A Food System Plan for Austin*. The University of Texas at Austin.

Blum-Evitts, S. (2009). *Designing a Foodshed Assessment Model*. University of Massachusetts Amherst.

Bobbio, E. (2009). *Coltivare in Città: Proposte di Agricoltura Urbana a Torino e Vancouver*. (Unpublished master thesis). Politecnico di Torino, Turin, Italy.

Boyle, D. & A. Simms (2009). *The New Economics: A Bigger Picture*, London: Earthscan.

Born, B., & Purcell, M. (2006). Avoiding the Local Trap: Scale and Food Systems in Planning Research. *Journal of Planning Education and Research, 26*(2), 195–207.

Bulkeley, H., Castan Broto, V., & Maassen, A. (2014). Low-carbon Transitions and the Reconfiguration of Urban Infrastructure. *Urban Studies, 51*(7), 1471–1486.

Bulkeley, H., Castán Broto, V., Hodson, M., & Marvin, S. (Eds.). (2011). *Cities and Low Carbon Transitions*. New York-Abingdon: Routledge.

Camagni, R. (2011). *Principi di economia urbana e territoriale*. Roma: Carocci editore.

Center for a Livable Future (2015). *Food Policy Council Directory, 2015 Update* [PowerPoint slides]. Retrieved from http://www.jhsph.edu/research/centers-and-institutes/johns-hopkins-center-for-a-livable-future/projects/FPN/directory/index.html

Coenen, L., Benneworth, P., & Truffer, B. (2012). Toward a spatial perspective on sustainability transitions. *Research Policy, 41*(6), 968–979.

Crutzen, P. J., & Stoermer, E. F. (2000). The Anthropocene IGBP Newsletter, 41. *Royal Swedish Academy of Sciences, Stockholm, Sweden*.

DiLisio, C. M. & Hodgson, K. (2011). *Food Policy Councils: Helping Local, Regional, and State Governments Address Food System Challenges*. Chicago, IL: American Planning Association.

Doglio, C. (1953). *L'equivoco della città giardino*. Napoli: Edizioni RL.

Geddes, S. P. (1915). *Cities in Evolution: An Introduction to the Town Planning Movement and to the Study of Civics*. London: Williams & Norgate.

Geels, F. W. (2002). Technological transitions as evolutionary reconfiguration processes: a multi-level perspective and a case-study. *Research Policy, 31*(8–9), 1257–1274.

Geels, F. W. (2006). The hygienic transition from cesspools to sewer systems (1840–1930): The dynamics of regime transformation. *Research Policy, 35*(7), 1069–1082.

Geels, F. W. (2007). Analysing the breakthrough of rock 'n' roll (1930–1970) Multi-regime interaction and reconfiguration in the multi-level perspective. *Technological Forecasting and Social Change, 74*(8), 1411–1431.

Geels, F. W., & Schot, J. (2007). Typology of sociotechnical transition pathways. *Research Policy, 36*(3), 399–417.

Gibson-Graham, J. K., Cameron, J., & Healy, S. (2013). *Take Back the Economy: An Ethical Guide for Transforming Our Communities.* Minneapolis-London: University of Minnesota Press.

Grin, J. (2010). The Governance of Transitions: An Agency Perspective. In J. Grin, J. Rotmans, & J. Schot (Eds.), *Transitions to Sustainable Development: New Directions in the Study of Long Term Transformative Change* (pp. 265–284). New York, NY: Routledge.

Hargreaves, T., Longhurst, N., & Seyfang, G. (2013). Up, down, round and round: Connecting regimes and practices in innovation for sustainability. *Environment and Planning A, 45*(2), 402–420.

Hielscher, S., Seyfang, G., & Smith, A. (2013). Grassroots Innovations for Sustainable Energy: Exploring Niche-Development Processes Among Community-Energy Initiatives. In M. J. Cohen, H. Szejnwald Brown, & P. J. Vergragt (Eds.), *Innovations in Sustainable Consumption: New Economics, Socio-technical Transitions and Social Practices* (pp. 133–158). Cheltenham-Northampton: Edward Elgar.

Hinrichs, C. C. (2014). Transitions to sustainability: A change in thinking about food systems change? *Agriculture and Human Values, 31*(1), 143–155.

Hodgson, K., Campbell, M. C., & Bailkey, M. (2011). *Urban Agriculture: Growing Healthy, Sustainable Places.* Chicago, IL: American Planning Association.

Hodson, M., & Marvin, S. (2010). Can cities shape socio-technical transitions and how would we know if they were? *Research Policy, 39*(4), 477–485.

Ilieva, R. T. (2013). *Growing Food-Sensitive Cities for Tomorrow: How to Integrate Sustainable Food Systems and Spatial Planning for a Brighter Urban Future in the 21st Century?* (Unpublished doctoral dissertation). Politecnico di Milano, Milan, Italy.

Kemp, R., Schot, J., & Hoogma, R. (1998). Regime shifts to sustainability through processes of niche formation: The approach of strategic niche management. *Technology Analysis & Strategic Management, 10*(2), 175–195.

Kirwan, J., Ilbery, B., Maye, D., & Carey, J. (2013). Grassroots social innovations and food localisation: An investigation of the local food programme in England. *Global Environmental Change, 23*(5), 830–837.

Knickel, K., Brunori, G., Rand, S., & Proost, J. (2009). Towards a better conceptual framework for innovation processes in agriculture and rural development. *Journal of Agricultural Education and Extension, 15*(2), 131–146.

Kunzmann, K. R. (2011, July 27). *Creative Planning for a Slow Society,* presentation at the Alta Scuola Politecnica Summer School, module on "The dynamics of creativity for a territory in stand-by," Sestriere, Torino, Italy.

La Cecla, F. (1998). *La pasta e la pizza.* Bologna: Il Mulino.

Loorbach, D. (2010). Transition management for sustainable development: A prescriptive, complexity-based governance framework. *Governance, 23*(1), 161–183.

Mansfield, E. (1961). Technological change and the rate of imitation. *Econometrica, 29,* 741–766.

Markard, J., Raven, R., & Truffer, B. (2012). Sustainability transitions: An emerging field of research and its prospects. *Research Policy, 41*(6), 955–967.

Mendes, W. (2006). *Creating a "Just and Sustainable" Food System in the City of Vancouver: The Role of Governance, Partnerships and Policy-Making.* (Doctoral dissertation). Retrieved from ProQuest Dissertations & Theses Global. (NR23888)

Mokyr, J. (1990). *The Lever of Riches: Technological Creativity and Economic Progress.* New York, NY: Oxford University Press.

Monaghan, A. (2009). Conceptual niche management of grassroots innovation for sustainability: The case of body disposal practices in the UK. *Technological Forecasting and Social Change, 76*(8), 1026–1043.

Morgan, K. (2009). Feeding the city: The challenge of urban food planning. *International Planning Studies, 14*(4), 341–348.

Morgan, K. (2013). The rise of urban food planning. *International Planning Studies, 18*(1), 1–4.

Morgan, K., & Sonnino, R. (2010). The urban foodscape: World cities and the new food equation. *Cambridge Journal of Regions, Economy and Society, 3*, 209–224.

Morris, D. H. (2009). *One Thousand Friends of Food: Strategies for the Implementation of Local Food Policy in New York City*. (Master thesis). Retrieved from DSpace@MIT (http://hdl.handle.net/1721.1/50108).

Moulaert, F., Martinelli, F., Swyngedouw, E., & González, S. (2005). Toward Alternative Model(s) of Local Innovation. *Urban Studies, 42*(11), 1969–1990.

Mulgan, G., Tucker, S., Ali, R., & Sanders, B. (2007). *Social Innovation: What It Is, Why It Matters and How It Can Be Accelerated*. Oxford Said Business School. Basingstoke, UK: The Basingstoke Press.

Pollan, M. (2008). *In Defense of Food: An Eater's Manifesto*. New York, NY: Penguin.

Pothukuchi, K., & Kaufman, J. L. (1999). Placing the food system on the urban agenda: The role of municipal institutions in food systems planning. *Agriculture and Human Values, 16*, 213–224.

Pothukuchi, K., & Kaufman, J. L. (2000). The food system: A stranger to the planning field. *Journal of the American Planning Association, 66*(2), 113–124.

Raja, S., Born, B., & Kozlowski Russell, J. (2008). *A Planners Guide to Community and Regional Food Planning*. Chicago, IL: American Planning Association.

Raven, R., Schot, J., & Berkhout, F. (2012). Space and scale in socio-technical transitions. *Environmental Innovation and Societal Transitions, 4*, 63–78.

Raven, R. P. J. M. (2006). Towards alternative trajectories? Reconfigurations in the Dutch electricity regime. *Research Policy, 35*(4), 581–595.

Richardson, J. M. (2010). *Foodshed Vancouver: Envisioning a Sustainable Foodshed for Greater Vancouver*. (Master thesis). Retrieved from UBC Theses and Dissertations (http://hdl.handle.net/2429/25491).

Rip, A. & Kemp, R. (1998).Technological change. In S. Rayner & E.L. Malone (Eds.), *Human Choice and Climate Change* (pp. 327–399), Vol. 2. Columbus, OH: Batelle Press.

Rogers, E. M. (1962). *Diffusion of Innovations*. New York, NY: Free Press of Glencoe.

Rotmans, J., Kemp, R., & van Asselt, M. (2001). More evolution than revolution: Transition management in public policy. *Foresight, 3*(1), 15–31.

Rutherford, J. & Coutard, O. (2014). Special Issue: Urban energy transitions: Places. processes and politics of socio-technical change. *Urban Studies, 51*(7), 1353–1536.

Schiff, R. (2007). *Food Policy Councils: An Examination of Organisational Structure, Process, and Contribution to Alternative Food Movements*. (Doctoral dissertation). Retrieved from Murdoch University Research Repository (http://researchrepository.murdoch.edu.au/id/eprint/293).

Schot, J., & Geels, F. W. (2008). Strategic niche management and sustainable innovation journeys: Theory, findings, research agenda, and policy. *Technology Analysis & Strategic Management, 20*(5), 537–554.

Seyfang, G. (2009). *The New Economics of Sustainable Consumption: Seeds of Change*. New York: Palgrave Macmillan.

Seyfang, G., & Haxeltine, A. (2012). Growing grassroots innovations: Exploring the role of community-based initiatives in governing sustainable energy transitions. *Environment and Planning C: Government and Policy, 30*(3), 381–400.

Seyfang, G., & Smith, A. (2007). Grassroots innovations for sustainable development: Towards a new research and policy agenda. *Environmental Politics, 16*(4), 584–603.

Shove, E. (2004). Sustainability, System Innovation and the Laundry. In B. Elzen, F. W. Geels, & K. Green (Eds.), *System Innovation and the Transition to Sustainability: Theory, Evidence and Policy* (pp. 76–94). Cheltenham: Edward Elgar.

Shumate, N. (2012). *Success on the Ground: Case Studies of Urban Agriculture in a North American Context.* (Master thesis). Retrieved from UWSpace at University of Waterloo (https://uwsapce.uwaterloo.ca/handle/100012/6819).

Smith, A. (2006). Green niches in sustainable development: The case of organic food in the United Kingdom. *Environment and Planning C: Government and Policy, 24*(3), 439–458.

Smith, A. (2007). Translating sustainabilities between green niches and socio-technical regimes. *Technology Analysis & Strategic Management, 19*(4), 427–450.

Smith, A., & Raven, R. (2012). What is protective space? Reconsidering niches in transitions to sustainability. *Research Policy, 41*(6), 1025–1036.

Spaargaren, G., Oosterveer, P., & Loeber, A. (Eds.). (2012). *Food Practices in Transition. Changing Food Consumption, Retail and Production in the Age of Reflexive Modernity.* New York-Abingdon: Routledge.

Stierand, P. (2008). *Food and the City: The Relevance of the Food System for Urban Development* (original title in German, *Stadt und Lebensmittel: Die Bedeutung des Ernährungssystems für die Stadtentwicklung*) (Doctoral dissertation). Retrieved from Eldorado Database, Technical University of Dortmund (http://hdl.handle.net/2003/25789).

Truffer, B., & Coenen, L. (2012). Environmental innovation and sustainability transitions in regional studies. *Regional Studies, 46*(1), 1–21.

United Nations, Department of Economic and Social Affairs, Population Division. (2014). *World Urbanization Prospects: The 2014 Revision, Highlights* (ST/ESA/SER.A/352).

United States Department of Agriculture. (2015). *2012 Census of Agriculture: Organic Survey (2014). Volume 3, Special Studies, Part 4* (AC-12-SS-4).

van den Ende, J., & Kemp, R. (1999). Technological transformations in history: How the computer regime grew out of existing computing regimes. *Research Policy, 28*(8), 833–851.

Viljoen, A., & Wiskerke, J. S. C. (Eds.). (2012). *Sustainable Food Planning: Evolving Theory and Practice.* Wageningen: Wageningen Academic Publishers.

2 Food and the city of tomorrow

the children, the women, the workers of the town can come but rarely to the country . . . we must therefore bring the country to them, . . . make the field gain on the
street, not merely the street gain on the field

–Patrick Geddes, *Cities in Evolution*

Transitioning to an urban age, in which food is an integral part of the design
and management of cities, depends on the development of new understandings
of what is and what ought to be a "normal" city as much as on the effective
shelving of obsolete ideas about its spatial ordering. The global wave of city-
driven sustainable food projects and initiatives, which manifested over the
past decade, is one concrete example of the rising determination of urbanites
to uproot dominant perceptions that food growing and direct sales of farm
produce have no place in the city. Yet, reintroducing farming in cities by
design is not an entirely new idea. Pioneer social reformists, who heralded
the institutionalization of modern city planning more than a century ago, all
considered productive landscapes as an essential element of the life and spatial
form of the ideal city of the future. This second chapter explores the rationale
behind these iconic models for alternative urban development in the age of
the industrial metropolis and provides a glimpse into two radically different
visions as to why agrifood systems can be a valuable source of inspiration for
post-industrial city-regions today.

Food in early-twentieth-century planning visions

Although present-day advocates for greater food systems sensitivity in urban
policy and planning barely draw on the work of early-twentieth-century planning theorists, they do share the common goal of bridging the gap between
cities and their rural hinterlands. In fact, the precursors of the town and country planning movement in the UK, the regional planning movement in the
US, and national planning in the Netherlands all took farmland and its integration in the physical and social fabric of cities as a centerpiece of their work.
In this first section of the chapter, we will look into four early city-regional

planning visions, which prompted the institutionalization of urban planning in public policy and contained valuable insights into some of the solutions their authors envisioned to the unsustainable alienation of urban life from the countryside.

In particular, we will explore four specific models intended to overhaul established urban growth patterns and bring about a more harmonious urban-rural relationship and, ultimately, a better society. The models are the Garden City (1898/1902) by UK parliamentary stenographer and inventor Ebenezer Howard, the City in Evolution (1915) by Scot biologist Patrick Geddes, the Randstad-Green Heart (1930s–1960s) by Dutch national planners, and Broadacre City (1932/1934) by world-renowned US architect Frank Lloyd Wright. The value of these visions for the nascent urban food planning discourses and practices is twofold: first, they present us with different scenarios of what a ubiquitous, urban scale of the food system could look like and what role planners, architects, and urban designers could play to enact it, and, second, they provide us with important lessons as to what transitioning the dominant regime of urban policy, development, and planning practices might entail throughout this chapter. It will become evident how, even if radical visions do succeed to ignite a social movement, the aspired transition can turn not in the way its pioneers intended to.

The garden city

The unsustainability of industrial cities can be overcome by fundamentally recasting the relationship between city and countryside into a new integrated model for urban growth, balancing dwelling, landscape, and working spaces and shifting from a mono- to a polycentric pattern of urbanization. This was the radical proposition that Ebenezer Howard – a London-based parliamentary stenographer – was advancing through his book *To-morrow: A Peaceful Path to Real Reform* (1898), later reissued as *Garden Cities of To-morrow* (1902), at the beginning of the past century. Besides being one of the germs of modern urban planning, consistently reiterated in planning textbooks for more than a century, Howard's city-regional development model offers also a number of design and implementation cues for the emergent niche of urban food planning.

Before examining the new urban model that Howard envisioned, however, two important considerations are due. First, for Howard, physical design was not an end per se, but a means to a wholesale social transition; in fact, there are only two chapters of the book devoted to the spatial layout of the new city and city-regional system. Second, the book was not a fiction about an unattainable utopian future, but a down-to-earth how-to manual for urban development of his time. The timely change of the book title and the minute analyses of the costs and forms of governance necessary for the realization of the Garden City occupy a large portion of the hundred-page manuscript and clearly show the pragmatic intent of Howard's endeavor.

The model

Between the late eighteenth and mid-nineteenth centuries, the population of London more than doubled, reaching a staggering 2.2 million inhabitants, and, at the time Howard was writing, this trend was still persistent. Uncontrolled inner-city densification, tenement overcrowding, and speculative urban expansion were all enduring symptoms of the long-unsolved urban question resulting in detrimental impacts on people's health and the built environment. The solution that Howard put forward in *Garden Cities of To-morrow* was to divert urban development away from the old metropolis through a polycentric system of fixed-size self-sufficient new towns – Garden Cities, surrounded by extensive agricultural belts and linked up through railway transportation. At the regional scale, the aggregation of several garden cities would form the Social City – a hybrid urban-rural space offering a superior kind of collective urban experience.

In terms of scale, Howard posited that a single urban center must not exceed the carrying capacity of a medium-sized town in order to preserve a healthy relationship between city and countryside and between working and living in the city. Thus, a model Social City would have comprised up to six standard Garden Cities, hosting no more than 32,000 people each (Figure 2.1), and one

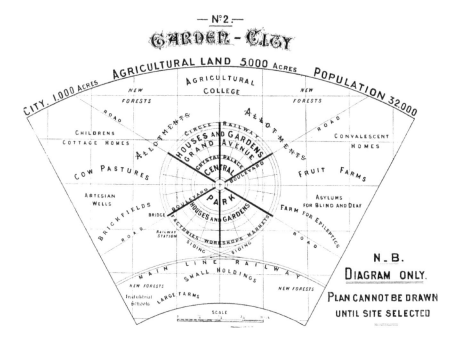

Figure 2.1 The Garden City by Ebenezer Howard. Diagram of a segment of plan.

Source: Howard (1902).

larger central Garden City hosting a maximum of 58,000 people, equating to 250,000 people in the Social City as a whole. In Howard's view, this new city-regional urban structure would have provided a much-needed "third way" for urban growth and force of attraction in the London metropolitan area; a new "town–country magnet" able to neutralize the downsides of town and country life as discrete experiences, while honing their major advantages. He exhibited this idea in the book through the famous three-magnets diagram – town, country, and town–country – each altering the nature and direction of the demographic pressures on the metropolis.

Where Howard rendered his idea of a unified town–country urban environment best, however, was at the scale of the Garden City. One of the basic planning principles he introduced was the neat separation between the different urban activities and the spaces where they take place throughout the day. There were four main types of specialized areas disposed in a sequence of concentric rings across the Garden City – public and leisure (the city core with parks, civic buildings, and the Crystal Palace, and, amidst the residences, the Grand Avenue), residential (in an intermediate ring), industrial (concentrated in the outermost urbanized ring), and agricultural (the green belt encompassing the whole city). Though spatially demarcated, these areas were not isolated. In fact, the scale of the city was such that one could experience them within the space-time of ordinary daily life. Moreover, a wide range of basic amenities, such as shops, playfields, libraries, gardens, and schools, had to be provided at the neighborhood scale. Howard envisioned that the city would be divided into six distinct wards of 5,000 residents each so that services could be equally distributed.

One important question for those of us interested in the insights this model can provide for urban food planning is what kind of connection to productive landscapes and the food system this new town would have offered. The physical layout imagined by Howard suggests that, at the urban scale, the relationship between built-up area and open space would be overtly in favor of the latter – of the overall 6,000 acres (2,400 ha) only one-sixth, 1,000 acres (400 ha), would be urbanized, while the remaining 5,000 (2,000 ha) would be left for landscape and farming. To achieve this, Howard maintained densities in residential areas relatively high – around 80–90 people/acre (200–220 people/ha), which was comparable to London's residential densities (Steel, 2009b) – contrary to what suburban development advocates would later misleadingly claim. The land would be farmed partly by farmers already in the area and partly by newcomers; of the 32,000 Garden City residents, 2,000 would be employed in farming.

The kinds of farming operations would vary depending on their scale and function – from large farms and cow pastures to small-scale family farms and allotments. Different crops, Howard figured, would require different spaces and forms of management. To be viable, wheat production, for instance, would necessitate extensive fields and the efficiency that only a capitalist farmer, or a group of cooperators, can provide, while growing fruits, vegetables, and flowers involves a greater personal care and creativity, and therefore would be best advanced by individuals or small groups of like-minded people who share "a common belief in the efficacy and value of certain dressings, methods of culture, or artificial and natural surroundings" (Howard, 1902, p. 26). This view on the distinct subculture of the community of urban farmers that Howard had greatly differed from previous model cities put forward in the nineteenth century, like the one conceived by Scottish cotton mill entrepreneur Robert Owen (1771–1858), in which farming was a mandatory occupation for all citizens.

Yet growing spaces were not confined to the green belt or the countryside alone. Small-scale horticulture could be practiced in housing estates across the city and in some public spaces as well. Howard praised the value of gardening as a means to stronger and more meaningful social and socioecological bonds in cities, but also a kind of urban culture. Every school in his view would have greatly benefited from a garden where pupils would have acquired knowledge and skills useful not only in school but long after throughout their adult life (Howard, 1902, p. 39, citing *The Echo*, Nov. 1890). In addition to gardens, a wide array of other local food infrastructure elements would have been located in each of the six wards of the Garden City: cooperative kitchens, local food stores, and local food depots – or food hubs, to say it in today's urban food planning jargon – were all part of the short food supply segment of the urban food system. While local food and farmland were central to the Garden City economy, they were not meant to operate for a closed self-sufficient market as some might expect. Rather, Howard was very vocal about preserving the "principle of freedom" for local enterprises and farmers who would "have the fullest right to dispose of their produce to whomsoever they please" (Howard, 1902, p. 26), thus not being constrained by the sole market of their town.

Seeds of transition

Instances of innovation in urban planning thinking from the past can provide useful insights not just into why changing the status quo makes sense or what physical solutions there could be, but also into the processes that allow some ideas to go beyond the drawing board, or the book for that matter, and make a lasting real-world impact. Transition theories offer one theoretical lens that could help us discern some of the key factors that influenced the genesis and implementation of Howard's Garden City vision.

A main postulate in transition theories is that radical sociotechnical transitions come about when complex, large-scale challenges stimulate the formation of niches for sociotechnical innovation, which together destabilize the dominant sociotechnical regime and urge it to change its institutions and course of action (e.g., Geels, 2006). The large-scale challenges are commonly referred to as landscape pressures, the landscape being the sum of structural or supralocal forces (e.g., global economy, culture, climate, physical geography, demographics, political traditions, etc.) in a given sociotechnical system. Some of the major landscape pressures that workers, entrepreneurs, and government officials were trying to cope with in nineteenth-century London were the unprecedented demographic growth and the detrimental coupling of rapid urban industrialization and economic distress in the countryside due to cheap foreign imports (Benevolo, 2012). Ebenezer Howard's Garden City proposal was a niche innovation offering a radical way out which, at the time, resonated with some of the powers that be, and, though it did not overhaul the dominant urban development regime, it did change how we think about cities and their management. Throughout the twentieth century many followed in his footsteps, often by tweaking the model to suit their own purposes, but on few fortunate occasions by developing his ideas even further and continuing to write the history of planning – as in some of the cases we will see further on in this chapter.

To fully appreciate the impact that *Garden Cities of To-morrow* had on thinkers, designers, and governments at the time, a closer look into the implementation efforts that took place over the first half of the twentieth century is warranted. The two projects that took off right after the publication of the book in Great Britain were Letchworth Garden City (1903), designed by Raymond Unwin, and Welwyn Garden City (1920), designed by Louis de Soissons, both in the county of Hertfordshire in the London metropolitan area. A later effort to put Howard's planning vision in practice is the town of Wythenshawe designed by Barry Parker and built south of Manchester in the 1920s–1930s (Hall & Tewdwr-Jones, 2011). These early episodes of experimentation, however, were soon dwarfed by the host of overseas attempts to translate and adapt the Garden City model. Two decades after the release of Howard's hundred-page booklet, cities in all corners of the world were seeking to apply his ideas, and an international Garden City movement had unfolded. The *cités jardins* in France (e.g., Ma Bicoque in 1912; Les Lilas in the 1920s; Suresnes, Châtenay-Malabry, and Plessis-Robinson in the 1930s), the *Gartenstadt* in Germany (e.g., Gartenstadt Rüppurr in 1907, Gartenstadt Hellerau in 1909, Gartenstadt Staaken in 1913, the Hufeisensiedlung in 1925), the *den-en toshi* in Japan (e.g., Sakurai in 1911, Ikeda-Takaracho in 1912, Tamagawadai in 1918), and many other in North America (e.g., Forest Hills Gardens in 1912, Sunnyside Gardens in 1924–1928, Radburn in the 1920s–1930s), Italy (e.g., Milanino in 1909), Poland (e.g., Sepolno in the 1920s–1930s), and Australia (e.g., Dacey Garden Suburb in 1911, the plan for Canberra in 1911, Electrona in 1918) were all part of this emergent urban planning niche and by the end of the 1930s were increasingly displaying its twists and contradictions, along with the sheer scale of its influence.

While all of the above claimed Garden City lineages, hardly any were truly cooperative self-sufficient new towns; most were simply "garden suburbs," which nevertheless provided the blueprint for a great part of post-war suburban planning (Taylor, 1998). Ironically, some of the early garden suburbs, like the Hampstead Garden Suburb (1905) of London or Forest Hills Gardens (1912) in Queens, New York, eventually morphed into high-end neighborhoods catering for the urban elite rather than low-income working-class families. A second important wave of new-town development, however, took place in the United States, in the aftermath of the Great Depression of 1929–1933, and in the United Kingdom, after the Second World War. At this point, the Garden City niche, or at least some of the innovative solutions it was believed to offer, was already robust enough to influence the dominant regime of urban policy and planning. In the United States, the National Industrial Recovery Act (NIRA) from 1933 and the Division of Subsistence Homesteads heralded the nationwide institutionalization of industrial decentralization coupled with subsistence agriculture to cope with the economic downturn. The Borough of Roosevelt (originally named Jersey Homestead) near Trenton, New Jersey, was one notable Garden City project developed as a result of the New Deal legislation. Later, Rexford Tugwell's Resettlement Administration (RA) sponsored the development of a series of other government-driven new towns like Greenbelt in Maryland, Greenhills in Ohio, and Greendale in Wisconsin (Wheeler & Beatley, 2014). In Great Britain, some of the milestones of the institutionalization of Howard's Garden City planning proposal – or at least of some of its elements – were the Housing, Town Planning, etc. Act (1909), the Green Belt Act (1938), Patrick Abercrombie's regional plan for Greater London (1944), the New Towns Act (1946), the Town and Country Planning Act (1947), and the National Parks and Access to the Countryside Act (1949) (Taylor, 1998). In the period between the 1940s and 1960s, the New Town Program brought about the implementation of as much as 32 new satellite towns in the London metropolitan area after the Second World War.

Thus, while Howard's ideal polycentric Social City never came true, his reformist ideas did influence – though often in unintended ways – many of his contemporaries and the subsequent generations of professional planners, policymakers, and real estate developers. What made his efforts in transitioning industrial cities to a new town planning regime so influential was the rare combination of conducive socioeconomic, cultural, and political factors with his great acumen in presenting and championing the Garden City idea. In fact, Howard was far from being the first to advance the idea of solving the urban question through the decentralization of economic activities in new agri-urban communities. He was, however, very successful in synthesizing the bulk of new-town experimentation and intellectual advancements that took place before him and in proving their practical importance. The Garden City model was rooted in much of the nineteenth-century ideal-city concepts and the trials and errors of their authors striving to put them in practice, among which were Charles Fourier's Phalanstery model buildings and community (1814) subsequently realized by Jean Baptiste Godin in Guisa (1825); Etienne Cabet's vision for Icaria (1848) and his efforts to implement it in North America during the 1880s; James S. Buckingham's model town Victoria (1849); and Benjamin W. Richardson's ideal city of health Hygeia (1875).

Howard's regional Garden City network vision, however, gained an unprecedented popularity at the turn of the century, not only for the long tradition of visionaries that preceded him, but because he proposed it at a time when it made sense to both industrialists and governments. By the early 1900s, dislocating factories from congested city centers to new company-owned towns in the countryside had already become a common practice among industrialists not only in Great Britain but all over Europe. Some of the well-known examples of industry-funded planned communities in the 1800s are New Lanark by cotton mill owner Robert Owen in Scotland (1800–1810) and his attempt to scale it up in North America with the plan for New Harmony in Indiana (1825); the Grand Hornu mining village started in 1825 by Henri De Gorge in Boussu, Belgium; Titus Salt's textile mill town in Saltaire near Bradford (1853–1863); the cluster of *Arbeiterkolonie* built by the steel company Krupp in 1863–1875 near Essen in Germany (e.g., Westend in 1863, Nordhof in 1861, Kronenberg in 1872–1874); the George Pullman's model company town for the workers in his Pullman car factories near Chicago (1880); and the model "garden village" of Bournville (1893–1895) by cocoa and chocolate manufacturer George Cadbury near Birmingham. Most importantly, not only were industry owners already convinced of the value of new-town projects, but, when *Garden Cities of To-morrow* was published, they had accumulated the necessary capital to scale up these endeavors (Hall & Tewdwr-Jones, 2011).

The gist of Howard's vision was to turn these scattered initiatives of industrial decentralization into a unified large-scale strategy for managing urban growth and use it to lay the groundwork for a broad societal transformation. Neither the scale nor the comprehensiveness of his approach were too far off from what different governments across Europe had already been aspiring to pursue throughout the previous century. Grandiose projects, such as the plan for Foro Bonaparte in Milan commissioned to Italian architect Giovanni Antonio Antolini by Napoleon Bonaparte in 1801 but eventually not carried out, the *grand travaux* in Paris conducted by Seine's Department Prefect Baron Georges-Eugène Haussmann during the 1850s–1860s, the Vienna's Ringstraße development works on the area of the former baroque city fortifications in 1857–1861, and Ildefons Cerdà's impressive grid plan for the renewal and expansion of Barcelona in 1859 after the demolition of the old fortifications, were all government-run planning efforts that reinforced the assumption that, to solve the nineteenth-century city's problems, adopting a large-scale reconstruction strategy is imperative. The fundamental difference in Howard's proposition was that the fresh start had to be pursued far from the old metropolis through a new crown of self-sufficient settlements. In addition to the prior proliferation of company towns, what made his vision plausible was one technological innovation that by the beginning of the twentieth century had become normalized in Great Britain – railway transportation. In 1830, the first steam-power public transport railway line was inaugurated, connecting Liverpool to Manchester, followed shortly after by the line between London and Birmingham in 1838. By 1900, UK's population exceeding 38 million was already extensively using the expanded railway network, generating nearly one billion journeys per year, equating to an overall distance of 15 billion miles per year (ATOC, 2007).

Yet another critical factor that made a difference to the advancement of Howard's ideas, compared to his predecessors in the 1800s, was that when his work was published discourses about the institutionalization of town planning powers and the rational organization of urban development were at their peak (Unwin, 1909). At the beginning of the 1900s, the first English manuals and university programs in town and country planning started being introduced in the UK and the US. In 1905, Alfred Richard Sennett's two-volume manuscript *Garden Cities in Theory and Practice* was issued, followed by Raymond Unwin's *Town Planning in Practice* in 1909 and, on the other side of the Atlantic, by the first US conference on Town Planning and Congestion and the first course in city planning, at Harvard University and launched the same year. Four years later, the first formal town planning organization – the Royal Town Planning Institute (RTPI) – was established in the UK, and, a decade after in 1923, the less formal but not less influential Regional Planning Association of America (RPAA) was instituted in New York City by the so-called "Decentrists" – Clarence Stein, Lewis Mumford, Henry Wright, and Catherine Bauer, among others. Many of the regional planning precepts advanced by this group drew on Howard's Garden City vision, as well as on those of his other prominent contemporaries, such as Scottish biologist and planner Sir Patrick Geddes (1854–1932), discussed next in this chapter.

Besides the mix of factors stemming from the broader context of intellectuals, industrialists, government, and physical infrastructure – or what in transition theories constitutes the sociotechnical regime, the micro-scale of who Howard was and how he presented and advocated for his ideas was equally key to the fortunes of the Garden City model. In fact, transitions are the outcome of the coevolution of niche, regime, and landscape-level societal transformations. Howard worked as a parliamentary stenographer in London, and this allowed him to appraise firsthand the major political issues of the day and the dominant beliefs and positions of elected officials on each matter. He aptly used this knowledge to frame both the problem at stake (i.e., how to improve living conditions in London) and its plausible solutions, stressing the need to act upon the cause of the problem (i.e., the unsustainable influx of people from the countryside to the city) rather than on its symptoms, as some parliamentarians had already argued (Howard, 1902, p. 11). Thus, the way he presented his radical idea was to a great degree aligned with many of the expectations and aspirations of regime actors trying to cope with a seemingly intractable problem.

But Howard was also able to speak to the minds and hearts of industrialists and, as Lewis Mumford observed (1965, p. 37), he devoted a substantial part of *Garden Cities of To-morrow* to the process of financing and execution of the Garden City enterprise. What arguably made Howard's proposal even more compelling to prospective stakeholders, however, was his ability to summarize the key concepts he extensively argued for in his writing in a few graphical representations – the Three Magnets diagram, the Social City network of Garden Cities, and the Garden City and its wards. Though intended as purely schematic and supplementary to the book, these diagrams stuck so strongly in people's imagination that they eventually took over the text and began to influence real-world projects on their own. It would have been hard, however, to imagine any of the early implementations of the Garden City without the *International Garden Cities and Town Planning Association* (1899) that Howard established to this end immediately after his book was released. This new institutional space proved instrumental in propelling the Garden City niche and in publicizing the idea of urban growth based on new Garden City towns and of town planning as a professional practice in its own right.

Transition roadblocks

Yet, from the vantage point of the late twentieth century, Sir Peter Hall – one of the most prominent scholars in the recent history of urban planning – critically assessed Howard's Garden City model as one that "promised so much and in practice delivered so little" (1988, p. 9). Indeed, the Social City never came about and the Garden Cities that were built had to sacrifice the core tenets of the model to be viable. In the process of implementation of Letchworth Garden City, for instance, the idea of common property and a cooperative management was abandoned – which was exactly what happened a century earlier to Etienne Cabet's phalanstery model when Jean-Baptiste André Godin was putting it into practice in the French town of Guisa – while the principle of limited growth and the green belt were skipped in developing the third Garden City of Wythenshawe, south of Manchester, resulting in a gargantuan garden city with a population of over 100,000 people. Despite the great intellectual influence the Garden City model exerted on society throughout the first half of the twentieth century, it eventually led neither to the creation of the town–country magnet rescuing London from overcrowding nor to a reformed society reconciling the place of work with the place of food. The question then is what possibly sabotaged the process of transition.

The transition theories framework of strategic niche management (Schot & Geels, 2008) suggests that niche innovations fail to influence dominant socio-technical regimes due to ill-defined or unrealistic expectations, insufficiently robust social networks to support them, or ineffective learning throughout the design and implementation process. Overly unrealistic expectations and blind belief in the potential of the physical environment to engender societal reform were, in Karl Marx's view, two of the main reasons for the failure of much of nineteen-century ideal-city endeavors (Benevolo, 2012). This holds true for Howard's Social City plan as well. In order for the plan to work, people, industrialists, and government had to concurrently change their worldviews and somehow be naturally inclined to give up certain privileges for the sake of common good. The rational choice that Howard had in mind, however, did not match that of his audience when the project had to be translated in practice.

People were expected to spontaneously come to the Garden City, seek employment only within its boundaries, voluntarily cooperate to manage land,

and be actively engaged in the tending of allotments and kitchen gardens. Each of these assumptions proved prone to flaws when confronted with reality. For renowned American urban planning critic Jane Jacobs, for instance, a Garden City lifestyle could appeal to you only "if you were docile and had no plans of your own and did not mind spending your life among others with no plans of their own" (Jacobs, 1992/1961, p. 17), hence the hesitancy of working-class families to choose newly built garden cities over London, or even Manchester for that matter. Shared-tenure arrangements were an equally shaky proposition since, as Nobel Prize–winner Elinor Ostrom demonstrated in *Governing the Commons* (1990), a conflict-less management of the commons is possible, but only when certain conditions are met (e.g., low-yield large-scale assets as grazing pastures are the object of shared management) and by relatively small groups of people, far from the city-regional scale at which Howard was aiming to accomplish it.

In addition, the model assumed that people's attitudes toward locally grown food and gardening would remain unchanged as the city develops. Still, after the world wars and the Victory Gardens efforts, leaving urban gardening behind was perceived as a sign of progress, not a practice to sustain in the long run and, even more so, in the face of the first suburban shopping malls and chain stores that mushroomed in the interwar period (Ambrose, 1986). But we know that the groups of like-minded urban gardeners whom Howard had in mind would emerge again for whole different reasons throughout the 1960s and now in the 2000s. These fluctuations in people's understandings of what is normal and desirable from one historic period to another can make or break the pathway of transition, normally necessitating 20 to 50 years of sustained effort (Raven, Schot, & Berkhout, 2012, p. 67), and its absence is what arguably made local food infrastructure in the Garden City pilots quickly impractical.

Howard's expectations from investors proved far too ambitious as well. He posited that "the rate-rent of a well-planned town, built on an agricultural estate, will amply suffice for the creation and maintenance of such municipal undertakings" (Howard, 1902, p. 49). As Mazza (2009) points out, assuming that capital investors would give up their profits and hand them over to the Garden City's cooperative for the development of infrastructures and services was a contradiction in terms. Moreover, while in his book Howard skillfully demonstrated that a Garden City would cost only half of what a traditionally built town of this size would, he largely underestimated the interest rates (4%) on invested capital; in fact, Letchworth Garden City finished paying the debts to its investors only in 1945 (Mazza, 2009, p. 18). But this is understandable given that Howard was neither an expert in finance nor in real estate, and, independently from the flaws in his estimates, he could hardly foresee the market disruptions that would occur with the two world wars and the collapse of Wall Street in 1929, shortly after the construction of the first Garden City pilots commenced.

Lastly, two additional roadblocks to the transition to a new regime of urban growth and synergic town-country development pertain to the dimensions of government and time. One paradox that Dutch government officials pointed out, in considering the application of the Garden City model in the Netherlands, was the tension between granting "larger measures of local self-government" (Howard, 1902, p. 124) and, at the same time, unconditional cooperation between garden cities and the old metropolises which they aim to be an alternative of (Faludi & van der Valk, 1994). The entire Social City vision indeed rests on the assumption of such cooperation. In reality, not only cities sharing the same geographic region tend to compete for resources and power, but different land-use allocations within the city itself are sources of multiple antagonisms as well. That is, unless a collective tenure or public ownership of the land is ensured in perpetuity, an arrangement highly unlikely to manifest in capitalist states economies. The other ambitious expectation of the model Howard advanced was the blocked dimension of the Garden City. The internal and regional-scale balance depended on the frozen dimension of the towns, the intact greenbelts, and the maintenance of out-of-commuting-range distances between them. The bundle of sweeping transitions that came with the normalization of electricity, electric trains, motorized transportation, and private car ownership in the 1930s – which in the UK alone rose from some 229,000 cars in 1918 to over 3 million in 1939 (Ambrose, 1986) – utterly dynamited the commuting-range propositions that Howard put forward at the turn of the century.

But despite all its flaws and imperfections, even more than a century after its release, *Garden Cities of To-morrow* cannot be easily dismissed as obsolete, and its seeds of transition continue to be fertile for scholars and communities working to pursue sustainable development goals today. Since 2011, the Town and Country Planning Association (TCPA) – which Howard founded in 1899 – launched a campaign to popularize the benefits of the Garden City model as a valuable guidance for development projects seeking to tackle the current housing shortages in the UK. More recently, in 2014, a Garden City Declaration was signed in Letchworth Garden City and a community interest company titled the New Garden Cities Alliance was established. The group seeks to obtain a trademark accreditation and publish a set of design principles for the development of new communities following the Garden City model tenets. In particular, their goal is to "create definable and measurable definitions of practices, principles and standards that are required to be adopted by any settlement to allow them be accredited to use the suffix 'Garden City'" (New Garden Cities Alliance, 2014). In February the same year, the TCPA published a report called "New Towns Act 2015?" to call for a holistic approach to present-day new-town development and point at some of the major issues for government that this Garden Cities renaissance might entail.

The city in evolution

The seeds of transition to a renewed relationship between city and countryside lie also in the work of Scottish biologist and sociologist Sir Patrick Geddes

(1854–1932) – commonly regarded as one of the "founding fathers" of modern urban planning. While Geddes was familiar with the work of Howard and praised the Garden Cities movement, his approach to addressing the plight of disordered and sprawling industrial cities was markedly different, if not the reverse. Unlike Howard, who had little interest in the old metropolis and overtly deemed it beyond repair, Geddes was deeply concerned with understanding the existing city and how it relates to the surrounding region. This, in his view, was a promising way to uncover not only effective solutions to unsustainable urban growth and inner-city decay, but also basic principles for the planning and development of cities. Even though Geddes lived at a time when ideal-city visions and model new towns were given great credence, his contribution did not consist of one single grand blueprint, but of a series of original concepts. His intellectual heritage provides the groundwork for present-day city-regional food planning endeavors and points to some of the factors that could facilitate or hinder the normalization of unconventional ideas into mainstream planning culture.

Biologist by training, but with research interests spanning multiple disciplinary fields, Geddes was able to promptly spot and blend different concepts from scientific areas as diverse as biology, sociology, and human geography, emerging as a stand-alone discipline in France at that time. Importantly, his background in the natural sciences drew him to a different entry point for approaching the urban question. Instead of asking himself what an ideal city looks like, Geddes started off with questioning what a city is. For Geddes, the city was a living organism whose evolution depended on both its internal organization and the external environment in which it was situated. One of the key arguments he made in his famous manuscript *Cities in Evolution* (1915) was that the industrial revolution had transformed cities and their surrounding environment so profoundly that it was fair to consider this process as a large-scale societal transition, from a "paleotechnic" to a "neotechnic" era of development, as he put it. Cities and their morphology, therefore, had to be studied and planned bearing this transition and new agents of change in mind.

There is little doubt that Geddes's interest in the study of cities through the lens of evolution was prompted by the groundbreaking discoveries made in the field of biology by Charles Darwin, presented in his masterwork *On the Origin of Species* (1859) just a few years after Geddes was born. Geddes's take on evolution, however, substantially differed from Darwin's in that, in his view, when applied to cities, evolutionary processes were far from linear, and cooperation, as opposed to sole competition, played a key role along the way. In fact, for Geddes, cities were the outcome of "social union and evolution" (Geddes & Thomson, 1889, p. 312) not just of survival of "the fittest" and natural selection. In studying the morphology of cities, he noted that the clustering of urban settlements in thriving industrial regions was one physical manifestation of the evolutionary forces of cooperation. He labeled this spatial phenomenon "conurbation" (Geddes, 1915, p. 25). The solution to the indiscriminate urbanization of natural environments for Geddes, however, was not so much in the development of new towns but in the strategic protection of land from development as the city expands. Contrasting his ideas with the Garden Cities approach, he underscores: "we, with our converse perspective, coming in from country towards town, have to see to it that these growing suburbs no longer grow together, as past ones have too much done" (Geddes, 1915, p. 96). Hence the goal of planning is to allow cities to grow in a more balanced fashion with "green leaves set in alternation with . . . golden rays" (Geddes, 1915, p. 97).

To bring about the harmonious alteration of nature and culture, for Geddes, meant to plan for urban growth in compliance with the natural resources available in its surrounding environment, much like living organisms normally do. He compellingly illustrated this idea in his "Valley Section," where he called attention to the intimate relationship between the evolution of cities, the availability of natural resources, and the economic activities that people would engage with depending on the proximity of such resources. His famous triad Place-Work-Folk, which summoned these interdependencies, was inspired by the work of French sociologist Frédéric le Play (1806–1882) and his formula "Lieu, travail, famille" (Place, Work, Family), which he used to inquire into the impact of industrialization on family structures. For le Play, place was a proxy for regional economy, which in turn was a proxy for the organization and quality of family bonds. Geddes found this conceptual framework convincing also on the grounds of evolutionary theory and the codependencies that one could observe between environment, conditions, and organism (Geddes, 1905, p. 71). The proper unit of analysis for town planning therefore had to be broader than the city itself and reflect the sociospatial relationships unfolding at the landscape scale. The "natural region" for Geddes offered a more inclusive unit of analysis reflecting the understanding that "it takes the whole region to make the city" (Geddes, 1905, pp. 105–106), and that regional identity, as Hough (1990, p. 180) puts it, is "the collective reaction of people to the environment over time."

One of Geddes's key arguments was that, to use the laws of city-regional interdependence to build healthier urban environments, one had to systematically study them through direct observation first. Importantly, he viewed the creation of this new body of scientific knowledge on the city and its natural region as a collective endeavor, involving not merely erudite scholars in academia but the general public at large. As Ferraro (2002, p. 37) points out, the urban plan for Geddes was the expression of the aspirations of society. If people felt that they were part of the evolutionary trajectory of the places they inhabited, they would begin to consider what their role in the process could be and this would engender an endogenous, organic way of repairing the system. The project for the brighter city thus could not be separated from that for a sound education in civics.

Contrary to the approach of Garden Cities proponents, Geddes directed his research not out of town in the green fields or at his office desk, but right at the heart of the poorest slum in his native Edinburgh, where he discovered the germs of endogenous renewal despite unsettling poverty and blight. In *Cities in*

Evolution (1915, p. 102) he writes "nowhere better shall we found smaller open spaces and people's gardens in the opening decade than in the very heart of present slums" and applauds the efforts of citizens, women's organizations, and supportive city departments to advance a "garden movement" across the UK and Ireland. The realization that a whole network of urban gardens had materialized in the least probable of all places was the result of the "Open Spaces Survey" that Geddes did in Old Edinburgh with the support of the Outlook Tower Committee. The Outlook Tower was both an institution that Geddes created to spearhead research for the new science of cities and a physical place where a wide array of public engagement activities for its popularization took place. He exhorted citizens to engage with the history and geography of their towns and regions with the slogan "Know Your City."

Besides through the Outlook Tower, Geddes was committed to spark public interest and fascination with the study of urban evolution also through itinerant exhibitions. One of the well-known exhibitions he made was the "Cities and Town Planning Exhibition" in Ghent, Belgium, in 1913. The role of these exhibitions however was beyond educating the public alone; Geddes conceived them as a quite pragmatic way to activate urban change on the ground. In recollecting the outcomes of the exhibition hosted in Saffron Walden in the UK, for instance, he notes the rise of gardening and greening initiatives citywide, a greater interest in public health, and, most importantly in his view, "a new tide of civic feeling" (1915, p. 333). His faith in the ability of cities to regenerate from within would later inform his "conservative surgery" approach to urban renewal, in stark opposition to dominant comprehensive rebuilding ideologies.

To achieve the botanical growth of modern towns and counter their detrimental "grease spots" morphology, Geddes argued, Garden Cities and new construction would not suffice. Planning endeavors for the existing city are thus equally germane to achieve this goal. He advocated for the development of a network of open spaces, both naturalistic and productive, within cities as a way to reconnect factory workers and their families to nature and the countryside, i.e., the natural region. Geddes spelled out his vision of remaking the relationship between town and country quite eloquently in *Cities in Evolution* when exhorting his fellow colleagues committed to repairing the old city to take action:

> While our friends the town planners and burgh engineers are adding street beyond street, and suburb beyond suburb, it is also for us to be up and doing, and make the field gain on the street, not merely the street gain on the field.
>
> (1915, p. 96)

While some of Geddes's most progressive proposals – such as the development of an evolutionary science of cities or the appreciation of place-based solutions to the urban question – arguably got lost with time passing, the bulk of his thinking shaped much of modern planning theory and practice. His argument about the inextricable connection between town and country development, the "natural region" as a unit of analysis, was part of the reasons why the "town planning" movement was rebaptized into "town and country planning." Yet his insistence on the importance of social surveys as the basis for urban plan making was the idea that affected mainstream planning practice the most. In fact, the maxim "survey before plan" influenced the work of all subsequent generations of city planners, though often in unintended ways, opening a gap between research and everyday life. The success of this specific idea, however, was due to the robust niche for innovation that Geddes managed to create by providing a new physical and organizational space – the Outlook Tower, its Committee, and related research campaigns and exhibitions – where survey practices could be advanced and popularized among experts and lay people.

In the UK, Geddes's influence can be seen in the work of AIA Gold Medal recipient Sir Patrick Abercrombie (1879–1957), author of the Greater London Plan (1944) – strictly devised at a regional scale and informed by multiple surveys and analysis of the current state, and, among numerous other publications, of the book *Town and Country Planning*, issued two years after his death (1959). He also pioneered the Campaign to Protect Rural England (1926) with the aim to limit loss of farmland and rural landscapes due to ever-sprawling cities. Across the Atlantic, another great thinker, Lewis Mumford (1895–1990), whom we already mentioned in relation to the Garden Cities movement influence overseas, also picked up and persuasively expanded much of Geddes's research and practice agenda for planning. Besides contributing to the establishment of the Regional Planning Association of America (1924), Mumford further developed the concept of transition from a "paleotechnic" to a "neotechnic" era of societal evolution in his internationally acclaimed book *The Culture of Cities* (1938), which later became the main rulebook for regional planning in the US.

More recently, with the resurgent interest in physical design in planning (Batty & Marshall, 2009) and the allure of complexity theory, which dismisses the existence of any perfect state of equilibrium of cities, or of any other complex system for that matter, Geddes's invitation to think of city-regional development in evolutionary terms has begun to regain significance for planners. But this was not the case for a great part of the twentieth century. The reason why Geddes's ideas on the application of evolutionary theory in planning did not receive the attention they deserved at the time was due both to the way in which he put them forward and to the broader cultural and political context which his audience was part of. His famous book *Cities in Evolution* (1915), which aimed to spark interest in the evolutionary perspective on cities and which he wrote toward the end of his career as a planner in the UK, was in great part an anthology of different works he had previously composed rather than a monograph focused entirely on the subject.

The wide array of topics he addressed and the rich body of references he used made the book very informative but at times hard to follow. In addition, unlike Howard's *Garden Cities* (1902) manuscript, in which the lengthy and detailed argumentation about why decentralized urbanization makes sense was followed by practical proposals for intervention, Geddes never offered one grand synthesis of his findings on urban evolution that could inform city building on the ground. The historical period in which his ideas had to diffuse was also one in which the dominant urban government and planning regime had espoused ideas which were the exact opposite to what he suggested – top-down approaches to planning were privileged over bottom-up ones and order and uniformity were valued over diversity (Batty & Marshall, 2009, p. 569). In fact, the prevalent planning doctrine at the time entirely rejected the idea that there might be solutions to the problems being addressed already present in the city and that these could be worthwhile exploring, for they had been the result of long evolutionary processes and collective problem-solving endeavors. The influence of the Garden City movement, moreover, was growing stronger and, because Geddes was sympathetic to its advancements, urban planning historians and critics like Lewis Mumford and Jane Jacobs would later misinterpret his evolutionary message.

Even though *Cities in Evolution* did not bring forth a paradigm change or the development of an evolutionary science of cities, Geddes's argument about the tight-knit connection between cities and their natural regions, as well as the importance of social research prior to planning, greatly transformed town planning theory. Today, Geddes's legacy can provide a host of valuable insights for emergent urban food planning efforts as well. As planners are beginning to map urban food systems and alternative urban-rural linkages, the use of direct observation and other in-depth research techniques, alongside large-scale quantitative analysis, is essential. Geddes's emphasis on the coevolution of geography, the economy, and urban life can moreover be a useful lens to examine the intricate interdependences between cities and their supportive agrifood systems. The work of British architect and urban food systems scholar Carolyn Steel, discussed in the second part of this chapter, offers some promising inroads to this end and a way to think of cities as part of a lager global-scale food system, while also acknowledging their quality of food system environments in their own right. But before turning to present-day elaborations of Geddes's ideas, the contributions of two other visionary experiences from the past century are worth exploring – the Randstad-Green Heart concept pioneered by Dutch planners since the 1930s and US architect and urbanist Frank Lloyd Wright's Broadacre City vision of a reformed urban-rural development pattern.

The city with a green heart

At the turn of the nineteenth century, uncontrolled urbanization, which plagued many large cities across the UK throughout the nineteenth century, was becoming a daunting concern for many national governments overseas as well. The "clock" of urban planning, to use Peter Hall's words (1988, p. 49), started ticking. But while political leaders and intellectuals in the UK saw town and country planning as a hopeful cure for the ills of the old metropolis, their mainland counterparts were eager to embrace it to prevent the metropolis from manifesting altogether. The Netherlands was one of the countries that famously turned to planning to safeguard existing town–country relationships and ensure that the worst effects of unbridled urbanization were avoided.

Between the mid-nineteen and early twentieth centuries, the population of the Netherlands grew by about two-and-a-half million people. The unmet demand for housing, particularly in the western part of the country where major cities like Amsterdam, Rotterdam, The Hague, and Utrecht are located, was unprecedented and, besides the first Housing Act (1901), prompted the establishment of the Netherlands Institute for Housing and Planning (1918). While these were not groundbreaking steps per se, half a century later, they would lead to the formulation of one of the most compelling principles of spatial organization in Dutch, and arguably European, planning history – the Randstad-Green Heart Metropolis; a concept which would shape much of Dutch town and country planning throughout the second half of the twentieth century and which continues to thrive, though under a transformed guise, in present-day planning discourses and practice as well.

As we will see from the analysis that follows, what makes the concept unique is not merely the physical configuration it suggests for urban development in the western part of the Netherlands, but the principle that town and countryside must be planned in tandem and at the national and regional scales of government. The Dutch experience is especially relevant for emergent urban food planning efforts, since it embodies the ambition to treat productive and built-up areas on equal footing. Policies for farmland preservation and a decentralized, but compact, urbanization are used concurrently to ensure the optimal evolution of the urban and rural domains, while safeguarding their distinctive features. This is the innovation gist of the Randstad-Green Heart Metropolis model and the endeavors for its implementation, which were sustained for over four decades during the past century.

The model

The overarching purpose of the Randstad-Green Heart concept was to provide a sound alternative to sprawling concentric urban expansion and bring about the development of a balanced polycentric metropolis, in which people could enjoy the benefits of industrialized societies, without experiencing their major disadvantages. If large-scale urbanization was inevitable, the ways in which towns and cities were about to coalesce could still be managed in a purposeful and orderly manner. The two core elements of the Randstad-Green Heart spatial development strategy, formally laid out in the late 1950s, when national-level urban planning was emerging in the Netherlands, are the "Randstad" (literally "Rim City") and the "Green Heart." The Randstad represents the horseshoe-shaped urban region encompassing the cities (now city-regions) of Amsterdam, Rotterdam, The Hague, and Utrecht, where currently over half of the Dutch population lives, while the Green Heart is the area of open spaces and agricultural land bounded by the Randstad and stretching east (Figure 2.2).

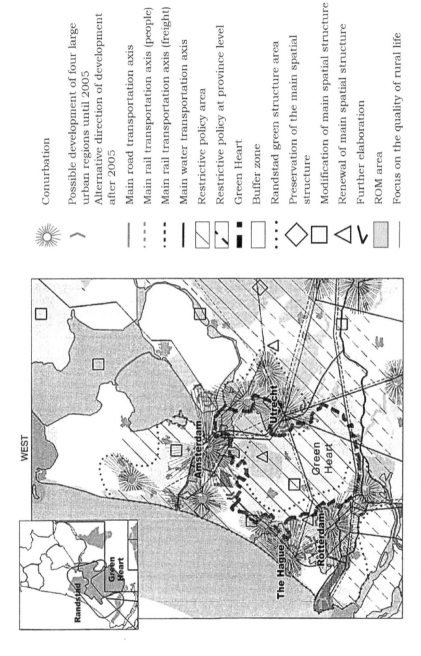

WEST

Conurbation

Possible development of four large
urban regions until 2005

Alternative direction of development
after 2005

Main road transportation axis

Main rail transportation axis (people)

Main rail transportation axis (freight)

Main water transportation axis

Restrictive policy area

Restrictive policy at province level

Green Heart

Buffer zone

Randstad green structure area

Preservation of the main spatial
structure

Modification of main spatial structure

Renewal of main spatial structure

Further elaboration

ROM area

Focus on the quality of rural life

Figure 2.2 The Randstad and the Green Heart.

Source: Elaboration based on Fourth National Spatial Planning Policy Extra (Vierde Nota Over de Ruimtelijke Ordening Extra), Dutch Ministry of Housing, Spatial Planning and the Environment (VROM), 1993.

Courtesy: The Directorate–General for Spatial Development and Water Affairs (DGRW) of The Netherlands.

In a nutshell, the Randstad-Green Heart principle of spatial organization was a tactic to bypass the metropolis in one of the most rapidly urbanizing regions in the Netherlands and preserve valuable agricultural land at its heart. The original building blocks and principles for its implementation were set by the Working Commission on the Western Netherlands (1951–1958), appointed by national government to inform the First National Spatial Planning Policy (Bureau for the National Plan, 1960). The core planning principles put forward by the Commission, and later regarded as the bedrock of the Dutch spatial planning "doctrine" (Faludi & van der Valk, 1994; Roodbol-Mekkes, van der Valk, & Korthals Altes, 2012), were to (1) concentrate urban development in bounded urban zones – conurbations, city regions, and agglomerations – along the Randstad and use green buffers and corridors to keep them morphologically distinct; (2) maintain the enclosed open area – the Green Heart – free from development; and (3) ensure that development proceeds in an outward direction, away from the historical cities and the Green Heart (see also Faludi & van der Valk, 1991).

Some of the specific measures that had to be observed in executing the Randstad-Green Heart vision were to cap the size of historical cities at one million inhabitants and accommodate housing demand beyond this threshold in so-called "overspill towns." Each overspill town had to host a maximum of 100,000 inhabitants and be built at least 15 km (9 miles) away from "donor" cities decentralizing their urban development. Large urban agglomerations had to be kept apart by means of green buffers no less than 4 km (2.5 miles) wide, while urban dwellers had to be able to travel no further than 4 km (2.5 miles) from any point in the town they lived to reach farmland or major recreational areas. This was the essence of the approach of "concentrated deconcentration," which Dutch planners developed to accomplish the Green Heart Metropolis ambition in practice (Faludi & van der Valk, 1994). The precise borders and internal organization of the Green Heart were discussed only in the early 1990s, after the release of the Fourth National Spatial Planning Policy and its follow-up plans and supplements, noting its articulation in three broad functional areas: a core area of agricultural and recreational activities, an intermediate green-buffer area of 10–15 km (6–9 miles) with some recreational facilities, and an outer urbanized ring where some development had taken place.

Compared to the previously discussed early-twentieth-century visionary concepts, such as Ebenezer Howard's Garden City or Patrick Geddes's natural region, the Randstad-Green Heart strategy appears to be a radically different approach to the urban question; yet, under closer scrutiny, several elements of continuity may be grasped. The bounded size of cities, the decentralization of urban growth in dedicated growth areas and towns, and the use of green buffers (similar to the British green belts) to contain urban expansion are some of the common threads that one can spot. Nevertheless, in reality, even though the Netherlands Institute for Housing and Planning was a member of the International Garden Cities and Town Planning Association and hosted a conference on the topic in Amsterdam in 1924, the Dutch planning community remained unconvinced of its desirability and practical application in the Dutch conditions. Some of the reasons were the dubious independence of Garden Cities from central government and large urban centers and the limited availability of agricultural land experienced in the Netherlands (Faludi & van der Valk, 1994, p. 57).

Arguably, of all town planning principles that the UK's town planning movement advocated for, the two that resonated with Dutch planners the most were planning for urban growth through a regional lens and conceiving of urban regions as organic wholes. These two were best exemplified in Geddes's Place-Work-Folk triad, whereby cities cannot be understood in isolation from their regions, and in the Greater London Plan (1944), devised by Geddes's renowned follower, Patrick Abercrombie, to guide postwar reconstruction. In fact, the scale of the Randstad-Green Heart Metropolis vision is above and beyond Howard's 250,000-people Social City agglomeration, although, truth be told, Howard never posed limits to the extension of his model, ideally replicable infinite times. The Randstad-Green Heart proposal, however, embodies an iconic image that completely overturns the Garden City construct of a fixed-size town, bounded by an agricultural belt, by offering an alternative vision of a protected agricultural heart bounded by an urbanized belt.

But more important than the relation between the Green Heart city concept and other pioneering ideas that came before is the question how it endured for over half a century and what the outcomes of the sustained efforts for its implementation are. Did Dutch planners succeed in building Randstad-Green Heart Metropolis in practice? With what major breakthroughs and what challenges? To answer these questions, we need to inquire into what constitutes the Randstad-Green Heart, not as a static image or planning "doctrine" per se, but as a complex sociotechnical process whose outcomes were subjected to a host of social, political, cultural, and economic factors.

Seeds of transition

There are at least three tangible outcomes of the efforts to normalize and deploy the Randstad-Green Heart principle of spatial organization in the Netherlands. First, the proponents of the idea have been successful in influencing Dutch planning discourses and practices to the point of transitioning the notions of Randstad and Green Heart from startling novelties into "household words" (Faludi & van der Valk, 1994). In fact, all five National Policy Reports on Spatial Planning that succeeded the first one (1960) – i.e., the Second (1966), the Third (1977), the Fourth (1990), the Fourth Extra (1993), and the Fifth (2001, not approved by parliament) – included explicit policies aimed at preserving the Randstad-Green Heart principle. Even recently, the Randstad 2040 Structural Vision released by the Ministry of Housing, Spatial Planning and the Environment (VROM) in 2008 (substituted by the National Structural Vision on Infrastructure and Space in 2012) overtly affirmed the importance of the Green Heart in strategizing for long-term sustainable development in the region. Considering that the Randstad-Green Heart is not a geographic concept, but a planning concept (IENM, 2012, p. 8), this is a remarkable achievement.

Second, 50 years after its inception, the core of the Dutch planning "doctrine" has not only survived on paper (Roodbol-Mekkes et al., 2012), but continues to influence important planning decisions. A case in point is the execution of an 8-km (5-mile) segment of the high-speed railway line between Amsterdam and Rotterdam (continuing further south to Belgium and France) underground, since it would have otherwise cut across the Green Heart. The tunnel, purposefully named "Green Heart Tunnel," connects Hoogmade with Hazerswoude-Dorp and was realized between 2000 and 2004 at the cost of about USD 349 million. The high cost of the project as well as the overall trajectory of the south high-speed line – respecting to great extent the boundaries of the Green Heart – made the decision contested. In addition, the project for the second high-speed railway line, aiming to connect the Netherlands to Germany and crossing a substantial portion of the Green Heart, has been, for the time being, downsized to an expansion of the existing line with additional tracks. Some of the reasons for this are geological – the soil is not stable enough to meet the carrying capacity requirements for the high-speed infrastructure – but some are related to the core of the planning "doctrine" (to say it with Faludi and van der Valk's analogy), which, in the 1990s, when decisions about the infrastructure were in the making, was highly regarded.

Third, considering the direct impact of the Randstad-Green Heart policies on the patterns of urbanization in the region, it is fair to say that planners succeeded in slowing down the encroachment of housing on farmland in the Green Heart. In the 1960s–1990s, the Randstad-Green Heart was the region where the greatest pressures for suburbanization manifested, yet the share of Dutch population hosted there remained about the same (Korthals Altes, 2007). The overspill towns and the "concentrated deconcentration" stratagem thus effectively countered part of the urban sprawl by meeting the projected housing demand at the planned locations. Several critics, however, have pointed out that there have been multiple breaches in the efforts to restrict suburbanization in the Randstad-Green Heart Metropolis (e.g., Bontje, 2003), but we will come back to this at the end of this section. Before that, let us see what key factors facilitated the Randstad-Green Heart Metropolis vision in becoming the "new normal" in Dutch national spatial planning policies. The lens of transition theories can uncover some helpful cues.

When the Dutch State Office for the National Plan (RNP) embarked on devising the first National Spatial Planning Policy in the 1950s, there were two critical landscape pressures shaping public perception – the severe famine of the winter of 1944 (*Hongerwinter*), which made the preservation of scarce agricultural land a top political priority, and the demographic boom and related ever-increasing demand for housing, making farmland protection highly unlikely without government intervention. Thus, when the Working Commission presented the Randstad-Green Heart spatial strategy for future development in the most densely populated part of the country, the idea, with very few exceptions (see Faludi & van der Valk, 1994, p. 107), strongly resonated with the aspirations of the wider community of government officials. The fear that uncontrolled, chaotic urbanization would threaten the integrity of Dutch society was another important factor that made the new course of action appear not only reasonable but desirable among decision-makers in the dominant planning regime. Moreover, the assumption that one could safeguard, or reform, society through the design of physical space was still profoundly embedded in the worldviews of planners at the time. Advocates of the Randstad-Green Heart approach in the Ministry and the Working Commission have most likely considered such preoccupations, since the single most influential image that they presented in their report was a metropolitan growth scenario, in which not only did the four historical cities in the region (i.e., Amsterdam, Rotterdam, The Hague, and Utrecht) coalesce, but the Green Heart was flooded by a sea of randomly arranged urban settlements. This struck a nerve in the political community and successfully got the idea across.

The sustained support for the Randstad-Green Heart by government was also due to the national and international acclaim the strategy received after the release of the first National Spatial Planning Policy (Bureau for the National Plan, 1960). British planner Gerald L. Burke, for instance, wrote a book titled *Green Heart Metropolis* (1966) using the term for the first time, while Peter Hall, an internationally renowned planning scholar, praised the Randstad-Green Heart approach in his book on world cities, also published in 1966. Thus, the concept gained further credibility in Dutch planning circles and in national government more broadly. These scholarly contributions, however, played an important role not only in acknowledging and popularizing the concept, but also in treating the region as one whole. Despite its fragmented structure, the Randstad was seen as a metropolis worthy of the label "world city." This reinforced the perception that Dutch government was on the right track and effectively resonated with its ambition to bring about a metropolitan region able to compete in the league of cosmopolitan cities like Paris and London, but without undergoing their major disadvantages.

The formation of an influential and diverse social network to support the Randstad-Green Heart idea was also key to its transition from a marginal niche, known only to rarefied planning elites, to the dominant principle of national spatial organization from the 1950s on. One leading figure responsible for the conception of the Randstad was the director of the Dutch national airlines, Albert Plesman, who around 1938 used the "Rim City" metaphor (or "Randstad" in Dutch) referring to the horseshoe-shaped urban region, stretching from Utrecht to Amsterdam, The Hague, and Rotterdam (Faludi & van der Valk, 1991). Plesman was connected both to urban planners and high-rank government officials, such as the Director of the Dutch State Office for the National Plan (RNP), Jasper Vink, who referred the idea to the Minister for Housing and Reconstruction, Joris in 't Veld. It was the minister who eventually insisted on the preservation of the Green Heart as the "commons" of the region and on the elaboration of the extreme urbanization scenario that would have occurred in the absence of planning, drawn by the chief planning consultant to the Working Commission J. P. Thijsse in 1956 (Faludi & van der Valk, 1994, p. 107).

The production of new knowledge about the urban system and how its evolution related to the processes of industrialization was also an important lever for the introduction of the Randstad-Green Heart vision in planning discourses and mainstream policy. More important, not only did pioneer investigations as those conducted in the 1920s by Th. K. van Lohuizen, deemed "the godfather of civic surveys" in the Netherlands (Faludi & van der Valk, 1991), or the 8-year-long research of the Working Commission in 1950–1958 yielded new sociospatial data at a monumental scale, but they also brought about to what transition scholars call "second-order learning" (Schot & Geels, 2008, p. 541). Rather than using this knowledge to optimize existing models of concentric urban growth in an incremental fashion, Dutch planners set on a radically different trajectory of regional planning and large-scale decentralization. The detrimental "grease-spot" fashion of urban expansion, which Geddes harshly criticized in *Cities in Evolution* (1915), was purposefully challenged through a new paradigm of spatial organization – the Randstad-Green Heart. Thus, rather than trying to cope with suburbanization in Amsterdam, Rotterdam, The Hague, or Utrecht in isolation, decisions for new construction sites had to be taken in concert, sharing the responsibility for maintaining the central green area open.

Of course, a similar level of top-down coordination, and at this scale, would have been inconceivable if the land earmarked for development were not public domain. In fact, this extensive land ownership granted Dutch government with planning powers that few, if any, other Western European countries enjoyed. But what set the ideal scene for government-led spatial planning were the two oil crises from the late 1970s, which abruptly paralyzed the private real estate market. In those years, almost the entire stock of new housing (80%) was built by the public sector, so the patterns of urbanization followed those prescribed in national spatial planning policies. This rare combination of a planning regime having a competitive advantage over the private sector both in terms of land tenure and market supply, due to the disruptive landscape pressures on the system (i.e., the oil crises), created conditions that were extremely conducive to the implementation of innovative and ambitious urban development approaches as the "concentrated deconcentration," put forward with the first National Spatial Planning Policy in 1960 and reiterated in subsequent planning reports.

The ability to lay out clear and sufficiently detailed expectations for the implementation of the Randstad-Green Heart strategy through national planning was yet another decisive factor in championing it across different state departments and levels of government. Some of the early national policy reports on spatial planning have even been criticized for their excessive specificity, resembling the level of detail typical for old-style blueprint plans. Yet, the meticulous codification of the grand vision of a Green-Heart Metropolis into a series of discrete pragmatic objectives was pivotal to its institutionalization and stabilization in the norms and practices of the mainstream planning regime. Indeed, the explanatory map number three, enclosed in the Second National Policy Report on Spatial Planning (1966), illustrating the four types of residential development planned for the Randstad and their exact locations, was proof of the wide consensus accomplished by the administration and the serious commitment to implementation. In fact, today, the map is regarded as expression of one of the highest moments in Dutch national planning (IENM, 2012, p. 17).

What kept the Randstad-Green Heart doctrine afloat, however, was also its relative ambiguity (Faludi & van der Valk, 1994, p. 16), which gave planners enough leeway for flexible interpretation and repurposing as socioeconomic and political conditions started to change. The Green Heart, for instance, which – in the shadow of postwar food insecurity crisis – was justified as a strategic "reserve" to cater for future needs (Faludi & van der Valk, 1994, 107), from the 1980s on began increasingly being portrayed through the lens of ecology, environmental protection, and biodiversity and much less through that of food production or urban development. This perspective is still consistently reflected in the 2012 Structural Vision on Infrastructure and Space presenting the Green Heart as a part of the national ecological network. In recent national planning reports, the Randstad metaphor has also partly been put aside in favor of the more open-ended concept of "urban network."

Transition roadblocks

The Randstad-Green Heart has by far been the most resilient concept in Dutch spatial planning history, yet from the vantage point of the early 2000s, critical observers have questioned the effectiveness of its implementation. Scholars are in accord on the transition of planning discourse and practice to a new "doctrine," but they are far less sanguine about the transition in physical space that should have taken place as well. There are three main criticisms that have been raised: national policies to contrast sprawl in the Green Heart have failed, since the area witnessed the highest pace of urbanization in the country; deconcentration policies decentralized housing, but led to severe traffic congestion and air pollution in the region, since jobs remained in central cities (Bontje, 2003); and the Randstad has never grown into the cohesive polynuclear metropolis able to outrun world cities such as Paris and London; rather, it remained an archipelago of relatively independent city-regions (VROM, 2008).

These outcomes, however, were not due to limitations inherent to the planning regime alone but resulted from changes in other sociotechnical systems as well, like the agrifood and transportation sectors, along with changes in people's dwelling preferences and lifestyles. One of the reasons for the high urbanization pressures in the Green Heart was that suburban and rural environments were a preferred dwelling setting and a growing number of families could afford to own homes there (Asbeek Brusse & Wissink, 2002). The areas in the Green Heart were also well connected to the big cities in the Randstad where the majority of jobs were. What is more, municipalities in the Green Heart were eager to welcome more suburban development because the revenues from it were essential to the development of new housing to meet internal demand (Faludi & van der Valk, 1994, p. 225).

All these mutually reinforcing phenomena were challenging established planning rules, and their effect was further amplified by radical innovations transitioning the farming sector. At the beginning of the twentieth century, Dutch agriculture was severely hit by cheap foreign imports and still catching up with the industrialization of farming practices that had occurred in the US and the UK. As a result, government resolved to invest heavily in the modernization and mechanization of the sector. The impacts of these policies started being felt in the years when the ambitious national spatial planning policies – and the Randstad-Green Heart vision – were advanced. In the period 1945–1995, domestic food production in the Netherlands increased from 15%–20% to 200%–300%, while the number of people employed in the sector dropped from 19% in 1947 to 5% in 1990 (Grin, Rotmans, & Schot, 2010). Agribusiness was becoming increasingly large-scale, centralized, and less land-based, making it easier for landowners to turn farmland to developers. Thus, despite the "compact city" policies of the 1980s, which succeeded the "concentrated deconcentration" of the 1960s–1970s, urbanization of farmland took place. Successful cases of inner-city redevelopment were rare also because of high cleanup costs, far less convenient than development of greenfields from scratch. Frequent renegotiations and compromises throughout the execution of national spatial policies and the slow processes of their implementation (Bontje, 2003) further put the development of the Randstad-Green Heart in jeopardy.

Notwithstanding the multiple breaches in the Randstad-Green Heart Metropolis principle, made during its translation in practice, the concept is still recognized as the most iconic vision in national planning history so far. It was deemed the number one "icon" of Dutch planning (IENM, 2012) in a catalog of 35 emblematic planning examples compiled through a participatory consultation process by the Dutch Ministry of Infrastructure and the Environment. The catalog was aimed at providing a source of inspiration for the future generations of planners and urge them to pair, or top, the high quality of past planning endeavors for which the Netherlands have earned an international reputation in the field. But the Randstad-Green Heart example offers food for thought for budding urban food system planners as well. It turns our attention to the power of good metaphors in supporting radical transitions in planning practice and to the complexities of changing urban development regimes on the ground, even in allegedly ideal circumstances. For instance, it faces us with questions such as: What strong metaphor could help us protect urban gardens and regional food systems while we are building a more robust set of research methods and analytical techniques to inform urban food plans and policies? Are metaphors like the "urban foodshed" (see Chapter 3) or "green infrastructure" sufficiently convincing? In considering these questions, one last early-twentieth-century proposal, proposing a radically different fix to the inefficient industrial metropolis, is worth examining – the Broadacre City model by US architect and urbanist Frank Lloyd Wright.

The Broadacre city

At the time when the Dutch Randstad-Green Heart concept was emerging and the early garden cities and suburbs were being built in the UK (e.g., Welwyn, 1920; Wythenshawe, 1930) and the US (e.g., Radburn, New Jersey, 1933), another bold vision of the city of tomorrow, where local foodscapes had a primary role, was being laid out on the other side of the Atlantic. It is world-renowned US architect Frank Lloyd Wright's (1869–1959) vision of "Broadacre City" (1934–1935). The model is a proposal for the radical transition to a new form of spatial organization of modern society that would allow individuals to reach their full potential; it aimed to free Americans from the oppressive forces of the industrial metropolis and empower them by using the most advanced technological innovations (e.g., automobiles, telecommunications, aircraft) as the basis for urban planning and design. With hindsight, Broadacre City blended many of the principles that imbued model town proposals in the nineteenth and early twentieth centuries – the integration of farming and gardening in the everyday life of citizens, the decentralization of urban growth, the regional and even national scale of spatial planning, the evolutionary view of the connection between cities and regions – yet, the synthesis it put forward was nothing close to them.

Much like Ebenezer Howard, some 30 years earlier, Wright also believed that the redesign of physical space could offer a "peaceful path to real reform," as Howard put it in his 1889 book title. Like Howard, Wright also felt that a superior form of urban environment, combining the benefits of town and country life while doing away with their respective downsides, was the best cure for the unhealthy and immoral society that the industrial metropolis had produced. Wright's "town–country magnet," however, was way more radical than Howard's Social City – not only did he do away with the flaws of the industrial city, but he proposed to overhaul the city as a form of spatial organization altogether. In fact, the "city" in Broadacre City is misleading. The model for new urban development that Wright put forward lacked two quintessential city hallmarks – a clear center and high density – suggesting a decentralized, diffused urban network instead of a new town, or a network of new towns, for that matter. Thus, Broadacre was not the American version of the Garden City nor should it be compared to the decentralized polynuclear metropolis that Dutch planners came up with later. It was a "non-city" and a "non-stop-city" at the same time, made possible by technological innovation and meant to set the scene for an evolutionary leap in the evolution of cities. The time was ripe, since suburban development in the US was already under-way and planning it on new terms would have potentially had nationwide repercussions.

The hybrid urban-rural space that Wright envisioned was not a mere turn back to the land. Broadacre City was an attempt to show that a "third" way of urbanization was possible, whereby even highly technologically advanced cit-ies can be actively engaged in stewarding an urban and even a domestic scale of the food system. Wright termed this hybrid space the "middle landscape" (1958). At the heart of the model was a new government policy by virtue of which each Broadacre citizen, current or yet to be born, would have received one acre (0.4 hectares) of farmland by law. Universal land ownership was thus one of the fundamental preconditions for the transition to a better urban soci-ety. It was also a key element in the development of an urban food infrastruc-ture. The surplus of fresh produce, that each family or individual would have grown, would have been picked up and sold to a local food outlet located near the super-speed highway bordering Broadacre. The hyperlocal food supply chain that Wright imagined was meant to provide citizens with access to "pro-duce fresh every hour" (Wright, 1932, p. 61); an overly ambitious goal even by today's local food movement standards. But, for Wright, local, fresh food was part of his strategy for liberating the individual from the unhealthy, parasitic urban existence, which he saw also in the growing consumption of processed foods. In his view, this was a perilous trend that was turning Americans into a "canned" nation (Wright, 1932, p. 65); therefore, all citizens had to acquire the necessary skills and resources to be part-time farmers.

Shortening the distance between food production and consumption and the direct engagement of citizens in gardening and farming, for Wright, was a means to a complete human existence. In line with the tenets of Russian philosopher Pyotr A. Kropotkin (1842–1921) and the UK industrialists who pioneered some of the early company towns we saw at the beginning of the chapter, as Robert Owen's New Lanark (1800–1810), Wright believed that a balanced combination of manual and intellectual labor was imperative. It would have created the ideal conditions for individuals to contribute to the best of their possibilities to the progress of society. Broadacre Cities would have thus provided the opportunities for reconnection with food through the acres of farmland that each household would have tended, but also through educa-tion in schools. At school, pupils would have learned how to grow, recognize, and cook different plants and vegetables (Wright, 1932, p. 80) – all skills that Wright felt were being lost in the blue-collar/white-collar functional, socio-economic, and spatial segregation of modern society.

Household food production however was not the only locus of the integra-tion of food into the built environment. Small-scale farms were also an integral part of Broadacre City. These urban farms were planned as a neighborhood amenity no different by importance from public bathhouses and were typically located near high-income urban dwellings. The assumption was that, thanks to technological progress, factories and other traditional productive activities, like farming, could operate in a nonpolluting fashion and therefore be placed in close proximity to residential and other nonindustrial city areas, resulting in an unproblematic mixed-use development pattern. While city-grown food was a key component of Broadacre's new urban economy, Wright was concerned with the ability of these small-scale farmers to stay in business and compete with large-scale agriculture enterprises. Two of the tactics he considered were land tenure – each farmer would have owned the land in production and there would have been a shared ownership of expensive technology and mechanical tools, like tractor vehicles, which would have otherwise indebted individual farmers to banks and insurance companies.

As its name hints, the design of Broadacre City was based on a very low-density yet mixed-use principle of spatial organization. A 4-square-mile section (2,560 acres, or 10.4 km^2) of the city would have hosted about 5,000 inhabitants. By way of comparison, Howard's standard Garden City would have hosted 30,000 inhabitants on 1,000 acres of land. Nelson (1995) estimates that, adjusted to a median household size of three, rather than six as Howard considered, Garden Cities would have been four times more populous than Wright's Broadacre Cities. The underlying assumption was that physical density and proximity were no longer vital to urban economic functions and distances could be seamlessly stretched thanks to technology – people could move rapidly from one place to another and, because of ubiquitous telecommunications, they would typically not even need to. Thus the one-acre plot, which was the building block of Broadacre and the means to a progressive American society in Wright's view, was not a step backwards vis-à-vis industrialization, but a leap forward propelled by it.

Wright called for a complete overhaul not only of established models of urban organization and design, but of the underlying institutional and governmental structures as well. For their decentralized layout, Broadacre Cities would have been best governed at the county level. More important, municipality and state jurisdictions had to be abolished, connecting county administrations directly to federal government (Wright, 1958). According to Wright's vision, the key elected official, overseeing the proper working of each Broadacre City in any given county, was the County Architect. The architect would have had the competencies to ensure that the principles of organic urban development and organic architecture – i.e., drawing on the natural features and topography of each site, thereby blurring the boundaries between nature and manmade environment – were respected as the city evolved.

While this was a fairly top-down take on urban planning – very distant, for instance, from Geddes's ideal of enabling citizens to directly partake in urban planning and transformation – Wright did place the expression of one's individuality at the heart of Broadacre's rationale. In fact, he viewed individuality as "the natural ideal of democracy" (1932, p. 15), and therefore Broadacre City would have provided the script for "the future city as a future for individuality" (1932, p. 17). Importantly, he contrasted individuality with individualism, deemed as the exact opposite of the effort of achieving an organic unity of the multifaceted dimensions of one's character. The obsolete centralized city, Wright argued, was inhibiting individuality. Capitalism, in the plutocratic form that Wright reproved, was either proliferating uniformity or blatantly mixing cultures and styles, hence obscuring rather than giving space for individuality to emerge. In Broadacre City, this would have been avoided by providing citizens with the opportunity to develop their property in full accord with their personal histories, needs, and tastes, yet within the framework of organic architecture – the hallmark of Wright's work. That is why high-rise apartment buildings – there were twelve 15-story towers in the typical Broadacre subsection – were considered only a temporary, transient accommodation for those newcomers who were not ready to move to the one-acre single-family-house properties as yet. This is, in fact, one of the few cases in which Wright deemed the new design possibilities granted by technological innovation undesirable for the city of the future.

Despite the fact that Wright was one of the most influential and accomplished architects of his time, Broadacre City was never realized in practice. The reasons why this transition failed to take off are to be sought in the gestation of the idea, the model itself, the efforts Wright put into its popularization, and the broader cultural and socioeconomic milieu in which the proposal was put forward. Broadacre was the outcome of a life-long research and an effort to transfer the tenets of organic architecture at the community scale. Many of the building typologies that Wright had developed over the course of his career could be found in Broadacre City. As a matter of fact, as Smith observes (1966, p. 155), to judge Broadacre is to judge the entire work of Wright, and the other way around. But Broadacre was more than a mere assemblage of Wright's signature buildings, it was a meticulous synthesis and a provocative statement of how a new social order could be established by reinventing the city of tomorrow. While Wright had started probing his ideas at the urban scale in various projects across the country, such as Usonia I in East Lansing, Michigan, and Usonia II in Pleasantville, New York, deemed as relatively successful (Burley, Deyoung, Partin, & Rokos, 2011), he first attempted to piece them together in a single urban planning manifesto in his book *The Disappearing City* (1932).

Like Geddes, who, approaching the sixth decade of his life, wrote *Cities in Evolution* (1915) bent on laying the groundwork for a new science of cities, Wright embarked on crafting the grand synthesis of his work in his sixties. While he first laid out the rationale and design principles for Broadacre City in *The Disappearing City* (1932), he continued refining and adjusting the model until the end of his life, writing two more manuscripts – *When Democracy Builds* (1945) and *The Living City* (1958). Conveying radical visions for the city of tomorrow through manifesto-like manuscripts was far from uncommon, in fact, it was necessary – Owen, Buckingham, Howard, and Geddes all turned to the written word, sparingly supplemented with evocative diagrams, as a means to real-world change. But, being an architect, Wright regarded visual representations as important, if not more important, as prose. Thus, besides in his writing, he portrayed Broadacre through breathtaking bird's-eye-view perspectives and a massive 12 × 12 feet (3.7 × 3.7 meters) three-dimensional model of a 4-square-mile section of Broadacre, which was displayed at the Industrial Arts Exhibition at the Rockefeller Center in New York City in 1935.

Wright's formidable reputation and the extensive social network he had developed throughout his professional practice were decisive in promoting Broadacre City and turning it into a promising niche innovation. One of Wright's clients funded the construction of the Broadacre model for the exhibition, while later, in 1943, some of the most prominent intellectuals of the time like Albert Einstein and John Dewey signed his "Citizen's Petition" to support the Broadacre City model (Don, 2010). Yet, despite all these efforts, Broadacre City never sparked the excitement that Howard's Garden City or the Dutch Randstad-Green Heart vision enjoyed. Much like Geddes's call for an evolutionary theory of cities, Wright's plea for a nationwide transition to a decentralized city regime largely remained on paper. Part of the neglect of Wright's ideas was due to his way of conveying them. If, for Howard, a central concern was to appeal to the political leaders and industrialists of his time, directly quoting and responding to many of their concerns, Wright's books were a harsh critique to both local governments and developers who, in his view, were selfishly profiting from the "parasitic" metropolis. While Howard was preoccupied with proving the financial feasibility of his proposal and its superiority to comparable developments, Wright was greatly relying on the strength of his ethical and technological innovation arguments.

The critical, vexing tone of Wright in setting forth his proposal and the paucity of pragmatic considerations made it less compelling to the US businessmen, governors, and planners of his time. In an era when the "middle-men" in both real estate and the food industry were expanding, his advocacy for an urban world without rents, landlords, food supply intermediaries, and traditional money (he suggested a bartering scheme based on social credit), was irritating, to say the least (Collins, 1963). Additionally, Wright's scheme of dispersed villages administered by counties, whereby two of the essential jurisdictions of the US's administrative structure − the city and the state − were taken out, was unthinkable for government officials and added up to the reasons why Wright's grand vision ended being neglected. One of Wright's prominent observers, Robert Twombly (1972, p. 547), hints that the vagueness of Broadacre as to implementation might have well been deliberate and its intended purpose could have been of a "platform for criticism and a standard against which to measure prevailing conditions." Still, the energy and resources Wright invested in developing it make it unlikely that he was aiming at a purely theoretical contribution. Yet, his strong individuality and uncompromising character left little room for second-order learning, which would have arguably tempered Broadacre's unrealistic expectations from government and society and eventually barred its widespread endorsement.

The impacts and implications of Wright's legacy, however, are still a moot point. While it is true that no social movement or government policies drew on Broadacre City as a direct source of inspiration, scholars tend to agree that Wright's vision was remarkably prophetic of the US transition to suburban and "exurban" development that took place during the second half of the twentieth century. But it would be misleading to consider suburbia as the fulfillment of Wright's prophecy – unlike residential-only suburban areas, Broadacre featured a great variety of functions, with housing next to small-scale farming and public amenities. Exurbs, on the other hand, defined as "semi-rural communities, beyond suburbs but within commuting range" (Oxford Dictionary of American English, introduced in 1955), resembled much more Wright's ideal of the city of tomorrow. Exurban development in the US boomed during the 1960s–1980s and coevolved with the consolidation of so-called "edge cities" – the alter ego of traditional downtowns – near major transportation arteries and intermodal junctions. Indeed, the revolution in telecommunications, the Internet, and highway infrastructures that society witnessed in those years opened up the possibility, for those who could afford it, to resettle beyond the suburbs, and in doing so proved right many of the propositions that Wright advanced in *The Disappearing City* (1932).

Indicative of the unfolding of a nationwide urban transition was the fact that in 25 years alone (1960–1985), about 16 million Americans moved out of suburbs and cities to live in exurbia (Nelson, 1995). This fundamental transition in dwelling practices greatly affected the relationship between people, the food system, and the environment. Shopping for food turned into a car-dependent practice with people inescapably driving to and from big-box supermarkets typically located out of urban centers, along major freeways, as Wright foresaw. This modernization, however, was seldom coupled with an authentic "return to the land," at least not in the sense that Wright intended. While people were allegedly driven to exurbs by ideals similar to the kind of agrarian individualism that US president Thomas Jefferson (1743–1826) advocated for a century earlier, their interest in small-scale farming had little to do with food growing as a source of income or secure food supply. Rather, tending a small plot of farmland or an orchard was seen as the kind of alternative leisure activity that only the affluent upper- and upper-middle-class citizens could afford to practice. As Nelson (1995, p. 345) aptly points out, exurbanites saw the great value of owning a piece of farmland mainly through the lens of the part-time "gentlemen farmer."

Neither suburbia nor the rise of exurbia led to the decommissioning of historical urban centers. In fact, people living exurbs and suburbs are still greatly dependent on the metropolis, or the "edge city" for that matter, for employment and basic public services. Most important, regardless of whether these forms of decentralized urbanization followed Broadacre's principles or not, they brought to light some of its potential weaknesses and hidden social and environmental costs. Soaring energy consumption, road congestion, air pollution, and extensive fragmentation of prime agricultural land are the corollary of a dispersed built environment, or at least in the conditions of today's advancements in technology and prevalent consumerism culture. The dominant food system regime has progressively pushed the real places of food production out of sight, alienating the majority of urban dwellers from the actual practices involved in feeding the city. Thus, it is unclear the extent to which a greater exposure to the rural environment brings about more sustainable food consumption practices. Evidence on the benefits of recovering an urban scale of agriculture in cities is nevertheless mounting.

So, looking back at Broadacre, some of the questions worth asking today perhaps are: How do we bring about the same level of organic integration of food-growing spaces in existing urban areas and downtowns? How do we reinstate local food infrastructure elements as neighborhood amenities, sited amidst schools, commercial centers, office towers, and residential buildings? What would it take to normalize food growing, cooking, and composting practices in the bundle of everyday urban routines of people of all socioeconomic strata? A revamped urban food environment has the potential to provide the "new scaffolding" for civilization that Wright was referring to, and a growing number of scholars today are seeking to re-envision the city of the twenty-first century through a food system lens. The next part of the chapter is about some of them.

A new generation of urban food visions

As we saw in the first part of the chapter, the ambition to reconnect cities to the countryside was pervasive in all reformist city models trying to fundamentally rectify the ills of the industrial city; it was, in fact, part of the pioneer experiences that laid the ground for city and regional planning as a professional field and a responsibility of government. But while the belief that the design of physical space alone can bring about a better society endured in modernist architecture and planning, the effort of making "the field gain over the street" – to use Geddes's metaphor – faded away. At first, leaving the urban food supply system largely to the private initiative seemed to work just fine, but, a century later, we have come to realize that this assumption cannot be further than the truth. In fact, toward the late 1990s, open-minded planners (e.g., Greenhow, 1994; Martin & Marsden, 1999; Pothukuchi & Kaufman, 1999, 2000; Quon, 1999; Sommers & Smit, 1994) started calling attention to the awry consequences of leaving the food system out of the public domain and out of the remit of their professions. In the 2000s a small, but rapidly expanding, group of urban scholars and professionals have begun to voice their concerns about this "puzzling omission" (Pothukuchi & Kaufman, 2000, p. 113) and lay out different strategies to address it.

Some of the proposals are overtly pragmatic, in the spirit of small-scale interventions at the scale of a building, street, or a neighborhood, while others are decidedly conceptual, focusing on the new theoretical foundations that this new design and government responsibility would necessitate to be enacted. In this second section of the chapter, we will explore two very distinctive and profoundly different conceptual visions as to how principles embedded in the agrifood system could lay the groundwork for designing an entirely new built environment, breaching the rigid functional barriers our cities inherited from the modernist architecture and urbanism movement. The two concepts are "Agronica" by Italian architect and designer Andrea Branzi and "Sitopia" by British architect and food systems scholar Carolyn Steel. Because both proposals were conceived in recent times, with Branzi's arguably well ahead of his time, looking at their impact vis-à-vis the dominant spatial planning regime through the lens of transitions would be misplaced. Yet, as we will see, they nevertheless provide important cues as to what the building blocks of this transition could be.

Agronica

The work of Italian architect and designer Andrea Branzi can be viewed as the missing link between early twentieth century ideal-city models, through which pioneer urban planners were seeking to recover the domestic scale of agriculture as a means to social reform, and early twenty-first-century food-city visions, whereby architects and urbanists argue for the reinstatement of local food spaces and practices as a means to sustainable development. One of Branzi's prominent commentators, Charles Waldheim, observes that his avant-garde projects and ideas lay the groundwork for a "new generation of urbanists interested in the economic and agriculture drivers of urban form" (2010a, p. 22). In fact, as we will see in this section, Branzi questions the opportunities for organically integrating urban and rural realities in the face of fast-paced technological innovation. Perhaps, most important, he calls attention to the key distinction between physical space as a means to transition and transitional space; the latter offering a much needed room for experimentation and reversible sociotechnical innovation processes. Branzi's proposals are often regarded as a source of inspiration for the agricultural urbanism approach to urban planning, but they offer important insights for the broader urban food planning "movement" as well.

Much like Wright, who envisioned a new space for the rapprochement between agriculture and modern urban life in Broadacre City, with his theoretical project called "Agronica" (1995), Branzi and his colleagues – Dante Donegani, Antonio Petrillo, Claudia Raimondo, and Tamar Ben David – put forward a new kind of urban space where high-tech, industrial farming and everyday public and private life are organically interwoven, but the relationships between them are open to multiple adjustments. Agronica can be viewed both as a "semi-urbanized agricultural park" (Shannon, 2006, p. 155) and a hybrid urban environment shaped by the fundamental principles of agricultural production (Waldheim, 2010b, p. 117) – such as seasonal adaptation, flexible repurposing, reversibility, and temporality. These are some of the essential ingredients of what Branzi termed "weak urbanization." Agronica is thus a provocation and a firm call for a disciplinary renewal that is perhaps best synthesized in Branzi's assertion that "contemporary architecture should start to look at modern agriculture as a reality with which to set new strategic relations" (2003, cited in Shannon, 2006, p. 154). In the same way in which advanced systems of industrial farming and food production promptly adapt to changing economic and environmental conditions, cities would benefit from abandoning the pursuit of some ideal finite form and instead be planned for the constant renegotiation of the balance between physical infrastructure, social practices and institutions, and regional ecosystems.

The rationale for Branzi's turn to agriculture is, thus, far from any normative claims about the virtues of reconciling a life augmented by technology with traditional stewardship of the land. Rather, it is the blending of advanced mechanization and the ability to respond to changes in the external environment in real time, promptly rearranging the "hardware" of cities, namely the built infrastructure, to reflect changes in the "software," i.e., the nonmaterial socioeconomic webs that make cities work. Branzi never used an IT metaphor to frame his proposal, but is essentially one of the strongest messages his work conveys. In Agronica, the turn to farming is driven neither by nostalgic romanticism nor by environmentalism and sustainable development concerns. It is rather a plea for the acknowledgement and integration of complexity into city planning, starting with rethinking the very image of the city – as a borderless bundle of diffused telecommunications or, as Branzi (2010a) puts it, a "personal computer every 20 square meters" (215 square feet).

Four years after the inception of Agronica, Branzi with two of his collaborators, Ernesto Bartolini and Lapo Lani, had the opportunity to apply the design principles of Agronica in developing the master plan (1999–2000) for the area of the former Philips industries in Strijp, Eindhoven, in the Netherlands. The project was by all means a "weak urbanization" manifesto; it rejected any possibility for strict functional subdivision of the area, openly overhauling the tenets of modernist land-use zoning, and posited that urban functions must be "manageable as agriculture" (Lani, 2011). A key concern for the design team was to convince the administration of Eindhoven to consider the project not as a definitive form that once implemented would remain more or less still in time and space, but as an intentionally mobile "experimental terrain" (Lani, 2011). As we will see in Chapter 6, this is also the overarching philosophy of the Almere Oosterwold master plan designed by the Dutch architectural office MVRDV for the City of Almere in the Netherlands.

Besides temporality and the possibility for indefinite spatial rearrangements by means of mobile infrastructures, the absence of fixed boundaries was another poignant provocation that Agronica and the Eindhoven master plan launched to the dominant planning and designing regimes in Italy and abroad. It is hard to distinguish inside from outside and rural from urban spaces as if the individual, and the many collectives that make up society as a whole, are challenged to redefine where the boundaries between urban and rural are, or should be. Urban planners, architects, and designers, working in the age of globalization, the Internet, and mass media, are thus invited to pause and reconsider the conceptual and methodological frameworks, and the very object they claim expertise in, before proceeding with shaping the urban environment for the next generations. The physical models that Branzi advanced represent his vision of the "Weak Metropolis" (Waldheim, 2010b, p. 114), shaped by design principles the exact opposite of the "Functional City" paradigm that modernist architects forged with the 1933 Athens Charter. But Branzi calls not just for abolishing the rigid functional boundaries ingrained in much of twentieth-century planning, but to reflect on the tracing of boundaries as an act of establishing power structures, which are made permanent through the fixity of the place, form, and function of built infrastructure. Importantly, his work draws attention to the inbuilt lock-ins in the dominant regime of planning practices that stifle urban innovation and creative adaptability.

The mobile multifunctional physical environment of the "weak" metropolis defies any attempt to impose a vertical hierarchy of power relations or a physically centralized system of management and control; in Agronica's decentralized and spread urban realm, there are no "cathedrals," as Branzi metaphorically puts it. Centralization and power structures could arguably be seen only by mapping the digital world and the networks of interest-based social collectives (e.g., work, leisure, government, family, mobility, etc.) that assemble and dismantle there. The germs for this *leitmotif* in Branzi's Agronica concept can be traced back to the unorthodox representations that he and his colleagues from the Archizoom Associati architectural collective he cofounded (with Gilberto Corretti, Paolo Deganello, Massimo Morozzi, and Lucia Bartolini), launched 30 years earlier with the thought-provoking name "No-Stop City" (1969–1972). In this model, the city is rendered as a diffused assemblage of heterogeneous objects rather than the traditional dense and compact aggregation of architectures and enclosed open spaces. No borders, no monuments, no stops indeed, just a universally inhabited space. As Branzi (2010b, p. 112) clarifies, his work is not about theorizing the ideal city of the future but providing new representations of the city of today. Thus, unlike the radical thinkers that we previously discussed, Branzi uses the project not as a model but as an analytical tool and a platform for enlightened critique – an investigative approach worth considering when approaching the challenge of redesigning city-regional food systems in the public interest. Fresh representations of the city through a food system lens can effectively challenge our conventional understandings of the places and spaces of food, their impacts on people and the environment, and our role in them.

This approach to radical urban transformation by making more room for complex self-organization, side-by-side linear top-down approaches to planning, is especially close to the point that sociotechnical transition management scholars make. It is not the ability to perfectly imagine the end-state of a several-generations-long transition that would ultimately take us there, but the right set of tools and rules to steer transition processes, while defining and redefining our normative goals – from the "slum-less" and "smoke-less" cities of the nineteenth century to the "smart cities" and "zero-carbon cities" of the twenty-first century. In his seven suggestions for a New Athens Charter, which offers a new "doctrine" for urban design and planning for the present century, Branzi (2010a, 2010b) offers a set of principles that could help direct change toward the redesign of the built environment for humanity in the digital age. The suggestions are the following: (1) Reuse and repurpose existing estates; (2) Enter in the interstices of daily life to foster large-scale transformation through microstructures; (3) Foster reversible facilities for new activities that are unforeseen; (4) Consider the city as a personal computer every 20 square meters (215 square feet); (5) Think of solutions that are less anthropocentric and more open to biodiversity; (6) Create threshold areas which are half urban and half agricultural with flexible discontinuous housing; and (7) Design new architectural facilities that make public/private and interior/exterior boundaries disappear (Branzi, 2010a).

The gist of Branzi's contribution is his emphasis on the need to create spaces aiding the development of diffused capabilities to adapt, respond, and finally overcome socioeconomic, political, and environmental pressures from the scale of the individual to entire urban regions, making the most of the informational revolution we live in, a prospect that dominant representations of the city as brick and mortar likely suppress. It is a space which can be configured ad hoc to express one's individuality at best. But unlike Wright's Broadacre City, the conundrum of how future individualities can be still allowed for once the single-family houses are organically built for their first dwellers is solved by using the stratagem of mobile buildings and infrastructures, so that one is free to accept or unmake inherited individualities. The beauty of this model, however, is also its major risk. To tap into its benefits in practice, great attention must be given to how it could be best equipped to allow for productive exploration and experimentation; in other words, how it could be best specialized for the practices of research and creative problem-solving and adaptation. Fertile spaces for innovation are essential, but fuzzy definitions of what this means at the urban scale can easily fall in the perilous trap of "everything goes" and thus succumb to mediocre generality and the apathy that empty, ambiguous spaces, suited for everything and nothing, engender.

Ultimately, Agronica's legacy is meaningful to the urban food planning movement not for the integration of agriculture per se – in fact, there is no trace of short food supply chains, artisan foods, or urban agriculture – but for drawing planners' attention to the value of intermediate transitional spaces where the best transition pathways can be forged, recurrently and in accordance with the specific environmental conditions available at any given time. Spaces are required where productive hybridization between urban and rural rationales of social and spatial organization can take place and where technology can be used to test multiple hypotheses for the reconciliation between cities and their local foodsheds and between agriculture and urban planning. The concept discussed next – Sitopia – is an attempt to view the city through a food system lens and an invitation to this kind of experimentation.

Sitopia

More than a century after Ebenezer Howard's stride to solve the problems of industrial London through his Garden City model for urban decentralization, London and the UK at large were hit by the detrimental effects of industrialization yet again; not on the city, but this time around on the agrifood system. As had many Western cities, post-industrial London had happily left the horrors of the nineteenth-century metropolis behind, but the stupendous scale of mechanization, standardization, and globalization of the food system – reflected in its displacement from cities' streets, squares, and hinterlands – which took place over the twentieth century began revealing its hidden costs for the well-being of urban and rural dwellers and the environment altogether. Like other developed-economies cities, London had taken its emancipation from the local food system too seriously. The exponential loss of farmland, an obesity "epidemic," and languishing food procurement and preparation skills are some of the glaring symptoms of another, subtler, urban crisis at work. In the early 2000s, London-based architect Carolyn Steel resolved to take the problem head on and expose the bundle of connections linking food and cities – from field to fork and beyond – and how these can purposefully be used to address the root causes of the nutritional and environmental anomalies that London and other Western cities are currently faced with.

In her book *Hungry City: How Food Shapes Our Lives* (2009b), Steel makes a persuasive call to unlearn what we know about cities and redefine them through the lens of food. She takes a historical approach to make her point and illustrates the complex coevolution between food system practices – such as farming, transportation, shopping, cooking, and waste disposal – and urban development, reflected in city form, urban economy, and the domestic and public spaces of urban life. Equally important, being trained in the domain of design disciplines, Steel does not stop with her plea for the new representations of the city that food can yield, but stresses food's importance as a means to actually transform the state of things. As she put it in a follow-up article on the book: "Once we recognize its power to shape our lives, we can harness food as a collaborative, multidisciplinary tool to address a wide range of issues, from resource depletion and poverty to obesity and climate change" (Steel, 2010, p. 34). The conceptual framework the British architect proposes to this end is "Sitopia" – a pragmatic utopia whereby the city is experienced and planned for as the "place of food." The term Sitopia stems from two ancient Greek words, sitos (food) and topos (place). But for Steel, Sitopia is altogether a worldview, a design tool, and an ideal city-regional environment, whereby the artificial schism between us and the organic realm to which we owe our very existence is intentionally disrupted, resulting in greater public health and environmental sustainability.

Steel's holistic analysis of the evolution of industrial and post-industrial London, and Western cities more broadly, uncovers how central urban planning challenges, like urban sprawl, social cohesion, vibrant city centers and public spaces, and effective waste management, can usefully be reframed through the lens of food. This makes it a particularly instructive contribution for those of us interested in the emergent domain of urban food planning. Steel meticulously unpacks the urban implications of the century-long transition of agriculture and food supply from a top responsibility of government and the public domain to an area of competency almost entirely managed by the private sector. She generously walks us though the consequences of the rise and consolidation of the so-called "middlemen" – i.e., the processing and distribution segment of the system – which Wright so forcefully was trying to bypass through his Broadacre City. In his view, this was the necessary next chapter of urban development in America; he dreamt about the elimination of leasehold from homes and farmland but also of any form of intermediation that would suppress one's connection to the land and his or her individuality. Unlike Wright, however, Steel (2009b, p. 10) invites us to reform these connections by changing the way we perceive existing cities, way before even considering the possibility of modeling those of the future: "In order to understand cities properly, we need to look at them through food."

By using the lens of food to appraise the city, one easily becomes aware of how, for example, the evolution of food transportation unfolded hand-in-hand with large-scale urban expansion and the coalescing of adjacent urban areas into amorphous conurbations at the regional scale. The advent of the first commercial railway lines and transatlantic steamships in the 1830s played a role as important as population growth in the indiscriminate consumption of periurban and regional farmland and the demise of market gardening and agriculture in and around industrial metropolises. Steel illustrates how this interdependence between urban development and food supply is at work in present times as well, arguably more than ever before. Cheap, high-speed truck and air transportation, advanced refrigeration technologies, and sophisticated logistics have given birth to an entire new kind of local food storage and distribution spaces and systems. Extensive regional and national food hubs, the size of airports, have been built on many greenfield sites across the UK (e.g., Crick in Northamptonshire county), while in North America some of the largest such facilities in the world have been developed – New York City's Hunts Point 60 acre (24 ha) terminal market in the Borough of Bronx and Toronto's 40 acre (16 ha) Ontario Food Terminal.

Not only have these mammoth depots swallowed up vast portions of periurban and rural land, but they have further perpetuated the physical and cultural disconnect of cities from the places and practices of food production and distribution. Using a historical map of seventeenth-century London, Steel (2009b, p. 118) illustrates how the role of the city as the locus of food exchange par excellence used to be easily recognizable and experienced on a daily basis by city dwellers. Back then one could seamlessly orient her- or himself where a certain kind of produce was sold by simply recalling the names of city's streets and squares (e.g., bread, fish, poultry, vegetables), but also they could draw accurate conclusions about food's provenance by looking at the direction from which it entered the city. Thus, after the railway, present-day food logistics have reinforced the widening cliff between the geography of food and public spaces in the city, making the food-related toponyms sound like some old-fashioned idiosyncrasies, vestiges of less fortunate times. The world of food supply has in fact effectively been concealed out of sight and out of mind, while locational and spatial planning decisions are being taken overwhelmingly in the private domain.

Looking at the city through a food lens reveals also the correlation between food shopping places and practices and the faith of inner-city areas. It becomes clear how the desertification of high streets and downtowns, which took place in the UK during the 1980–1990s, was tightly connected to the advent of big-box supermarkets at the city edges. In Steel's view, the reason for the detrimental effects of these new venues for food shopping lies in their fundamental incompatibility with the city as a locus of food exchange. To be viable, large supermarkets and shopping malls need cheap land and easy access to major transportation junctions that could seamlessly connect them to the nearest food hub, both conditions at odds with dense inner-city cores. But it was the concurrent possibility of handling large quantities of food both at the supermarket and at home that made the real difference. Suburban supermarkets flourished also because domestic fridge, television, and car ownership became ubiquitous in that same period. Thus, "one-stop" food shopping became a practice technically possible and culturally appealing to the majority of urban and suburban households.

Moreover, as the power of retail and centralized food supply operations grew, retailers developed, for the first time in history, an appetite for large-scale urban development projects and new residential districts. With supermarket CEOs wearing the hat of real-estate developers and the consolidation of retail in few large names, urban planners started being faced with even stronger market opponents. In fact, appreciating the mechanisms of urban development through the lens of food, Steel argues, unmasks the manifestation of unexpected phenomena such as "supermarket urbanism" or "supermarket cities" (e.g., a 2,500 acre brownfield site redevelopment in Hampton in the UK). Not only are global supermarket chains filing urban development applications, but, to overcome planning restrictions, they have started purchasing large tracts of urban land in concert to form shared "land banks," thus obtaining an insurmountable bargaining power and effectively undermining local administrations' control over land-use decisions. But there are also isolated instances where the modern shopping-mall culture has been used by city governments as a means to inner-city urban renewal and the preservation of old indoor urban markets structures. Boston's Faneuil Hall Marketplace conservation and the revitalization effect it had on adjacent public spaces is one successful case in point Steel brings our attention to. What becomes evident from this approach to urban analysis is that "control of food gives control over space and people" (Steel, 2009b, p. 145), hence food can, indeed, be used as a powerful design tool that can make or destroy cities and their local and distant hinterlands.

Casting a food-sensitive light on city life can help us also discover surprising connections between mundane everyday practices, like cooking or the disappearance thereof, and expert practices, like architecture and interior design. In fact, as Steel shows in her analysis, the widespread disappearance of cooking practices in the UK over the past decade was not due to a fascination with ready meals and convenience alone, but, equally important, to building codes and regulations constantly shrinking the minimum kitchen-size requirements down to 6.5-square-meter (70-square-feet) spaces that would discourage just about anyone to cook from scratch at home. Being a compound practice, at the intersection of shopping, eating, and waste disposal, a departure from cooking immediately translates in shunning certain food procurement practices, particularly of fresh and raw ingredients. This in turn further stretches and adulterates the umbilical cord connecting cities and urban populations to the soil and organic matter where food originates from. As Steel (2009b, p. 198) notes, "Cooking . . . is pivotal point in the food chain: the one that, arguably, affects everything else in it."

The current arrangement of cities' organic waste disposal infrastructures is one other often neglected cause for the entrenched disconnect of cities from the organic realm that sustains them. Steel calls attention to how past decisions to dispose of rather than reuse human waste for urban and periurban agriculture in London, once it had been collected through the sewages, have heavily impacted people's attitudes and sentiments toward it over the past two centuries. If in preindustrial times "cities formed part of an organic cycle in which the food supply was fuelled by the waste it generated," Steel (2009b, p. 260) points out that today, in an era of increasingly heterogeneous urban waste streams, this organic cycle has been disrupted and organic waste ends up either in landfills or in incinerators. Back in the early 1660s, when London was far less populous and lacked its current underground sewage infrastructure, organic waste was collected by market gardeners' associations and reused as fertilizer in vegetable gardens tended along the river Thames or in the city outskirts.

The transition to a sophisticated network of sewages able to effectively purge the city from its waste occurred following a transition in people's perception of human dung from a valuable resource to a superfluous and harmful matter. The reason for that was the great spike in urban density that London experienced in the second half of the sixteenth century, which made the old system of human waste management overly unsustainable. The first sewage network built then, however, only postponed the true solution to the problem, which came in the 1800s, after London's first sewages were completely clogged. This caused multiple backups in people's homes, an unbearable smell, and multiple overflows in nearby rivers, thereby polluting Londoners' drinking water. To pose an end to this and effectively prevent the nightmarish cholera outbreaks that plagued the city as a result, engineers designed an innovative system of sewages and pumping centrals, which eventually dumped the hazardous waste far away into the open sea. While London's sewage crisis was solved for good, the realization that this is going to perpetuate the depletion of a finite natural resource, phosphorus, essential to soil fertility and farming, would hardly come to mind to any modern urbanite.

In the final part of her seminal study, Steel raises the important question of how can we use the codependency between urban development and the agrifood system – from seed to sewage/landfill – purposefully, as a means to enhance our living environment and ensure its long-term sustainability. In other words, what if the concept of Sitopia, namely the city as the place of food, was deployed not just as an analytical but a normative framework as well, guiding future city planning and architectural decisions – from the scale of the single dwelling to the building, the neighborhood, and the city-region at large. In Steel's view (2009a, p. 21, 2009b, p. 322), a "sitopic" city – that is, a city designed entirely through the lens of food – would ideally enjoy the following qualities: strong links with its regional hinterland, strong sense of food identity, an ubiquitous local food infrastructure (e.g., farmers markets, independent grocery stores, allotments, abattoirs, comfy domestic kitchens), mandatory food education in city schools, comprehensive urban food system plans, government protection from food monopolies, access to medium-scale industrial food production, a high degree of food sovereignty, and no urban growth boundaries, provided that the integrity of local organic cycles is ensured since its inception.

The model of Sitopia thus provides a glimpse into what a "third way" of urban food supply, a food-literate citizenry, and food-aware built environment could look and feel like. Industrial agribusinesses would step out of their profit-centered comfort zone toward agroecology and land stewardship practices, while real-estate developers and local government would acknowledge food as a matter of public interest and lend support for the development of sustainable city-regional food links, a diverse retailscape, and closed ecological cycles. In her "third" scenario, Steel likewise suggests the transition of citizens from consumers to active agents of urban and food system sustainability, or to "co-producers," to say it with the term used by Carlo Petrini, founder of the Slow Food Movement. But Steel's main point and *leitmotif* in *Hungry City* is that just making the effort to look at cities through the prism of food would bring about a transition in its own right. One of the greatest urban planning critics and scholars of the twentieth century, Jane Jacobs (1916–2006), half a century ago exhorted planners to pause and, before undertaking any sweeping urban renewal endeavor, study and theorize how the present city works, especially when it works well in the absence of or despite government planning interventions. Food, as Steel convincingly argues, can be one entry point to do just that.

From the standpoint of sociotechnical transitions, one important takeaway from Steel's work is that we cannot plan for the sustainability transition of the city by ignoring that of the food system and vice versa. The two systems are tightly interlocked. The question then becomes how to transition the institutionalized separation between the two and turn the notion of Sitopia from a quirky novelty into a commonplace concept. Steel gives limited cues to this end. The transition of the national planning "doctrine" in the Netherlands we examined in the first part of the chapter and the concepts of "Rim City" and "Green Heart" as new principles of spatial organization allude to the power of metaphors in shifting established ideas and routines, but, as we saw, metaphors alone might not be enough for the transition to unfold.

Concluding remarks

In this chapter, we cruised through some of the most compelling comprehensive visions of how a new equilibrium between cities and their natural regions can be achieved through the radical redesign of urban morphology. Four emblematic models from the early days of city and regional planning shed light on the rationale behind purposefully integrating agricultural land uses in plans for the city of tomorrow. We then fast-forwarded to the late 1990s and early 2000s to explore two additional conceptual proposals, suggesting that not only can agrifood system infrastructures be integrated into the built environment, but, most importantly, they can provide the basic principles for steering new urban development. Broadly, past and recent proposals differ by their attitude toward the existing city – with nineteenth- and early-twentieth-century models decidedly advocating for abandoning it and starting anew in the region (with the notable exception of Geddes and Dutch national planners) and recent proposals suggesting to reform it from within.

With hindsight, one can perhaps argue that the root cause of the problems that eventually spurred radical proposals for social and spatial reform, from Garden Cities through Broadacre City to Sitopia, was essentially the same – society's unreserved belief that the private sector on its own would provide the best response to cities' needs. The 1800s proved this belief wrong with respect to housing, while the 2000s proved it wrong with respect to the food system. So a central question is how to transition a sociotechnical system whose negative externalities have become socially unacceptable; put otherwise, what sociotechnical processes are best suited to do away with detrimental professional and social practices and the tools and spaces that shape them. The four historical cases provided some clues as to why some of them were more influential than others.

As noted previously, Howard's success was greatly due to the interplay of several personal and contextual factors: his proposal was the corollary of a long history of model-town plans by nineteenth-century industrialists and intellectuals, so his ideas for decentralized self-reliant new towns made sense to many potential investors; the time was ripe for his large-scale proposal also because industrialists had grown a critical mass of capital unthinkable half a century earlier; his calculations illustrated that the model would be more convenient compared to similar developments; he aptly framed the problem at stake and its solution through quotes and references to daily political debates thus making his proposal approachable and appealing to political circles at the time; and his position as a parliamentary stenographer gave him access to important social networks and ways of framing the problems of the day. The simplicity and expressiveness of his diagrams as well as the endorsement of his ideas by leading architects, such as Raymond Unwin, who could commit to their translation in practice, were crucial in championing the Garden Cities model.

Geddes's prose was less penetrable, but he managed to galvanize a whole new community of practice and establish a physical and institutional space for civic surveys and civic engagement, the Outlook Tower in Edinburgh, which convincingly passed his message about the study of cities in relation to their regions on for multiple generations of urban planners, in the UK and overseas. The Dutch concept of Randstad–Green Heart successfully thrived for over half a century because of its endorsement by committed and powerful individuals at the national level of government, the inception of national spatial planning, and the right dose of flexibility and adaptability when it came to implementation through specific local planning policies and projects over the years. Finally, Wright's grand vision for a decentralized America never went beyond his 12-by-12 feet model and his manuscripts, because of its overt hostility to existing government and market arrangements and the inflexibility of Wright himself. He continued to work on the model for several decades, however, out of conviction that the time for a similar transition was ripe. And in fact it was – the rise of suburbia and, later of exurbia, followed suit during the subsequent years.

Ironically, independently from the immediate influence, or lack thereof, that these pioneer planned communities models had, critical observers would later deem all of them as de facto transition failures – radical on paper, but inconclusive in reality. Some of them were widely accepted and even spread out into an international movement (i.e., the Garden Cities movement), but this only proved that neither popularizing a new idea nor institutionalizing it in government practices is enough to transition business-as-usual urban development regimes, relying on certain landownership arrangements and forms of social cooperation. Worse still, widely diffused ideas that have succeeded to influence popular culture can even spur unintended transitions. Many satellite garden suburbs developed in the UK, which had nothing to do with the original model of self-reliant communities that Howard envisioned, were nevertheless marketed through the Garden City rhetoric. And, in the US, none of the hundreds of suburban communities built after World War II got anywhere close to Wright's Broadacre City model, yet many commentators would later blame the architect for having inspired the most unsustainable urban pattern of urban growth. Even Geddes's motto "survey before plan" would not be spared and would be used to promote an approach to town and country planning the exact opposite of what he envisioned – desk-based data collection and analysis rather than field work, top-down expert-only decision-making rather than broad civic participation, sweeping urban renewal plans rather than place-based "conservative surgery."

Besides drawing attention to the opportunities and challenges of advancing radically new models of urban development, the legacy of these visionaries is meaningful for present-day efforts to integrate a food systems competency into planning also for the substantive part of their proposals. All four of the historical models reviewed were grounded in the conviction that ensuring a strong connection to land through the redesign of urban space – e.g., spaces for urban gardening and farming, outdoor food and agriculture classes in schools, and protected areas of periurban and regional farmland – was pivotal to social reform. An urban scale of agriculture was conceived as a means to instill traditional virtues in working classes and preserve the integrity of those family structures and morals that had endured. Spatially, however, the models greatly differed from one another: Howard proposed a decentralized regional urban web of fixed-size new towns, the Garden Cities, whereby food growing practices were woven into the urban fabric through allotments, school gardens, and agricultural belts where agriculture colleges were to be established; the Randstad-Green Heart model advanced by Dutch planners suggested the development of a decentralized metropolis hinged on existing cities in the region, separated by green buffers and expanding in outward direction to preserve the extensive agricultural land at its core intact; while Wright ensured that agriculture was generously integrated in the domestic and public life of its decentralized Broadacre City communities by means of universally distributed one-acre family homesteads, local neighborhood farms elevated to the status of important buildings and public amenities, and a series of small-to-medium-scale farms and allotments located along the superhighway that would have connected one Broadacre settlement to the next one.

Both of the contemporary visions that we examined – Agronica and Sitopia – called for acknowledging complexity and coming to terms with the notion that there is no such thing as a perfect urban form that can be accomplished. Thus, instead of trying to design universal model-city environments, the authors argue, it would be more productive to focus our efforts on equipping present cities with new codes of conduct and ephemeral infrastructures that could help us incrementally rethink our relationship to soil and our supportive ecosystems. In other words, the role of urban planners and designers is to aid the development of a food-system-aware evolutionary pathway that could allow for recursive adaptation and progressive sophistication as we restore our knowledge of the system and rediscover our place in it. This position is in many ways aligned with Geddes's plea for a new science of the evolution of cities that could uncover the intricate, coevolutionary relationships between people's well-being, occupation, and the places they inhabit. This, in Geddes's view, would have provided the much-needed scientific backcloth for all new urban interventions.

In a way, with her seminal book *Hungry City*, Steel argued that food could be one promising lens through which to develop such new fields of urban research and practice. Though still amorphous and in the making, urban food planning is well poised to be one of the domains of research and practice where this new knowledge is generated and normalized. Starting with attempts to conceptually demarcate the scope and area of competency of this emergent domain, over the next six chapters, we will get a closer look of some of the forerunners seeking to provide the analytical, design, and organizational grounding for urban food planning as a discipline and professional practice.

Questions for further consideration

- What new relationship between cities and the food system did each of the six models examined in the chapter envision?
- Were any of these models translated in practice? To what extent and with what outcomes? What were some of the major weaknesses that they displayed?
- What factors proved critical for the stabilization and popularization of some of the early twentieth-century models in planning and government circles?
- How do recent visions compare to those from the past? Are there any of the urban planning approaches advanced in the twentieth century still meaningful today, particularly for the advancement of sustainable food system goals in cities? How so?

References

Ambrose, P. (1986). *Whatever Happened to Planning?* London: Methuen Publishing.

Asbeek Brusse, W., & Wissink, B. (2002). Beyond town and countryside? A Dutch perspective on urban and rural policies. *Built Environment, 28*, 290–298.

ATOC. (2007). *The Billion Passenger Railway Lessons from the Past: Prospects for the Future.* London: The Association of Train Operating Companies.

Batty, M., & Marshall, S. (2009). Centenary paper: The evolution of cities: Geddes, Abercrombie and the new physicalism. *Town Planning Review, 80*(6), 551–574.

Benevolo, L. (2012). *Le origini dell'urbanistica moderna* (23rd ed.). Bari: Editori Laterza.

Bontje, M. (2003). A "Planner"s Paradise' Lost? Past, present and future of Dutch national urbanization policy. *European Urban and Regional Studies, 10*(2), 135–151.

Branzi, A. (2003). Weak and spread. Public Lecture at Berlage Institute, Rotterdam, The Netherlands.

Branzi, A. (2010a). For a Post-Environmentalism: Seven Suggestions for a New Athens Charter. In M. Mostafavi & G. Doherty (Eds.), *Ecological Urbanism* (pp. 110–111). Zürich: Lars Müller Publishers.

Branzi, A. (2010b). The Weak Metropolis. In M. Mostafavi & G. Doherty (Eds.), *Ecological Urbanism* (pp. 112–113). Zürich: Lars Müller Publishers.

Bureau for the National Plan (1960). *(First) National Physical Planning Report.* The Hague: Ministry of the Interior.

Burke, G.L. (1966). *Green Heart Metropolis: Planning in the Western Netherlands.* London: Macmillan.

Burley, J., Deyoung, G., Partin, S., & Rokos, J. (2011). Reinventing Detroit: Reclaiming grayfields – new metrics in evaluating urban environments. *Challenges, 2*, 45–54.

Collins, G. R. (1963). *Broadacre City: Wright's Utopia Reconsidered.* New York, NY: Columbia University Press.

Darwin, C. R. (1859). *On the Origin of Species by Means of Natural Selection, or the Preservation of Favoured Races in the Struggle for Life*. London: John Murray.

Don, K. (2010, April 8). Frank Lloyd Wright's Utopian Dystopia. *Next City*. Retrieved from https://nextcity.org/daily/entry/frank-lloyd-wrights-utopian-dystopia

Faludi, A., & van der Valk, A. (1994). *Rule and Order: Dutch Planning Doctrine in the Twentieth Century*. Dordrecht- Boston- London: Kluwer Academic Publishers.

Faludi, A., & van der Valk, A. J. J. (1991). Half a million witnesses: The success (and failure?) of Dutch urbanization strategy. *Built Environment, 17*(1), 43–52.

Ferraro, G. (2002). Un manuale di educazione allo sguardo. In P. Di Biagi (Ed.), *I classici dell'urbanistica moderna* (pp. 31–40). Roma: Donzelli editore.

Geddes, P. (1904). *Civics: as Applied Sociology*. Read before the Sociological Society at a Meeting in the School of Economics and Political Science (University of London). Retrieved from www.guthenberg.org/files/13205/13205-h/13205-h.htm

Geddes, P. (1915). *Cities in Evolution: An Introduction to the Town Planning Movement and to the Study of Civics*. London: Williams & Norgate.

Geddes, P., & Thomson, J. A. (1889). *The Evolution of Sex*. London: Walter Scott.

Geels, F. W. (2006). Co-evolutionary and multi-level dynamics in transitions: The transformation of aviation systems and the shift from propeller to turbojet (1930–1970). *Technovation, 26*(9), 999–1016.

Greenhow, T. (1994). *Urban Agriculture: Can Planners Make a Difference* (Cities Feeding People Report, 12). Ottawa, ON: IDRC.

Grin, J., Rotmans, J., & Schot, J. (2010). *Transitions to Sustainable Development: New Directions in the Study of Long Term Transformative Change*. New York-Abingdon: Routledge.

Hall, P. (1988). *Cities of Tomorrow: An Intellectual History of Urban Planning and Design Since 1880*. Oxford: Basil Blackwell Ltd.

Hall, P., & Tewdwr-Jones, M. (2011). *Urban and Regional Planning* (5th ed.). New York City: Routledge.

Hough, M. (1990). Principles for Regional Design. In *Out of Place: Restoring Identity to the Regional Landscape* (pp. 179–213). New Haven-London, CT: Yale University Press.

Howard, E. (1898/1902). *Garden Cities of To-morrow*. London: Swan Sonnenschein & Company.

IENM. (2012). *Icons of Dutch Spatial Planning*. The Hague: Dutch Ministry of Infrastructure and the Environment.

Jacobs, J. (1992/1961). Introduction. In *The Death and Life of Great American Cities* (Reissue ed., pp. 3–25). New York: Vintage Books.

Korthals Altes, W. K. (2007). The impact of abolishing social-housing grants on the compact-city policy of Dutch municipalities. *Environment and Planning A, 39*(6), 1497–1512.

Lani, L. (2011). Masterplan Strijp Philips a Eindhoven. Retrieved from http://europaconcorsi.com/projects

Martin, R., & Marsden, T. (1999). Food for urban spaces: The development of urban food production in England and Wales. *International Planning Studies, 4*(3), 389–412.

Mazza, L. (2009). Plan and constitution – Aristotle's Hippodamus: Towards an "ostensive" definition of spatial planning. *Town Planning Review, 80*(2), 113–141.

Mumford, L. (1938). *The Culture of Cities*. London: Secker & Warburg.

Mumford, L. (1965). The Garden City Idea and Modern Planning. In F. J. Osborn (Ed.), *Garden Cities of Tomorrow* (2nd ed., pp. 29–40). Boston, MA: MIT Press.

Nelson, A. C. (1995). The planning of exurban America: Lessons from Frank Lloyd Wright's Broadacre city. *Journal of Architectural and Planning Research, 12*(4), 337–356.

New Garden Cities Alliance (2014). *The Letchworth Declaration*. Retrieved from https://gardencities.info/the-letchworth-declaration

Ostrom, E. (1990). *Governing the Commons.* Cambridge: Cambridge University Press.

Pothukuchi, K., & Kaufman, J. L. (1999). Placing the food system on the urban agenda: The role of municipal institutions in food systems planning. *Agriculture and Human Values, 16*, 213–224.

Pothukuchi, K., & Kaufman, J. L. (2000). The food system: A stranger to the planning field. *Journal of the American Planning Association, 66*(2), 113–124.

Quon, S. (1999). Planning for urban agriculture: A review of tools and strategies for urban planners (Cities Feeding People Report, 28). Ottawa, ON: IDRC.

Raven, R., Schot, J., & Berkhout, F. (2012). Space and scale in socio-technical transitions. *Environmental Innovation and Societal Transitions, 4*, 63–78.

Roodbol-Mekkes, P. H., van der Valk, A. J. J., & Korthals Altes, W. K. (2012). The Netherlands spatial planning doctrine in disarray in the 21st century. *Environment and Planning A, 44*(2), 377–395.

Schot, J., & Geels, F. W. (2008). Strategic niche management and sustainable innovation journeys: Theory, findings, research agenda, and policy. *Technology Analysis & Strategic Management, 20*(5), 537–554.

Shannon, K. (2006). From Theory to Resistance: Landscape Urbanism in Europe. In C. Waldheim (Ed.), *The Landscape Urbanism Reader* (pp. 141–162). New York: Princeton Architectural Press.

Smith, N. K. (1966). *Frank Lloyd Wright: A Study in Architectural Content.* Englewood Cliffs, NJ: Prentice-Hall.

Sommers, P., & Smit, J. (1994). Promoting urban agriculture: A strategy framework for planners in North America, Europe and Asia. *Cities Feeding People Report, 9*, 1–15.

Steel, C. (2009a). City, sitopia. *Ecologist, 39*(5), 19–21.

Steel, C. (2009b). *Hungry City: How Food Shapes Our Lives.* London: Random House.

Steel, C. (2010). Sitopia, un nuovo antico modo di vivere: Sitopia, a new-old approach to living. *Abitare, 501*, 33–34.

Taylor, N. (1998). *Urban Planning Theory Since 1945* (1st ed.). London: SAGE Publications.

Twombly, R. C. (1972). Undoing the city: Frank Lloyd Wright's planned communities. *American Quarterly, 24*(4), 538–549.

Unwin, R. (1909). *Town Planning in Practice: An Introduction to the Art of Designing Cities and Suburbs.* London: Adelphi Terrace.

VROM. (2008). *English Summary of Randstad 2040 Structuurvisie.* Delft: TU Delft.

Waldheim, C. (2010a). Notes Towards A History of Agrarian Urbanism. In M. White & M. Przybylski (Eds.), *On Farming: Bracket 1* (pp. 18–24). Barcelona: Actar Publishers.

Waldheim, C. (2010b). Weak Work: Andrea Branzi's "Weak Metropolis" and the Projective Potential of an "Ecological Urbanism." In M. Mostafavi & G. Doherty (Eds.), *Ecological Urbanism* (pp. 114–121). Zürich: Lars Müller Publishers.

Wheeler, S. M., & Beatley, T. (Eds.). (2014). *The Sustainable Urban Development Reader.* New York: Routledge.

Wright, F. L. (1932). *The Disappearing City.* New York, NY: Stratford Press.

Wright, F. L. (1945). *When Democracy Builds.* Chicago: University of Chicago Press.

Wright, F. L. (1958). *The Living City.* New York: Horizon Press.

3 Bridging food and planning

Food affects the economic, environmental, and social wellbeing of every place, yet food choices and the issues that surround them are rarely part of the urban planner's agenda.

—Arly Cassidy and Bowen Patterson, *The Planner's Guide to the Urban Food System*

Food, as a manmade artifact, and planning, as the endeavor to purposefully manage change, are two of the most distinctive markers of our human ingenuity and have always coevolved. The invention of agriculture enabled us to plan our food supply and likely led to the creation of the first cities, cities enabled us to better collaborate and led to the creation of a sophisticated, globalized agrifood industry, which, in turn, catalyzed the creation of new urban forms – metropolises, post-metropolises, and mega-city-regions. The twentieth-century transition of both food and urban development to highly engineered and standardized commodities, while boosting cities' profits and efficiency, was traded off for social equity and public and environmental health. This became evident at the turn of the 1960s, when Jane Jacobs's seminal critique of urban planning in *The Death and Life of Great American Cities* (1961) and Rachel Carson's groundbreaking *Silent Spring* (1962), documenting the detrimental effects of industrial agriculture on the environment, exhibited the "hidden" costs of the kind of agrifood and the urban planning systems we had so successfully developed. The idea that these two problems may, or even should be, tackled in tandem and can share some of their solutions, however, was still hard if not impossible to imagine.

This chapter, and indeed the whole book, is about urban food planning – an effort to conceptually and practically bridge food and planning. It is an emerging domain of theory and practice, which, far from replacing the dominant agrifood and planning systems, aims to reconfigure them so that they can serve us better as individuals and as a society. While urban food planning requires the co-creation of novel networks for place-based food governance encompassing state, market, and civil society spheres of social and economic practice, planners in the public domain and in private practice have a distinct role to play. As we saw in Chapter 2, the idea to plan for cities with local food infrastructure in mind is far from new to architects and urbanists, but, for the host of reasons we mentioned, it did not get to be implemented as envisioned. The recent resurfacing of the topic, however, suggests that these ideas may be "seeds of transition" which are yet to germinate. Over the past decade, in an era of unprecedented abundance, a growing community of urban planners has begun to see the absence of food in their profession not as a sign of prosperity but as a worrisome and unwise omission. They have set on a course to bridge food and planning and show the benefits of this challenging union. After briefly defining the urban food system and urban planning, in this chapter we will delve into the emerging domain of urban food planning to discover why planning for the food system from the vantage point of cities matters and how it can be done.

The urban food system

Talking about an urban food system, rather than simply the food system, is relevant for two reasons. Succinctly put, an urban food system can be viewed as the food system *in* the city and the food system *of* the city. The food system *in* the city consists of all the people, physical infrastructures, organic and inorganic inputs and outputs, as well as ideas, discourses, rules, and social practices that make food procurement, consumption, and disposal in the city possible. It can be just one link in the globalized food supply chain, or it can comprise shorter circuits through city-based food production, distribution, and recycling initiatives. The food system *of* the city is not defined by what one experiences in the city alone, yet it is urban because it serves and is driven by an increasingly urban world. It also prompts us to ask whether there is something unique that makes a food system specific to a given locale (e.g., this element of the urban food system is of this and this city only and I cannot find it elsewhere). It helps us keep our eyes open for emerging city-driven food system innovations and consider how a transition to a more hybrid food system *of* the city can be achieved by remaking the food system *in* the city. In short, an urban food system lets mayors, planners, just and sustainable food system advocates, and common citizens enter the scene as problem solvers and not as the problem.

Depending on how one views the urban food system, different entry points for transition come to the fore. The extent to which our lens is functional, geographic, or people-centered can change the way we perceive food issues, their solutions, and the role of planners altogether. The overwhelming majority of definitions in circulation tend to emphasize the functional distinctions within the food system by the five industrial sectors it comprises – production, processing, distribution, consumption, and waste management – and the regulations and institutions that accompany them (e.g., Pothukuchi & Kaufman, 2000). From an urban standpoint, this definition is useful in that sheds light on food as a multifaceted system with a cyclic nature. It helps reframe food in the city from a static object we merely purchase, eat, and dispose of to a component of a much more complex industrial and organic process. The inclusion of regulations and institutions can help us also think of the food system beyond the physical infrastructure – made of fields, factories, food trucks, supermarkets, eateries, landfills, and sewages – as a sociotechnical system (e.g., Geels, 2004) comprised of both material and nonmaterial components. To be precise, the current level of sophistication of the food system makes it very hard to pin it down to a single sociotechnical system as can more easily be done with energy or water, so it would be more accurate to talk about a system of sociotechnical systems.

This systematic definition effectively portrays the food system as a bundle of infrastructures, regulations, and related activities, but somewhat leaves places and people in the background. It may prompt planners to examine how all elements play out in space and what impacts one sector has for the sustainability of the other – e.g., farming practices on water quality, food transportation and distribution fluxes on air quality, consumption practices on waste management. Joint solutions like diverting food waste from landfills and increasing the fertility of urban and regional soils, or preventing food waste and fighting hunger, can also begin to come to mind.

Another way to demarcate the urban food system is through geography. It is a more slippery terrain for crafting definitions, but with some due precautions can augment our perception of the present and potential food system *of* the city. Concepts like the urban foodshed – the geographical area that feeds a city (N. Cohen, 2011; Getz, 1991; Kloppenburg, Hendrickson, & Stevenson, 1996), or the local food web – the network of links between people who buy, sell, produce, and supply food in an area (Campaign to Protect Rural England, 2010), are two influential examples of place-based definitions. Other demarcations distinguish between community and regional food systems, though the boundaries are not clear-cut. For land use specialist Rebecca Roberts (2007, p. 1), the notion of community food system "weds the concept of a food system to a particular place" (e.g., town, village, city, county, region, bioregion). For others, what distinguishes a regional from a "global" food system is instead the emphasis on specific qualities of the system, such as food security, proximity, self-reliance, and sustainability (Baumbrough, Aasen, Gunner, Whiting, & Kalina, 2009, p. 18). Seen through a spatial lens and the question of food security, the urban food system has also been demarcated as an archipelago of areas with uneven access to fresh, healthy, and affordable food sources, where the areas with the lowest access to such options are referred to as "food deserts" (Blanchard & Matthews, 2007; Larsen & Gilliland, 2008; LeClair & Aksan, 2014).

The value of a place-based food system definition is that it draws attention to the centrality of space. This makes the connection between food and planning more immediate because the management of urban development through the organization of human activities in space is the defining feature of urban planning. Thus, they may see their role in supporting the local food economy by protecting farmland or facilitating the development of new local food infrastructure, or in safeguarding public health by incentivizing new fresh food outlets in underserved neighborhoods and introducing new public transportation connections to improve food access. Moreover, a spatial perspective can draw our attention to the urban food system as a contested space. All food system activities, no matter their scale, coalesce in a single space, be it a neighborhood, a city, or a region. Because land is a finite resource, this can be the source of tensions between the food system and other systems, like housing and transportation, and between the different parts and scales of the food system itself (e.g., a community garden vs. a new residential development with a fresh food store). However, critical observers warn that a geographically bound demarcation of the food system – local, global, community, regional – is susceptible to several conceptual "traps" – the risk to confound scale (e.g., local) with normative values, such as equitable and sustainable (Born & Purcell, 2006), or with a specific quality of the food system, such as mainstream or alternative (Whatmore, Stassart, & Renting, 2003).

A third way to define the urban food system is through the lens of everyday social practices (N. Cohen & Ilieva, 2015). Seen as a bundle of social practices, the food system is neither solely a complex of economic sectors and institutions nor a geographic phenomenon; rather, it is made of the sum of mundane and seemingly inconsequential food practices that people, independently from their profession, do in the city every day. Shopping for food, having a meal out, and disposing of leftovers and food packaging are all routines that often pass unnoticed in strategizing for radical and systemic food system transitions. Yet, in the aggregate, these everyday practices do produce environmental, social, and economic impacts as significant as those of large infrastructures. A practice perspective on the urban food system can also help us overcome the false dichotomies local/global and mainstream/alternative and help us see how grassroots innovations in the food system are pieced together and integrated in the chains of activities that constitute everyday life.

This practice-based way to demarcate the urban food system as a unit of analysis gets us closer to the understanding of food as "relationship" (Kirschenmann, 2008) and to all people (and objects) as food system makers, but if applied too narrowly it might fail to reconnect us to the "big picture." The challenge is thus to maintain a twofold focus on how social practices change *and* how micro-changes bring about large-scale infrastructural and societal transformations. Planners might work with sociologists, anthropologists, environmental psychologists, and behavioral economists to map conceptually and physically how such social practices are co-constructed in the food system and enacted through public and private spaces in the city. Using planning competencies to strategically steer the transition of unsustainable urban food practices to sustainability thus emerges as the kind of activity that planners could engage with in approaching the food system through a social practice perspective.

Independently from what specific definition of the urban food system one espouses, the food system remains the only urban system that so viscerally connects public to ecological health and the quality of the city-regions we inhabit. It is hard to imagine that we still need to be convinced that it is a system worth planning for.

Urban planning

Urban planning is a relatively young scientific field and administrative practice and aims at the balanced organization of social activities in space. It is commonly pursued through the management of existing and prospective uses of land, as well as the coordination of policies having implications for such uses (CEMAT, 1983; Hall & Tewdwr-Jones, 2010). For its inclusive subject matter – space, or better, the relationship between space and society – it is an endeavor inherently comprehensive in scope and multidisciplinary in practice. Yet, as an institutionalized technique, it tends to be distinguished by its rigidity and path-dependency (Van Assche, Beunen, Duineveld, & de Jong, 2013), causing the reproduction of established routines and regulations and only seldom sparking creative, nonlegitimized solutions (Kunzmann, 2011).

The planning system, which encompasses all organizations that ensure the stability and enforcement of established rules and regulations and oversee the development of new courses of action through provisions such as plans, laws, policies, programs, and projects, is unique to every nation and may significantly vary between different jurisdictions at the subnational level of government. Designations of planning may also vary between nations – spatial planning (e.g., the UK, Germany), urban and territorial planning (e.g., Italy), or physical planning (e.g., the Netherlands), to mention a few. Though without a legally binding status, in 1999, a supranational spatial planning framework – the European Spatial Development Perspective (ESDP) – was adopted by the Ministers for Spatial Planning of the European Union. In the US, most states have a planning framework and cities are generally in a stronger position to enforce planning policies than their European counterparts, but there is no national planning system and the need for government-led planning remains contested (Gawroński, Van Assche, & Hernik, 2010; Warner, 2000).

Among the tools that local governments use to influence the organization of social activities in space are land use and zoning plans (and related laws and regulations), determining the admissible uses of land and their spatial organization, as well as comprehensive and strategic spatial plans, having the aim to guide future urban development and give a geographic expression to the aspirations of local communities and administrations (typically these plans are not legally binding). The role of government in the development and implementation of urban plans may vary – in some area-specific plans, like planned unit developments (PUD) in the US or neighborhood agreements ("contratti di quartiere") in Italy, public–private partnership is key. In others, for example, like the plans for integrated intervention ("piani integrati di intervento") in Italy, private initiative is central, while in others still, such as New York City's community-based plans (also known as "197-a plans"), community initiative may be at the heart of the planning process. Independently from their specific form, initiators, and regulatory strength, the gist of urban plans is to provide a shared template for collective action, not a single expert solution. In addition to plans, administrative procedures like environmental quality review and land use review are also essential parts of the planning system at different levels of government.

As a scientific field, urban planning is still evolving and trying to establish its distinctive contribution and intellectual identity. Some observers attribute this to its relatively short history (Lloyd Rodwin, 2000) and to the fact that it started "maturing" only in the 2000s (Davoudi & Pendlebury, 2010). As we saw in Chapter 2, the germs of the majority of modern planning systems originated in the late nineteenth century and were progressively institutionalized in many national and local governments during the first half of the twentieth century. The flaws of early planning theories and models, often due to a hastened incursion in the domain of hard sciences, attracted much of twentieth-century criticism and led to a diffused mistrust in the core values of planning, the unfortunate schism between physical and policy-oriented approaches, and the distancing of planning theory from planning practice. Planning theorists resolved that the key reason for planning's undelivered promises was the poorly understood and designed planning process. This realization moved planning closer to the social sciences and greatly enriched its architecture, engineering, and surveying lineages. Communicative (Forester, 1989; Innes, 1995; Sager, 1994, 2006) and collaborative (Healey, 1998) planning theories are two notable outcomes of this encounter with philosophical and sociological areas of scholarly research.

More recently, however, planning scholars have called attention to the need to resume research on the core subject and end-goal of planning practice as well. Normative planning frameworks such as the just city (e.g., Fainstein, 2010), the healthy city (e.g., Corburn, 2007; World Health Organization, 2001), and the sustainable city (e.g., UN-Habitat, 2009; Wheeler, 2013) have gained prominence and the spatial dimension of planning has reemerged (Davoudi & Pendlebury, 2010). Thus, the time for food systems – as a means to achieve social equity, public health, and environmental sustainability goals in urban regions – to reenter the planning scene might be just ripe.

But how to take advantage of this opening window of opportunity if much of planning is routine, business-as-usual, and change is path-dependent? Theories about "creativity" in planning (Albrechts, 2005; Balducci, Kunzmann, & Sartorio, 2004; Kunzmann, 2005) can provide us with some useful pointers. According to Klaus R. Kunzmann (2011), renowned German planning scholar and founder of the Association of European Schools of Planning (AESOP), among the key tactics that planning organizations and local governments can use to spur creativity in planning are to allow decision-making processes beyond daily routine, learn from creative (not reactionary) grassroots initiatives, encourage the formation of international creative platforms and networks, and reward creative bureaucrats. In keeping up with a relational perspective on institutional change, Healey (2006, 2012) suggests that unconventional ideas and behaviors – like those needed to allow for creativity and innovation – get normalized in planning by means of specific episodes, which can transform established practices, and through practices transition dominant planning and governance cultures. This view echoes the niche-regime-landscape lens of the multilevel perspective on sociotechnical transitions (see Chapter 1) we adopted when we commenced our exploration and helps us further appreciate where entry points for systemic change may lie.

Urban food planning

Urban food planning is an emerging domain of theory and practice advanced by a broad constituency of urban food policy "entrepreneurs" having the common goal to make the urban food system work in the public interest to generate healthy, prosperous, and ecologically sound human settlements. It is concerned with the repair of inefficiencies in existing city-regional food infrastructures and the development of new ones, hinged on emerging grass-roots innovations. While it has "urban planning" in its name, urban planners are just one group of practitioners in the many organizations at the forefront of its development (Morgan, 2013), including private practice professionals, activists, and government officials from a wide range of economic sectors and disciplines. Planners have, however, played a key role in advancing the urban food planning agenda by developing dedicated policy guides on the subject, creating working groups in their professional and academic associations on both sides of the Atlantic (e.g., the Food Interest Group of the American Planning Association and the Sustainable Food Planning group of the Association of European Schools of Planning), and popularizing the topic through scientific journals, books, and academic conferences. Urban food planning has grown into a new conceptual niche for research and practice and, as we will see from the remainder of this section, there are plenty of reasons and unique opportunities for planners to make a difference, while doing what they already do, only better.

Why plan for the urban food system?

When planning scholars Pothukuchi and Kaufman (2000) did their pioneering 1997–1998 survey of US planners and their engagement with food system issues, they found that the absence of food from the urban planner's agenda was ubiquitous. Food was not a focus in the planning field and remained unacknowledged in the work planners already did; the main reasons participants in the survey gave for this were that there was no need to focus on it because the food system was not "broken," they had no formal mandate or funding to do food planning work, they did not have sufficient knowledge on the topic and no clarity on who to work with, and food was not really an urban issue and not quite in the remit of the public domain. While planners who see food as priority in their work are still a minority (Raja, 2015), some of the conditions that prompted the responses to the survey done by Pothukuchi and Kaufman, almost two decades ago, have begun to change. The public understanding that food is an urban system and that ensuring its integrity is part of the responsibilities of local governments (in both developed and developing counties) has started gaining prominence. A quick scan of the landscape of emerging arguments for why it is in the planners' interest to engage with urban food planning can yield at least 10 good reasons worth considering. The list that follows does not have the aim to be exhaustive, but rather give a sense of the wide gamut of rationales (some might say "ideologies") planners have at their disposal to take food on board.

The urban food system is powerful but "broken"

There is already a plethora of global and local indicators signaling major dysfunctions in our highly sophisticated and globalized food systems. It is no secret that our state-of-the art food supply chain has provided (at least the privileged of) us with a bounty of year-round fruits, vegetables, ready-made meals, and cheap fish and meat, but the real cost of it has been perilously "externalized" (Lappe, 2010). Most of us would be familiar with the grim statistics of deforestation (Achard et al., 2002; Hansen et al., 2013), carbon dioxide (CO_2) emissions (Cole et al., 1997), methane (CH_4) emissions – contributing 25 times more to global warming than CO_2 (EPA, 2015), and the huge food losses – about a third of all world produce, along the chain (Barilla Center for Food & Nutrition, 2009; Parfitt, Barthel, & Macnaughton, 2010). Forests, molecules, and landfills might be hard to see from the busy city streets, but inadequate nutrition – including both undernourishment and obesity – is not (Cutts, Darby, Boone, & Brewis, 2009; Winne, 2008). The effects of "supermarket urbanism" on independent shops, food security, public health, and vitality of inner-city areas are all there before our eyes (e.g., Steel, 2009). For several decades now, around cities, small- and medium-scale farms have been steadily pushed out of business (Gardner, 1996; Osservatorio Nazionale sui Consumi di Suolo, 2009), putting in jeopardy not only regional economies, but the integrity of cities' watersheds and the host of related social and environmental benefits, or ecosystem services as urban ecologists teach us (Andersson, Tengö, McPhearson, & Kremer, 2015; Jenerette, Harlan, Stefanov, & Martin, 2011), resulting from their healthy functioning.

It is in the DNA of the profession

The reintegration of local foodscapes in the urban environment and the reconnection of cities to their natural regions were ideas deeply engrained in the early days of urban planning; that is, when planning was still a social movement (see Chapter 2). At the beginning of the twentieth century, pioneers of the planning profession sought to devise new spatial and economic models for an integrated, polycentric urban–rural development as a means to healthier cities and an escape from the horrors of the unruly industrial metropolis. Ebenezer Howard's Garden Cities, Patrick Geddes's city in the natural region, the American regional planning movement, Patrick Abercrombie's Plan for Greater London, Frank Lloyd Wright's vision for a hypermodern yet dispersed American city with ubiquitous farmsteads and local food supply circuits, and the envied Randstad-Green Heart principle for spatial organization of Dutch national planners, are all part of planning's "icons" one can find in every planning textbook. But a biological metaphor may serve us better and we could say that urban food planning is in the "genetic code" of the planning profession, thus, rather than merely contemplating it as an intellectual heritage, we can feel compelled to cautiously reactivate it. Moreover, since 2000, when the seminal survey by Pothukuchi and Kaufman was published in the *Journal of the American Planning Association*, several US planners have set out to research whether and to what extent we are really dealing with a "stranger" to the planning field. A number of influential contributions (e.g., Donofrio, 2007; Lawson, 2004; Vitiello & Brinkley, 2014) have pointed out that there is a "hidden" history of planners' engagement with the urban food system, much more articulated than the few canonic examples we tend to recall. For each city this history may be unique, but the germs of urban food planning (and the lessons from them) are already there, it just will take some time to uncover them. In short, urban food planning is not entirely new but it had gone in recess, and both planning and cities seem to have lost more than they have gained from dismissing it.

Planning claims a holistic approach

As a whole, urban planning professes a holistic approach to tackling complex sociospatial problems and puts emphasis on the relationships between urban systems (e.g., land use *and* transportation) rather than on their management as discrete units of analysis. Food is an inherently cross-sectoral system and thus is a natural connector between the different city-regional systems and can ease planners' efforts to plan for them in concert. Planning also claims comprehensiveness in that it considers all basic infrastructures essential to the sustenance of urban life, like housing, employment, recreation, and transportation and related underground infrastructures (e.g., piped water, sewages, energy, communications), and yet has kept food out of its field of expertise and influence (Pothukuchi & Kaufman, 2000). This means leaving out a substantial share of the interconnections between food and the urban systems planners commonly plan for and thus failing to see the impact it has on them and vice versa. The urban planning profession is also intrinsically concerned with the anticipation of change and with "caring for people in the city" (Kunzmann, 2011) and, thus, if a vital urban system as the food system is "broken," it makes sense to include it in long-term comprehensive urban plans, as well as in everyday planning routines and review procedures.

There is a rapidly expanding community of practice to work with

Planners willing to take on food as part of their research and practice agenda are no longer alone and are likely to be less so in the near future. Without the need to rehearse all spheres where urban food planning practices are being advanced, it is enough to mention that very active food systems planning interest groups already exist in planning associations, the literature on the topic is steadily growing, and university courses are offered by more and more planning schools across North America, Europe, and Australia. The knowledge gap between theory and practice is being filled also by a growing number of food planning guides (Cassidy & Patterson, 2008; Raja, Born, & Kozlowski Russell, 2008; Sustain, 2014) and policies (American Planning Association, 2007) that provide both general and city-specific directions as to how to take action. The first edited volume of contributions, featuring more than 40 examples of urban food governance, planning, and design cases (Viljoen & Wiskerke, 2012), gives insights into the many entry points planners and other urban professionals have to engage with the urban food system and the diverse community of scholars and practitioners they can collaborate with. Emerging international networks of urban food planning experts (e.g., CITYFOOD by ICLEI and RUAF, see also Chapter 7) are also a valuable resource for newcomers to the field. The challenge of integrating food issues in present-day planning systems has for much longer been a concern of local administrations and planners in the Global South (Greenhow, 1994; Quon, 1999) and some cities have emerged as leaders in the field. While these planning contexts are very different compared to their developed countries counterparts, some of the food planning challenges and expertise on effective approaches to cope with them may be shared (e.g., soil quality, reliable land tenure arrangements, public nuisance concerns).

Demand for urban food planning is rising

Mayors, community organizations, and developers are becoming increasingly interested in developing comprehensive city-regional food system assessments, strategies, action plans, and monitoring indicators. To date, there have been released over 90 city and regional food system strategies in developed economies cities, and, while many administrations are already updating them, others are just commencing the development of their first food system assessment. These are increasing the opportunities for urban planners to enter the field. In addition, a market niche for food-sensitive master-planning and urban development services is also taking shape (see also Chapter 6) and opens unforeseen opportunities for planning professionals in private practice to engage with the urban food system (Raja, 2010). The planning and design for agri-urban subdivisions, integration of rooftop agriculture in public housing projects, conversion of vacant lots into productive landscapes and high-quality community spaces, and improving food security in underserved neighborhoods are all areas of intervention that require synergies between a wide range of professionals, including urban planners in the public and the private spheres. As cities are moving towards the implementation of their food system and urban agriculture plans, funding opportunities for plans, projects, and consultancy services in urban food planning are going to increase.

Planning might be part of the problem

Planners might not be aware of it, but many regulations, land use review procedures, environmental quality reviews, rezonings, and new urban development projects do have an impact on the urban food system – either by reducing opportunities for grassroots innovations to emerge or by reinforcing spatial (and power) asymmetries the system and thus its inefficiencies. Labels, professional jargon, and dominant narratives about food and agriculture in the planning field can be as influential. For many years, urban plans have labeled periurban lands around cities as "awaiting development" and hatched them as blank space, disregarding the great diversity of rural infrastructures and landscapes that distinguished one periurban area from the other. Urbanization proceeded regardless of these diversities and thus has had a detrimental impact on many periurban farms and rural heritage sites, particularly in European urban regions. Dominant understandings of what is "urban" and what is "rural" and what is the "best and highest" use of land have also perpetuated the schism between planning and urban food systems. Without doubt, ideas, conventions, and practices in the private sector – from field to fork – greatly shape city, regional, and national food infrastructures, but the way they are reproduced or challenged at the local level, including through land use and comprehensive city plans and overall urban planning culture, has a nonnegligible effect on the system as well.

Planners are part of the solution

Systems thinking, statistical and geospatial analysis, civic engagement, communication, and deliberation skills, as well as the ability to combine multiple qualitative and quantitative research and representation techniques, are just a handful of the many talents that planning scholars and professionals have and can use to advance urban food planning research and practice. Helping communities and cities, and the institutions that govern them, "see" themselves through a food system lens is one of many productive ways in which planners can contribute to bridging the divide between food and planning and between the sustainability of urban and food systems. Planning for sustainability entails not just thinking how to reduce inputs and outputs in our complex sociotechnical systems and everyday lives, but mediating conflict between competing goals and objectives (Campbell, 1996). Indeed, urban food planning, as planning for all other urban systems, entails the skillful recognition and management of "trade-offs" in the face of uncertainty. Many of the trade-offs between different planning approaches to pursuing the normative goals of greener, healthier, and more equitable cities, and achieving them through the promotion of local food infrastructures, are not considered, not even acknowledged, and this is a key area of opportunity in which planners are well positioned to contribute to.

Food can help address "big" planning issues

Evidence from a growing body of food systems planning research and mayoral food system strategies and progress reports suggests that a food system lens offers untapped opportunities for planners and local administrations to tackle a host of entrenched, "big" planning issues. Urban sprawl, traffic congestion, social cohesion, poverty, hunger, crime, obesity, disaster preparedness, clogged sewage infrastructures, waste management, and brownfields redevelopment are some of them. Planners and other urban experts have begun to question many of the assumptions framing these problems and their solutions. For instance, the perception of obesity as only a matter of individual choices and appropriate medical treatments is being challenged through holistic approaches taking into account the whole spectrum of built and nonmaterial elements shaping the urban food environment. This view can lead to the reframing of proximate city-regional foodsheds (and short food supply chains) as "infrastructure for public health" (Urban Design Lab, 2011a). While it is true that anomalies in the urban food system – like hunger and inadequate nutrition – need to be addressed by attacking their root causes (e.g., poverty, gender, age, and racial disparities), expanded opportunities for city-driven food systems innovations offer a complementary means to address them while eradicating structural inequalities within and beyond the food system (Reynolds & Cohen, 2016).

Food can help consolidate planning's positions

For its visceral connection to human well-being and manifestation in multiple urban infrastructures and geographical scales – from the single dwelling to the neighborhood, city, region, and, indeed, the planet – food can provide a unique avenue to address some of planning's fundamental dilemmas and limitations. At the turn of the twenty-first century, distinguished Indian-American urban planning scholar Bishwapriya Sanyal (2000) suggested that there were three major challenges that the urban planning profession has yet to address in order to consolidate its position as a discipline: integrate spatial and socioeconomic planning, produce theories that meet the needs of practitioners, and rejustify government intervention. To these we can add the challenge of interdisciplinarity – the ability to build new knowledge by occupying the space between different disciplines – underscored by renowned UK urban planning scholars Simin Davoudi and John Pendlebury (2010).

It is hard to ignore that food matters both as a discrete, physical object, landscape, and infrastructure *and* as a relationship – social, economic, cultural, and ecological. Planning for food issues, one would therefore expect, is the kind of issue naturally prone to bringing physical and socioeconomic planners together. Middle-range theories emphasizing the importance of the material components of social practices like theories of social practice (Reckwitz, 2002; Schatzki, 2001; Shove, Pantzar, & Watson, 2012), increasingly being tested to explore the role of local governments and citizens in food system change (N. Cohen & Ilieva, 2015; Hargreaves, Longhurst, & Seyfang, 2013; Spaargaren, 2011), may be one promising conceptual space to develop planning theories with immediate relevance to planning practitioners concerned or not with food issues.

Because, with the sole exception of drugs, the agrifood industry is the only industry whose products we ingest (Goodman, 1999; Morgan, 2009), planning to ensure safe, healthy, ecologically sound, and fair urban food systems may help rejustify planning and government intervention. While direct attacks at the industry, though bans and moratoriums, have hitherto failed to legitimate mayoral action, evidence from multi-stakeholder watershed planning experiences (e.g., New York City) show that when a territorial approach to preserving a scarce resource – clean water, and a finite resource – farmland, is taken, government interference in private property rights and planning beyond a city's administrative boundaries are not unattainable planning objectives. An urban food system focus can expand opportunities to this end and provide a powerful lens for reframing contested sustainability-oriented planning endeavors.

The 2030 Sustainable Development Goals (SDGs) mandate it

On September 25, 2015, the new 2030 Agenda for Sustainable Development of the United Nations was adopted by the leaders of 193 countries. Unlike their predecessors, the Millennium Development Goals (2000–2015), the Sustainable Development Goals (SDGs) mandate local action in both developed and developing countries (United Nations, 2015, p. 3). Food security, healthy nutrition, and sustainable agriculture are explicitly stated in goal number two, though, in practice, fair and sustainable urban food systems are a crosscutting theme encompassing public health, sustainable consumption, sustainable cities and communities, and sustainable terrestrial and marine ecosystems, among other goals. Urban planners in lead academic and professional positions can now use this overarching framework to support the integration of sustainable city-regional food system goals in their research and practice agenda and steer the work of their project teams or university departments in this direction.

The list, of course, could go on, and the arguments that both planners and other members of the urban food planning community are advancing to encourage planners to resume work on the urban food system abound. The point is, as we are approaching the third decade of the new millennium, food is no more a complete absentee from the planning domain, or at least a good conversation about it has started.

How to plan for the urban food system?

When in the 1980s public health and nutrition scholar Betsy Haughton (1987, p. 191) analyzed one of the "seeds" of today's urban food planning movement – the Knoxville municipal food policy (in 1981) and food policy council – she concluded that

> Food policy is an important parameter of city planning to guide decision-making at each point of the food system. It defines socially-approved goals and objectives from which public and private planners may look to guide and evaluate their programs and activities.

Since then, however, the bulk of purposeful urban food planning practices have been carried out of government, and certainly out of the planning domain, under the auspices of the rising movement of food policy councils. Even if planners were engaged in different ways by community food security advocates and the food planning initiatives of food policy councils, a comprehensive policy about how urban planning professionals can contribute was yet to be developed.

The need to provide a general framework showing how food issues relate to and can be normalized through the everyday work that planners do, the skills they have, and the tools they use to pursue their day-to-day tasks, surfaced only two decades later with the research of two of the pioneers of "modern" urban food planning – city planning scholars Kameshwari Pothukuchi and the late Jerome Kaufman (Kaufman, 2002, 2004; Pothukuchi & Kaufman, 1999, 2000). In those same years, Toronto food policy pioneer Wayne Roberts (2001) was also making efforts to provide a holistic view of why and how urban planners can integrate a food systems perspective in their work, grounding it in detailed recommendations for Toronto's Official Plan (2000). Over the past decade, an unprecedented joint effort of university scholars, civil society organizations, and private practice professionals tried to fill the gulf between the need for urban food planning expertise and action and the lack of adequate guidance to support them.

In just a few years, an impressive number of food policy and planning guides addressed specifically to urban planners have been devised in the US, the UK, Canada, and Australia, among which are the American Planning Association's *Policy Guide on Community and Regional Food Planning* (2007), *Planner's Guide to Community and Regional Food Planning* (Raja, Born, & Kozlowski Russell, 2008), and briefing paper on *Food Policy Councils* (DiLisio & Hodgson, 2011); *The Planners Guide to the Urban Food System* by Cassidy and Patterson (2008); the *Food-Sensitive Planning and Urban Design* report by Donovan, Larsen, and McWhinnie (2011); and the *Good Planning for Good Food* (2011) and *Planning Sustainable Cities for Community Food Growing* (2014) by Sustain in the UK. Local administrations have also begun to commission such reports tailored specifically to the needs of their city planning departments. Examples for such guidelines are *A Guide to Local Food System Planning for Scott County, Minnesota* by Aitchison (2009), the *Food System Planning Municipal Implementation Tool* of the Delaware Valley Regional Planning Commission (2010), the *Planning for the Food System* guidelines by the Maryland Department of Planning (2012), and the report *Integrating Food Policy in Comprehensive Planning* (2012) for the City of Seattle by the Puget Sound Regional Council. Master's theses in city and regional planning have also begun to provide practical guidance on the topic (Eckert, 2010; Jacobsen, 2006; Winter, 2009).

As we saw early on in this chapter, from a transition theories perspective (e.g., Geels, 2004; Geels & Schot, 2007), the agrifood sector can be portrayed as a sociotechnical system reproduced through the work of industries, regulators, researchers, sponsors, civil society organizations, end users, and infrastructures and technologies. Urban planners can be viewed perhaps more easily as part of government institutions and regulators, affecting the system (directly or indirectly) through land-use decisions. Yet, as we saw in the opening chapter of the book, planners are also making efforts to purposefully transform the urban food system though research, advocacy, and design. Because land is such a pervasive feature of all food system sectors – from agriculture to waste management, and from industrial to artisan food purveyors – planners contribute to the transitioning multiple segments of it in the cities and regions they are working. It goes without saying that every planning system is different in every country, and even every city, and the prevalence and influence of different planning tools local governments adopt may greatly vary (e.g., zoning plans may be more prevalent than comprehensive plans, or planning policies may have replaced physical plans). The very power of cities to enforce unconventional land use decisions could be overshadowed by policies and decision-making structures in higher tiers of government. Nevertheless, there are some commonalities. For one, the organization of social activities by means of functional zones and related policies and regulations, and the emerging literature on how planners can engage with food systems planning, can provide insights applicable in more than one geographical context.

Preserving and expanding opportunities for sustainable regional and urban food growing is perhaps the fastest shortcut from planning to urban food planning. Planners can help protect prime farmland (and its value) not only through restrictive policies and zoning but also alternative tactics such as the transfer of development rights, allowing the reallocation of development rights closer to already urbanized areas with public services, roads, and utilities infrastructures in place (Pruetz & Standridge, 2008; Renard, 2007), or by encouraging conservation easements, protecting land from development, typically, in perpetuity (Merenlender & Huntsinger, 2004; Morrisette, 2001). Providing a more nuanced understanding and representation of the different faming enterprises, ecological systems, and food production infrastructures in and around cities can help better direct future urban development, and is yet another way for planners to contribute to the preservation of periurban and regional farmland and operating businesses. The point here is that, rather than relying on

simplistic definitions of "urban" and "rural," planners can help local administrations identify the most suitable periurban land for development, as opposed
to universally allowing urbanization or banning development altogether.

Effective farmland preservation strategies would furthermore need to be
coupled with affordable and high-quality infill development in cities and the
effective development of new rural-urban economic linkages and physical
infrastructure. Making room for regional food distribution infrastructure, such
as "food hubs" (Blay-Palmer, Landman, & Knezevic, 2013), to facilitate the
aggregation of regional produce and its processing and transportation in bulk,
is also a key strategy to the conservation farmland and the resiliency of small-
and medium-scale farming businesses. Reframing the role of institutional food
procurement as a tool for combating urban sprawl and diet-related diseases
like obesity, while encouraging sustainable farming practices, clean water, and
biodiverse regional landscapes, is a further opportunity for planners to advance
urban food planning goals. Stronger connections with regional farmers may
also help effectively plan for the redistribution and recycling of urban organic
waste, reducing its transportation costs and environmental impact. By using
their spatial and statistical analysis skills, planners can help municipalities and
regional planning authorities conduct comprehensive food system assessments,
such as foodshed analyses (discussed in the next chapter), on the basis of which
develop plans and policies transcending traditional segregations between farming, food, and urban waste management.

Ensuring safe and resilient spaces for urban food production is another key
area of urban food planning that planners can help advance. Securing land
tenure for existing gardens through municipal programs, land use review procedures, or collaborating with land trusts for community gardens is an important step toward the development of a city-based urban food infrastructure.
Considering the introduction of minimum standards of community gardens
per capita (e.g., Seattle's, 2005 Comprehensive Plan), walking or cycling distance from community gardens (Cassidy & Patterson, 2008), and minimum
maintenance or production standards for undeveloped land (Knight & Riggs,
2010, p. 123), so that owners are kept responsible for the quality of landscapes
on vacant properties, are some of the additional provisions that could support
more diverse and productive urban landscapes.

Building and zoning codes and regulations are both tools urban planners
are familiar with in their day-to-day practice and can enable the integration
of quality urban foodscapes in the built environment. Removing restrictions
for food growing and selling practices (including beekeeping and small animal
husbandry) on private properties (yards and rooftops) and in public spaces,
introducing overlay urban agriculture districts, and including specific lan-
guage reflecting a variety of subtypes of urban agriculture activities (e.g.,
allotments, community gardens, community farms, institutional gardens,
commercial farms, etc.) are all provisions that can facilitate the planning and
implementation of a sound urban agriculture system. The redefinition of
general designations such as "green infrastructure," "public amenities," and

"healthy housing" to include spaces for urban food production can be small but consequential changes of the regulatory system that currently shapes the urban food environment.

Planning for new urban development and urban expansion projects through the lens of local food systems, as a whole, constitute an emerging domain of professional practice. Conceptual frameworks such as agricultural urbanism (de la Salle & Holland, 2010; Mullinix et al., 2008), food urbanism (Verzone, 2012), continuous productive urban landscapes (Bohn & Viljoen, 2010; Viljoen & Bohn, 2005; Viljoen, Bohn, & Howe, 2005), and agrarian urbanism (Duany & DPZ, 2012), among others, have been supplemented with practical how-to guidelines and methodologies for planners, architects, and urbanists to engage with this new field of practice. Gaining a better understanding of what institutional and regulatory barriers may hinder the translation of new agri-urban plans in practice, as well as the standards that would ensure their quality, effectiveness, and longevity, would be increasingly important, and both government and private planning professionals can make a key contribution to this end.

Besides regulations that could enable sustainable urban food growing practices, urban food planning entails also the comprehensive assessment of the current and potential spaces that can host them. Productive and vacant land inventories, assessments of the production potential of urban farms and gardens, and soil quality maps, as well as valuations of the benefits of urban agriculture beyond food production (N. Cohen, Reynolds, & Sanghvi, 2012), are all tools planners can help develop and are essential building blocks in the development of urban food planning capacities at the local level. Local government officials and urban planners can use them either for the development of dedicated urban agriculture plans (e.g., Minneapolis) or the inclusion of urban agriculture goals in comprehensive urban plans (e.g., Portland, Seattle, Toronto, London), sustainability plans (e.g., Baltimore, New York City, Chicago, Philadelphia), and food systems strategies (e.g., New York, Seattle, Los Angeles, London, Amsterdam). Systematic scans for best practices in community and commercial food growing and effective solutions to common challenges can also inform the development of formal tools to guide new development applications such as the Planning Advice Notes in the UK (Brighton & Hove City Council, 2011).

Transportation, distribution, and retail are equally significant domains for advancing urban food planning. Addressing the uneven geographies of access to fresh, healthy, and affordable produce, found predominantly in cities in Anglo-Saxon countries (but not exclusive to them; most European countries have a growing elderly population facing similar challenges) is a mayoral task that urban planners can help with. Developing indicators and maps that can adequately represent the spatial distribution of a wide range of urban food outlets – from large supermarkets to corner stores and farmers markets and the kind of produce they offer to communities – can be decision-support tools in devising municipal programs and incentives to amend current disparities. Gathering in-depth qualitative and quantitative data on current food procurement practices pursued by families and individuals in underserved communities is an important supplementary research that can help avoid misplaced assumptions about local food culture and practices. Some of the research tools planners could use to this end include community food assessments (B. Cohen, Andrews, & Kantor, 2002; Pothukuchi, 2004) and the mapping of healthy and affordable food retailers that accept government food subsidies, as the US "food stamps," later renamed supplemental nutrition assistance program (SNAP) benefits.

Providing zoning and financial incentives to attract new fresh food retailers or to facilitate the integration of fresh food options in existing local food outlets are two planning strategies that can help address food access anomalies in the urban food system. These apply to underserved communities both in urban and rural communities. Other options involve rethinking the relationship between food access and public transportation by, for example, introducing new bus routes or shuttle services, sponsored by supermarkets themselves, that can connect people living in areas with few or no healthy food outlets – commonly referred to as "food deserts" or "food swamps" (Fielding & Simon, 2011), to access them. As with the establishment of new city-regional food distribution infrastructure, densifying transportation linkages requires the attentive coordination of transportation policies at multiple government scales to ensure effective implementation and avoid undesired outcomes (Pothukuchi & Wallace, 2009).

Supporting the development and integration of new "hybrid" community food infrastructures – featuring urban agriculture, emergency food, small-scale food processing, compost drop-off, community supported agriculture, and educational uses – such as community food centers, can be an additional way to creatively plan for food in the city. Valuating the negative impacts of existing large-scale food distribution hubs on nearby neighborhoods and urban areas, in terms of traffic congestion, noise, and air pollution, is equally key, and most municipalities already have the data necessary to account for them. Such representations can support the development of strategies to reduce traffic, monetize its impact, and require mitigation interventions like the densification of tree canopies and other vegetation filters and infrastructures. Agrifood business parks can also be held to higher environmental standards, including air quality (Carey, 2011, p. 114) and overall site design.

For its inherently interdisciplinary, interdepartmental, and cross–sectoral subject matter, doing urban food planning entails devoting time and energy to fostering the cooperation and coordination between disparate and often competing communities of practice. By supporting the development of and directly participating in new platforms for urban food planning and policy-making, like food boards and food policy councils, is another valuable avenue for city and regional planners to engage with urban food planning (DiLisio & Hodgson, 2011). Other crosscutting areas for immediate food planning action include assessments of how existing regulations and policies at different government scales affect the integrity of the city-regional food environment and how regional and national governments can learn from innovations in urban policy and planning (Sonnino, 2009) and facilitate their further development and potential scaling up and replication.

As we will see in the next chapters, these are just few of the many directions that planners can begin to explore and use as entry points to join emerging endeavors of urban food governance and planning. We just began uncovering some of the possibilities and limitations that planners and other government and private practice professionals have before them to enter the field. As we continue our journey, we will keep adding up to and reconnecting these fragments with the help of context-specific examples.

Concluding remarks

In this chapter, we started charting the contours of the reemerging interface between urban food systems and urban planning, which constitutes a subset of practices in the broader domain of urban food planning. We laid the groundwork for our subsequent exploration of this nascent field by considering different ways to the demarcate food as an urban system – functional/sociotechnical, geographical, and sociological – and their implications for food as an object of study and a means to society-wide transitions toward sustainability. Depending on how current and prospective urban food planners define the urban food system – a bundle of industrial sectors and institutions, a specific place, or a bundle of everyday social practices – they will likely develop different problem definitions and, thus, problem management strategies. We also briefly introduced some of the distinctive features of urban planning, which is an evolving field of theory and professional practice in and of itself. This brief summary called our attention to two main points: first, while planning systems tend to be rigid and unsusceptible to radical change, under certain circumstances, they too can be loci for creativity and innovation; and, second, after several decades of shying away from physical space as the matter of urban planning theory and of food as a matter of urban planning practice, the growing saliency of normative frameworks such as sustainable cities, just cities, and healthy cities, in urban politics and across disciplines suggests that the time for the food system to reenter the planning field might be just right.

We might be amidst the predevelopment of a transition toward a normalized competency in food systems in the planning field, also judging from the changing milieu of reasons for and ways to engage with food system issues for planners. While the majority of planners may still not be fully aware of the emerging niche of urban food planning in their domain, much has changed since the turn of the century when the food system was first documented as a missing focus in planning practice. Today, it was argued, there are at least 10 compelling reasons for planners to take on food as a focus in their work, or at least rebut historical claims as to why food is not an urban planning issue. On the backdrop of this emerging mosaic of "new" rationales for urban food planning, a growing literature suggesting concrete ways in which planners can engage with food systems planning (even if not formally trained to do so) and advance food system goals more broadly is now taking shape. The dominant understanding that urban planners do not have the expertise to plan for food systems is progressively being dismantled by an increasing number of guidelines, white papers, and informative reports specifically addressed to urban planners. There may still be institutional, economic, and political barriers to the thorough bridging of food and urban planning, but if one thing is sure it is that planners are uniquely positioned to help cities see the need for urban food policy in the first place.

Questions for further consideration

- Why does it make sense to talk about an "urban" food system? What is in and what is out of an urban food system? Can you think of two alternative ways to define the urban food system? What strengths, limitations, and implications for policy and planning does each definition exhibit?
- Why are planners reluctant to take on a food systems perspective in their work? Considering the emergent urban food planning "movement" and prevalent concerns of urban planning scholars and practitioners, what may be some new arguments for urban planners to engage with food as part of their remit? How, do you think, planners may rebut such arguments?
- What are some concrete examples of how planners can pursue urban food planning goals and practices? Can you think of specific cases illustrating the implementation of such practices in the city or country where you live or work?

References

Achard, F., Eva, H. D., Stibig, H. J., Mayaux, P., Gallego, J., Richards, T., & Malingreau, J. P. (2002). Determination of deforestation rates of the world's humid tropical forests. *Science, 297*(5583), 999–1002.

Aitchison, K. (2009). *A Guide to Local Food System Planning for Scott County, Minnesota.* Minneapolis, MN: Community Growth Options (U-CGO), University of Minnesota.

Albrechts, L. (2005). Creativity as a drive for change. *Planning Theory, 4*(3), 247–269.

American Planning Association (APA). (2007). *Policy Guide on Community and Regional Food Planning.* Retrieved from https://www.planning.org/policy/guides/adopted/food.htm

Andersson, E., Tengö, M., McPhearson, T., & Kremer, P. (2015). Cultural ecosystem services as a gateway for improving urban sustainability. *Ecosystem Services, 12*, 1–4.

Balducci, A., Kunzmann, K. R., & Sartorio, F. S. (2004). Towards creative city region governance in Italy and Germany. *Dokumentations Und Informationsstelle Für Planung, 158*, 2–45.

Barilla Center for Food & Nutrition. (2009). *Cambiamento climatico, agricoltura e alimentazione.* Parma, Italy: Author.

Baumbrough, B., Aasen, W., Gunner, A., Whiting, D., & Kalina, L. (2009). *A North Okanagan Food System Plan: Strengthening the Regional Food System.* Coldstream, BC: The Regional District of the North Okanagan.

Blanchard, T. C., & Matthews, T. L. (2007). Retail Concentration, Food Deserts, and Food-Disadvantaged Communities in Rural America. In C. C. Hinrichs & T. A. Lyson (Eds.), *Remaking the North American Food System: Strategies for Sustainability (Our Sustainable Future)* (pp. 201–215). Lincoln, NE: University of Nebraska Press.

Blay-Palmer, A., Landman, K., & Knezevic, I. (2013). Constructing resilient, transformative communities through sustainable "food hubs". *Local Environment: The International Journal of Justice and Sustainability, 18*(5), 521–528.

Bohn, K., & Viljoen, A. (2010). The edible city: Envisioning the Continuous Productive Urban Landscape (CPUL). *Field Journal, 4*(1), 149–161.

Born, B., & Purcell, M. (2006). Avoiding the local trap: Scale and food systems in planning research. *Journal of Planning Education and Research, 26*(2), 195–207.

Brighton & Hove City Council. (2011, September). *PAN 06 Food Growing and Development*. Brighton-Hove. Retrieved from http://www.brighton-hove.gov.uk/content/planning/planning-policy/planning-advice-notes-pans

Campbell, S. (1996). Green cities, growing cities, just cities? Urban planning and the contradictions of sustainable development. *Journal of the American Planning Association, 62*(3), 296–312.

Carey, J. (2011). "Who Feeds Bristol? Towards a Resilient Food Plan." Retrieved from www.bristol.gov.uk/whofeedsbristol

Carson, R. (1962). *Silent Spring*. Boston, MA: Houghton Mifflin.

Cassidy, A., & Patterson, B. (2008). *The Planner's Guide to the Urban Food System*. Los Angeles, CA: University of Southern California.

CEMAT. (1983). *European Regional/Spatial planning Charter: Torremolinos Charter*. Strasbourg: Council of Europe. European Conference of Ministers Responsible for Regional Planning.

Cohen, B., Andrewvs, M., & Kantor, L. S. (2002). *Community Food Security Assessment Toolkit*. Washington, DC: USDA Economic Research Service.

Cohen, N. (2011). How great cities are fed revisited: Ten municipal policies to support the New York city foodshed. *Fordham Environmental Law Review, 22*(3), 691–710.

Cohen, N., & Ilieva, R. T. (2015). Transitioning the food system: A strategic practice management approach for cities. *Environmental Innovation and Societal Transitions, 17*, 199–217.

Cohen, N., Reynolds, K., & Sanghvi, R. (2012). *Five Borough Farm: Seeding the Future of Urban Agriculture in New York City*. New York: Design Trust for Public Space.

Cole, C. V., Duxbury, J., Freney, J., Heinemeyer, O., Minami, K., Mosier, A., . . . Zhao, Q. (1997). Global estimates of potential mitigation of greenhouse gas emissions by agriculture. *Nutrient Cycling in Agroecosystems, 49*(1–3), 221–228.

Corburn, J. (2007). Reconnecting with our roots: American urban planning and public health in the twenty-first century. *Urban Affairs Review, 42*(5), 688–713.

Cutts, B. B., Darby, K. J., Boone, C. G., & Brewis, A. (2009). City structure, obesity, and environmental justice: An integrated analysis of physical and social barriers to walkable streets and park access. *Social Science and Medicine, 69*(9), 1314–1322.

Davoudi, S., & Pendlebury, J. (2010). Centenary paper: The evolution of planning as an academic discipline. *Town Planning Review, 81*(6), 613–646.

de la Salle, J., & Holland, M. (2010). *Agricultural Urbanism: Handbook for Building Sustainable Food & Agricultural Systems in 21st Century Cities*. Winnipeg: Green Frigate Books.

Delaware Valley Regional Planning Commission. (2010). *Food System Planning Municipal Implementation Tool*. Philadelphia, PA. Retrieved from http://www.dvrpc.org/MIT018/#googtrans/en

DiLisio, C., & Hodgson, K. (2011). *Food Policy Councils: Helping Local, Regional, and State Governments Address Food System Challenges*. Chicago, IL: American Planning Association.

Donofrio, G. A. (2007). Feeding the city. *Gastronomica, 7*(4), 30–41.

Donovan, J., Larsen, K., & McWhinnie, J. (2011). *Food-Sensitive Planning and Urban Design: A Conceptual Framework for Achieving a Sustainable and Healthy Food System*. Melbourne: National Heart Foundation of Australia.

Duany, A., & DPZ. (2012). *Garden Cities: Theory & Practice of Agrarian Urbanism* (2nd ed.). London: The Prince's Foundation for the Built Environment.

Eckert, J. (2010). *Food Systems, Planning and Quantifying Access: How Urban Planning Can Strengthen Toledo's Local Food System*. (Master Thesis). Retrieved from utdr.utoledo.edu/these-dissertations/829

EPA. (2015). *Inventory of U.S. Greenhouse Gas Emissions and Sinks*. Washington, DC: U.S. Environmental Protection Agency.

Fainstein, S. S. (2010). *Just City*. Ithaca, NY: Cornell University Press.

Fielding, J. E., & Simon, P. A. (2011). Food deserts or food swamps?: Comment on "fast food restaurants and food stores". *Archives of Internal Medicine, 171*(13), 1171–1172.

Forester, J. (1989). *Planning in the Face of Power*. Berkeley, CA: University of California Press.

Gardner, G. (1996). *Shrinking Fields: Cropland Loss in a World of Eight Billion. Worldwatch Paper* (Vol. 131). Washington, DC: World Watch Institute.

Gawroński, K., Van Assche, K., & Hernik, J. (2010). Spatial planning in the United States of America and Poland. *Infrastructure and Ecology of Rural Areas, 11*, 53–69.

Geels, F. W. (2004). From sectoral systems of innovation to socio-technical systems: Insights about dynamics and change from sociology and institutional theory. *Research Policy, 33*(6–7), 897–920.

Geels, F. W., & Schot, J. (2007). Typology of sociotechnical transition pathways. *Research Policy, 36*(3), 399–417.

Getz, A. (1991). Urban foodsheds. *Permaculture Activist, 7*(3), 26–27.

Goodman, D. (1999). Agro-food studies in the "age of ecology": Nature, corporeality, bio-politics. *Sociologia Ruralis, 39*(1), 17–38.

Greenhow, T. (1994). Urban agriculture: Can planners make a difference (Cities Feeding People Report, 12). Ottawa, ON: IDRC.Hall, P., & Tewdwr-Jones, M. (2010). *Urban and Regional Planning* (5th ed.). London-New York, NY: Routledge.

Hansen, M. C., Potapov, P. V., Moore, R., Hancher, M., Turubanova, S. A., Tyukavina, A., . . . Townshend, J. R. G. (2013). High-resolution global maps of 21st-century forest cover change. *Science, 342*(6160), 850–853.

Hargreaves, T., Longhurst, N., & Seyfang, G. (2013). Up, down, round and round: Connecting regimes and practices in innovation for sustainability. *Environment and Planning A, 45*(2), 402–420.

Haughton, B. (1987). Developing local food policies: One city's experience. *Journal of Public Health Policy, 8*(2), 180–191.

Healey, P. (1998). Building institutional capacity through collaborative approaches to urban planning. *Environment and Planning A, 30*(9), 1531–1546.

Healey, P. (2006). *Urban Complexity and Spatial Strategies: Towards a Relational Planning for Our Times*. London-New York, NY: Routledge.

Healey, P. (2012). Re-enchanting democracy as a mode of governance. *Critical Policy Studies, 6*(1), 19–39.

Innes, J. (1995). Planning theory's emerging paradigm: Communicative action and interactive practice. *Journal of Planning Education and Research, 14*(3), 183–189.

Jacobs, J. (1961). *The Death and Life of Great American Cities*. New York, NY: Vintage Books.

Jacobsen, C. T. (2006). *Planning for Farmers Markets and Sustainable Food Systems* (Master thesis). Retrieved from UBC Theses and Dissertations (http://hdl.handle.net/2429/17598).

Jenerette, G., Harlan, S., Stefanov, W. L., & Martin, C. A. (2011). Ecosystem services and urban heat riskscape moderation: Water, green spaces, and social inequality in Phoenix, USA. *Ecological Applications, 21*(7), 2637–2651.

Kaufman, J. L. (2002). Viewpoint of Jeromy Kaufman. *APA Planning, 68*(2), 46.

Kaufman, J. L. (2004). Introduction. *Journal of Planning Education and Research, 23*(4), 335–340.

Kirschenmann, F. L. (2008). Food as relationship. *Journal of Hunger & Environmental Nutrition, 3*(2), 106–121.

Kloppenburg, J., Hendrickson, J., & Stevenson, G. W. (1996). Coming in to the foodshed. *Agriculture and Human Values, 13*(3), 33–42.

Knight, L., & Riggs, W. (2010). Nourishing urbanism: A case for a new urban paradigm. *International Journal of Agricultural Sustainability, 8*(1), 116–126.

Kunzmann, K. R. (2005). Creativity in planning: A fuzzy concept? *Dokumentations Und Informationsstelle Für Planung, 162*(3), 5–13.

Kunzmann, K. R. (2011, July 27). *Creative Planning for a Slow Society.* Keynote presentation at the Alta Scuola Politecnica, Module on the dynamics of creativity for a territory in "stand-by." Sestriere, Italy.

Lappe, F. M. (2010). *Diet for a Small Planet.* New York, NY: Random House Publishing Group.

Larsen, K., & Gilliland, J. (2008). Mapping the evolution of "food deserts" in a Canadian city: Supermarket accessibility in London, Ontario, 1961–2005. *International Journal of Health Geographics, 7*(1), 16.

Lawson, L. (2004). The planner in the garden: A historical view into the relationship between planning and community gardens. *Journal of Planning History, 3*(2), 151–176.

LeClair, M. S., & Aksan, A.-M. (2014). Redefining the food desert: Combining GIS with direct observation to measure food access. *Agriculture and Human Values, 31*(4), 537–547.

Maryland Department of Planning. (2012). *Planning for the Food System* (Publication No. 2012-003). Baltimore, MD: State of Maryland.

Merenlender, A., & Huntsinger, L. (2004). Land trusts and conservation easements: Who is conserving what for whom? *Conservation Biology, 18*(1), 65–75.

Morgan, K. (2009). Feeding the city: The challenge of urban food planning. *International Planning Studies, 14*(4), 341–348.

Morgan, K. (2013). The rise of urban food planning. *International Planning Studies, 18*(1), 1–4.

Morrisette, P. (2001). Conservation easements and the public good: Preserving the environment on private lands. *Natural Resources Journal, 41*(2), 373–426.

Mullinix, K., Henderson, D., Holland, M., De Salle, J., Porter, E., & Fleming, P. (2008). Agricultural Urbanism and Municipal Supported Agriculture: A New Food System Path for Sustainable Cities. Proceedings from the *2008 Surrey Regional Economic Summit* (pp. 1–12). Surrey, BC: Kwantlen Polytechnic University.

Osservatorio Nazionale sui Consumi di Suolo. (2009). *Osservatorio Nazionale sui Consumi di Suolo: Primo rapporto 2009.* Segrate: Maggioli Editore.

Parfitt, J., Barthel, M., & Macnaughton, S. (2010). Food waste within food supply chains: Quantification and potential for change to 2050. *Philosophical Transactions of the Royal Society B: Biological Sciences, 365*(1554), 3065–3081.

Pothukuchi, K. (2004). Community food assessment: A first step in planning for community food security. *Journal of Planning Education and Research, 23*(4), 356–377.

Pothukuchi, K., & Kaufman, J. L. (1999). Placing the food system on the urban agenda: The role of municipal institutions in food systems planning. *Agriculture and Human Values, 16*, 213–224.

Pothukuchi, K., & Kaufman, J. L. (2000). The food system: A stranger to the planning field. *Journal of the American Planning Association, 66*(2), 113–124.

Pothukuchi, K., & Wallace, R. (2009). Sustainable food systems: Perspectives on transportation policy. In S. Malekafzali (Ed.), *Healthy, Equitable Transportation Policy: Recommendations and Research* (pp. 113–129). Oakland, CA: Policy Link, Prevention Institute, and Convergence Partnership.

Pruetz, R., & Standridge, N. (2008). What makes transfer of development rights work? Success factors from research and practice. *Journal of the American Planning Association, 75*(1), 78–87.

PSR Council (2012). *Integrating Food Policy in Comprehensive Planning: Strategies and Resources for the City of Seattle*. Seattle, WA: Author.

Quon, S. (1999). Planning for urban agriculture: A review of tools and strategies for urban planners (Cities Feeding People Report, 28). Ottawa, ON: IDRC.

Raja, S. (2010). Food systems planning: An opportunity for planners in private practice. *APA Private Practice Division Newsletter*, Fall 2010, 1–3. Retrieved from www.planning.org/divisions/privatepractice

Raja, S. (2015, April 3). Why all cities should have a Department of Food. *The Conversation*. Retrieved from http://theconversation.com/why-all-cities-should-have-a-department-of-food-39462

Raja, S., Born, B., & Kozlowski Russell, J. (2008). *A Planner's Guide to Community and Regional Food Planning*. Chicago: American Planning Association.

Reckwitz, A. (2002). Toward a theory of social practices: A development in culturalist theorizing. *European Journal of Social Theory, 5*(2), 243–263.

Renard, V. (2007). Property rights and the "transfer of development rights": Questions of efficiency and equity. *Town Planning Review, 78*(1), 41–60.

Reynolds, K., & Cohen, N. (2016). *Beyond the Kale: Urban Agriculture and Social Justice Activism in New York City*. Athens, GA: University of Georgia Press.

Roberts, R. (2007). Planning for community food systems. *The Land Use Tracker, 7*(3), 3–12.

Roberts, W. (2001). *The Way to a City's Heart is Through Its Stomach*. Toronto: Toronto Food Policy Council.

Rodwin, L. (2000). Images and Paths of Change in Economics, Political Science, Philosophy, Literature and City Planning: 1950–2000. In L. Rodwin & B. Sanyal (Eds.), *The Profession of City Planning: Changes, Images, and Challenges 1950–2000* (pp. 3–23). Piscataway, NJ: Transaction Publishers.

Sager, T. (1994). *Communicative Planning Theory*. Aldershot: Avebury.

Sager, T. (2006). The logic of critical communicative planning: Transaction cost alteration. *Planning Theory, 5*(3), 223–254.

Sanyal, B. (2000). Planning's Three Challenges. In L. Rodwin & B. Sanyal (Eds.), *The Profession of City Planning: Changes, Images, and Challenges 1950–2000* (pp. 312–333). Piscataway, NJ: Transaction Publishers.

Schatzki, T. R. (2001). Practice Theory. In T. R. Schatzki, K. Knorr Cetina, & E. von Savigny (Eds.), *The Practice Turn in Contemporary Theory* (pp. 10–23). London: Routledge.

Shove, E., Pantzar, M., & Watson, M. (2012). *The Dynamics of Social Practice: Everyday Life and How It Changes*. New York: Sage.

Sonnino, R. (2009). Feeding the city: Towards a new research and planning agenda. *International Planning Studies, 14*(4), 425–435.

Spaargaren, G. (2011). Theories of practices: Agency, technology, and culture. *Global Environmental Change, 21*(3), 813–822.

Steel, C. (2009). *Hungry City: How Food Shapes Our Lives*. London: Random House.

Sustain. (2011). *Good Planning for Good Food: Using Planning Policy for Local and Sustainable Food*. London: Author.

Sustain. (2014). *Planning Sustainable Cities for Community Food Growing: A Guide to Using Planning Policy to Meet Strategic Objectives Through Community Food Growing*. London: Author.

Toronto City Planning Division (2000). *Toronto Official Plan (Consolidated December 2010)*. Toronto, ON: City of Toronto.

UN-Habitat. (2009). *Planning Sustainable Cities*. London-Sterling, VA: Earthscan.

United Nations. (2015). *Transforming Our World: The 2030 Agenda for Sustainable Development* (A/RES/70/1). New York, NY: Author.

Urban Design Lab. (2011). *Infrastructure-Health: Modeling Production, Processing and Distribution Infrastructure for A Resilient Regional Food System*. New York, NY: Columbia University.

Van Assche, K., Beunen, R., Duineveld, M., & de Jong, H. (2013). Co-evolutions of planning and design: Risks and benefits of design perspectives in planning systems. *Planning Theory, 12*(2), 177–198.

Verzone, C. (2012). The Food Urbanism Initiative. In A. Viljoen & J. S. C. Wiskerke (Eds.), *Sustainable Food Planning: Evolving Theory and Practice* (pp. 517–531). Wageningen: Wageningen Academic Publishers.

Viljoen, A., & Bohn, K. (2005). Continuous productive urban landscapes: Urban agriculture as an essential infrastructure. *Urban Agriculture Magazine, 15*, 34–36.

Viljoen, A., Bohn, K., & Howe, J. (2005). *Continuous Productive Urban Landscapes: Designing Urban Agriculture for Sustainable Cities*. Oxford: Elsevier Architectural Press.

Viljoen, A., & Wiskerke, J. S. C. (Eds.). (2012). *Sustainable Food Planning: Evolving Theory and Practice*. Wageningen: Wageningen Academic Publishers.

Vitiello, D., & Brinkley, C. (2014). The hidden history of food system planning. *Journal of Planning History, 13*(2), 91–112.

Warner, S. B. (2000). Do Americans Like City Planning? In L. Rodwin & B. Sanyal (Eds.), *The Profession of City Planning: Changes, Images, and Challenges 1950–2000* (pp. 231–236). Piscataway, NJ: Transaction Publishers.

Whatmore, S., Stassart, P., & Renting, H. (2003). What's alternative about alternative food networks? *Environment and Planning A, 35*(3), 389–391.

Wheeler, S. M. (2013). Tools for Sustainability Planning. In *Planning for Sustainability: Creating Livable, Equitable and Ecological Communities* (2nd ed., pp. 86–104). New York: Routledge.

Winne, M. (2008). *Closing the Food Gap: Resetting the Table in the Land of Plenty*. Boston, MA: Beacon Press.

Winter, J. (2009). *Comprehensive Planning for the Napa County Food System*. Napa, CA: Author.

World Health Organization. (2001). Urban and peri-urban food and nutrition action plan (WHO European Health 21, Publication No. E72949). Copenhagen, Denmark: WHO Regional Office for Europe.

4 Seeing the city through a food system lens

> If food planning continues to solidify as a planning sub-discipline, it may prove a useful prism through which to explore and influence the processes that govern land-use and human health.
>
> – Catherine Brinkley, *Avenues into Food Planning*

The credibility of urban food planning as a necessary practice in the public domain largely depends on its ability to convey the importance of its object of study and the problems it addresses. The development of a robust toolbox of analytical tools that can enable the generation, accumulation, and exchange of agrifood system knowledge tailored specifically to the needs of urban professionals, activists, and policymakers is an essential step to this end. This chapter explores some of the different "lenses" researchers are developing to uncover missing, emergent, and potential geographies of urban food procurement – from food retail to city and regional farming – and assess their impact on human and environmental well-being. The analytical tools considered vary from specialized to comprehensive and encompass both expert and community-based approaches of inquiry. The last part of the chapter provides an overview of some of the metrics and indicators that local administrations have hitherto developed to link specific food system features to sustainable food system goals and objectives and measure progress toward their implementation.

Spotting "hidden" city foodscapes

While there is no single way to portray the city through a food system lens, what all food system practices have in common is that they are all carried out in specific places. This holds true for both relocalized and global food practices. In fact, globalized systems, including the food system, are not "placeless," only their operational logic is (Castells, 2002). The term "foodscape" is thus used in this section to draw attention to emerging efforts to represent the interplay of material and nonmaterial features of the urban food system in space. Etymologically, foodscape is a neologism that results from the synthesis of food and landscape. The notion of landscape is especially pertinent, even mandatory, in a conversation about food and the city, because it helps us make the connection between nature and culture. In short, the foodscape is a manmade landscape, and as Pierce Lewis (1979, p. 15) notes in his *Axioms for Reading the Landscape*, the manmade landscape "provides strong evidence of the kind of people we are, and were, and are in process of becoming." This section focuses on research aimed at unmasking two of the many "hidden" foodscapes in the city: the uneven geographies of community food access and the emerging spaces of urban food production. Before we proceed, one caution is warranted. This is not a review of the possible ways to analyze the urban food system in general, but a closer view of some of the analytical tools used to answer prevalent questions in the urban food planning research agenda to date.

The hungry city

Out of the circles of urban food systems research, the notion that there is a "food gap" (Winne, 2008) in our prosperous and abundant food supply is hardly commonplace. Most of us who live in industrialized economies still find it hard to imagine that within most of the cities we deem wealthy and global, there are consistent geographies of hunger, not just hungry individuals. Hence the "hidden" hungry city. The fact that this hungry city within the wealthy city happens also to be disproportionately affected by chronic diseases like overweight and obesity, which we historically associate with affluence and not with hunger, conceals it even further. Yet, more than three decades of community food security research in North America and the UK have revealed that this is a paradox only on the surface. The modern foodscapes of hunger are not simply due to scarce nutrition, but to high-calorie foods with scarce nutritional value. This realization led to the substantial revision of old ideas of urban food security, measuring simply the ability of single households to acquire food, and to the transition from household to community food security as the condition in which "all community residents obtain a safe, culturally acceptable, nutritionally adequate diet through a sustainable food system that maximizes community self-reliance and social justice" (Hamm & Bellows, 2003, p. 37).

How then to unmask the hungry city and make it visible at least to local administrations, if not to the general public? Two of the earliest examples of urban investigations challenging preconceived ideas about food access in Global North cities were undertaken by forward-looking faculty members at urban planning schools in the US. In 1977, a precedent-setting community food access study in Knoxville, Tennessee, was conducted by a group of graduate planning students supervised by professor Robert Wilson at the University of Tennessee. The study, *Food Distribution and Consumption in Knoxville* (Blakey et al., 1977), pointed at a wide range of food system issues in the city, among which the stark food insecurity of inner-city areas where seniors and households of limited financial means were struggling with inadequate access to food and no public programs were addressing their needs or monitoring their health (Haughton, 1987; Schiff, 2005). These findings, together with the awareness that there was no city agency to oversee community food access, prompted the Knoxville city council to adopt the first urban food policy and establish a municipal food policy council in 1981 (see also Chapter 7).

More than a decade later, in 1992, Robert Gottlieb, currently director of the Urban and Environmental Policy Institute (UEPI) at Occidental College in Los Angeles, guided his students at the graduate school of planning at the University of California in developing a pioneer food access study in South Central Los Angeles. The study, *Seeds of Change* (Ashman et al., 1993), purposefully adopted a community food security rather than an anti-hunger frame of reference to underscore the systemic and social justice facets of the issues at stake (Gottlieb & Joshi, 2010). Together with the organization of community meetings, over 1,000 scholarly, industry, and government reports were reviewed and more than 200 interviews were conducted (Hammer, 2004). The findings, summarized in a 400-page report, are still considered "one of most far-reaching and broadly constructed reports on an inner-city food system to date" (Winne, 2008, p. 42) and led to the institution of a food partnership to advise the city council on food issues in 1996 (Gottlieb & Joshi, 2010).

Some of the first formal guidelines developed to support systematic research of community food security in the US are the guide by Mark Winne and colleagues titled *Community Food Security: A Guide to Concept, Design, and Implementation* (Winne, Joseph, & Fisher, 2000), the US Department of Agriculture's *Community Food Security Assessment Toolkit* (B. Cohen, Andrews, & Kantor, 2002), and the *What's Cooking in Your Food System?* (Pothukuchi, Joseph, Burton, & Fisher, 2002) guide to community food assessment. The two nongovernmental guides were published by the Community Food Security Coalition, one of the most influential nonprofit organizations engaged in food security in North America, which during the time of its operation, from 1994 through 2012, spearheaded much of the present-day community food planning movement. Among the cities that have conducted such assessments in the US are Austin, Texas (1994), Berkeley, California (1998), Detroit, Michigan (1999), Madison, Wisconsin (1997), San Francisco, California (2001), Portland, Oregon (2006), Chicago, Illinois (2008), Lowell, Massachusetts (2013), and Baltimore, Maryland (2013). Examples from Canada include Toronto (2000), Vancouver (2003), Thunder Bay (2004), St. Vital (2012), and Brandon (2015).

As a means for construing the city though a food system lens, community food assessments represent a departure from previous top-down and problem-focused approaches in that they not only redefine the concept of food security but also how to tackle it. Importantly, the assessment is conceived not as separate from but part of the means directly addressing community food insecurity (Pothukuchi, 2004; Pothukuchi et al., 2002). Community members are provided with guidance and training that enable them to take an active role in the implementation of the assessment (e.g., conducting interviews with family members). Moreover, rather than focusing on problems alone, the quality of the urban foodscape is assessed by juxtaposing both needs *and* "assets" present in the community and takes into account the broader goals that the community is interested in pursuing, which may include but are not limited to better food access, a stronger local economy, vibrant neighborhoods, and the preservation of cultural heritage. To summarize, instead of merely detecting the "food gap," community food assessments aim at empowering the communities they are addressed to. Thus, they potentially carry long-term implications as a means for preventing food insecurity (Corburn, 2007) rather than just signaling the need for government intervention.

While constituting only a subset of the tools necessary for a comprehensive community food assessment, urban food access studies have gained an increasing saliency in scholarly literature on public health, urban planning, and community food systems over the past two decades. The notion of "food deserts" – originally used to describe urban areas lacking adequate access to healthy and affordable food (Beaumont, Lang, Leather, & Mucklow, 1995) – has by now become a household word in food justice advocacy, public health (nutrition and epidemiology), and emerging urban food planning circles. The concept was initially conceived in the UK at a time when leaders in national government were debating the interconnection between sociospatial segregation and patterns of poor public health (Furey, Strugnell, & Mcilveen, 2001; Wrigley, Warm, & Margetts, 2003). More recently, food deserts studies have been used to inform the development of municipal and metropolitan food system plans and policies in the US, such as New York City's FoodWorks plan (Brannen, 2010), featuring a map of the urban areas with a high supermarket need across the five boroughs (Figure 4.1), which prompted the development of fresh food store zoning and financial incentives (The City of New York, 2009, 2013), and Chicago's Metropolitan Area long-term sustainability plan GO TO 2040 (CMAP, 2010), featuring a map of the areas with low food access and low median household income in the metro region. The Chicago study, which was part of the Northeastern Illinois Community Food Security Assessment (Block, 2008) mentioned earlier, found that over 700,000 people in the metropolitan area (or 9% of the population) lived in food deserts. Consequently, the plan set the goals to reduce this percentage to 7% by 2015 and to eliminate food deserts by 2040 (CMAP, 2010, p. 149).

Since the inception of the concept, a broad range of food deserts studies have been carried out to uncover foodscapes of hunger and food insecurity across the UK, Canada, and the US. Researchers have sought to verify the presence of food deserts at the urban (e.g., Eckert & Shetty, 2011; LeClair & Aksan, 2014), regional (e.g., Furey et al., 2001), and national scales of government (DoH, 1996; USDA, 2013). Besides mapping the current state of food-insecure areas, food deserts investigations have also been carried out to trace the historical formation of urban areas with inadequate food access, exposing the progressive disappearance of supermarkets from inner-city areas (Larsen & Gilliland, 2008) or the impact of the introduction of new fresh food outlets, such as a chain store (Wrigley et al., 2003) or a farmers market (Larsen & Gilliland, 2009), in a food-insecure neighborhood. Other studies have focused specifically on school districts, showing the tendency of fast food outlets to cluster

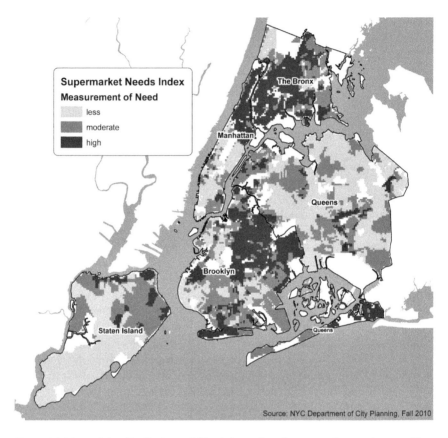

Figure 4.1 Map of the distribution of "food deserts" and supermarket need across New York City (2010).

Courtesy: © The Department of City Planning (DCP) of the City of New York.

around schools and, at the same time, the lack of adequate access to alternative food destinations near schools (Frank et al., 2006; Schafft, Jensen, & Clare, 2009). An in-depth review of the different approaches to the study of food deserts deployed to date has been compiled by Walker, Keane, and Burke (2010), while Kelly, Flood, and Yeatman (2011) provide a detailed overview of the methods researchers have hitherto deployed to describe local food environments, including techniques for measuring food access.

Despite its popularity, the "food desert" metaphor, and the food deserts assessments strand of community food security research as a whole, have been the object of considerable scholarly concern and criticism. Some scholars have called attention to the fact that the designation "desert" is in many instances misplaced. For one, in urban areas where supermarkets are missing, there still can be an abundance of fast food and other food venues offering less healthy options. Hence, some have suggested that the term "food swamps" may be more appropriate (e.g., Fielding & Simon, 2011). The availability of good public transportation connections to fresh food stores and supermarkets in adjacent neighborhoods also challenges the demarcation of food access in areas deemed to be food deserts (LeClair & Aksan, 2014). In addition, critical observers have argued that supermarket-centered definitions of food deserts can fail to acknowledge the current and potential contribution of small grocery stores to community food security (Raja, Ma, & Yadav, 2008; Short, Guthman, & Raskin, 2007). Using national-level data, food systems and social equity scholars (Blanchard & Matthews, 2007) have moreover debunked the assumption that food deserts are an exclusively urban phenomenon; in fact, rural areas can be as food insecure as urban areas. Other studies have proved that the common supposition that socioeconomic status can be a proxy for identifying urban areas where access to healthy and affordable food is impaired is not reliable and, for some urban areas, can prove entirely wrong (Eckert & Shetty, 2011).

As we saw in Chapter 2, with the suggestive images of the "Town–Country Magnet," the "Garden City," the "Green Heart," the "Natural Region," and the "Broadacre City," metaphors can powerfully shape the way we perceive a problem *and* its solutions. Wholesale sociotechnical transitions to sustainability largely depend on the capability of societies to collectively develop (and continually revise) a shared "basket of images" (Loorbach & Rotmans, 2006) that can guide experimentation and innovation toward the desired goal. The "food desert" metaphor has been effectively normalized both in academic and government discourses and has brought about the replication and alignment of multiple novelties in food access research. Yet, this seeming alignment of ideas and practices may be a symptom not of a large consensus about its effectiveness or desirability, but of the relative easiness of approaching the intricate question of community food security by measuring food access. In fact, scholars are raising concerns not just about the need for refining food deserts analyses but of their overall desirability.

Some analysts have underscored that planning policies to reintroduce supermarkets in underserved areas, prompted by food deserts studies, can not only be a waste of investments due to undetected availability of smaller-scale grocery stores, but can even worsen food insecurity in a given area; supermarkets may come to the food desert, push independent stores out of business, and then eventually decide to leave (Short et al., 2007). Others have overtly challenged the very idea of measuring food access and community food security through the technical tools planners are familiar with and have suggested that food deserts analyses are most usefully considered as a "first-wave empiricism" in urban food systems research (Born, 2013). Standing to the tenets of transition theories, the manifestation of critical concerns about how we create our urban food system "lens" is good news for urban food planning. Niche innovations are successful only when they go beyond the mere accumulation of new knowledge about the system they aim to transform and engage with "second-order learning" (e.g., Schot & Geels, 2007), fundamentally questioning the overarching paradigms and assumptions guiding their practices and innovation endeavors.

The edible city

Disparities in community food security across urban areas reflect the many deficiencies of what in the previous chapter we referred to as the urban food system *in* the city. The need to bridge food and urban planning however is driven also by the newly emerging urban food system *of* the city – that is, a food system rooted in a given urban area or region. The rise of urban farming in developed economies cities has raised an important question for urban planners, which their colleagues in developing counties have been facing for several decades now (Greenhow, 1994; Quon, 1999; Redwood, 2009): How can planners play an enabling rather than a hindering role in the development of urban agriculture infrastructures in cities? As we will see from the next chapters, there is much that can be done, in terms of both regulatory reforms and comprehensive planning. A first indispensable step, however, is to learn to see the city anew and learn from the "hidden" geographies of urban food production, which are unique to every city. Much like in the case of the foodscapes of urban food retail, there is a high risk to oversimplifying both the question and its answers. Seeing the city through the lens of urban agriculture therefore requires patience and research able to consider multiple scales, from the single project to the community and the entire city, and multiple domains, from land use to water and organic waste management and the regulations and institutions that shape them, in tandem. It would be perhaps fair to say that researching urban agriculture as a diverse system of places and practices can prepare both planning professionals and common citizens to approach the complexity of food as an urban system and thus see the opportunities for steering its transition through city-driven interventions.

How one defines urban agriculture determines what he or she is prepared to see as urban agriculture and where one would look for it. Considering that maps, or any synthetic representation for that matter, are not innocuous images but can drive community and political action in specific directions, definitions and descriptions of urban agriculture warrant special attention. So far, significant effort has been made to dismiss the idea that urban agriculture is simply about growing food in the city. In their comprehensive investigation of the rich realm of urban agriculture in New York City, boasting more than one thousand community gardens, Cohen, Reynolds, and Sanghvi (2012, p. 13) define urban agriculture as the process of "growing fruits, herbs, and vegetables and raising animals in cities . . . accompanied by many other complementary activities such as processing and distributing food, collecting and reusing food waste and rainwater, and educating, organizing, and employing local residents." In Europe, landscape scholars, like Pierre Donadieu (1998), have called attention to the fact that urban agriculture may well reside not only in the interstices of the built environment but also in the ambiguous periurban spaces between city and countryside, or what Donadieu calls the "urban countryside." Because this land is too close to the city to be suitable for intensive farming, but is not as urbanized as to be considered part of the built environment, many small-scale multifunctional urban agriculture projects may well be sited there and still be economically and socially linked to the everyday life of cities.

Analyses of the state of the art of urban agriculture in Global North cities have revealed a remarkable diversity in what an urban farm may look like. In their study of urban agriculture initiatives in US cities, Kaufman and Bailkey (2000) noted that entrepreneurial urban agriculture initiatives – defined as community or institutional urban farming projects selling all or part of their produce to the market – can greatly differ in their sources of funding, organizational structure, type of production techniques, scale, location, and connection to market outlets (e.g., farmers markets, residents, supermarkets, community-supported agriculture schemes). In-depth investigations of urban agriculture in New York City, for example, have distinguished between community farms, commercial farms, institutional farms, community gardens, educational gardens, and demonstration gardens and farms (N. Cohen & Reynolds, 2014; N. Cohen et al., 2012) and between ground-based, rooftop, and controlled-environment urban agriculture operations (Ackerman, 2012; Ackerman et al., 2014), which are not necessarily mutually exclusive.

Thus, alongside the burgeoning realm of community-driven mapping projects, governments, universities, and other nongovernmental organizations are increasingly becoming involved in the systematic mapping of cities heritage of longstanding and more recent urban agriculture sites and initiatives. Examples of comprehensive efforts to make urban agriculture visible and approach it as a full-fledged social and ecological system rather than the mere collection of isolated projects and best practices are the three-stage *Five Borough Farm* (2014; 2012) research project of the Design Trust for Public Space in New York City and the research on *The Potential for Urban Agriculture in New York City* (Ackerman, 2012) conducted by the Urban Design Lab at Columbia University. Some scholars, like Taylor and Lovell (2012) in Chicago, have focused on developing viable mapping and analytical methods to effectively include private urban agriculture spaces, such as home gardens, in addition to community and institutional urban farming projects citywide, suggesting that missing them may omit a substantial, if not the largest, part of a city's urban agriculture system. In informing the development of their comprehensive plans, some cities, like Portland (Rhoads & Guenin, 2009), have also included maps portraying urban agriculture sites and the unmet demand for them by spatializing community gardens waiting lists across the city.

Seeing the "edible city" entails also gauging the untapped potential of urban resources, like vacant land or abandoned buildings, to support the expansion of urban agriculture initiatives and reap the benefits of its transformation into a stable and ubiquitous urban infrastructure. One approach to the development of effective representations of the underused opportunities for future urban agriculture development is the use of land inventories. Land inventories of potential sites for urban agriculture have been compiled by many cities across North America and can be initiated by both municipal agencies and community organizations, as the experiences of Portland and Vancouver, thoroughly documented by Mendes, Balmer, Kaethler, and Rhoads (2008), have shown. There is no single approach to the design of such inventories and they may reflect both public and private plots as well as contain different suitability criteria (Horst, 2011); such criteria may include plot size, sun exposure, access to water and transportation, and surrounding neighborhood demographics.

Besides design, who initiates and implements the land inventory also matters. Community-driven projects like "The Diggable City" in Portland (Mendes et al., 2008) or "596 Acres" in New York City (Segal, 2015), whose organizers work closely with the communities where vacant land is available to raise awareness about the opportunities to connect with municipal agencies and turn it into community space, are more likely to engage the public and go beyond the inventory as an outcome in and of itself. Yet, community-based initiatives often rely on scarce financial resources, the pro bono work of experts, and an extensive cadre of volunteers, which raises questions about their ability to sustain such efforts in the long run. On the other hand, government agencies may be better positioned to run recurrent vacant land assessments over time, but the risk is that communities and the public fail to perceive the opportunities that such inventories may translate into or simply not be aware of their existence. A weaker connection between land inventories and the communities they are addressed to may jeopardize their effectiveness as a means to decreasing the amount of vacant land and buildings in cities and through community-based entrepreneurship.

While food production is only one of the many social and ecological benefits of urban agriculture land uses, making visible the extent to which a city is able to "feed itself" relying on its own resources has been a growing area of political and scholarly interest. Analysts have begun to use vacant land inventories as a basis for evaluating the food production potential of available land in cities and the extent it can meet incumbent demand for fresh produce. Building on a community-based vacant land inventory in Oakland, California, McClintock, Cooper, and Khandeshi (2013) have, for instance, identified over 1,500 acres of urban plots suitable for vegetable production, estimating that, in the most conservative production scenario, the city would be able to meet between 2.9% and 7.3% of its vegetables demand through city-grown produce. An earlier study on the City of Cleveland, Ohio, by Grewal and Grewal (2012) has shown that for some cities the potential for self-sufficiency through urban agriculture can be significantly higher. The researchers found that there were about 6,300 acres of available vacant land and rooftop surface in the city, which, if turned to production, in the most conservative scenario would be able to meet as much as 22% through 48% of the city's demand for fresh produce, a quarter of its demand for poultry and eggs, and its entire demand for honey.

Researchers in large metropolises as dense as New York City have also approached the challenge of estimating the extent to which their city can become self-reliant in food by tapping into the underutilized network of vacant land and flat-roofed buildings. Findings from New York City (Ackerman, 2012, p. 22) suggest that currently there are almost 5,000 acres of space suitable for urban farming, which can meet the need of fresh produce of about 174,000 residents if farmed through biointensive growing methods. Other pioneer self-sufficiency assessments based on available vacant land suitable for food production in large North American cities include Toronto (MacRae et al., 2010), Detroit (Colasanti & Hamm, 2010), and Philadelphia (Kremer & DeLiberty, 2011). Some community organizations have also initiated experimental projects to directly measure the volume of fresh produce that is already grown in the city in community gardens and farms. In New York City, Farming Concrete (2012) found that the 106 participating community gardens (4.5 acres or 1.8 ha) in their survey collectively produced over 195 varieties of crops and about 87,000 pounds (39,462 kg) of produce during the growing season in 2012.

The development of advanced approaches for assessing cities' self-reliance in food and the role of urban agriculture in it has importantly been accompanied by a new wave of research aimed at exhibiting the benefits of urban agriculture beyond food production per se. In New York City, for instance, Farming Concrete has recently partnered with the Design Trust for Public Space to develop a detailed data collection toolkit (Farming Concrete, 2015) and an online open-data platform to gauge environmental, social, health, and economic data, alongside harvest variety and weight. This progressive approach to the systemic metering of urban agriculture stemmed from an earlier metrics framework developed by research fellows at the Design Trust for Public Space (N. Cohen et al., 2012). The in-depth investigation of the contribution of urban agriculture to New York City's sustainability – considering land use, food security, water, energy, and waste management altogether – developed by the Urban Design Lab at Columbia University (Ackerman, 2012) constitutes another important milestone toward the development of a holistic lens for appraising emergent urban foodscapes and their socioecological value.

We are now beginning to ask questions about the extent to which urban agriculture contributes to healthy eating, physical activity, safety in public spaces, job training, storm water management, biodiversity, urban heat island reduction, and disaster preparedness, in a synoptic fashion. Considering the traditional divisiveness between sociological, spatial, cultural, economic, and ecological approaches to urban food system research, this is a hopeful step forward. More than that, it is a necessary step forward and not just for the sake of normalizing urban food planning as a field of expertise per se, but because making these connections can enable emerging urban agriculture projects to connect with priority issues on mayoral agendas and related financial and other resources. Two cases in point are the inclusion of rooftop farming in municipal incentives for green roofs in Toronto (Roberts, 2010), thanks to advocacy of the Toronto Food Policy Council (more about this in Chapter 7) and the inclusion of urban agriculture projects in the green infrastructure grant program of New York City's Department of Environmental Protection. The largest rooftop soil-based farm in the US, Brooklyn Grange in the Brooklyn Navy Yards area in the Borough of Brooklyn in New York City, has been awarded nearly $600,000 through the grant program (EPA, 2011), on the grounds that it would be able to divert over one million gallons of storm water from the city's sewage system per year.

Though in its infancy, research on how existing laws, programs, and government agencies affect the development and longevity of urban agriculture and other local food initiatives in industrialized cities is also taking shape. In investigating the institutional environment in which urban agriculture had evolved in New York City, Cohen et al. (2012) found that as many as 13 city agencies and departments were involved in some form of policymaking or planning for urban agriculture. Faculty and graduate students at the University of Virginia have developed a specialized community food assessment with a focus on policy – a food policy audit (O'Brien & Cobb, 2012) – to assess the presence and role of local laws, policies, and regulations in influencing food production, sale, and consumption in Charlottesville and the surrounding five-county region in the State of Virginia. Rather than simply inventorying legislation, the audit was supplemented by a second phase in which stakeholder meetings allowed for validation of the preliminary findings and a greater community engagement. Comparative multicity audits of policies, programs, and plans in support of urban agriculture and other urban food systems initiatives also started being put forward (Budge, 2013; N. Cohen, 2012; Neuner, Kelly, & Raja, 2011; Sonnino & Spayde, 2014).

Recharting the urban foodshed

Food is a powerful lens through which to unmask the social and organic fabric of cities and how they codetermine one another. This knowledge is essential for pursuing any sustainable city planning endeavor. Yet, as twentieth century urban planning theorists have insisted, the city can never be properly understood if considered in isolation from its region. Where one can draw the boundaries of this urban region is a highly contested question. Local landscape features, commuting patterns of regular city users, or the places of origin of goods and services used in the city are all plausible criteria, though, with profoundly different implications for how one perceives and plans for the urban region. Being both a globalized industry and a product inherently bounded to local ecosystems and landscapes, food offers an ideal entry point to address this question.

The urban foodshed – or the aggregate of places, people, institutions, and infrastructures that keep a city fed – is both a theoretical concept and a tool for inquiry into the present and potential geography of a city's food supply. The term "foodshed" is likely to have been first introduced by Walter P. Hedden, Chief of the Commerce Bureau of the Port Authority of New York, in his book *How Great Cities Are Fed* (1929), which he wrote in the wake of a major railroad strike initiated by some of the largest railroad worker unions in the US. The potentially catastrophic disruption of the city's food supply revealed how little government agencies knew about how much and what food the city needed, where food was coming from, and how it was transported and distributed. Back then, the concept was used to reacquire knowledge of the system and consider what could be done to ensure that a large city like New York stays food secure even in the face of major external disruptions. Today, the need to recover knowledge about the urban foodshed has resurfaced, but is largely driven by public health and environmental concerns. The social and ecological, rather than merely the infrastructural, integrity of the urban food-shed have thus come to the fore of public, scholarly, and political attention.

Before examining the present-day definitions and applications of the food-shed concept, it is however useful to consider how the broader community of urban scholars have recurrently turned to food as a useful prism for under-standing the modern city. The urban food system has indeed often been used to substantiate claims about the globalization of the urban region and redefine it as a networked space of flows in the context of the new world economy. Through the lens of urban food supply, Sassen (1994) has noted how cities tend to disconnect from their hinterlands, while Amin and Thrift (2002, p. 71) have observed that cities no longer experience a "self-expanding growth based on local consumption" and that the geographies of food delivery have departed from those of production and consumption. In his essay *Goods*, Stetter (2000, p. 41) has called attention to the highly complex and dynamic urban food system that shapes cities and, at the same time, constitutes an intricate journey in which every step entails different transportation, packaging, storing, refrig-eration, produce selection, price negotiation, demand estimates, ordering, and delivery practices "until finally, the produce appears, as if by magic, in our local shop". Seen through this lens, the modern urban foodshed is an incred-ibly complex sociotechnical and ecological system in which the outcome of any planned action is largely unpredictable.

During the 1990s, ecologists, rural sociologists, and community food sys-tems scholars began to consider the need to study the urban food system not just to better describe how cities work, but also to purposefully change the sys-tem itself. If considered purely as a complex of industries, the food system does appear as a tremendously efficient machine, working seamlessly and effectively meeting unprecedented urban food demand, but, taken as a social or eco-logical system, disparities and inefficiencies are quick to emerge. In his essay *Urban Foodsheds*, Getz (1991) made a strong plea for considering the foodshed along the same lines as a watershed, not so much for its structural properties, which concerned Hedden in the 1920s, but for its ability to remind us that, as water, the source of food requires attentive care and protection. A few years later, Kloppenburg, Hendrickson, and Stevenson (1996, p. 34) advanced this idea further to emphasize both the ecological and societal values of the urban foodshed concept which, in their view, could be used as a means to "reas-semble our fragmented identities, reestablish community, and become native not only to a place but to each other." Perhaps, most importantly, the authors called attention to the need for a systematic foodshed analysis to inform strate-gies to protect local food sources and make visible emerging local networks of production and consumption.

Thus, while the concept of the urban foodshed is not entirely new, its primary meaning and intended use is. This transition is well reflected in the definition that Lister (2007, p. 151) provides in discussing Toronto's foodshed as the area which "captures the food products that flow from local farms surrounding a given urban area, and routes them into the city." This variation from the original is not trivial. It enables analysts to tentatively demarcate the boundaries of the urban foodshed based on the time one would need to travel from a local farm to the city (or vice versa) to supply fresh produce. Hence, the 200-mile (321-km) radiuses used in foodshed analyses of large metropolitan areas like Toronto, Los Angeles, Chicago, and New York City (Figure 4.2), or the 100-mile (161-km) radiuses used for cities like Boston, Vancouver, Philadelphia, and San Francisco. Some towns in the UK, like Totnes, Sheffield, Hastings, and Norwich, among others, all part of a national Mapping Local Food Webs project initiated by the charity Campaign to Protect Rural England in 2007, have adopted radiuses as proximate as 30 miles (48 km), while a research project assessing the urban foodshed of Rennes Metropole in France used 17- and 14-mile (28- and 22-km) radiuses (Darrot, 2012). Clearly, there is no universal perception of the distance beyond which produce ceases to be "local," but fixing it universally is neither necessary nor desirable. What seems relevant instead is that the notion of the urban foodshed is now being used to investigate a set of questions quite different from what Hedden (1929) originally was concerned with, such as to what extent the urban foodshed can be re-regionalized and what alternative agrifood networks are already present in it.

Over the past decade, a growing number of studies have sought to use the urban foodshed as a unit of analysis and translate the directions for a systematic foodshed analysis put forward by Kloppenburg et al. (1996) in practice. Across North America and Europe, researchers have assessed the self-reliance potential for food of urban regions like San Francisco (Thompson, Harper, & Kraus, 2008), New York (Scenic Hudson, 2013; Urban Design Lab, 2011a, 2011b), Toronto (Lister, 2007), Philadelphia (Delaware Valley Regional Planning Commission, 2010), Vancouver (Richardson, 2010), Rennes (Darrot, 2012), and Milan (Porro, Corsi, Scudo, & Spigarolo, 2014). Statewide foodshed analyses have been conducted for New York (Peters, Bills, Lembo, Wilkins, & Fick, 2009, 2011; Peters, Bills, Wilkins, & Fick, 2008) and Washington (Born & Martin, 2011), while scholars in Japan have suggested an intraregional foodshed analysis focusing on the micro-scale of mixed-use urbanization patterns in the Kanto Plain, where the Tokyo metropolitan area is located (Kurita, Yokohari, & Bolthoise, 2008). Building on the ecological footprint concept (Rees & Wackernagel, 1996), in Sweden, Johansson (2008) has developed an "ecological foodprint" metrics and used it to design a national foodshed assessment model. Food systems analysts at the Urban Design Lab of Columbia University (Urban Design Lab, 2010), in collaboration with MIT, have also conceived a nationwide foodshed analysis to assess the potential for an integrated foodshed infrastructure in the US.

Mapping the geographies of existing short food supply chains has also grown into a burgeoning area of scholarly research. Besides the already mentioned Mapping Local Food Webs project undertaken in the UK, emergent urban-rural

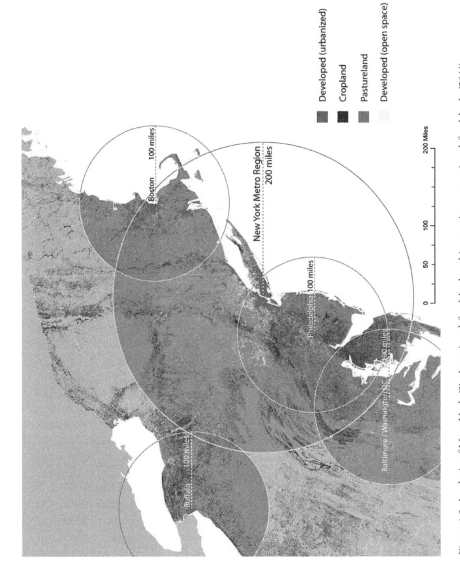

Figure 4.2 Analysis of New York City's regional foodshed and its contiguous regional foodsheds (2011).

Courtesy: © Urban Design Lab, Columbia University.

linkages have been mapped in Milan (Coviello, Graglia, & Villa, 2009), Venice (Ferrario, 2009), Paris (Aubry & Kebir, 2013), and the US (Galt, 2011). Pioneering multicity studies, such as the FoodMetres research project in Europe (Sali et al., 2014), which comparatively analyzes London, Ljubljana, Milan, and Rotterdam, have also begun to take shape. Overall, there is a need for a more articulated set of foodshed analysis metrics that can help us concurrently account for the social, economic, public health, and ecological benefits of shorter food supply networks. Drawing inspiration from the latest generation of urban agriculture assessments, urban planners, ecologists, rural sociologists, nutritionists, and the communities engaged in local food procurement practices can forge productive partnerships to fill this gap. An additional challenge is the development of more comprehensive accounts of organic waste – from manure through food scraps to human waste (Ackerman-Leist, 2013; Sonnino & McWilliam, 2011); finding creative ways to address it would make the foodshed analysis a more robust tool for inquiry and sustainable food systems planning.

A toolkit in the making

The host of endeavors to represent and reimagine the city through a food system lens we briefly explored so far has produced a great variety of analytical tools and approaches, which collectively make up an important part of the emerging urban food planning "toolkit." It is by all means a toolkit still in the making and in need of validation, but the mere fact that these studies have been advanced and that multiple research techniques are being devised, refined, or surpassed constitutes an import advancement. Food is coming to be considered as a system, and important connections between scattered sustainable food system outcomes (e.g., public health, hunger, environmental stewardship, job training) are being exposed. Anomalies and untapped opportunities "hiding in plain view," because residing in Global North cities, such as food insecurity, grassroots urban farming networks, and emergent urban-rural linkages, are now increasingly being made visible.

Overall, there is a need for consolidation of the approaches that work but also of consistent crossovers between overlapping analyses, for instance, by devising a foodshed analysis that attends to both urban vacant land and regional farmland, or that bridges geospatial analysis with immersive investigation techniques like participatory action research. A more comprehensive research approach is not without limitations, but it would enable us to both represent and learn from emergent urban food practices. Much of the primary data used for pioneer urban food systems research is now being made public and available for researchers beyond the communities where it was gathered (e.g., the open data platform of Farming Concrete in New York or the online Food Environment Atlas of the US Department of Agriculture), which significantly adds to the opportunities for testing and expanding the urban food planning toolkit. Without claims for comprehensiveness, the Table 4.1 summarizes some of the typologies of food system assessments we came across in our exploration so far and which are becoming a recurrent term of reference in urban food systems research (for a thorough review see Freedgood, Pierce-Quiñonez, & Meter, 2011).

Table 4.1 Towards a food systems assessment toolbox

Scale	Tools being tested	Authors
Local	Community food security assessment	B. Cohen et al. (2002), Pothukuchi et al. (2002), Pothukuchi (2004)
	Urban food deserts analysis	Beaumont et al. (1995), Eckert and Shetty (2011), LeClair and Aksan (2014)
	Progressive disappearance of supermarkets from inner-city areas	Larsen and Gilliland (2008)
	Impact of new food outlets in food deserts	Larsen and Gilliland (2009), Wrigley et al. (2003)
	Analysis of the distribution of unhealthy food destinations near schools	Frank et al. (2006), Schafft et al. (2009)
	Land inventories of vacant land suitable for urban agriculture	Mendes et al. (2008), Segal (2015)
	Assessment of a city's self-reliance in food	Colasanti and Hamm (2010), Grewal and Grewal (2012), Kremer and DeLiberty (2011), MacRae et al. (2010), McClintock et al. (2013)
	Assessment of urban food yields	Farming Concrete (2012), Farming Concrete (2015)
	Comprehensive urban agriculture assessments	Ackerman (2012), Altman et al. (2014), N. Cohen et al. (2012)
	Urban food systems reports	Brannen, 2010, DVRPC (2011), Fisher and Roberts (2011)
	Food policy audit	O'Brien and Cobb (2012)
Metropolitan/ Regional	Regional food deserts assessment	Furey et al. (2001)
	Regional foodshed assessment	Darrot (2012), Peters et al. (2008), Porro et al. (2014), Scenic Hudson (2013), Thompson et al. (2008), Urban Design Lab (2011)
	Mapping local food webs	Kneafsey, Lambie, Dowler, and Inman (2008)
	Counting and mapping community supported agriculture webs	Aubry and Kebir (2013), Coviello et al. (2009), Galt (2011)
	Multicity studies of short food supply chain networks	Sali et al. (2014)
Supraregional/ National	National food deserts assessment	DoH (1996), USDA (2013)
	Intraregional foodshed analysis	Kurita et al. (2008)
	National foodshed assessment	Johansson (2008), Urban Design Lab (2010)

(Continued)

Table 4.1 (Continued)

Scale	Tools being tested	Authors
Crosscutting	Review of approaches to food deserts analysis	Walker et al. (2010)
	Review of approaches to measuring local food environments	Kelly et al. (2011)
	Review of food system assessment tools	Freedgood et al. (2011)
	Comparative multicity analysis of urban food policy initiatives	N. Cohen (2012), Neuner et al. (2011), Sonnino and Spayde (2014)

Considering this group of approaches, four broad thematic foci can be discerned: community food security, urban agriculture, regional agriculture, and policy and governance. To these can be added civil society and government-led comprehensive food system reports (see Chapter 5) seeking to provide a bird's-eye view of the state of the system and recognize emerging local food initiatives. Historical accounts of the evolution of the urban food system and its influence on urban development (e.g., Steel, 2009) have also been advanced and constitute another means to the holistic investigation of the city through a food system lens. One area in need of further research that all assessments tend to share is how national or supranational legislation, like the Farm Bill in the US and the CAP in the EU, affects urban food systems in terms of barriers and opportunities (Fry & Wooten, 2012) and how urban food planning concerns can be linked with policies developed at higher jurisdictional levels (Pothukuchi, 2004).

Toward sustainable food city metrics

Since the turn of the century, over 90 city and regional food system strategies and action plans have been released by local administrations in the Global North (see Chapter 1). Yet, few of them have been equipped with a distinct set of metrics and indicators that can help local administrations track progress toward the implementation of their overarching goals and objectives. This gap is increasingly being addressed in recent food system strategies, which started including designated sections for indicators either as an integral part of the strategy (e.g., Vancouver, Philadelphia, Chicago) or as a follow-up food metrics report (e.g., New York, London, and the State of Massachusetts).

In isolated instances, the development and monitoring of urban food system metrics have been institutionalized through legislative provisions, such as New York City's Local Law 52 of 2011 Food Metrics for New York City and the subsequent Food Metrics Bill (S.4061/A.5102) of the State of New York passed into law in 2013. The latter, for instance, has mandated the tracing of the type, cost, and place of origin of the produce supplied through government procurement contracts and the development of guidelines for the increased procurement of local food by state agencies. In London, Sustain – a leading nonprofit organization for sustainable food systems in the UK – has supported the development and implementation of comprehensive sustainable food system benchmarks to assess the progress made by each London borough in pursuing the objectives of the London Food Strategy (2006) and Action Plan (2007). Monitoring has been periodically conducted every year since 2011 and the results have been summarized in five annual *Good Food for London* reports (e.g., Sustain, 2015).

Despite the progress made, many cities still feel the need for greater knowledge on which indicators and metrics can best help them move toward accomplishing their stated food system goals. In the UK, this concern provided the impetus for the creation of the Sustainable Food Cities coalition, initiated by cities having a food system charter, strategy, or action plan but in need for sharing knowledge on how to effectively track progress throughout their execution. This section aims to provide an overview of some of the main indicators that local administrations have hitherto put forward to this end. A sample of 93 local food system reports was examined, of which about a quarter either had an integrated food metrics section or were accompanied by a stand-alone food metrics report. Overall, more than 200 different indicators were identified and summarized in five broad categories reflecting prevalent definitions of sustainable food systems (Figure 4.3). The categories

Figure 4.3 The five goals of urban food system sustainability.

Source: Own elaboration based on review of recurrent goals in urban and regional food systems plans.

encompass metrics aimed to support the development of healthier, environmentally sound, fair, economically diverse, and resilient urban food systems. While subdivided into separate categories, many of the indicators can help measure progress toward more than one sustainable food systems goal.

Health and well-being for all

Metrics falling under the rubric of health and well-being for all are targeting two chief aspects of the urban food environment – access and consumer practices. Access is measured both in terms of physical access to healthy and unhealthy food options and in terms of economic access, considering the affordability of fresh and healthy food produce for all residents (Table 4.2). Metrics aimed at gauging consumer practices focus mainly on available knowledge and consumer behavior in the urban food system. Knowledge-oriented indicators assess current awareness of healthy nutrition practices, as well as available government programs to improve it through dedicated educational initiatives, while behavior-oriented indicators look at consumption habits and

Table 4.2 Urban food system goal: health and well-being for all

Focus	Suggested indicators in urban and regional food strategies
Access to healthy and sustainable food for all: spatial	The percent of the region's population who live in a "food desert"[1]
	Accessibility to transportation[2]
	Emergency food services availability[2]
	Number of Department of Education vending machines and revenue generated[3]
	Number of stores participating in healthy food initiatives[3,4]
	Number of salad bars in schools, hospitals, and public offices[3]
	Grocery stores per capita and new opened[3]
	Number of local food options accessible within walking distance[5,6]
	Reliable access to healthy foods[7]
	Number of food shelves serving fresh fruits and vegetables[8]
	Percent of residents within one-quarter mile of a healthy food access point[4]
	Distance (and distance distribution) from eaters to nearest full-service food store[9]
Access to healthy and sustainable food for all: economic	Annual cost of a nutritious food basket as a proportion of median income for a two-parent family in the food strategy area[10]
	Annual cost of a nutritious food basket as a proportion of after-tax low income cut-off for single parent families with two children in the Food Strategy area[10]
	Boroughs that have developed healthier catering scheme for businesses[11]
	Number of farmers markets that accept food stamps[9]
	Number of farmers markets with EBT machines[8]
	Pounds of food gleaned and distributed from local farms to local food pantries and organizations[8]
	Value of EBT benefits redeemed at farmers markets[4]
	Number of SNAP retailers accepting incentives[12]

Focus	Suggested indicators in urban and regional food strategies
Awareness of the importance of healthy and sustainable diet: knowledge	Consumer knowledge, determined from surveys, regarding the importance of buying and consuming local food and drink[7,13] Funds spent on nutrition education[3,12] Number of restaurants participating in the Chef's Collaborative[9] Number of schools participating in healthy and sustainable food consumption/system education programs[8,9,10,11]
Awareness of the importance of healthy and sustainable diet: behavior	Proportion of residents that eats fruits and vegetables 3/5 or more times per day[5,8,10] Proportion of the Food Strategy–area residents with overweight or obese self-reported[7,10] Proportion of the Food Strategy–area residents with Type II Diabetes[5,10] Obesity rate in adults[5,8,9] Daily per capita servings of fruits and vegetables[8,9] Weight of food consumed by food source (store/home; restaurant with fast food/pizzas; restaurant with waiter/waitress; bar/tavern/lounge; Meals on Wheels; community food program; cafeteria not at school; vending machine; soup kitchen/food pantry; others)[14]

Strategies where the indicator is suggested: [1]Chicago Comprehensive Regional Plan "GO TO 2040," 2010; [2]British Columbia's Capital Region Food Security Assessment, 2004; [3]Food Metrics Report NYC, 2015; [4]Seattle Food Action Plan, 2012; [5]State of the Food System Report, Austin 2012; [6]Fresh, Edmonton's Food & Urban Agriculture Strategy, 2012; [7]Greater Philadelphia's Food System Plan, 2011; [8]Regional Food System Plan for Vermont's Northeast Kingdom, 2011; [9]The New Mainstream – A Sustainable Food Agenda for California, 2005; [10]Vancouver Regional Food System Strategy, 2011; [11]Good Food for London, 2015; [12]Massachusetts Local Food Action Plan, 2015; [13]Food for Wales, Food from Wales 2010–2020; [14]San Francisco Foodshed Assessment, 2008.

the incidence of chronic diseases, such as diabetes, overweight, and obesity, attributed to poor nutritional intake in urban and rural communities.

Environmental sustainability

Environmental sustainability appeared to be one of the most populous clusters of local food systems indicators. Besides system-wide metrics, such as ecological footprint and use of fossil fuels, indicators targeted the five traditional functional domains of the food system: production, processing, distribution, consumption, and waste disposal (Table 4.3). Sustainable farming and waste disposal appeared to be the thematic areas equipped with the richest battery of sustainability metrics, while processing seemed to be the least developed so far. The place of consumption was considered as a relevant reference for environmental sustainability in just a couple of strategies, but it should be noted that the importance of local food production and consumption was found to be a persistent theme across all five food metrics areas.

Fairness

Metrics assessing fairness in the food chain and labor are a relatively recent addition to the urban food system research and policy agenda. Cities are

Table 4.3 Urban food system goal: environmental sustainability

Focus	Suggested indicators in urban and regional food strategies
Concerning the entire food system	Business targeting efficiencies and terms usage and GHG emissions[1,2,3] Food ecological footprint (city/region/state)[4,5] Development (urbanization) efficiency and future development in the foodshed study area[6] Use of fossil fuel in local food production[5,7]
Food production	Number of farmers participating with Environmental Farm Plans or the like[8,9] Value of ecological services provided by local farms[5] Farmland preservation (acres)[7,10,11,12,13] Farmland lost each day/acres[11,14] Number of farms protected per year under various farmland conservation programs[7] Area of natural areas affected by farming[5] Number of cultivars for selected commodities for top 75% of harvested acres[10] Number of crops statewide for top 75% of the harvested acres[7,10] Land planted in cover crops[11] Total resource use[4] Use of fossil fuel per net harvested energy (l/m Cal)[2] Fuel, fertilizer and chemical expense in agriculture; as % of total expenses[7,10] Soil quality[2,4] Farmworker pesticide poisonings[2,10] Number/ratio of organic farms; organic producers[1,2,7,8,10] Size of organic farms (acres)[7,10] Number of farms generating energy or electricity on the farm as a percentage of the total number of farms[7] Tons topsoil lost/year due to erosion[2,10] Water resource management[2,4,12] Total water usage (acre-feet) in agriculture[2,10] Water quality[4,10,12] Levels of phosphorus in lakes and ponds[7] Number and identity of humane animal certification programs[10] Number of certified humane raised and handled animal producers[2,10] Number of grass-fed animal producers[2,7,10] Waste produced by cattle[2] Nutrient management plans[11] Boroughs that adhere to animal welfare programs[15] Fish habitat health[10,11,15]
Food processing	Number of federal and state inspected slaughterhouses[10] Percentage of local food production processed and consumed within the given municipality,[5,11,14]
Food distribution	Distributors of certified organic produce[6] Wholesale markets purchases of locally produced foods[6] Compliance with food standards[9] Food transportation patterns (e.g. "food miles"); Number of paths for direct transportation from farmer to consumer[6,9]

Focus	Suggested indicators in urban and regional food strategies
Food consumption	Consumption of locally grown products[11]
	Consumption of locally raised and landed seafood[11]
	Where locally produced food is consumed[6]
Food waste disposal	Waste increase[4]
	Number of composters accepting food and agricultural waste (current) in relation to total number of composters/processors of organic materials (mostly urban)[2,10]
	Number of farms/organizations that are certified compost facilities[7,16]
	Number of operating food diversion programs[2,10]
	Funds spent on bottled water[9]
	Value of wasted food[14]
	Food wasted annually[14]
	Food waste landfilled[11]
	Anaerobic digester production[11]
	Percentage of food waste diverted from disposal[2,5,8,10,13,14]
	Number of schools that compost their waste or have it hauled to a compost facility[7]
	Food diverted from waste stream to emergency hunger relief[11]
	Food diverted from waste stream to energy production[11]
	Food diverted from waste stream for compost[7,11]

Strategies where the indicator is suggested: [1]Food for Wales, Food from Wales 2010–2020; [2]Multnomah Food Report, 2010; [3]South Australian Food Strategy 2010–2015; [4]One Wales: One Planet, 2009; [5]Fresh, Edmonton's Food & Urban Agriculture Strategy, 2012; [6]San Francisco Foodshed Assessment, 2008; [7]Regional Food System Plan for Vermont's Northeast Kingdom, 2011; [8]Vancouver Regional Food System Strategy, 2011; [9]Food Metrics Report NYC, 2015; [10]The New Mainstream – A Sustainable Food Agenda for California, 2005; [11]Massachusetts Local Food Action Plan, 2015; [12]Greater Philadelphia's Food System Plan, 2011; [13]Seattle Food Action Plan, 2012; [14]State of the Food System Report, Austin 2012; [15]Good Food for London, 2015; [16]City of Vancouver Food Strategy, 2013.

becoming increasingly cautious not only about where their food comes from and how it is produced, but also about who is producing it and under what economic and environmental conditions. Some of the indicators being introduced to measure progress toward greater fairness in the food chain take into account the wages of workers, but also their ethnicity, age, gender, and access to healthcare services (Table 4.4). A fair food system is also being defined as a system in which hunger and food poverty are systematically dismantled. The level of food-insecure citizens relying on government subsidies or civil society organizations for their sustenance is considered to be an important lens through which to assess social equity objectives in the urban food system. One strategy pointed also to the need to ensure that local food partnerships are equitable and transparent and explicit ethical codes of conduct are being adopted.

Local economic diversity and prosperity

Indicators measuring diversity and prosperity in the local agrifood economy are by far the largest group of indicators found across the five thematic areas. Cities are feeling the need to provide sound economic reasons as to why supporting

Table 4.4 Urban food system goal: fairness in the food chain

Focus	Suggested indicators in urban and regional food strategies
Workers involved: recognized and fairly rewarded	Food workers' wages, compared to the living wage and self-sufficiency standards[1,2,3]
	Percentage of farmworkers employed through farm labor contractors[3]
	Average wage paid to grocery workers (compared to other industries)[3]
	Average wage paid to food service and processing workers (compared to other industries)[3]
	Share of gross domestic product per capita[4]
	Total number of ethnic minority farmers[3]
	Total number of ethnic minority farmers, farms, acreage (Hispanic, Asian, African American, American Indian)[3]
	Total women farmers (principal operator) and acreage controlled[3,5]
	Age distribution of farmers[3,5,6,7,8]
	Boroughs that have achieved fair trade status[2]
	Percentage of farmers with health care[5]
	Average wage paid to processing employees[9]
	Average wage paid to farmworkers/fishermen[5,10]
Open and equitable partnerships	Upheld complaints to supply chain ombudsman[11]
	Food service outlets adopting supermarket code of practice[11]
Tracing food poverty	Efforts to abate hunger[1]
	Number/percentage of households suffering from "food insecurity"[1,3,5,6,9,12]
	Uptake of nutrition programs for SNAP recipients[9]
	Food security planning[9]
	Number of people connected to food banks[7]
	Percentage of population in poverty[3]
	Number of people using SNAP benefits[6,9,13]
	"Meal Gap": the meals missing from the homes of families and individuals struggling with food insecurity[13]

Strategies where the indicator is suggested: [1]Greater Philadelphia's Food System Plan, 2011; [2]Good Food for London, 2015; [3]The New Mainstream – A Sustainable Food Agenda for California, 2005; [4]South Australian Food Strategy 2010–2015; [5]Regional Food System Plan for Vermont's Northeast Kingdom, 2011; [6]State of the Food System Report, Austin 2012; [7]British Columbia's Capital Region Food Security Assessment 2004; [8]Vancouver Regional Food System Strategy, 2011; [9]Massachusetts Local Food Action Plan, 2015; [10]Multnomah Food Report, 2010; [11]The Welsh Food Strategy Report; [12]Seattle Food Action Plan, 2012; [13]Food Metrics Report NYC, 2015.

shorter food supply chains matters and why they should be part of their urban policy agenda. Five specialized areas of interest were identified, among which are diversity of food enterprises throughout the food chain, local food business profitability, the role of regional foods in strengthening regional identity and tourism, public procurement, and collaboration capabilities throughout the food chain (Table 4.5). Some of the indicators suggested for assessing economic diversity include the number and size of farms, retailers, and food manufacturers and the number of urban farms, food hubs, co-ops, farmers markets, and food business incubators. The proportion of local food in public sector food

Table 4.5 Urban food system goal: local economic prosperity

Focus	Suggested indicators in urban and regional food strategies
Concerning the entire food system	Personal income generated by farm, manufacturing, retail food and eating/drinking establishments[1,2]
	Number of workers in various food sectors[1,3]
	People employed in farms/fisheries[4]
	Number of food manufacturers by size classes (number of employees)[1,3,5]
	Number of dairy processing facilities[5]
	Number of people employed in food processing[3]
	Number of retail food businesses by size classes (number of employees)[1,6]
	Aggregate income earned by workers in various food sectors[1]
Diversity of food enterprises throughout the food chain	Number of outlets (farm shops, farmers markets, box schemes, Internet) retailing local food; number of farmers markets and vendors[1,2,7,8,9,10]
	Number of green carts[9]
	Number of food business incubators[2]
	Number of urban farms[2,10]
	Number of food hubs[10]
	Number of horticultural producers and area of land[7]
	Number of wholesalers; restaurants selling/serving local food[5,11]
	Number of farms served by produce distribution companies[5]
	Quantity of local fish in markets[7]
	Effective infrastructure: number of small abattoirs in the area considered by the food strategy[7]
	Number and size of farms[1,11]
	Number of commercial fishing licenses and permits[1]
	Value of agricultural products sold directly to individuals for human consumption in the region[5,15,16]
	Value of seafood products sold directly to consumer[3]
	Number of community food co-ops sourcing local fruit and vegetables[12]
Local food business profitability	Farms operating with deficits[13]
	Farms without off-farm income[3]
	Number of farm operators working more than 200 days off of the farm[5]
	Value of production per hectare of agricultural land[4,8,3]
	Value of agricultural production by food group (production, processing, distribution, consumption)[2,4,14]
	Ratio of farm business gross receipts to operating expenses[8]
	Annual gross receipts for farmers markets[1,4,5,8]
	Retail price spread[1]
	Percentage of consumers now buying local products more often than six months ago[1]
	Total receipts/income/employment from fishing and fish processing[1,3,8]
	Ratio local food/imported food prices[11]
	Direct and organic sales as percentage of total agricultural sales (per county)[1,14]
	Food manufacturers receiving monetary benefits[9]
	Total sale of seeds to markets (farmers, individuals, and wholesale)[5]
	Market value of milk and other dairy products sold[5]
	Average all milk price (dollars per hundredweight) paid to farmers[5]

(*Continued*)

Table 4.5 (Continued)

Focus	Suggested indicators in urban and regional food strategies
	Number of dairy farms receiving federal subsidies[5]
	Generated gross food revenue[2,3,17]
	Net farm/fishery/food processing industry income[1,3,4,5]
	Total value of crop/livestock production[3,5]
	Value of individual crops production[3]
	Annual sales of locally produced products[3,6]
	Economic multiplier analysis[6]
	Value added to the local economy[6]
	Volume of activity (sales) in processing and storage facilities[5,6]
	Annual per household spending on local food[6]
	Number of jobs generated in local food and agriculture sectors[3,5,6]
	Unemployment rate[5]
	Number of new local food related businesses[3,6]
Role of regional foods identity and tourism	Accurate provenance labelling of regional food[7]
	Quality local foods awards entries and winning products[7]
	Local food brands awareness of consumers and trade[18]
	Protected food name products[7]
	Number of counties and producers participating in "Buy Fresh, Buy Local" campaigns[1]
	Number of Slow Food Convivia and number of members in the organization[1]
	Number of farms that offer agri-tourism[1,5]
	Perception of "Sustainable Food Cities" as destinations where high quality and distinctive food is widely available[19]
	Number of visible food-related landmarks[6]
	Number of neighborhood and community destinations and gathering places related to local food[6]
	Number of times information portals related to local food are accessed[6]
	Provision of an exceptional food experience to visitors based on locally sourced and distinctive food[19]
Public procurement	Increased uptake of local food and drink by the public sector[11]
	Farm to institution purchases[3,5]
	Public school purchases of local food[3]
	Amount of funding (loans and grants) provided through economic development agencies for food systems development[5]
	Number of clients served by food systems business support programs[5]
	Number of meals served[9]
	Percentages of local diary, meat, fruit/vegetables sourced by public sector[9,20]
Enhanced capabilities and collaboration throughout the food supply chain	Farmers working with Food Centre Network or the like[20]
	Number of farms associated with food hub distribution models[5]
	Number of agencies/organizations working together on mutual projects/programs for food systems job placement and/or food systems training[5]
	Number of career and technical schools that will have articulation agreements with at least one college to allow transfer of credit for food systems courses[5]

Focus	Suggested indicators in urban and regional food strategies
	Number of food security programs with one or more organizations working in partnership[5]
	Collaborative initiatives established and sustained and number of farmers, processors, and retailers engaged[5,7]
	Stakeholders' reported grade of collaboration among the different organizations and across the political jurisdictions[13]
	People recognizing the importance of working together to make the region more economically competitive[13]

Strategies where the indicator is suggested: [1]The New Mainstream – A Sustainable Food Agenda for California, 2005; [2]State of the Food System Report, Austin, 2012; [3]Massachusetts Local Food Action Plan, 2015; [4]Multnomah Food Report, 2010; [5]Regional Food System Plan for Vermont's Northeast Kingdom, 2011; [6]Fresh, Edmonton's Food & Urban Agriculture Strategy, 2012; [7]Farming, Food & Countryside – Building a Secure Future, Wales 2009; [8]Vancouver Regional Food System Strategy, 2011; [9]Food Metrics Report NYC, 2015; [10]City of Vancouver Food Strategy, 2013; [11]British Columbia's Capital Region Food Security Assessment, 2004; [12]Food for Wales, Food from Wales 2010–2020; [13]Greater Philadelphia's Food System Plan, 2011; [14]San Francisco Foodshed Assessment, 2008; [15]Chicago Comprehensive Regional Plan "GO TO 2040," 2010; [16]Seattle Food Action Plan, 2012; [17]South Australian Food Strategy 2010–2015; [18]Local Sourcing Action Plan – "Food and Drink for Wales," 2009; [19]Cardiff University Report on Wales Food Strategy; [20]Food Tourism Action Plan – "Food and Drink for Wales," 2009; 2009.

procurement is yet another recurrent metric to gauge diversity in the urban food supply. Farm income per acre is a frequently used indicator used to track the profitability of local farms, while the number of receipts has been used to assess profitability of local food retailers. Diversity and quality of cross-sectoral partnerships and collaborations constitute one original area of urban food system assessment deemed relevant by a handful of strategies.

Resilient communities

The pursuit of resilient communities by means of food system change is a broad area of concern which encompasses, and depends upon, progress in all four of areas of local food policy – from public health and fairness to environmental and economic sustainability. The concept of resilience has its origins in ecology studies and calls attention to the ability of a system to withstand major shocks. According to the scientific definition, resilience is "the capacity of a system to experience disturbance and still maintain its ongoing functions and controls" (Holling & Gunderson, 2001, p. 50). Each locale where the urban food system is embedded possesses unique features that determine its ability to respond or adapt to such disturbances. The food system metrics sections and reports examined recognize the availability of knowledge (e.g., local food growing, cooking, and buying skills), resources (e.g., land, water, fertilizers, financial means), and collaborative networks and partnerships (e.g., degree of social interconnectedness) as essential community assets that need to be safeguarded to ensure community food resiliency (Table 4.6).

Table 4.6 Urban food system goal: resilient communities

Focus	Suggested indicators in urban and regional food strategies
Increased capacity to produce food close to home	Acres harvested for direct consumption[1,2]
	Number of community and backyard gardens, total and per person[2,3,4,5,6,7]
	Acres of city-owned land used for food production[8,9]
	Total acres of productive land available in the area interested by the food strategy[4,6,10,11]
	Distribution of agricultural land within the foodshed study area; percentage of irrigated cropland within the same[12]
	Number of acres and quality of land urbanized[1,12,13]
	Urban land in food production[8]
	High quality farmland as percentage of land developed since 1990[12]
	Number of community-based urban growing operations[7,8,14]
	Number of people engaged in community-based growing operations[8]
	Value of crops raised in community-based urban growing operations[8]
	Households with chickens/total number of chickens[5]
	Households with curbside composting[8]
	Volume of locally produced foods[15]
	Number of different local products produced annually[6,15]
	Annual number of hectares excluded from the available productive land[10]
	Annual number of hectares included from the available productive land[10]
	Estimate of the amount of land actively farmed[10]
	Number of fish bearing streams in the region[10]
Opportunity to develop food growing, cooking, and buying skills	Number of participants completing food skill programs[15]
	Number of participants in local food and agriculture related activities[15]
	Number of farm-to-school programs[4,6,13]
	Number of school gardens[5,13]
	Number of community kitchens[7]
	Number of food systems education programs in career and technical education centers[6]
	Number of career and technical centers offering food systems education and training for adult learners[6]
	Local school leavers pursuing land- and food-chain-based careers[16]
	Number of food-related job training programs[3,8]
Organizational/ advocacy support	Boroughs that have a local food partnership[14]
	Number and type of agrifood organizations and programs[2]

Strategies where the indicator is suggested: [1]Chicago Comprehensive Regional Plan "GO TO 2040," 2010; [2]British Columbia's Capital Region Food Security Assessment, 2004; [3]Food Metrics Report NYC, 2015; [4]Multnomah Food Report, 2010; [5]State of the Food System Report, Austin, 2012; [6]Regional Food System Plan for Vermont's Northeast Kingdom, 2011; [7]City of Vancouver Food Strategy, 2013; [8]Massachusetts Local Food Action Plan, 2015; [9]Seattle Food Action Plan, 2012; [10]Vancouver Regional Food System Strategy, 2011; [11]Greater Philadelphia's Food System Plan, 2011; [12]San Francisco Foodshed Assessment, 2008; [13]The New Mainstream – A Sustainable Food Agenda for California, 2005; [14]Good Food for London, 2015; [15]Fresh, Edmonton's Food & Urban Agriculture Strategy, 2012; [16]Food Tourism Action Plan – "Food and Drink for Wales," 2009; 2009.

Concluding remarks

Getting better at describing the city through a food system lens is critical to urban food planning not just for the sake of devising better food policies and plans, but for reminding us why we should question the food system's sustainability in the first place. Developing a robust set of research techniques and holistic urban food system representations thus plays an important role in the normalization of urban food planning as both an academic field and a professional practice. What emerged from the examination of the multiple directions of research taken to fill the knowledge gap between cities and food is a plethora of novelties and ongoing processes of experimentation. In some instances, novelties are already being replicated, adapted, and improved (e.g., community food assessments, land inventories, foodshed analyses) while in others (e.g., food deserts assessments) novel approaches are being fundamentally challenged. Both incremental and substantial criticisms have been put forward – the latter calling attention to the relation between assessments and solutions. Because defining the problem is already part of the solution, each analytical technique calls attention to certain solutions and excludes others. Although the emerging set of metrics and indicators accompanying local food system plans is still in its embryonic state, it constitutes an important stride toward a more holistic appreciation of the urban foodscape.

Finally, it is important to keep in mind that measuring the food system's inefficiencies and underused resources alone is no guarantee for a societal transition. Not only connections to policy, legislation, and funding need to be in place, but there is also the subtler risk that we end up managing only what we can measure. That is why it is imperative that we do not underestimate the value of ethnographic, case study, and grounded theory strategies to food system inquiry and keep an open mind about what analytical tools the urban food system toolkit ought to be made of. Ultimately, learning to see the city through a food system lens is not merely about reforming science and politics, but laying the foundations for an enlightened citizenship. As Geddes's Outlook Tower undertaking at the beginning of the twentieth century reminds us, no one is born a citizen, but one can become one by learning from the city and the region where they live and challenging preconceived ideas about how people, technology, and place shape one another. The urban food system offers a great place to start and can train us to see through the complex realm of socioecological interrelations that sustain it.

Questions for further consideration

- Why do we need to reacquire the ability to see the city through a food system lens? What are some of the elements or relationships in the urban foodscape that we commonly tend to overlook? Why, do you think, this is so?
- What is community food security? If you were to assess the extent to which a community is food insecure, what research techniques would you use and why?

- What are some of the different forms of urban agriculture enterprises? In what ways can cities assess the potential for and benefits of urban agriculture?
- How has the notion of the "urban foodshed" evolved since its inception at the beginning of the twentieth century? What are some of the key goals of a foodshed assessment?
- Among the food system metrics reviewed, are there any further indicators you would advise local administrations to add or revise? Which ones and why?

References

Ackerman, K. (2012). *The Potential for Urban Agriculture in New York City: Growing Capacity, Food Security, & Green Infrastructure* (2nd ed.). New York, NY: Urban Design Lab.

Ackerman, K., Conard, M., Culligan, P., Plunz, R., Sutto, M. P., & Whittinghill, L. (2014). Sustainable food systems for future cities: The potential of urban agriculture. *Economic and Social Review, 45*(2), 189–206.

Ackerman-Leist, P. (2013). *Rebuilding the Foodshed: How to Create Local, Sustainable, and Secure Food Systems.* White River Junction, VT: Chelsea Green Publishing.

Altman, L., Barry, L., Barry, M., Kühl, K., Silva, P., & Wilks, B. (2014). *Five Borough Farm II: Growing the Benefits of Urban Agriculture in New York City.* New York, NY: Design Trust for Public Space.

Amin, A., & Thrift, N. (2002). *Cities: Reimagining the Urban.* Cambridge: Polity Press.

Ashman, L. et al. (1993). *Seeds of Change: Strategies for Food Security for the Inner City.* Los Angeles, CA: UCLA Urban Planning.

Aubry, C., & Kebir, L. (2013). Shortening food supply chains: A means for maintaining agriculture close to urban areas? The case of the French metropolitan area of Paris. *Food Policy, 41*, 85–93.

Beaumont, J., Lang, T., Leather, S., & Mucklow, C. (1995). *Report from the Policy Sub-group to the Nutrition Task Force Low Income Project.* Hertfordshire: Department of Health, Radlett Institute of Grocery Distribution.

Blakey, R. C. et al. (1977). *Food Distribution and Consumption in Knoxville: Exploring Food-Related Local Planning Issues.* Knoxville, TN: University of Tennessee–Knoxville.

Blanchard, T. C., & Matthews, T. L. (2007). Retail Concentration, Food Deserts, and Food-Disadvantaged Communities in Rural America. In C. C. Hinrichs & T. A. Lyson (Eds.), *Remaking the North American Food System: Strategies for Sustainability (Our Sustainable Future)* (pp. 201–215). Lincoln, NE: University of Nebraska Press.

Block, D. (2008). *Finding Food in Chicago and the Suburbs – The Report of the Northeastern Illinois Community Food Security Assessment.* Chicago, IL: Chicago State University.

Born, B. (2013). A research agenda for food system transformation through autonomous community-based food projects. *Journal of Agriculture, Food Systems, and Community Development, 3*(4), 213–217.

Born, B., & Martin, K. (2011). *Western Washington Foodshed Study.* Seattle, WA: University of Washington.

Brannen, S. (2010). *FoodWorks: A Vision to Improve NYC's Food System.* New York, NY: The New York City Council.

Budge, T. (2013). Is Food a Missing Ingredient in Australia's Metropolitan Planning Strategies? In Q. Farmar-Bowers, V. Higgins, & J. Millar (Eds.), *Food Security in Australia* (pp. 367–379). New York, NY: Springer.

Castells, M. (2002). Local and global: Cities in the network society. *Tijdschrift Voor Economische En Sociale Geografie, 93*(5), 548–558.

The City of New York. (2009). *Special Regulations Applying to FRESH Food Stores*. New York, NY: The City of New York, Department of City Planning.

The City of New York. (2013). Food Retail Expansion to Support Health (FRESH). Retrieved from http://www.nyc.gov/html/misc/html/2009/fresh.shtml

CMAP. (2010). *GO TO 2040: Comprehensive Regional Plan*. Chicago, IL: Chicago Metropolitan Agency for Planning.

Cohen, B., Andrews, M., & Kantor, L. S. (2002). *Community Food Security Assessment Toolkit*. Washington, DC: USDA Economic Research Service.

Cohen, N. (2012). Planning for urban agriculture: Problem recognition, policy formation, and politics. In A. Viljoen & J. S. C. Wiskerke (Eds.), *Sustainable Food Planning: Evolving Theory and Practice* (pp. 101–112). Wageningen: Wageningen Academic Publishers.

Cohen, N., & Reynolds, K. (2014). Urban agriculture policy making in New York's "new political spaces": Strategizing for a participatory and representative system. *Journal of Planning Education and Research, 34*(2), 221–234.

Cohen, N., Reynolds, K., & Sanghvi, R. (2012). *Five Borough Farm: Seeding the Future of Urban Agriculture in New York City*. New York: Design Trust for Public Space.

Colasanti, K., & Hamm, M. (2010). Assessing the local food supply capacity of Detroit, Michigan. *Journal of Agriculture, Food Systems, and Community Development, 1*(2), 41–58.

Corburn, J. (2007). Reconnecting with our roots: American urban planning and public health in the twenty-first century. *Urban Affairs Review, 42*(5), 688–713.

Coviello, F., Graglia, A., & Villa, D. (2009). *Produrre e Scambiare Valore Territoriale*. (G. Ferraresi, Ed.). Firenze: Alinea.

Darrot, C. (2012). Rennes Ville Vivriere: Scenarios of Food Autonomy for Rennes Metropole (France) [PDF document]. Retrieved from www.reseaurural.fr/files/catherine_darrot_rennes_metropole_ville_vivriere_0.pdf

Delaware Valley Regional Planning Commission. (2010). *Greater Philadelphia Food System Study*. Philadelphia, PA. Retrieved from http://www.dvrpc.org/Food/FoodSystem Study.htm

DoH. (1996). *Low Income, Food, Nutrition and Health: Strategies for Improvement*. London: Department of Health.

Donadieu, P. (1998). *Campagnes Urbaines: Transl. It. Campagne Urbane. Una nuova proposta di paesaggio della città*. Rome: Donzelli Editore.

DVRPC. (2011). *Eating Here: Greater Philadelphia's Food System Plan*. Philadelphia, PA: Delaware Valley Regional Planning Commission.

Eckert, J., & Shetty, S. (2011). Food systems, planning and quantifying access: Using GIS to plan for food retail. *Applied Geography, 31*(4), 1216–1223.

EPA. (2011). DEP Awards $3.8 Million in Grants for Community-Based Green Infrastructure Program Projects. Retrieved from http://www.nyc.gov/html/dep/html/stormwater/grant_program.shtml

Farming Concrete. (2012). *Farming Concrete 2012 Harvest Report*. New York, NY: Farming Concrete.

Farming Concrete. (2015). Data Collection Toolkit. Retrieved September 23, 2015, from https://farmingconcrete.org/toolkit/

Ferrario, V. (2009). Agropolitana: Dispersed City and Agricultural Spaces in Veneto Region (Italy). In L. Qu, C. Yang, X. Hui, & D. Sepúlveda (Eds.), *The 4th International Conference of the International Forum on Urbanism (IFoU)* (pp. 637–646). Amsterdam-Delft: IFoU.

Fielding, J. E., & Simon, P. A. (2011). Food deserts or food swamps?: Comment on "fast food restaurants and food stores". *Archives of Internal Medicine, 171*(13), 1171–1172.

Fisher, A., & Roberts, S. (2011). *Community Food Security Coalition: Recommendations for Food Systems Policy in Seattle.* Venice, CA: Community Food Security Coalition.

Frank, L., Glanz, K., Mccarron, M., Sallis, J., Saelens, B., & Chapman, J. (2006). The spatial distribution of food outlet type and quality around schools in differing built environment and demographic contexts. *Berkeley Planning Journal, 19,* 79–95.

Freedgood, J., Pierce-Quiñonez, M., & Meter, K. (2011). Emerging assessment tools to inform food system planning. *Journal of Agriculture, Food Systems, and Community Development, 2*(1), 83–104.

Fry, C., & Wooten, H. (2012). "Complete eats" legislation: The farm bill and food systems planning. *Planning & Environmental Law, 64*(4), 3–8.

Furey, S., Strugnell, C., & Mcilveen, H. (2001). An investigation of the potential existence of "food deserts" in rural and urban areas of Northern Ireland. *Agriculture and Human Values, 18,* 447–457.

Galt, R. E. (2011). Counting and mapping Community Supported Agriculture (CSA) in the United States and California: Contributions from critical cartography/GIS. *Acme, 10*(2), 131–162.

Getz, A. (1991). Urban foodsheds. *Permaculture Activist, VII*(3), 26–27.

Gottlieb, R., & Joshi, A. (2010). *Food Justice.* Boston, MA: MIT Press.

Greenhow, T. (1994). *Urban agriculture: Can planners make a difference* (Cities Feeding People Report, 12). Ottawa, ON: IDRC.

Grewal, S. S., & Grewal, P. S. (2012). Can cities become self-reliant in food? *Cities, 29*(1), 1–11.

Hamm, M. W., & Bellows, A. C. (2003). Community food security and nutrition educators. *Journal of Nutrition Education and Behaviour, 35*(1), 37–43.

Hammer, J. (2004). Community food systems and planning curricula. *Journal of Planning Education and Research, 23*(4), 424–434.

Haughton, B. (1987). Developing local food policies: One city's experience. *Journal of Public Health Policy, 8*(2), 180–191.

Hedden, W. P. (1929). *How Great Cities Are Fed. Atlantic.* New York: D.C. Heath and Company.

Holling, C. S., & Gunderson, L. (2001). Resilience and Adaptive Cycles. In L. Gunderson & C. S. Holling (Eds.), *Panarchy: Understanding Transformations in Human and Natural Systems* (p. 50). Washington, DC-Covelo-London: Island Press.

Horst, M. (2011). A review of suitable urban agriculture land inventories. *APA Food System Writing Competition Winners.* Retrieved from https://planning-org-uploaded-media. s3.amazonaws.com/legacy_resources/resources/ontheradar/food/pdf/horstpaper.pdf

Johansson, S. (2008). The Swedish Foodshed: Re-Imagining Our Support Area. In C. Farnworth, J. Jiggins, & E. V. Thomas (Eds.), *Creating Food Futures: Trade, Ethics and the Environment* (pp. 55–78). Hampshire: Gower Publishing, Ltd.

Kaufman, J. L., & Bailkey, M. (2000). Farming inside cities: Entrepreneurial urban agriculture in the United States (Working Paper, Inventory ID WP00JK1). Cambridge, MA: Lincoln Institute of Land Policy.

Kelly, B., Flood, V. M., & Yeatman, H. (2011). Measuring local food environments: An overview of available methods and measures. *Health & Place, 17*(6), 1284–1293.

Kloppenburg, J., Hendrickson, J., & Stevenson, G. W. (1996). Coming in to the foodshed. *Agriculture and Human Values, 13*(3), 33–42.

Kneafsey, M., Lambie, H., Dowler, E., & Inman, A. (2008). *Mapping Local Food Webs Concepts and Methods.* Coventry, UK: SURGE.

Kremer, P., & DeLiberty, T. L. (2011). Local food practices and growing potential: Mapping the case of Philadelphia. *Applied Geography, 31*(4), 1252–1261.

Kurita, H., Yokohari, M., & Bolthoise, J. (2008). The potential of intra-regional supply and demand of agricultural products in an urban fringe area: A case study of the Kanto Plain, Japan. *Geografisk Tidsskrift-Danish Journal of, 109*(2), 147–159.

Larsen, K., & Gilliland, J. (2008). Mapping the evolution of "food deserts" in a Canadian city: Supermarket accessibility in London, Ontario, 1961–2005. *International Journal of Health Geographics, 7*(1), 16.

Larsen, K., & Gilliland, J. (2009). A farmers' market in a food desert: Evaluating impacts on the price and availability of healthy food. *Health & Place, 15*(4), 1158–1162.

LeClair, M. S., & Aksan, A.-M. (2014). Redefining the food desert: Combining GIS with direct observation to measure food access. *Agriculture and Human Values, 31*(4), 537–547.

Lewis, P. S. (1979). Axioms for Reading the Landscape. In D. W. Meinig (Ed.), *The Interpretation of Ordinary Landscapes* (pp. 11–32). New York, NY-Oxford: Oxford University Press.

Lister, N. M. (2007). Placing food: Toronto's edible landscape. *FOOD, 47*(3), 150–185.

Loorbach, D., & Rotmans, J. (2006). Managing Transitions for Sustainable Development. In X. Olsthoorn & A. J. Wieczorek (Eds.), *Understanding Industrial Transformation: Views from Different Disciplines* (pp. 187–206). Dordrecht: Springer.

MacRae, R., Gallant, E., Patel, S., Michalak, M., Bunch, M., & Schaffner, S. (2010). Could Toronto provide 10% of its fresh vegetable requirements from within its own boundaries? Matching consumption requirements with growing spaces. *Journal of Agriculture, Food Systems, and Community Development, 1*(2), 105–127.

McClintock, N., Cooper, J., & Khandeshi, S. (2013). Assessing the potential contribution of vacant land to urban vegetable production and consumption in Oakland, California. *Landscape and Urban Planning, 111*, 46–58.

Mendes, W., Balmer, K., Kaethler, T., & Rhoads, A. (2008). Using land inventories to plan for urban agriculture: Experiences from Portland and Vancouver. *Journal of the American Planning Association, 74*(4), 435–449.

Neuner, K., Kelly, S., & Raja, S. (2011). *Planning to Eat? Innovative Local Government Plans and Policies to Build Healthy Food Systems in the United States.* Buffalo, NY: The State University of New York.

O'Brien, J., & Cobb, T. D. (2012). The food policy audit: A new tool for community food system planning. *Journal of Agriculture, Food Systems, and Community Development, 2*(3), 177–192.

Peters, C. J., Bills, N. L., Lembo, A. J., Wilkins, J. L., & Fick, G. W. (2009). Mapping potential foodsheds in New York state: A spatial model for evaluating the capacity to localize food production. *Renewable Agriculture and Food Systems, 24*(1), 72.

Peters, C. J., Bills, N. L., Lembo, A. J., Wilkins, J. L., & Fick, G. W. (2011). Mapping potential foodsheds in New York state by food group: An approach for prioritizing which foods to grow locally. *Renewable Agriculture and Food Systems, 27*(2), 125–137.

Peters, C. J., Bills, N. L., Wilkins, J. L., & Fick, G. W. (2008). Foodshed analysis and its relevance to sustainability. *Renewable Agriculture and Food Systems, 24*(1), 1–7.

Porro, A., Corsi, S., Scudo, G., & Spigarolo, R. (2014). The contribution of bioregione research project to the development of local sustainable agri-food systems. *Scienze Del Territorio, 2*, 319–326.

Pothukuchi, K. (2004). Community food assessment: A first step in planning for community food security. *Journal of Planning Education and Research, 23*(4), 356–377.

Pothukuchi, K., Joseph, H., Burton, H., & Fisher, A. (2002). *What's Cooking in Your Food System? A Guide to Community Food Assessment.* Venice, CA: Community Food Security Coalition.

Quon, S. (1999). *Planning for urban agriculture: A review of tools and strategies for urban planners* (Cities Feeding People Report, 28). Ottawa, ON: IDRC.

Raja, S., Ma, C., & Yadav, P. (2008). Beyond food deserts: Measuring and mapping racial disparities in neighborhood food environments. *Journal of Planning Education and Research, 27*(4), 469–482.

Redwood, M. (Ed.). (2009). *Agriculture in Urban Planning: Generating Livelihoods and Food Security.* London-Sterling, VA: Earthscan.

Rees, W., & Wackernagel, M. (1996). Urban ecological footprints: Why cities cannot be sustainable – and why they are a key to sustainability. *Environmental Impact Assessment Review, 9255*(96), 223–248.

Rhoads, A., & Guenin, H. (2009). *Portland Plan Background Report: Food Systems.* Portland, OR: City of Portland, Bureau of Planning and Sustainability.

Richardson, J. M. (2010). *Foodshed Vancouver: Envisioning a Sustainable Foodshed for Greater Vancouver* (Master thesis). Retrieved from UBC Theses and Dissertations (http://hdl.handle.net/2429/25491).

Roberts, W. (2010). Food Policy Encounters of a Third Kind: How the Toronto Food Policy Council Socializes for Sustain-Ability. In A. Blay-Palmer (Ed.), *Imagining Sustainable Food Systems: Theory and Practice* (pp. 173–200). Surrey- Burligton: Ashgate Publishing.

Sali, G., Corsi, S., Mazzocchi, C., Monaco, F., Wascher, D., van Eupen, M., & Zasada, I. (2014). *FoodMetres: Analysis of Food Demand and Supply in the Metropolitan Region.* Retreived from http://foodmetres.eu

Sassen, S. (1994). *Cities in a World Economy.* Thousand Oaks, CA-London-New Delhi: Pine Forge Press.

Scenic Hudson. (2013). *Securing Fresh, Local Food for New York City and the Hudson Valley: A Foodshed Conservation Plan for the Region.* Poughkeepsie, NY: Scenic Hudson, Inc.

Schafft, K. A., Jensen, E. B., & Clare, H. C. (2009). Food deserts and overweight school-children: Evidence from Pennsylvania. *Rural Sociology, 74*(2), 153–177.

Schiff, R. (2005). Public Policy and Planning for Sustainability in the Urban Food System. In P. Troy (Ed.), *Refereed Proceedings of the 2nd Bi-Annual Conference on The State of Australian Cities.* Brisbane, Queensland: Griffith University.

Schot, J., & Geels, F. W. (2007). Niches in evolutionary theories of technical change. *Journal of Evolutionary Economics, 17*(5), 605–622.

Segal, P. Z. (2015). From open data to open space: Translating public information into collective action. *Cities and the Environment, 8*(2), 1–9.

Short, A., Guthman, J., & Raskin, S. (2007). Food deserts, oases, or mirages?: Small markets and community food security in the San Francisco bay area. *Journal of Planning Education and Research, 26*(3), 352–364.

Sonnino, R., & McWilliam, S. (2011). Food waste, catering practices and public procurement: A case study of hospital food systems in Wales. *Food Policy, 36*(6), 823–829.

Sonnino, R., & Spayde, J. J. (2014). The "New Frontier"? Urban Strategies for Food Security and Sustainability. In T. Marsden & A. Morley (Eds.), *Sustainable Food Systems: Building a New Paradigm* (pp. 186–205). London-New York, NY: Routledge.

Steel, C. (2009). *Hungry City: How Food Shapes Our Lives.* London: Random House.

Stetter, A. (2000). Goods. In N. Barley (Ed.), *Breathing Cities: The Architecture of Movement* (pp. 40–42). Basel: Birkhäuser.

Sustain. (2015). *Good Food for London 2015: How London Boroughs Can Help Secure a Healthy and Sustainable Food Future.* London: Sustain.

Taylor, J. R., & Lovell, S. T. (2012). Mapping public and private spaces of urban agriculture in Chicago through the analysis of high-resolution aerial images in Google Earth. *Landscape and Urban Planning, 108*(1), 57–70.

Thompson, E. J., Harper, A. M., & Kraus, S. (2008). *Think Globally – Eat Locally: San Francisco Foodshed Assessment.* San Francisco, CA: American Farmland Trust.

Urban Design Lab. (2010). National Integrated Regional Foodshed Model. Retrieved October 12, 2015, from http://urbandesignlab.columbia.edu/projects/food-and-the-urban-environment/national-integrated-regional-foodshed-model/

Urban Design Lab. (2011a). *Infrastructure-Health: Modeling Production, Processing and Distribution Infrastructure for A Resilient Regional Food System.* New York, NY: Columbia University.

Urban Design Lab. (2011b). NYC Regional Foodshed Initiative. Retrieved October 12, 2015, from http://urbandesignlab.columbia.edu/projects/food-and-the-urban-environment/nyc-regional-food-shed-initiative/

USDA. (2013). Food Environment Atlas. Retrieved from http://www.ers.usda.gov/data-products/food-environment-atlas/go-to-the-atlas.aspx

Walker, R. E., Keane, C. R., & Burke, J. G. (2010). Disparities and access to healthy food in the United States: A review of food deserts literature. *Health & Place, 16*(5), 876–884.

Winne, M. (2008). *Closing the Food Gap: Resetting the Table in the Land of Plenty.* Boston, MA: Beacon Press.

Winne, M., Joseph, H., & Fisher, A. (2000). *Community Food Security: A Guide to Concept, Design, and Implementation.* Venice, CA: Community Food Security Coalition.

Wrigley, N., Warm, D., & Margetts, B. (2003). Deprivation, diet, and food-retail access: Findings from the leeds "food deserts" study. *Environment and Planning A, 35*(1), 151–188.

5 Urban food planning in the public domain

> To accord priority to the protection of the environment, health, consumers, and social justice will require considerable adjustment in policy and food practices, but can society and the environment afford not to do this?
>
> – Tim Lang, *The Complexities of Globalization*

While the dominant food system regime is far from sustainable as yet and urban food planning is still in its infancy, the growing saliency of food in the mayoral agenda has heralded a new phase of food policy in the public domain. The local level of food policy is gradually being reactivated. In less than a decade, over 100 local, regional, and state administrations in the Global North have adopted a food charter or a food system plan for the first time. The institutionalization of food in local government is now underway, and entrenched societal perceptions, dismissing food as a rural issue or food insecurity as the concern only of developing economies countries, have started being challenged. This chapter is about why and how these processes are taking place and what some of their recurrent institutional outcomes are. We will look into the inception of new conceptual frames such as "food citizenship" and "food democracy" and the advancement of shared agendas for their translation in practice by means of urban food charters, comprehensive food system plans, and local laws and regulations.

Food citizenship

The notion of citizenship has recently emerged as a central concern both in urban planning and in urban food policy scholarship. The questions of how urban planning shapes citizenship and how food can be a means to active citizenship, resulting in the reshaping of the dominant food system, have become increasingly pressing concerns for urban planning and food systems theorists.

In the domain of urban planning, Italian scholar Luigi Mazza (2009, 2014) has compellingly called attention to the neglected intellectual lineages of planning from the nineteenth-century philosophical school of British Idealists who greatly influenced the work of one of the "founding fathers" of modern planning, Patrick Geddes (see Chapter 2). A central tenet of the school is that the notion of citizenship goes well beyond the notion of national citizenship and "naturally" acquired rights and duties. Rather, true citizenship entails "a consciousness of the moral ends of human life as embodied within the institutional structure of the State, in other words, a consciousness of the common good" (Mazza, 2014).

Simply put, caring for the common good means ensuring that everyone is in the condition of "making the best of oneself in one's social function and seeking the same for others" (Mazza, 2014). Decisions about a city's physical space thus inevitably affect, directly or indirectly, the integrity of citizenship. On these grounds, Mazza (2012) suggests that citizenship ought to be considered as a standard against which urban planning decisions are evaluated. In his analysis on the nexus between planning and citizenship, Chiodelli (2013) calls attention to the contribution of Lefebvre's concept of "right to the city" and the inequalities in citizenship reproduced through urban development projects. A key point that Chiodelli makes is that not only is citizenship a higher form of social belonging than the national citizenship, but that this citizenship is never given and can only be gained through purposeful and active participation in society. Put in other terms, citizenship is a "prerequisite of true democracy based on respect" (Mazza, 2014).

In the domain of just and sustainable food systems research and activism, the notion of citizenship has been introduced through critical reflections about democracy and the extent the current food system regime enables or hinders the possibilities for democratic participation. The notion of "food democracy" thus has been introduced since the 1990s, thanks to the work of British food policy scholar Tim Lang (1998) and Canadian municipal food policy pioneers Welsh and MacRae (1998). In Lang's view (1998, p. 18), food democracy is "the inverse of food control" and an effort "to achieve the right of all citizens to have access to a decent, affordable, health-enhancing diet, grown in conditions in which they can have confidence." This effort exemplifies not so much the work of the industrial complex in the food system but the "process of holding food systems accountable from the 'bottom up'" (Lang, Barling, & Caraher, 2009).

A key prerequisite for food democracy is the transition of urban residents from consumers to active and educated citizens (Welsh & MacRae, 1998), or what Carlo Petrini (2005) defines as the move from consumers to "co-producers," conscious of crafting a shared destiny determined by their choices. In theorizing food democracy, Hassanein (2003, p. 85) calls attention to the instrumental value of the concept, which can be used as a "method for making choices when values come into conflict and when the consequences of decisions are uncertain." In a subsequent contribution (Hassanein, 2008), she further elaborates on this idea and suggests five key dimensions that can help demarcate and study the manifestation of food democracy: collaborating, becoming knowledgeable, sharing ideas, developing efficacy, and caring about the public good, bearing in mind both human and nonhuman communities.

The idea of "food citizenship" is thus tightly related to the notions of citizenship and food democracy and entails "belonging and participating, at all levels of relationship from the intimacy of breastfeeding to the discussions at the World Trade Organization" (Welsh & MacRae, 1998, p. 241). Food citizenship has also been usefully framed a "social skill" that needs to be cultivated and recognized alongside other sustainable food system values like health, quality, biodiversity, and affordability in the *Sustainability and UK Food Policy 2000–2011* report of the UK Sustainable Development Commission (Lang, Dibb, & Reddy, 2011). In the US, the term is likely to have been first introduced by Lyson (2004) and his elaboration of the idea of "civic agriculture," which defines the complex of grassroots urban food growing initiatives that have "the potential to transform individuals from passive consumers into active food citizens" (Lyson, 2005, p. 97). The role of urban agriculture as a vehicle for food citizenship has been the focus of research also for Baker (2004), who in analyzing emergent urban food practices in Toronto conceives of food citizenship as enacted through the relocalization of food systems and the collective care for "place," encompassing both people and the environment. McClintock (2014, p. 153) has recently expanded the notion of food citizenship through the concept of "agroecological citizenship," which can help us transition to a food system regime in which public gain is privileged over private gain, healthy food is considered a public good, and healthy food access is safeguarded as an unalienable human right.

Though often associated with decisions and actions directly reshaping the relationship between people and the food system, food citizenship can be enacted also by influencing ideas, discourses, and public opinion through civic engagement and the media (Renting, Schermer, & Rossi, 2012). The nonmaterial expression of food citizenship has also been underscored through the concept of "ethical foodscapes," encapsulating the idea that place-based food practices have a distinctive normative dimension (Psarikidou & Szerszynski, 2012). Yet, the transformation of physical space is what makes the footprints of the performance of a food citizenship visible in cities and urban regions. In fact, Baker's (2004, p. 323) investigation of exemplary cases of urban agriculture in Toronto led him to the conclusion that a commitment to food citizenship brings about the transformation of both the urban landscape and the food system.

Despite its many conceptual merits, one should however pay attention to the intricacies inevitably accompanying the translation of the tenets of food citizenship in practice. In his critical assessment of the urban agriculture movement, McClintock (2014) warns that, in practice, the enactment of food citizenship can be greatly uneven; either because of divisiveness between elite and marginalized social groups in the city disconnected from the geographies of short and healthy food supply altogether, or because of the overwhelming dependency of local food initiatives on nonprofit organizations whose work is greatly tailored through the goals and interests of funding agencies and sponsors.

To summarize, citizenship, food, and urban planning intersect at multiple levels, either through the shared objective of the public good or through their physical manifestation in the transformation of urban land. In her exploration of the interconnections between community food systems and urban planning, Campbell (2004) suggests that "food citizens" and planners sit at the same table and jointly work toward the goal of sustainable food systems through their unique sources of power, positions in society, and competencies. Of course, this does not preclude the possibility that planners can also be food citizens. There is also another emergent connection between urban planning and food citizenship, which we saw in the growing attention given to the planning system by civil society organizations working toward the implementation of sustainable food system goals (e.g., Chapters 1, 3, and 7). This phenomenon has been conceptualized by urban planning theorists (e.g., Friedmann, 2002; Miraftab, 2006; Sandercock, 1998) as "insurgent planning" driven by the manifestation of an "insurgent citizenship" (Holston, 1998), whereby urban planning practice and planners are seen as an opportunity to influence the system and expand participation in mainstream decisions.

Ultimately, one of the yet underexplored contributions of the concept of food citizenship is its potential to serve as a standard against which to measure the value of both urban food planning and urban planning practices, affecting wittingly or unwittingly the opportunities for food democracy.

Urban food charters

One emergent form of the codification of food citizenship, and in some instances its institutionalization in local governments, is the urban food charter ("urban" is used here to denote locally driven initiatives in the broadest sense of the term and thus includes urban areas, but it is not necessarily limited to them). A food charter constitutes a civic declaration of values and principles intended to guide the creation and execution of local food policies, projects, and programs. It is a guiding document that can be developed either through civil society or government initiative and at different levels of government and sites of community mobilization: city (e.g., Toronto, Vancouver, New York), district (e.g., Bradford), regional (e.g., Capital Region, York Region, Peel Region), province (e.g., Manitoba), state (e.g., Minnesota, Michigan), and international (e.g., Milan Urban Food Policy Pact). Food charters can be the means for bringing together a wide range of social groups invested in shaping the urban food system – from farmers to institutional food catering companies, government officials, and food justice advocacy organizations – and can result in the creation of a new political space (Hajer, 2003) to strategize how a fairer, healthier, and more environmentally sound urban food system can be pursued.

Over the past decade, more than 20 food charters have been devised in Global North countries. Table 5.1 provides an overview of some, certainly not all, food charters released to date. One of the earliest food charters is the

Table 5.1 City and regional food charters released in the period 2001–2015 by local governments in Canada, the United States, and the United Kingdom and the first international urban food charter

Country	Food Charter	Year
Canada	Toronto's Food Charter	2001
	Saskatoon Food Charter	2002
	City of Greater Sudbury Food Charter	2004
	Vancouver Food Charter	2007
	Capital Region Food Charter	2008
	Region of Durham Food Charter	2008
	Thunder Bay Food Charter	2008
	London's Food Charter	2010
	Guelph-Wellington Food Charter	2011
	Kawartha Lakes Food Charter	2011
	York Region Food Charter	2012
	Manitoba Food Charter	2013
	Peel Region Food Charter	2015
United States	New Orleans Community Food Charter	2007
	Philadelphia Food Charter	2008
	New York City Food Charter	2009
	Michigan Food Charter	2010
	Minnesota Food Charter	2013
United Kingdom	Bradford District Food Charter	2001
	Plymouth Food Charter	2008
	Bristol Food Charter	2010
	Gwynedd Food Charter	2012
	Cardiff Food Charter	2012
	Durham County Food Charter	2013
	Oxford Food Charter	2014
	Cambridge Food Charter	2014
	Glasgow Food Charter	2014
	Carlisle Food Charter	2015
	New Castle Food Charter	2015
International	Milan Urban Food Policy Pact	2015

Toronto Food Charter adopted by the Toronto City Council in 2001. The development of the charter was spearheaded by The Food and Hunger Action Committee with the support of the Toronto Food Policy Council instituted in 1991 (see Chapter 7) and has ever since been an inspirational example for many other food charters in Canada and internationally. The key focus of the charter is urban food security and the possible ways to ensure economic and spatial access to healthy and culturally appropriate food for all citizens in Toronto. Even though the charter was promoted and developed under the auspices of the Department of Public Health, the actions it suggests espouse a holistic view of the food system, from seed to table to sustainable waste management. This more inclusive framing of the notion of community food security is well reflected in two of the priorities of the charter: to "protect local agricultural lands and support urban agriculture" and to "encourage the recycling of organic materials that nurture soil fertility." Thus, to pursue this comprehensive effort, the city recognizes the need for an interdepartmental collaboration, which is built-in as a key principle in the charter and represents one of its original features.

In the UK, one of the pioneer food charters is the Bradford District Food Charter put forward by The Bradford and Airedale District Food Network in 2001, which is a local nongovernmental partnership. Much like the Toronto Food Charter, the principles stated in the Bradford Charter transcend the conventional compartmentalization of food system sectors and the perilous local/global and mainstream/alternative segmentation of the urban food system. The 10 principles stipulated by the charter address both infrastructural improvements and social practices and stress the importance of urban agriculture as part of a broader agenda for diversity across all functional departments of the food chain, therefore including manufacturing and distribution. Fairness in the food system is an explicit principle and addresses injustices stemming from the exploitation of people and the environment. Moreover, the outlook of the charter is "cosmopolitan" (Morgan, 2010), in that it urges the fulfillment of the charter goals both with respect to near and distant urban and rural communities. Although born under the auspices of a nongovernmental organization, the Bradford District Food Charter managed to influence local government practices and policies and brought about the development of one of the earliest food system strategies in the UK, The Bradford District Food Strategy, in 2003. The strategy was later updated and adopted as a formal food system plan by the City of Bradford Metropolitan District Council in 2012.

The chief driver for a food charter may also not be long-standing food system inefficiencies or new opportunities to strengthen the local economy, but an abrupt disruption of the system. This was the case with the New Orleans Community Food Charter developed in the wake of two devastating hurricanes, Katrina and Rita, in 2005. These catastrophic events exposed just how vulnerable urban food systems can be even in developed economies cities. The major disruption of food supply in the city led to unprecedented community mobilization and efforts to make the city more food secure. In 2007, the New Orleans Food and Farm Network, with the support of the Grow New Orleans community food justice group, gathered community input and developed the New Orleans Community Food Charter. According to Harper, Alkon, Shattuck, Holt-Giménez, and Lambrick (2009), the charter has been an effective tool for raising awareness about food justice issues and effectively integrating them in the New Orleans reconstruction agenda. It also ignited a dynamic urban agriculture movement, led by those most affected by the hurricane, and brought about the conversion of many vacant or abandoned urban areas into vegetable gardens.

On a more critical note, Everett (2012, p. 468) observes that, while the charter has been an effective tool for convening the community around a shared agenda, it has not been as successful in influencing mainstream policies and urban planning processes. She points at the limited attention to food policy issues in the city's long-term comprehensive master plan and zoning ordinance, *Plan for the 21st Century: New Orleans 2030,* released by the City Planning Commission in 2010. Yet, the mere fact that the plan addresses urban agriculture in a separate section (*Urban Agriculture, Gardening, and Open Space*) and commits to removing zoning and other barriers to encourage urban agriculture activities throughout the city is a significant sign of progress in this direction.

Overall, food charters are an important institutional novelty that can support the creation of a food planning niche in the public domain (e.g., Toronto, Vancouver, London, Brighton and Hove, Bristol). In some instances, food charters have been a first step toward the institutionalization of healthy, sustainable, and ethical food system goals and values in the urban policy agenda and have facilitated the creation of food policy councils, food system strategies, and food security programs. An increase in urban agriculture practices and localized urban-rural food networks have been among the tangible outcomes of the collaborative process of developing a food charter. Some hurdles along the way, however, do exist. In their commentary on the recent rise of food charters, Hardman and Larkham (2014) note that some of the challenges that the development of a food charter may pose are the difficulty in conveying the need for and purpose of such a document and reservations about the ability of charters to get signatories to actually commit to the principles stated. In the UK, since the establishment of the nationwide Sustainable Food Cities coalition, which provides knowledge and guidance to cities with established food policy agendas as well as to newcomers to the field, some of these hurdles are being overcome and the number of food charters has continued to grow. One could hope that, following the 2015 Milan Urban Food Policy Pact, which constitutes a de facto international food charter signed by over 100 local administrations worldwide, the credibility, available knowledge, and guidance toward the development and implementation of urban food policy and planning is going to increase in the future.

Urban food policies, plans, and strategies

Along with the growing number of urban food charters, local authorities and communities have increasingly become engaged in the preparation of more detailed and comprehensive urban food policy frameworks. Such frameworks are commonly referred to as food system plans or strategies and can either be found as stand-alone documents or integrated in long-term planning and sustainability strategies. Unlike food charters, which succinctly lay out the general principles for urban food policy, urban food plans are much more comprehensive and usually comprise an assessment of the urban food system, pointing at its major issues and opportunities; a set of goals and objectives to address these issues and take advantage of untapped opportunities, but also support autonomously emerging solutions; and, in some instances, a set of metrics and indicators against which the implementation of the plan will be evaluated. In brief, urban food plans provide a more cohesive and systematic agenda for food policymaking at the local level. Though rarely legally binding, urban food plans contribute to the development of strategic capacities for urban food governance in local administrations (Mendes, 2008) and are the result of an emergent place-based food governance, whereby new linkages between government and civil society organizations are forged (Wiskerke, 2009).

Food policies in comprehensive plans

The integration of food policies in comprehensive city and regional plans constitutes a small yet important part of the instances in which established urban policy and planning mechanisms have made room for urban food planning. Comprehensive plans are typically long-term visions devised to guide the development of a city or an urban area over the course of several decades. Among those that have explicitly included a focus on the urban food system are comprehensive sustainable development plans (e.g., in San Francisco, Vancouver, Baltimore, Newquay) and general urban plans (e.g., in Toronto, Chicago, Portland, London), see also Table 5.2. A nationwide scan of comprehensive plans in the US carried out by Hodgson (2012) revealed that food-sensitive plans are still a tiny fraction (about 9%) of all comprehensive plans released thus far. Nevertheless, as we will see, these forerunners shed light on the ways in which sustainable food system goals can become an integral part of local governments' practices, and some provide arguments as to why food is an urban planning matter. Of course, this is not to say that general plans do not already affect the urban food system; in fact, they do. The point is rather that they do so, but implicitly, not as a purposeful and systematic endeavor as is the case of food-system-centered policies. Thus, what makes the latter relevant is their role in consolidating the idea that food is an important urban infrastructure in its own right and, in doing so, prompting questions about how other urban systems match or compete with just and sustainable food system goals.

A pioneer example of the incorporation of food issues in a comprehensive sustainability plan is the San Francisco Sustainability Plan developed in 1997 (City of San Francisco, 1997). Even though the plan is nearly two decades old now, its Food and Agriculture Strategy section represents one of the best-articulated urban food system plans to date. The strategy outlines six overarching goals to guide the design of specific urban and regional food policies. In a nutshell, these are to increase and expand participation in the food system, ensure access to healthy food for all, support sustainable regional farming

Table 5.2 The integration of food policies in comprehensive plans

Country	Comprehensive plan	Released by	Food system	Year
Canada	Toronto Official Plan	City Planning Division	Elements	2010
	Vancouver Greenest City 2020 Action Plan	Greenest City Planning Team	Chapter	2012
United States	San Francisco Sustainability Plan	Commission on San Francisco's Environment, City Planning Department	Chapter	1997
	PlanNYC 2030	Office of Long–Term Planning and Sustainability (OLTPS)	Chapter	2007, 2011*
	Portland Plan	Bureau for Sustainability and Planning	Background report	2009
	Baltimore Sustainability Plan	Commission on Sustainability, City Planning Commission, City Council	Chapter	2009
	Chicago GO TO 2040 Comprehensive Regional Plan	Chicago Metropolitan Agency for Planning	Chapter	2010
	Philadelphia 2035 Citywide Vision	City Planning Commission	Elements	2011
United Kingdom	Newquay Growth Area Sustainable Development Plan	Duchy of Cornwall Council, Food Section: Sustain, Camco	Chapter	2007, 2009*
	One Wales: One Planet, The Sustainable Development Scheme of the Welsh Assembly Government 2020	Welsh Assembly Government	Elements	2009
	The London Plan: Spatial development strategy for greater London 2020	Greater London Authority, London Plan Team	Elements	2011

(*) Indicates the latest update.

practices, maximize urban food production, recycle all organic waste and ban the use of chemicals in agriculture and landscape operations, and initiate a community-based policy and educational program to implement the plan.

Each goal is broken down into a set of specific long-term visions, five-year targets, and immediate actions. For instance, in relation to regional farming, the plan envisions a city where in every neighborhood there are farmers or gardeners markets and community supported agriculture projects, and all food purchased by public institutions is organic and extensively grown by farmers in the region. The five-year targets set were to source at least a quarter of institutional food from the San Francisco Bay area and at least 70% from farmers in the State of California. Boosting urban agriculture within the city is an equally ambitious goal, articulated in visions for a city where rooftop farms are tended in every neighborhood, all public vacant land unsuitable for biodiversity reserves is turned to urban farming, there are plenty of fruit-bearing trees, spaces for food growing are mandated in every new project for residential development, and new public–private partnerships are established to ensure that land is maintained productive.

More recent examples of sustainability plans that have included explicit food policies are the Baltimore Sustainability Plan (2009), the Philadelphia Green-Works plan (Dews & Wu, 2013), the New York City PlaNYC 2030 plan (City of New York, 2011), the Vancouver Greenest City 2020 Plan (Greenest City Action Team, 2012), and the Newquay Growth Area Sustainable Development Plan (Sustain & ESD, 2007; Duchy of Cornwall & Restormel Borough Council, 2009). Often food makes its way into these plans under the rubric of actions to "green" the city. This is the case of Baltimore and Vancouver, for instance. The Baltimore sustainability plan advances the ambitious goal for the city to become a leader in local food systems and outlines specific objectives to expand urban agriculture, develop a dedicated Urban Agriculture Plan, improve access to healthy food, encourage demand for local produce citywide, and start systematically gathering data about the urban food system (Baltimore Office of Sustainability, 2009, pp. 72–75). The plan also requires that policy recommendations developed by the city's advisory body on sustainable food – the Baltimore Food Policy Task Force – be implemented.

The Vancouver sustainability plan includes the food system alongside a wide range of commonly considered urban systems like water, mobility, buildings, and parks and stresses its importance in pursuing multiple sustainability goals – from reducing greenhouse gases emissions to increasing biodiversity and greening the economy. Part of the original approach that the plan takes to urban food planning is the framing of the different components of the urban food system in terms of "food assets." Food assets encompass a variety of locally oriented food system infrastructures, such as urban farms and gardens, farmers markets, community kitchens, community composting facilities, and food hubs, among others. For each asset, a specific 2020 growth target is set and, as a whole, the plan aims to increase the city's food assets by 54.4% by 2020 with respect to 2010 levels. This is consistent with the plan's goals to increase urban food production and ensure that the adequate connections between local food producers and city-run facilities are in place. While containing already a quite detailed set of directions, the plan sees the necessity for a food system strategy that can help the city coordinate cross-sectoral urban food policies and their implementation.

Besides sustainability-centered comprehensive plans, general urban and regional plans are another urban policy document that has been used in several instances to advance sustainable food system goals. A recent example of this "hybridization" is the section on local food of the Chicago long-term metropolitan plan GO TO 2040 released by the Chicago Metropolitan Agency for Planning (CMAP) in 2010. Two of the core local food goals the plan advances are to increase local food production for human consumption and to improve food access so that no community in the metropolitan area lives in a "food desert," that is, an area where access to fresh, nutritious, and affordable food is impaired (see also Chapter 4). Like many of the other urban food plans, Chicago's plan also calls attention to the need to raise awareness about the local food system by addressing the paucity of food system data and instituting a Regional Food System Policy Organization that could oversee the process and help the region lead in the field.

One of the unique features of the background food systems report (The Chicago Food Policy Advisory Council & The City of Chicago, 2009), which informed the local food section of the plan, is the specific set of arguments it provides as to why food is a planning issue and why planners are strategically positioned to support positive food system change. The report, authored by the Chicago's Department of Zoning and Land Use Planning and the Chicago Action Food Policy Council (formerly Advisory Food Policy Council), which operates as a nonprofit organization, makes the strong case that the city "must plan for food now," because there is an unparalleled public engagement with the issue, the fate of farmers in the region depends on sound public policy, and planners are well positioned to reverse structural disinvestment in underserved communities by food retailers and make sure that opportunities for local food growing are not jeopardized by urban development projects in the future (The Chicago Food Policy Advisory Council & The City of Chicago, 2009, pp. 12–13).

Another general plan reflecting a new sensitivity toward food policy in the planning domain is the Portland Plan released by the City of Portland Bureau of Planning and Sustainability in 2010. While the final plan contains just a handful of specific food system goals and policies, its background report on food systems (Rhoads & Guenin, 2010) provides a thorough overview of the urban food system and exhibits two innovative features when compared to other plans. The first is the rich compendium of maps providing a multilayered snapshot of the urban food system; the second is the decision to frame local food systems as an "infrastructure." Twelve different food system maps were developed to gauge different facets of the urban foodscape, among which are full-service grocery stores, food banks, usage of government subsidies for food purchases, direct market farms, and community, backyard, and school gardens. The report was developed by city planners and a wide range of community food experts and stakeholders and the support of the Portland Multnomah Food Policy Council, which was operative until 2012 (Coplen & Cuneo, 2015).

A major breakthrough in the integration of food policy in the British planning system is the London Plan of 2011, which features a number of key food-related policies (e.g., 2.18 Green infrastructure, 3.2 Improving health and addressing health inequalities, and 7.22 Land for food, among others). The policies are nested in several overarching policy goals, among which are Quality of Life, including specific policies for the improvement of healthy food access and for the limitation of fast food stores near schools, and Living Places and Spaces, supporting the expansion of land uses for food growing in London and its Green Belt. As was the case for the other comprehensive plans, the decision to weave food policy into the plan was not made overnight but was the outcome of a much longer process of introduction and gradual stabilization of food policy in the mayoral agenda. Before work on the London Plan commenced, the London Food Strategy (LDA, 2006) and Implementation Plan (LDA, 2007) were released under the auspices of the office of the mayor, and a comprehensive report linking local food growing initiatives and planning, titled *Cultivating the Capital: Food Growing and the Planning System in London* (2010), was produced by the Planning and Housing Committee of the London Assembly. Moreover, the government was already invested in the citywide urban agriculture project Capital Growth, which had set the ambitious goal of creating 2,012 new urban food-growing plots by 2012.

Thus, while seen in isolation each food policy or plan might seem inconsequential, if considered as part of a broader, emergent network of urban food governance novelties, it can be reevaluated as a potential seed of transition. Seemingly fragmented episodes of urban food planning, as the food-sensitive comprehensive plans we saw in this section, can also be used as entry points for examining the circumstances under which food issues succeeded to enter into the planning agenda and the institutional and food system outcomes this led to.

Stand-alone food system plans and strategies

One of the earliest attempts to outline a comprehensive urban food policy framework, connecting public health and environmental concerns in developed economies counties, is the Urban and Peri-Urban Nutrition Action Plan released by the Regional Office for Europe of the World Health Organization (WHO) in 2001. The plan stands out for its holistic approach to poor nutrition and environmental degradation, the inclusion of considerations of both urban and periurban areas, and the inclusion of countries from both Western and Eastern European regions. It moreover provides guidelines as to how the planning process for a community food system plan can be structured and calls attention to the role of community food councils. Both opportunities and barriers to the increase of local food growing and procurement practices are moreover examined. The new edition of the plan, the European Food and Nutrition Action Plan 2015–2020 released in 2014, however, appears to have dropped the focus on local food systems and the inclusive orientation to food policy, including both nutrition and urban and regional farming goals, of its predecessor. As we will see, this turn is somewhat anomalous compared to the recent wave of urban and regional food system plans and strategies devised by local administrations in the Global North.

The WHO Urban and Peri-Urban Nutrition Action Plan of 2001 attests that the idea of developing a comprehensive urban food system policy is not entirely new. What is new, however, is its growing popularity and scale of diffusion, which started unfolding about a decade after its publication. Over the past 15 years, over 90 city and regional food system plans and strategies (Table 5.3) have been released in industrialized countries (see also Chapter 1, Figure 1.2). From New York City to Seattle and from Vancouver to Amsterdam, cities and regions are taking on the challenge of reintegrating food in the public domain and rethinking it as a means to equitable and sustainable urban development. While the plans may vary substantially in terms of who initiates and develops them (e.g., a public health department, city planning department, mayor's office of food initiatives, food policy task forces, or food policy councils), what they all have in common is their holistic take on assessing and planning for the urban food system, from field to fork to waste disposal (at least, the urban part of it that cities already administer). There is also a relative consistency across all plans in the way their authors frame the need for involvement of the local state in food policy issues.

Rationale and suggested courses of action

By far, the two most frequent arguments put forward to legitimize the need for a local food system plan or a strategy are the need to ensure and safeguard public health and the lost opportunity for local economic development through shorter food supply chains. Environmental sustainability concerns are an integral part of all strategies but are rarely the main trigger for their development. Typical problem frames depicting the causes of complex public health challenges, such as obesity and inadequate nutrition, more broadly point at economic, physical, and cultural factors that limit the opportunities for healthy diets and lifestyles. The recurrent concepts of "food poverty," used to designate households using more than 30% of their income for food in the UK, "food deserts," and "food literacy" encapsulate well this threefold orientation.

Some of the frequent solutions advanced are thereby policies to diversify the urban retail environment by incentivizing chain stores in underserved communities, increase opportunities for consumption of fresh, unprocessed food through new outlets for food grown in the city or in the region (e.g., farmers and gardeners markets, mobile food vendors, edible schoolyards, local public food procurement), and to strengthen knowledge and skills about food

Table 5.3 Overview of urban, regional, and national food system plans released in industrialized nations over the past decade

Country	Urban or regional food system plan or strategy	Released by	Year
Canada	A Healthy Community Food System Plan for Waterloo Region	Region of Waterloo – Public Health, Grand by Design	2007
	Capital Region Food and Health Action Plan (2007–2010)	Food and Agriculture Initiatives Roundtable CRD Roundtable on the Environment	2007
	North Okanagan Food System Plan. Strengthening the Regional Food System	Regional District of the North Okanagan	2009
	District of North Saanich Growing Toward Food Self-Reliance	District of North Saanich	2009
	Cultivating Food Connections: Toward a Healthy and Sustainable Food System for Toronto	Public Health Department, Toronto Food Policy Council	2010
	Plant It! A Healthy Community Food System Plan for the City of Peterborough	Community Food Network	2011
	A Healthy Community Food System Plan for Sarnia-Lambton	Sarnia-Lambton Food Coalition	2011
	Vancouver Regional Food Systems Strategy	Metro Vancouver	2011
	Edmonton Food and Agriculture Strategy	Edmonton Food and Agriculture Advisory Committee	2012
	Saskatoon Regional Food Action Plan	Saskatoon Regional Food System Assessment and Action Plan Team	2013
	What Feeds Us: Vancouver Food Strategy	City of Vancouver, Vancouver Food Policy Council	2013
United States	Food for Growth: A Community Food System Plan for Buffalo's West Side	Massachusetts Avenue Project	2003

(Continued)

Table 5.3 (Continued)

Country	Urban or regional food system plan or strategy	Released by	Year
	The New Mainstream: A Sustainable Food Agenda for California	Ecotrust	2005
	Vermont Farm to Plate Strategic Plan	State of Vermont	2010, 2013*
	FoodNYC: A Blueprint for a Sustainable Food System	Office of Manhattan Borough President	2010
	FoodWorks: A Vision to Improve NYC's Food System	New Your City Council	2010
	Transforming the Oakland Food System: A Plan for Action	Oakland Food Policy Council	2010
	The Good Food for All Agenda Creating a New Regional Food System for Los Angeles	The Los Angeles Food Policy Task Force	2010
	From Farm to Fork: A Guide to Building North Carolina's Sustainable Local Food Economy	Center for Environmental Farming Systems, NC State University	2010
	Iowa – A Healthy Seasonal Local Food System Plan	Iowa Corridor Food and Agriculture Coalition	2010
	Eating Here: Greater Philadelphia's Food System Plan	Delaware Valley Regional Planning Commission (DVRPC)	2011
	Northeast Kingdom Food System Plan	Northeastern Vermont Development Association, The Center for an Agricultural Economy	2011
	Seattle Food Action Plan	City of Seattle	2012
	Local Sustainable Food System Plan	Grant County, New Mexico	2012
	Fargo-Moorhead Metropolitan Food Systems Plan	Fargo-Moorhead Metropolitan Council of Governments (Metro COG)	2013
	Washington County Food System Plan	Washington County	2013
	From Opportunity to Achievement: Canadian Food Strategy	The Conference Board of Canada	2014

Country	Plan	Organization	Year
	Food System Plan to Promote Healthy, Local Food Production and Consumption in Davidson, NC	The Town of Davidson	2014
	Feeding Kansas: A Statewide Farm & Food System Assessment with a Plan for Public Action	Kansas Rural Center	2014
	Planning for Santa Fe's Food Future	Santa Fe Food Policy Council	2014
	Massachusetts Local Food Action Plan	Massachusetts Food Policy Council	2015
	Delta Roots: The Mid-South Regional Food System Plan	Memphis Shelby County Office of Sustainability	2015
	A Food System That Works for All in New Hampshire	Food Solutions New England	2015
	Rappahannock-Rapidan Farm and Food Plan	Rappahannock-Rapidan Regional Commission	2015
United Kingdom	The Mayor's Food Strategy: Healthy and Sustainable Food for London	London Development Agency, London Food Board	2006
	Spade to Spoon: Making the Connections, a Food Strategy and Action Plan for Brighton & Hove	Food Matters	2006, 2012*
	Lewisham Food Strategy	NHS Lewisham	2006
	Leeds Food Matters Strategy	NHS Leeds	2006
	Food Futures: A Food Strategy for Manchester	Manchester Food Futures Board	2007
	Cardiff Food and Health Strategy	Cardiff Health Alliance	2008
	A Sustainable Food Strategy for Bristol and Bristol Food Network	Bristol Food Network	2009
	Islington Food Strategy	NHS Islington	2010
	Liverpool Food and Health Strategy	NHS Liverpool	2010
	Haringey Sustainable Food Strategy 2010–2015	Haringey Council	2010
	Bristol Good Food Plan	City of Bristol, Bristol Food Policy Council	2013
	Sheffield Food Plan	NHS Sheffield Sheffield First Partnership	2011, 2014*

(Continued)

Table 5.3 (Continued)

Country	Urban or regional food system plan or strategy	Released by	Year
	Middlesborough Food Sustainability Action Plan	Middlesbrough Environment City	2011
	Plymouth Food Action Plan	Food Plymouth	2012
	Bradford District Food Strategy	Bradford Metropolitan District Council	2012
	Food for Wales, Food from Wales 2010–2020 – A Food Strategy for Wales	Welsh Assembly Government	2010
	Bath and North East Somerset Local Food Strategy 2014–2017	Bath and North East Somerset Council	2014
	County of Durham Sustainable Local Food Strategy 2014–2020	County of Durham Food Partnership	2014
	Solihull Food Strategy and Action Plan	Solihull Metropolitan Borough Council	2015
Ireland	Donegal Food Strategy	Donegal County Enterprise Board	2012
Australia	City of Darebin Urban Food Production Strategy 2014–2018	City of Darebin	2014
Netherlands	Amsterdam Metropolitan Food System Strategy	Amsterdam Physical Planning Department (DRO)	2006
	Amsterdam Food Vision	Amsterdam Economic Board, Amsterdam Physical Planning Department (DRO)	2013
	Rotterdam Food Strategy	Urban Planning Department	2012
	The Hague Food Strategy	Labor Party, GroenLinks, Haagse Stads Patij, PvdV	2011
Italy	Pisa Food Plan	City of Pisa	2010
Finland	Finnish Food Strategy	Ministry of Forestry and Agriculture	2014
Europe	Urban and Peri-Urban Food and Nutrition Action Plan	WHO Regional Office for Europe	2001

(*) Indicates the latest update.

purchasing and preparation (e.g., cooking workshops, school food curricula, outreach programs at farmers markets). One original proposal to this end, for instance, is to encourage the development of community supported agriculture (CSA) schemes tailored specifically to meet the needs of low-income residents (e.g., Greater Philadelphia Food System Plan, 2011). One concrete example of a viable CSA model of this kind is the Corbin Hill Road Farm Share in New York City (Cohen & Derryck, 2011), connecting low-income communities in the Borough of Bronx to farmers in upstate New York.

Economic arguments for the development of public policies for food in cities and regions are as prevalent. In particular, the rising demand for locally sourced food in urban areas is often seen as an underused lever to counter traditional obstacles to open space and farmland preservation through economic development. The development of a thriving local economy through the revitalization of both artisan and larger-scale independent farming and food processing enterprises in and around cities is an area of consistent priority across most of the food strategies released to date. Facilitating access to high-quality farmland, training, fair wages, and decent retirement plans for present and future generations of farmers in metropolitan areas are some of the policies advanced to preserve and expand land-based urban and periurban economies. While urban agriculture is often included in sections focused on local food growing and production, it is rarely depicted as an economic development tool. Rather, the rationale for policies seeking to expand city farming and gardening is above all linked to the educational, ecological, social cohesion, and public health benefits they bring about.

Creating new opportunities for local food processing and marketing is one further policy area that urban and regional food plans focus on. Among the concrete strategies envisioned are the rehabilitation of underutilized or abandoned public markets sites and buildings to promote innovative startups, like kitchen incubators and polyfunctional local food hubs, and the institution of dedicated food enterprise zones where incentives for such startups are concentrated. Economic strategies aiming to catalyze new local food and farming businesses, however, are not exclusively focused on the creation of new infrastructure. The diversification of existing food terminals, typically serving national and global food circuits, is also an untapped opportunity stressed particularly by large cities. The integration of services dedicated specifically to local farmers at some of the world's largest food distribution terminals, like the Hunts Point Distribution Center in New York and the Ontario Food Terminal in Toronto, contemplated by the New York City's FoodWorks plan (2010) and Toronto's Cultivating Food Connections (2010) strategy respectively are two cases in point.

Institutional food procurement, or the acquisition of food for collective consumption at schools, prisons, hospitals, and other public institutions, is one greatly underused urban lever and food policy area to which all food system plans and strategies draw attention. The area is strategic both for its scale – for example, over 800,000 meals are served in public schools in New York City every day – and for its ability to influence the source and quality of the food and promote healthier eating habits at once. Some scholars have furthermore stressed the value of public food procurement as a potential strategy for combating urban sprawl (Vallianatos, Gottlieb, & Haase, 2004). The Amsterdam Food Strategy (Brand, van Schendelen, & Vermeulen, 2007), for instance, set a policy to increase the share of organic food supplied by the city's municipal canteens from 32% in 2009 to 40% by the end of 2010 and to 60% by the end of 2011 and to increase organic food production in the region (Noord Holland) from 3.4% in 2007 to 7% in 2011 (Brand, van Schendelen, & Vermeulen, 2010). Other cities, like New York, have pushed further the local food procurement policies stated in their comprehensive, yet not legally binding, food plans by translating them into local laws and standards by the force of which city agencies are required to consider opportunities for prioritizing local food sources. In some US states, like Illinois (Public Act 96–0579 of 2009), local food procurement has also been encouraged through legislation which allows for premiums (10% in the case of Illinois) to be used by state-funded agencies to encourage procurement of locally grown produce in their bids (CMAP, 2010).

Environmental sustainability concerns are generally most pronounced in the plans' sections devoted to the management of urban waste production and disposal. Policies are commonly organized along two main strategic lines of intervention: prevention and recycling. In some cities, organic waste separation and composting are still largely devolved to community-based initiatives, so food system plans seek to encourage pilot projects that could test the viability of a curbside food scraps collection service to be offered citywide. Educational pilots targeting the separation of school food waste from the generic waste stream are also part of the policies put forward. Cities are moreover using their food system plans to advance strategies for the more sustainable management of their solid food waste, particularly packaging (e.g., takeaway trays, cups, plastic bottles), by suggesting, for example, water fill stations to reduce the use of bottled water where high-quality tap water is available. Some urban food strategies have gone as far as to suggest bans on nonrecyclable packaging (e.g., Vancouver Greenest City Strategy, New York City FoodWorks Plan). Additionally, policymakers are now rethinking an often-neglected urban food waste, used cooking oil, which can be used as a valuable resource for the production of city-made biodiesel to fuel public transportation and residential heating systems.

Food-related traffic, contributing to congestion and air pollution in cities, is another area of environmental concern targeted by urban and regional food system plans. Policies aim to reduce traffic, incentivize the use of cleaner fuel, and shorten the distance between food destinations and residents by encouraging the introduction of healthy food vendors near major transit stations. Some strategies recognize the need to engage policymakers working at higher tiers of government to mobilize changes in national programs, subsidies, and tax mechanisms that have greater influence on the geography of food transportation. Similar concerns are expressed also in relation to policies aiming to transition farming operations in metropolitan regions to more ecologically sound models that can help safeguard biodiversity, watersheds, and soil quality. Conflicting sustainability goals are seldom discussed, though one food system strategy did recognize the need to introduce a policy that can prioritize the localization of greenhouses and solar panels on already developed land and thus protect valuable open space and farmland (DVRPC, 2011).

Last but not least, the need to forge new partnerships and establish stable institutional spaces (or support the work of already existing ones), like mayoral food offices and food policy councils, that can oversee the implementation of the food system plans is a widely shared concern by all food system plans and strategies. As we saw in Chapter 4, not all strategies are equipped with a detailed set of metrics that can help local administrations track progress, so the creation of a specialized advisory body is an often-recommended policy to this end. To accelerate the normalization of food policy in government agencies, partnering with and learning from other long-established policy areas, like transportation, energy, and housing, is a strategy suggested as a potential tactic for local administrations to consider. Overall, more than an agenda for radical food system change, the overarching purpose of this first generation of local food system plans and strategies is to scan the field for ways in which local governments are already advancing food policy initiatives, explore what innovative grassroots initiatives and solutions are already available, and contemplate how to best support, replicate, and scale them up.

Dynamics of inception

The way each food system strategy comes about is fairly unique but usually is the result of a combination of change agents at work, both within the local institutional environment and at larger scales out of the direct reach of local institutions. In transition theory terms, novelties, like the local food system strategies, policies, and legislative provisions this section discusses, can be viewed as the result of the interplay of niche innovations, incumbent landscape pressures, and regime actors perceiving the innovations as an advantageous means to tackle such pressures and urgent policy issues. The reason why regime actors, in this case local government leaders and officials, come to consider food policy as a relevant area for their policy agendas can be related to multiple factors. Among these is the internal institutional history of the social groups they are part of, which in some instances can contain a long series of food-related precedents (e.g., consider the rich history of food system reports and programs that preceded the 2010 food system strategy of Toronto, or the integration of local food growing objectives in the 2011 London Plan).

Often, however, it is not just a matter of accumulation of a critical mass of novelties that bring about institutional change, but the presence of urban food policy "champions," "risk-taking bureaucrats" (Kunzmann, 2011), and "policy entrepreneurs" (Block & Paredis, 2013), who are ready to go beyond institutional constraints and forge strategic partnerships to get things done and normalize food in urban policy. Examples of such entrepreneurs are the late mayor of Boston, Thomas M. Menino, who for his pioneering food policy initiatives was referred to as the "mayor of food" and elected as the first chair of the food policy task force of the US Conference of Mayors (see Chapter 7); the former Manhattan Borough President Scott Stringer, who spearheaded the report *Food in the Public Interest* (2009) and several other policy statements on why the food system as a whole – from farming to distribution and waste management – ought to be a municipal concern in New York City; the former Mayor of San Francisco Gavin Newsom, who passed an Executive Directive on Healthy and Sustainable Food for San Francisco in 2009 (more about this in the next section); and many others. Of course, food policy champions can well reside outside the mayor's office, as the chairs of some of the most successful food policy councils, boards, coalitions, and partnerships, testify.

Besides the internal qualities of local governance networks, however, there are hosts of "external" factors that can influence decision-makers and determine the way food policy goals travel to the mayoral agenda. Such factors can range from concerns about social inequality and food poverty to public health crises (e.g., the understanding that there is an obesity "epidemic"), uncertainties due to climate change and fossil fuels depletion, or the rapid urbanization of prime agricultural land. Pressures can be also "positive," which is often the case of perceived unique opportunities (e.g., the 2012 Olympic Games in London, the 2015 World EXPO on sustainable food in Milan, the 2022 Floriade in Almere) or an impetus to stay competitive and match or exceed the accomplishments of other administrations already championing the advancement of the issue.

Overall, public health is arguably one of the most pervasive drivers for the introduction of food in public policy at the local scale. Indeed, many of the strategies released in the UK have hitherto been developed under the auspices of the National Health Service (NHS) agency. Some of them put the emphasis on nutrition (e.g., Leeds, Liverpool, Cardiff), while others outline a more holistic agenda and devote equal attention to all spheres of the urban food system (e.g., Lewisham, Islington, Sheffield). In general, while hosting the urban food planning process in a public health department might tailor the food system agenda using consumption as an entry point, this is not always the case.

The pioneer experience of municipal food policymaking in Toronto and the 2010 food strategy Cultivating Food Connections developed through the city's Department of Health are good examples of this. The work of the department has, for instance, contributed to the introduction of incentives for rooftop gardens and farms in the city (Roberts, 2010) and, through its comprehensive food strategy, is now providing policy recommendations for greening the local economy through food-related initiatives and even reconsidering the role of large-scale facilities like the Ontario Food Terminal (Toronto Public Health, 2010). In this case, the holistic orientation of the strategy owes much to the work of the Toronto Food Policy Council, which operates within the department but advocates for a systemic approach to public health and food system issues (see Chapter 7). Thus, rather than judging a food strategy by its institutional home, it is more useful to look at the governance networks and the kind of partnerships that had brought it about. Championing an urban agenda for food policy through an established government agency or department has overwhelmingly proved to be an effective strategy for the inception of food system discourses and ideas in the public domain. Even if the agenda is initially filtered through a handful of issues, the influence, reputation, and resources that established public agencies have are critical in getting the conversation started and preparing the institutional ground to subsequently transition it to more holistic agendas.

Seeds of transition or ephemeral outliers?

While the support of a mayor or a city agency is an essential precondition for advancing food system goals in the public domain, it is by no means a guarantee for the longevity of local food initiatives. In fact, oftentimes shifts in administrations and the transition from one political orientation to another can relegate emergent food policy novelties to inconsequential episodes and preclude them from further influencing mainstream government practices. But then, are urban food plans and strategies just ephemeral outliers, or are they the seeds of an institutional and societal transition? The short answer is that they are both.

The evolution of urban food policy in Amsterdam proves well this point. The idea of taking on food in local policy was introduced through concerns about how to preserve valuable landscapes in the Green Heart area enclosed by the four major cities in the Western Netherlands – Utrecht, Amsterdam, The Hague, and Rotterdam, collectively forming the Randstad (see Chapter 2, Figure 2.2). In particular, Vermeulen (2012, p. 70) notes that while focused meetings were convened to debate potential strategies to cope with the challenge, Dutch planners and other representatives of national and local government agencies came across the London Food Strategy. The connection between the objective of halting urban sprawl and the opportunity to promote healthy and active urban lifestyles through food systems planning thus became obvious.

The City of Amsterdam took the issue further and embarked on the development of a sustainable urban food system agenda through its Physical Planning Department (DRO), the first one of this kind in the Netherlands. The Amsterdam Food Strategy, *Proeftuin Amsterdam*, was released in 2007 (Figure 5.1), the same year when the Implementation Plan for the London Food Strategy was published. Overall, the policymaking process was predominantly government-driven and involved the creation of an intergovernmental coalition between the City of Amsterdam, Zaanstad, the Province of North Holland, the Dutch Ministry of Agriculture and Food Quality, and the Steering Committee National Landscape Green Heart.

While the strategy was funded as a short-term program, the expectations were that it could set a precedent and further initiatives would have followed.

food processing

consumer demand

urban agriculture

dairy farming

polders, mixed landuse

greenhouses

national landscapes

Figure 5.1 The Amsterdam food region and local food system infrastructure in Proeftuin Amsterdam (January 2010), Amsterdam Metropolitan Area (AMA).

Courtesy: © The Physical Planning Department (DRO) of the Municipality of Amsterdam.

Yet, three years after its inception, the administration changed and the prospects of continuity of the urban food policy agenda became unlikely. This is far from unusual even by sociotechnical transitions standards and, as Wiskerke and van der Ploeg (2004, p. 2) note, the most common scenario in emergent niche innovations is that the first outcome of an innovation passes unnoticed and niche novelties – like urban food systems plans in our case – remain "hidden" and "might even be nipped in the bud." However, the Amsterdam Food Strategy regained saliency two years later when in 2012 the city resolved to participate in the bid competition for the Floriade 2022: Growing Green Cities horticultural exhibition. The strong focus on the promotion of local food growing practices and landscapes of the bid made the local administration reconsider the role of local food policies in the future development of the city. A key part of the process was the continuity in internal leadership at the department of city planning and the contribution of one of the champions of the Amsterdam food strategy – senior urban planner Pim Vermeulen.

Though the Floriade 2022 competition was eventually won by the neighboring municipality of Almere, many of the ideas that were developed were kept, among which a pilot project for creating a continuous productive urban landscape (Bohn & Viljoen, 2010; Viljoen & Bohn, 2005) along a mobility infrastructure planned for reconstruction. Perhaps, most important, the institutional and political mobilization for the bid gave the impetus for the development of a new edition of the food strategy, the Amsterdam Food Vision (2014–2024) (*Voedsel en Amsterdam*), which put emphasis on the economic value of integrating a food systems perspective in urban policy and was issued in 2013. A budget of €200,000 was settled for the first year of implementation of the Vision. More recently, this second-generation food planning novelty, and the intergovernmental coalitions that stemmed from it, catalyzed a wider process of planning and visioning around food in the region and a Regional Food Strategy is now in the making. Some of the partners are the municipalities in the Amsterdam metropolitan area (including Amsterdam, Almere, Amstelveen, Haarlemmermeer, Hilversum, and Velsen), the Amsterdam Economic Development Board, the Province of North Holland, Greenport North Holland, and Greenport Aalsmeer.

The role of planning

While urban planning per se is rarely the focus of policy in comprehensive food system plans and strategies, it is often mentioned when food system goals and land-use regulations and plans explicitly intersect. Planners are also frequently recognized as a necessary party in the formation of focus groups and partnerships to develop and implement local food policies. A handful of food policy frameworks, however, like the Newquay Growth Area Food Strategy (Sustain & ESD, 2007), the Waterloo Region Food System Plan (2007), and the Seattle Food Action Plan (2012), as well as the Recommendations for Food Systems Policy (2011) preceding it, do devote significant attention to the role that planning professionals and local planning systems can play in the implementation of policies for a more equitable and environmentally sustainable urban food system.

The Newquay Growth Area Food Strategy, for instance, stresses the importance of spatial and community planning in revamping public spaces to host a wide range of local food outlets and events such as farmers markets, food festivals, and cooperatives, as well as permanent facilities and infrastructures. The importance of equipping local food venues with ancillary services such as onsite waste management for food markets and public transportation connections are indicated as additional policy areas to which spatial and community planners can contribute. The strategy also underscores the importance of planners in developing food access assessments to inform mainstream planning processes. The attentive consideration of the planning domain in this case was fixed at the outset of the plan-making process and in the goal to provide a model "for how the infrastructure for a sustainable food system can be addressed as a core component of local spatial and retail planning, environmental protection, and social/health policy" (Sustain & ESD, 2007, p. 8).

The Seattle Food Action Plan and food systems policy recommendations call attention particularly to the role of land use and planning departments in ensuring access to full-service healthy food outlets across the city (City of Seattle, 2012, p. 15; Fisher & Roberts, 2011, p. 19). Specific food policy goals are addressed to transportation planners, who can play a key role in promoting pedestrian- and bicycle-friendly neighborhoods and the availability of diverse food destinations in every urban community. The city's department of transportation is advised to consider the introduction of a shuttle service for food shoppers to reduce car traffic. Other non-legally-binding planning policies put forward in the preliminary report, though not explicitly integrated in the final plan, are the recommendation for emergency planners to develop a strategic food self-reliance plan and the recommendation for the city to invest in the training of staff with expertise in the integration of food system issues in transportation plans. A crosscutting recommendation the report suggests is the integration of food systems analysis in all major policymaking areas that the city has competencies in – from transportation to land use, comprehensive planning, and climate change.

Planning for local food systems, however, entails also the skillful management of competing goals or, as Lang et al. (2009) put it, food policy is above all a "contested terrain" and requires the "constant 'juggle' of competing interests and perspectives." In reporting the feedback of urban planners on each of the food policy objectives advanced, The Waterloo Region food system plan (Miedema & Pigott, 2007) well reflects this point. Three contested areas that affect the promotion of local farming enterprises in the region are zoning for on-farm businesses, minimum size farm policies, and farm-gate sales. A first point of contention is that while allowing for on-farm processing activities can help farmers stay in business, in the long run, these can take over food-growing land uses and thus jeopardize farmland preservation. A second contested area relates to minimum farm size limits set at 40 hectares (about 100 acres) in the region. While these limits prevent excessive farmland fragmentation, they are also likely to hinder smaller-scale farming operations, particularly the growing of herbs, fruits, and vegetables for community supported agriculture schemes. Lastly, while roadside stands enable farmers to market their produce closer to potential buyers, planners are hesitant to remove zoning restrictions since expanding the practice may compromise road traffic.

Spatial planning is considered to have a "special status" when it comes to implementing food policy, according to the London Food Strategy. The brief comment on the role of planners made in the strategy suggests that planners have a role to play in supporting "the development of on-farm processing facilities, the provision of sub-regional food distribution systems, the protection of street markets, farmers' markets and specialist markets, the maintenance of the High Street, tackling food 'deserts' and a host of other food-related issues," yet the strategy also acknowledges that "many other strategic and institutional forces will need to make a contribution too" (London Development Agency, 2006, p. 22). Simply put, there is no shortage of ways in which planners can champion and implement urban food policies, but they cannot do it alone. This view is shared by the Toronto food strategy, which draws attention to the fact that many of the planning and legislative competencies that cities can potentially use to shape food policy are actually influenced by higher-tier authorities at the provincial and federal level of government (Toronto Public Health, 2010, p. 18), thus advocacy and creative partnerships with decision-makers at these levels are necessary.

New York City's FoodWorks plan points also to the unique challenges to sustainable transportation planning the food system poses. The plan underscores that while planners have for long advocated for alternative modes of transportation, particularly trains and public transit, the current food system inevitably relies on fast transportation and large refrigerated trucks (Brannen, 2010). Thus, transitioning food transportation to sustainability is inherently "more complicated" than shifting passenger traffic. In sum, while there are limitations to what planning and planners can do to advance sustainable food system goals at the local level, the ways in which they can engage with urban food planning abound. As Pim Vermeulen, senior urban planner at the Department of Physical Planning in Amsterdam and pioneer of the Amsterdam Food Strategy (Brand, van Schendelen, & Vermeulen, 2007), eloquently puts it – two of the unique ways in which planners can contribute to the advancement of food policy are by using their ability to connect "tunnel visions" and by creating evidence about the urban food system to policymakers.

Mayoral food policy directives

Though generally rare, mayoral executive directives are one alternative mechanism that has been used to advance urban food policies in the US. Executive directives provide instructions for multiple city departments, agencies, and divisions as to how food policy should be implemented and outline specific tasks and responsibilities for each. Like food system plans and strategies, executive directives do not carry the force of law and are vulnerable to shifts in the electoral cycle, since they are only valid for the duration of the mandate of the mayor that issues them. Yet, from an administrative point of view, these provisions are better suited to advance a coordinated, interdepartmental approach to urban food planning than food policies developed by a single division of local government.

One notable example of an executive directive that has been used to advance food policy at the municipal level is the San Francisco's Executive Directive 09–03 Healthy and Sustainable Food for San Francisco released in 2009 by the then-Mayor Gavin Newsom. The food policy principles the directive put forward echoed the comprehensive approach advanced by the Food and Agriculture Strategy of San Francisco's Sustainability Plan of 1997 (examined at the beginning of this section) and translated well the normative goal of "ecological public health," which food policy scholars Lang, Barling, and Caraher (2009) have theorized, into actionable policy. The policy principles advanced by the directive were to ensure food access for all, reduce the environmental impacts of the food system from seed to table, increase urban food growing initiatives, preserve valuable farmland, create more green jobs through the local food sector, encourage sustainable farming practices, invest in healthy and sustainable food systems education, promote local food in municipal food procurement contracts, and advocate for policies that can support and strengthen the impact of the executive directive at higher tiers of government.

The directive also provided detailed instructions for the establishment of a food policy council with the responsibility to monitor progress on each of the directive's policies and aid their implementation. It contained specific indications on the composition of the council, specifying the city departments and potential external stakeholder groups that would take part. One of the most salient parts of the executive directive is arguably the articulation of duties and responsibilities of each city department. Sixteen specific actions were outlined and addressed to different city agencies, among which were the Planning Department, the Department of Public Health, the Department of Aging and Adult Services, and the Department of Recreation and Parks. A deadline of 60 days from the adoption of the directive was fixed, by which all departments mentioned in the directive were required to prepare detailed plans for its implementation.

While the food policy council disbanded in 2010 and the city administration changed in 2011, the directive managed to influence both the institutional and physical environment of the city's food system. Since 2009, over 40 city agencies have started working on the policies outlined, the city planning code was amended to facilitate food growing and selling operations across the city, a designated Urban Agriculture Program was established, and all bids for publicly financed food procurement now need to source food within a 200-mile radius from the city. Additionally, a dedicated Food Systems Policy Program with two staff members is now hosted within the city's Department of Planning, which initiated and coordinated the *San Francisco Food and Beverage Industry Cluster Study*, released in 2014, with specific recommendations on how to reinforce the city's food and beverage economy. Many of these accomplishments undoubtedly owe much to the support of the incumbent mayor of San Francisco Ed Lee, yet the executive directive of 2009 set a national precedent in openly declaring the development of healthy and ecologically sound urban food systems a responsibility of local governments and outlined a cohesive framework of the concrete actions that municipal administrations can take to this end.

Urban food laws, incentives, and regulations

Alongside the growing number of local food system plans and strategies released by local administrations, a new wave of food-related legislation, regulations, and incentive programs has risen over the past decade. These provisions are arguably the urban food planning novelties best representing the emergent interface between food policy and the public domain. Some of them pioneer the establishment of new administrative bodies (e.g., food policy councils) and practices (e.g., systematical collection of food system data), while others attempt major overhauls of the laws and regulations (e.g., city charters, local laws, zoning and building codes) that influence the urban food system's physical layout, the dominant understandings of what is a normal urban food environment, and the choices that residents and entrepreneurs make in it.

Organizational innovations

Some of the earliest examples of formal government provisions to reconsider food's place in the organizational structure of the local state in the US are resolutions and ordinances sanctioning the establishment of a food policy council. Unlike resolutions, which represent a formal policy or position statement, ordinances are legally binding. Examples of food policy councils instituted through a resolution are the Knoxville-Knox County Food Policy Council (1981), the Portland Multnomah Food Policy Council (2002), Dane County Food Policy Council (2006), and the Santa Fe City and County Food Policy Council (2008), while among those sanctioned through an ordinance are the City of St. Paul Food and Nutrition Commission (1992) and the New Haven Food Policy Council (2005). New urban food planning practices can be introduced also in the absence of food policy councils. In 2011, the City of New York enacted a specific local law (Local Law 50, introduced as the Food System Metrics Bill) to ensure the integration of food system monitoring practices in local government through the Office of Long-Term Planning and Sustainability. To consolidate the city's planning and other administrative practices related to urban agriculture, the City of San Francisco amended its administrative code, adding Sections 53.1 through 53.4 in 2012, and established an Urban Agriculture Program to better coordinate these efforts.

Urban agriculture

The bulk of legislative provisions undertaken by cities and other local government administrations have however hitherto focused mainly on facilitating and promoting the development of new physical infrastructure to reinstate the local layer of the urban food system. By far, efforts to revise zoning codes and regulations to accommodate urban agriculture land uses within and near urban areas are the most numerous among urban food systems legislative provisions. Because in some cities food growing and selling practices are explicitly prohibited by law, to reintroduce them, a change of the city's zoning code (or ordinance) is required. Cities that have recently amended their zoning codes to formally recognize and support urban agriculture uses are San Francisco (San Francisco Planning Code Sections 102.35 and 204.1), distinguishing between neighborhood agriculture, allowed everywhere in the city, and large-scale urban agriculture, allowed only in industrial zones; Chicago (Chicago Municipal Code, Section 17–2–0207), distinguishing between community gardens and urban farms (commercial farms up to 25,000 square feet are now allowed in the city); and Atlanta (Atlanta Zoning Ordinance, Section 16–29.001), regulating urban gardens and market gardens land uses to address specifically disparities in fresh food access in the city.

In addition to the introduction of explicit land use classifications for urban agriculture, some cities have amended their zoning codes to allow for the development of designated urban agriculture districts. Among these in the US are Cleveland (Cleveland Zoning Code, Title 7, Chapter 336), Madison (Madison Zoning Code, Section 28.093), and Chattanooga (Chattanooga Zoning Ordinance, Article V, Section 1600). Though relatively rare, a city's zoning code can include also an exclusively agricultural district, usually for periurban areas with a more rural character and potentially threatened by urbanization. Two examples of such districts are the City of Vancouver (British Columbia) Limited Agriculture District (Zoning Category RA-1, since 1955) and the City of Madison's newly introduced Agriculture District (Madison Zoning Code, Section 28.092). The City of Boston, which has some of the oldest zoning provisions for community gardens districts (Boston Zoning Code, Section 33–8, since 1988), has recently introduced an Urban Agriculture Overlay District (see Figure 5.2) in its zoning code for a specific urban area within the Greater Mattapan Neighborhood District (Boston Zoning Code, Article 60, Section 60–28). Proposals for pilot projects for the conversion of city-owned land in the overlay district to urban agriculture uses were subsequently formally solicited by the Boston Redevelopment Authority.

Small animals, like chickens and rabbits, and bees are often excluded from the list of domestic animals permitted in residential areas in cities. Yet, with the increasing popularity of local food and "locavore" lifestyles and the frequent informal reintroduction of such animals in residential areas, some cities have felt the need to update their regulations to legalize these emerging practices. For instance, in 2008, the City of Denver amended its zoning code (City

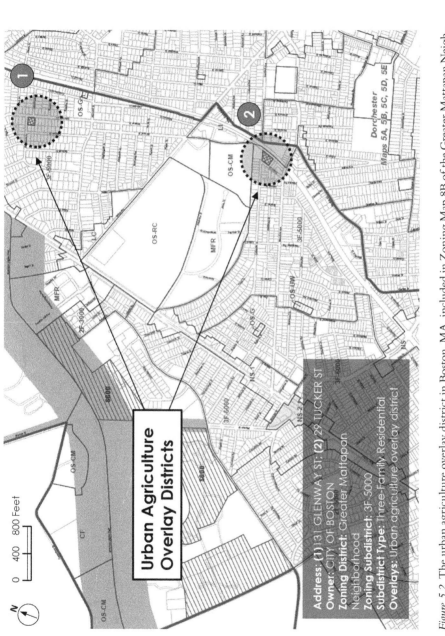

Figure 5.2 The urban agriculture overlay district in Boston, MA, included in Zoning Map 8B of the Greater Mattapan Neighborhood District (last update April 25th, 2012).

Courtesy: Boston Redevelopment Authority, Office of Digital Cartography and GIS.

Within the figure:

Urban Agriculture Overlay Districts

Address: (1) 131 GLENWAY ST; **(2)** 29 TUCKER ST
Owner: CITY OF BOSTON
Zoning District: Greater Mattapan Neighborhood
Zoning Subdistrict: 3F-5000
Subdistrict Type: Three-Family Residential
Overlays: Urban agriculture overlay district

Dorchester
Maps 5A, 5B, 5C, 5D, 5E

0   400   800 Feet

N

and County of Denver Zoning Code, Section 59–2) to permit beekeeping and apiaries in residential areas. The Madison Zoning Code (Section 28.151) now also allows beekeeping as well as keeping chickens in the city with some limitations: a maximum of six beehives and four chickens per lot in residential zoning districts and up to six chickens at schools or museums in the downtown core district. For both practices, residents need to obtain a license. In Portland, residents can keep up to three small animals (e.g., chickens, ducks, pygmy goats, rabbits) without the need to apply for a license (Portland City Code, Section 13.05.015).

In recent times, the rise of interest in rooftop farming, both ground-based and in greenhouses, has made cities reconsider their zoning and building regulations and even the mechanisms through which this productive use of flat roofs in cities can be encouraged, particularly atop nonresidential buildings. In 2009, the Planning Department of the City of Toronto launched an Eco-Roof Incentives Program thanks to which edible green roofs could receive a subsidy of C$50 per square meter up to a maximum of C$100,000 (City of Toronto, 2009). The program specifically targeted existing commercial, industrial, and institutional buildings. In the US, in 2007, the City of Philadelphia promoted a similar incentive called Green Roofs Tax Credit (Bill No. 070072), which initially offered developers of a tax rebate 25% (now 50%) of the green roof actual construction costs up to a maximum of $100,000. The program also required that applicants adequately maintain the roof for at least five years after its completion.

The City of New York has also promoted the development of edible roofs and other urban agriculture projects through its Green Infrastructure Grants Program and subsequently through amendment of its zoning code, or the so-called Zone Green Text Amendment (N120132 ZRY) in 2012, with the aim to promote a wide range of sustainability-oriented initiatives. The amendment waived floor area and height limits for greenhouses constructed over roofs of nonresidential buildings. One of the few instances in which fiscal incentives to ground-based urban agriculture operations have been advanced is Baltimore's Urban Agriculture Tax Credit Bill enacted in 2015 (City Council Bill 14–0420, enacted 15–350), which grants 90% in property tax breaks for urban farmers who manage to grow and sell fruits and vegetables worth a minimum of $5,000 over a one-year period.

Another innovative use of zoning incentives is the Landscape Conservation and Local Infrastructure Program (LCLIP) of the City of Seattle. The program uses an incentive zoning mechanism to require developers in the South Lake Union and Downtown areas of the city to purchase development rights from farmland owners in Western Washington (City of Seattle, 2012). The aim of the program is to halt the encroachment of urbanization on prime agricultural land in the region and, at the same time, densify existing urban areas. Developers in the city are allowed to partly exceed established limits of floor area, number of units, and building height restrictions mandated by the city zoning code as long as they provide the equivalent gain in purchased development rights from the farms. According to city estimates, the program, which commenced in 2013, will help to preserve more than 25,000 acres of forests and farmland (City of Seattle, 2012, p. 26).

To encourage the preservation of open space in urban and periurban areas while encouraging urban agriculture uses in rezoned urban lots, some cities have used the so-called planned unit development (PUD) mechanism. The PUD is a planning tool introduced in the US in the 1950s and consists of an agreement between a city administration and a developer, allowing the developer to disregard some zoning restrictions in turn of accepting to comply with alternative obligations, such as the provision of additional neighborhood amenities, required by the city. One historical precedent in which a PUD has been used to incorporate community gardens and farms in residential development is the Troy Gardens projects in Madison (Campbell & Salus, 2003, see also Chapter 7). The idea has since been institutionalized as an incentive for urban agriculture projects by the City of Minneapolis, where developers are being given some leeway as to the siting of buildings and the uses of land, as long as permanent gardens, greenhouses, or other onsite food production activities of a minimum of 60 square feet (5.6 square meters) per dwelling unit are integrated in the PUD scheme (City of Minneapolis, 2015, p. 4).

Land tenure constitutes a key concern for many gardeners in cities and, given the tension between built and open-space uses on expensive city land, is typically hard to ensure through legislation. A widely renowned pioneer example of a city program seeking to overcome this challenge and extensively promote urban agriculture uses on city-owned land is Seattle's P-Patch Community Gardening Program established in 1973. As part of the program, the Seattle P-Patch Trust has directly acquired the land of six sites to allow for their use as community gardens in perpetuity. An additional mechanism put in place by the city in its 2005 comprehensive plan is the requirement to maintain and create one dedicated community garden for every 2,500 households in urban center villages (Seattle Comprehensive Plan, Urban Village Appendix B, UV-A5). The encouragement of community gardens and other local food infrastructure elements citywide is also an integral part of the latest Draft Comprehensive Plan for Managing Growth 2015–2035 (Policy CW3.8) that the city is finalizing. Another pioneer legislative provision to formally integrate land tenure considerations for community gardens is the New York City's Garden Review process instituted in 2010 through the addition of a new chapter in the City Rules (Title 56: Department of Parks and Recreation, Section 6–05).

Fresh food retail

As cities are increasingly becoming aware of the socioeconomic and spatial disparities perpetuated by the current urban food system and the impact that asymmetries in access to fresh, nutritious, and affordable food have on public health, a new set of food-retail-oriented legislative provisions and programs has begun to take shape. These provisions stem from the novel understanding that unhealthy or insufficient nutrition is not merely a matter of individual choices, but a mix of material and nonmaterial factors that determine the urban food environment, and that the quality and diversity of physical infrastructure is an important part of these factors. Among the provisions that cities have advanced to date are incentives for chain supermarkets to locate in underserved communities (e.g., New York City, Baltimore), ordinances requiring corner stores in urban areas with limited access to fresh food to include perishable goods in their offerings (e.g., Minneapolis), the removal of zoning barriers for farmers markets (e.g., King County, Portland) and mobile food vendors (e.g., Boston, New York City, Philadelphia), and a limit on the localization of new fast food outlets in vulnerable areas (e.g., San Francisco, Los Angeles, Concord) and school districts (e.g., London Borough of Newham).

A well-known example of zoning and financial incentives to encourage the localization of supermarkets in areas identified as lacking adequate access to healthy and affordable food is the New York City's FRESH (Food Retail Expansion to Support Health) program. The program was launched after a joint study by the Department of City Planning (DCP), the New York City Economic Development Corporation (NYCEDC), and the Department of Health and Mental Hygiene (DOHMH), called *Going to Market: New York City's Neighborhood Grocery Store and Supermarket Shortage*, was released in 2008. The study was commissioned by the Mayor's Food Policy Task Force and revealed that about three million New Yorkers lived in neighborhoods where few or no supermarkets were available. As a result, DCP, in collaboration with NYCEDC, launched FRESH in the subsequent year.

Among the zoning incentives the program offers are additional development rights, reduction in required parking, and the development of larger stores in manufacturing districts. The financial incentives include real estate tax reductions, sales tax exemption, and mortgage recording tax deferral. Stores need to be at least 6,000 square feet (557 square meters), at least half of the floor area must be used for the sale of foods that are intended for home consumption and preparation, and at least 500 square feet (46 square meters) must be used for the sale of fresh produce (New York City Zoning Code, Section 63–01). Initially, the eligible areas comprised community districts in the boroughs of Brooklyn and Bronx. They were later expanded to include underserved communities in the boroughs of Queens and Manhattan (see Figure 5.3). In 2015, the City of Baltimore launched a similar program through a tax credit bill waiving 80% of the personal property taxes of supermarkets in or near neighborhoods lacking adequate access to fresh and affordable food, identified as "food deserts" (see Chapter 4), throughout the city for a period of 10 years.

The reintegration of farmers markets in the urban food retail infrastructure is another challenge that local administrations have started approaching in recent years. Sometimes, however, incentive programs alone are not sufficient and a change in the city's regulations is necessary to effectively implement the policy. This was the case in King County in the State of Washington, where an incentives program for the development of new farmers markets did not

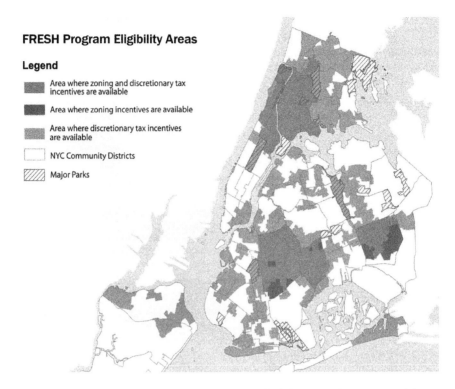

FRESH Program Eligibility Areas

Legend

■ Area where zoning and discretionary tax incentives are available

■ Area where zoning incentives are available

■ Area where discretionary tax incentives are available

☐ NYC Community Districts

▨ Major Parks

Figure 5.3 The New York City's FRESH Program eligibility areas for zoning and financial incentives (2015). Data based on the American Community Survey 5-Year estimate (2009–2013).

Courtesy: © The New York City Economic Development Corporation (NYCEDC).

lead to the expected outcomes because of stringent public health regulations. The functional category regulating open markets was requiring that all open markets had hot running water and bathrooms, thus automatically excluding the establishment of farmers markets. Two years after the regulations were amended, the number of farmers markets in the county increased by 50% (Born, 2009). In 2012, the City of Portland amended its zoning code to formally recognize farmers markets as an urban activity and provide specific indications as to their location, frequency, types of vendors, certification of organic produce, and use of parking space (City of Portland Zoning Code, Section 33.296). Except for zones with prevalent single-family and low-density multidwelling units, farmers markets were since allowed citywide.

Critical observers have often pointed out that the designation of some urban communities disproportionally affected by chronic diet-related diseases, like obesity and diabetes, and lacking access to healthy food sources are improperly labelled "food deserts." For the high density of unhealthy food destinations in such communities, these authors have suggested that they could be more usefully considered as "food swamps" (Fielding & Simon, 2011). One of the earliest uses of zoning regulations to hinder the clustering of large fast food outlets in certain urban areas is the San Francisco's Geary Boulevard Formula Retail Eating and Drinking Subdistrict introduced in 1987 (San Francisco Planning Code, Section 781.4). More recently, the City of Los Angeles also tried to use its land-use regulations to restrict the further concentration of fast food establishments in South Los Angeles, where 63% of the residents living there were overweight or obese. In 2008, the city passed a one-year ban on new fast food outlets, which, in 2010, became a permanent part of the planning guidelines for the 32-square-mile (83-square-kilometer) area. The outcomes of the ban have since been highly debated. Recent studies have suggested that the public health crisis has deepened (Chandler, 2015) and that, in general, the regulations might have been misplaced given the lower density of fast food outlets in the area compared to other urban areas (Maggio, 2009), which were however as much as 1,000 in 2008 (Worrel, 2012).

Healthy nutrition

Besides changing the geography of food retail, cities have also started reconsidering the way public institutions and individuals make choices about healthy food procurement beyond physical access. Institutional food procurement has come to be recognized as the strongest lever governments have to reshape the geography of urban food systems and play an active part in tackling its inefficiencies. While most local food procurement legislative provisions in the US have been done through state legislation (e.g., Illinois, Massachusetts, Alaska) or through policy change of single institutions like colleges and universities (e.g., the Real Food Challenge initiative), some local government administrations have also started adopting food purchasing standards and policies to allow institutions express preference of fresh, local, organic, humanely raised, or fairly traded produce.

New York City's Local Law 50 of 2011, which was part of the bundle of legislative provisions put forward after the release of the city's comprehensive food plan FoodWorks in 2010, required, for instance, the development of guidelines for food procurement of government agencies. The guidelines enabled city agencies to give preference to local produce and were tightly connected to New York State's General Municipal Law (Article 5-A Public Contracts), which granted municipalities with a 10% margin of the lowest responsible bidder's price to encourage them to give preference to New York State produce. In San Francisco, the Department of Public Health issued specific guidelines for the food procured for events, programs, or institutions of the department in 2006 to promote the purchase of healthy and environmentally sound foods. The guidelines include preferences for local produce, defined as sourced within about 150 miles (241 km) from San Francisco (SFDPH, 2011). Another example is that the Los Angeles Food Policy Council has managed to enlist the Los Angeles Unified School District in its Good Food Purchasing Pledge and encourage it to purchase food grown within a 200-mile radius from the city. In 2012, about 70% of produce in the district was procured from local sources (LAFPC, 2012). In Canada, the City of Toronto adopted a Local Food Procurement Policy in 2008, which was jointly implemented by the division of Children's Services and the Toronto Environment Office. In 2008–2009, the amount of food procured from local sources by the two institutions grew by 20% (Oates & Matthews, 2009).

Individual food purchasing practices have also been the subject of much policy attention over the past decade in North American cities. Among the incentives-oriented programs, the distribution of vouchers to increase the purchasing power of individuals relying on government subsidies for their food purchases (e.g., SNAP and WIC benefits in the US) and encourage them to shop at healthy food outlets has been at the fore of political, research, and public attention in recent times. For example, in 2005, the New York City's Department of Health and Mental Hygiene (DOHMH) launched a Health Bucks program, which offered participants in federal food subsidies programs a free $2 coupon for every $5 of government subsidies spent at the city's farmers markets. Similar initiatives have been pioneered also in Boston through the Bounty Bucks program, funding half of purchases under $20 or reimbursing $10 for larger purchases made through the electronic benefits transfer (EBT) system at farmers markets, and in Seattle through the Fresh Bucks program, providing residents with $10 extra for every $10 EBT purchase made at a city's farmers market or P-Patch market garden. In terms of restrictions and regulations, to ensure healthy nutrition some cities have adopted bans on the use of trans fats in foods sold within their jurisdiction and mandated calorie labelling in restaurant menus.

Solid and organic waste management

Food-related waste makes up a substantial part of the urban food system and, with the growing saliency of long-term municipal sustainability plans, it has reemerged as one of the important areas of direct intervention that cities can contribute to, both in terms of waste prevention and recycling. The New York City's 2030 sustainability plan PlaNYC released in 2007, for instance, set the goal of diverting 75% of municipal waste from landfill by 2030. Urban food waste currently accounts for about 1.2 million tons per year, and the diversion of organic waste was estimated to be able to reduce municipal waste management expenditure by $100 million per year. Local Law 77 of 2013 amended the city administrative code and mandated the implementation of a minimum two-year residential and schools curbside organic waste collection pilot project. The pilot commenced in 2013, involving about 30,000 households in the boroughs of Bronx, Brooklyn, and Staten Island and, in the subsequent year, 100,000 households in Manhattan. In 2014, the city enacted another law, Local Law 146, which sanctioned the assessment of available organic waste processing capacity to divert all commercial organic waste from landfills.

Back in 2009, the City of San Francisco mandated the separation of all recyclables and compostables by amending its Environment, Public Works, and Health Codes (City of San Francisco, Ordinance 100–09) and is now boasting a waste recycling rate of 80%. In 2015, the City of Vancouver in

Canada also mandated the separation of food scraps and launched the new legislation with the motto "Food isn't garbage." To avoid public health risks due to residential compositing operations, in 2007, the City of Chicago enacted a set of nuisance controls though a designated Composting Ordinance (#92607) and updated its municipal code (Chicago Municipal Code, Sections 7–28–710, 7–28–715). One often-neglected food-related waste is used cooking oil, which frequently causes clogs in urban sewage infrastructures (Marvin & Medd, 2010) and has proportionally increased with the rise of fast food outlets and deep-frying practices over the past several decades. Repairing such clogs can be very costly, and some cities, like New York, have started encouraging its collection and recycling into biofuels not only by enforcing restrictions on its disposal but also by introducing new laws requiring a minimum percentage of biodiesel blend in household heating systems (e.g., 3% in New York City), thus changing both restaurants' and household practices (Cohen & Ilieva, 2016).

Unlike organics, regulating the use of food packaging materials has turned out to not be an easy task for some local administrations so far. For instance, in 2014, New York City successfully banned the use of Styrofoam containers for take-home foods and beverages on the grounds of its significant environmental impact, yet, in 2015, the ban was overturned by the Supreme Court based on evidence of instances in which the material has been recycled. The City of San Francisco, however, has banned the material since 2006, as well as plastic bags since 2007 and, more recently, since 2015, plastic water bottles of size less than 21 ounces (620 milliliters). This goes to show that the leeway that each city has to enforce progressive food waste management laws and regulations is uniquely constrained by local institutions, politics, and culture, which can be more or less conducive to innovation or to the very idea that food packaging policies pertain to the public domain.

Concluding remarks

Food has long been absent from the public domain and from the remit of municipal governments. In industrialized nations, this has widely been perceived as a positive sign of economic and overall societal progress. Yet, having left the food system entirely to the private sector has been already revealed to be an unwise decision, and some of its outcomes are being dramatically felt in wealthy cities. Governments are coming to realize that being unaware of the workings of the urban food system and its impacts is not the same as being unaware of the workings of other sociotechnical systems we rely on, and that this is so at least for two reasons: first, we ingest the system's products and, second, few other urban systems affect human and environmental well-being so forcefully in tandem. Public health has always been a central concern of local governments and was one of the early drivers for the inception of the town and country planning movement in the nineteenth century. As the urban planning discipline is coming of age (Davoudi & Pendlebury, 2010) and the field of urban food planning is taking shape, a window of opportunity to reconcile food and the local state has started opening.

What emerged from this chapter is that a host of urban food policy novelties has started to take shape and that, in the aggregate, they make up an emerging interface between food and planning in the public domain. Some are isolated policy episodes focused on a single issue (e.g., food access), while others seek to create a coherent framework for urban food policy at the local level that can help governments connect traditionally compartmentalized policy areas (e.g., waste management, environmental protection, and parks and open space through urban agriculture) and position themselves as active decision-makers with respect to the food system. While most of the urban food system plans and strategies released to date are not legally binding and are vulnerable to changes in political leadership, they constitute potential seeds of transition. As we saw with the case of the Amsterdam Food Strategy, the landscape of urban food policies is very dynamic and even seemingly inconsequential precedents can resurrect to influence mainstream policy and planning processes.

But it is not just the bundle of urban food charters, policies, and strategies that has dramatically expanded. A growing cluster of laws, regulations, and incentives to facilitate and spur the development of local food system initiatives has also started taking root. Together, food charters, policies, strategies, laws, and new incentives programs point at the increasing degree of institutionalization and normalization of food in some, certainly not all, cities in the Global North. The replication and alignment of many of the food planning novelties and niche innovations (e.g., comprehensive food system strategies, zoning codes amendments to allow for ground and rooftop urban agriculture, fresh food retail stores incentives, local food procurement guidelines) has already commenced. This suggests that, while still in the making, the field of urban food planning is gradually transitioning from its initial stages of predevelopment and tentative experimentation to the take-off and acceleration phases of its evolutionary trajectory (Rotmans, Kemp, & van Asselt, 2001).

What is still missing to effectively stabilize urban food planning as a practice in the public domain are provisions that are both comprehensive in scope and have the force of law, and whose implementation is followed through by stable, well-staffed collectives of food system experts and practitioners. As the boundaries of the remit of local governments and urban planners are being redefined, this gap might become easier to address in the future. Ultimately, what our exploration of the realm of emerging urban food planning novelties revealed is that there are multiple opportunities to engage with urban food system change, yet, to be effective, policies, infrastructures, and social practices must change in tandem. Neither cities nor urban planners can steer this change alone, but they do have an important role to play. They are ideally positioned to connect our food system "tunnel" visions and mobilize both citizens and higher levels of governments to co-create otherwise unattainable societal transitions.

Questions for further consideration

- What does the concept of "food citizenship" stand for? Can you imagine a process in which government officials or urban food planners use food citizenship as a standard to evaluate the effectiveness of their policies, plans, and projects?
- What role do food charters play in the integration of food in urban policy and planning in the public domain? How are food charters different from food systems strategies and plans?
- How can food policies be integrated in comprehensive plans and sustainability strategies? With what advantages and what limitations?
- What roles can cities play in shaping food policy? Are they marginal players or can they be drivers for food system transitions? How so?
- Is there something missing from the food policy menu that cities have come up with so far? If so, what and how do you think they can fill the gap?

References

Baker, L. E. (2004). Tending cultural landscapes and food citizenship in Toronto's community gardens. *Geographical Review, 94*(3), 305–325.

Baltimore Office of Sustainability. (2009). *The Baltimore Sustainability Plan.* Baltimore, MD: Author.

Block, T., & Paredis, E. (2013). Urban development projects catalyst for sustainable transformations: The need for entrepreneurial political leadership. *Journal of Cleaner Production, 50*(1), 181–188.

Bohn, K., & Viljoen, A. (2010). The edible city: Envisioning the Continuous Productive Urban Landscape (CPUL). *Field Journal, 4*(1), 149–161.

Born, B. (2009). Food Access and Food Policy: Local Examples from Seattle. *Washington State Food and Nutrition Council 2009 Podcast Series.* Retrieved from http://pccnatural markets.com

Brand, L., van Schendelen, M., & Vermeulen, P. (2010). *Proeftuin Amsterdam: Naar een metropolitane voedselstrategie.* Amsterdam: Dienst Ruimtelijke Ordening (DRO).

Brannen, S. (2010). *FoodWorks: A Vision to Improve NYC's Food System.* New York, NY: The New York City Council.

Campbell, M. C. (2004). Building a common table: The role for planning in community food systems. *Journal of Planning Education and Research, 23*(4), 341–355.

Campbell, M. C., & Salus, D. A. (2003). Community and conservation land trusts as unlikely partners? The case of Troy Gardens, Madison, Wisconsin. *Land Use Policy, 20*(2), 169–180.

Chandler, A. (2015, March 24). Why the fast-food ban failed in South L.A. *The Atlantic.* Retrieved from http://www.theatlantic.com

The Chicago Food Policy Advisory Council, & The City of Chicago. (2009). *Food Systems Report.* Chicago, IL: The Chicago Community Trust.

Chiodelli, F. (2013). Planning and urban citizenship: Suggestions from the thoughts of Henri Lefebvre. *Planning Perspectives, 28*(3), 487–494.

City of Minneapolis. (2015). *Planned Unit Development Application.* Minneapolis, MN: City of Minneapolis, Department of Community Planning and Economic Development.

City of New York. (2011). *PlaNYC: A Greener, Greater New York.* New York, NY: Author.

City of San Francisco. (1997). *Food and Agriculture Strategy: Sustainability Plan*. San Francisco, CA: The City of San Francisco, Commission on the Environment.

City of Seattle. (2012). *Seattle Food Action Plan*. Seattle, WA: City of Seattle, Seattle Office of Sustainability and the Environment.

City of Toronto. (2009). Eco-Roof Incentive Program. Retrieved from http://www1.toronto.ca/

CMAP. (2010). *GO TO 2040: Comprehensive Regional Plan*. Chicago, IL: Chicago Metropolitan Agency for Planning.

Cohen, N., & Derryck, D. (2011). Corbin hill road farm share: A hybrid food value chain in practice. *Journal of Agriculture, Food Systems, and Community Development, 1*(4), 85–100.

Cohen, N., & Ilieva, R. T. (2016). Fooding the City: Everyday Food Practices and the Transition to Sustainability. In R. Roggema (Ed.), *Finding Space for Productive Cities: Proceedings of the 6th AESOP Conference on Sustainable Food Planning* (pp. 1–32). Newcastle upon Tyne: Cambridge Scholars Publishing.

Coplen, A. K., & Cuneo, M. (2015). Dissolved: Lessons learned from the portland multnomah food policy council. *Journal of Agriculture, Food Systems, and Community Development, 5*(2), 91–107.

Davoudi, S., & Pendlebury, J. (2010). Centenary paper: The evolution of planning as an academic discipline. *Town Planning Review, 81*(6), 613–646.

Dews, A., & Wu, S. (2013). *GreenWorks Philadelphia – 2013 Progress Report*. Philadelphia, PA: Mayor's Office of Sustainability.

Duchy of Cornwall & Restormel Borough Council. (2009). *Newquay Growth Area – Sustainability Strategy* (2nd ed.). Newquay, England: Duchy of Cornwall.

DVRPC. (2011). *Eating Here: Greater Philadephia's Food System Plan*. Philadelphia, PA: Delaware Valley Regional Planning Commission.

Everett, B. (2012). Food Seams: Planning Strategies for Urban Borders in New Orleans. In A. Viljoen & J. S. C. Wiskerke (Eds.), *Sustainable Food Planning: Evolving Theory and Practice* (pp. 467–478). Wageningen, the Netherlands: Wageningen Academic Publishers.

Fielding, J. E., & Simon, P. A. (2011). Food deserts or food swamps?: Comment on "fast food restaurants and food stores." *Archives of Internal Medicine, 171*(13), 1171–1172.

Fisher, A., & Roberts, S. (2011). *Community Food Security Coalition: Recommendations for Food Systems Policy in Seattle*. Community Food Security Coalition.

Friedmann, J. (2002). *The Prospect of Cities*. Minneapolis, MN-London: University of Minnesota Press.

Greenest City Action Team. (2012). *Vancouver 2020: A Bright Green Future*. An Action Plan for Becoming the World's Greenest City by 2020. Vancouver, BC: City of Vancouver.

Hajer, M. (2003). Policy without polity? Policy analysis and the institutional void. *Policy Sciences, 36*(2), 175–196.

Hardman, M., & Larkham, P. J. (2014). The rise of the "food charter": A mechanism to increase urban agriculture. *Land Use Policy, 39*, 400–402.

Harper, A., Alkon, A., Shattuck, A., Holt-Giménez, E., & Lambrick, F. (2009). *Food Policy Councils: Lessons Learned*. Development Report No. 21. Oakland, CA: Food First.

Hassanein, N. (2003). Practicing food democracy: A pragmatic politics of transformation. *Journal of Rural Studies, 19*(1), 77–86.

Hassanein, N. (2008). Locating food democracy: Theoretical and practical ingredients. *Journal of Hunger & Environmental Nutrition, 3*(2-3), 286–308.

Hodgson, K. (2012). *Planning for Food Access and Community-Based Food Systems: A National Scan and Evaluation of Local Comprehensive and Sustainability Plans*. Chicago, IL: American Planning Association.

Holston, J. (1998). Spaces of Insurgent Citizenship. In L. Sandercock (Ed.), *Making the Invisible Visible: A Multicultural Planning History* (pp. 37–56). Berkeley, CA: University of California Press.

Kunzmann, K. R. (2011, July 27). *Creative Planning for a Slow Society.* Keynote presentation at the Alta Scuola Politecnica, Module on "The dynamics of creativity for a territory in stand-by." Sestriere, Italy.

LAFPC. (2012). *Good Food Purchasing Guidelines for Food Service Institutions.* Los Angeles, CA: Los Angeles Food Policy Council.

Lang, T. (1998). Towards a Food Democracy. In S. Griffiths & J. Wallace (Eds.), *Consuming Passions: Food in the Age of Anxiety* (pp. 13–23). Manchester: Manchester University Press.

Lang, T., Barling, D., & Caraher, M. (2009). *Food Policy.* Oxford: Oxford University Press.

Lang, T., Dibb, S., & Reddy, S. (2011). *Looking Back, Looking Forward: Sustainability and UK Food Policy 2000–2011.* London: Sustainable Development Commission.

LDA (London Development Agency). (2006). *Healthy and Sustainable Food for London.* London: London Development Agency.

LDA (London Development Agency). (2007). *Healthy and Sustainable Food for London: The Mayor's Food Strategy Implementation Plan.* London: London Development Agency.

London Assembly. 2010. *Cultivating the Capital: Food Growing and the Planning System in London.* London: London Assembly.

London Development Agency. (2006). *Healthy and Sustainable Food for London: The Mayor's Food Strategy.* London: London Development Agency.

Lyson, T. A. (2004). *Civic Agriculture: Reconnecting Farm, Food, and Community.* Lebanon, NH: Tufts University Press.

Lyson, T. A. (2005). Civic agriculture and community problem solving. *Culture Agriculture, 27*(2), 92–98.

Maggio, E. (2009). South Los Angeles Ban on Fast-Food Chains Misses the Mark. Santa Monica, CA: RAND Corporation.

Marvin, S., & Medd, W. (2010). Clogged Cities: Sclerotic Infrastructure. In S. Graham (Ed.), *Disrupted Cities: When Infrastructure Fails* (pp. 85–96). Abingdon-New York: Routledge.

Mazza, L. (2009). Plan and constitution – Aristotle's Hippodamus: Towards an "ostensive" definition of spatial planning. *Town Planning Review, 80*(2), 113–141.

Mazza, L. (2012). Spatial planning rules and regulations: Between nomocratic and teleocratic perspectives. *Progress in Planning, 77*(2), 60–71.

Mazza, L. (2014). State, citizenship, and common good: British idealists' influence on social philosophy and planning culture. *City, Territory and Architecture, 1*(1), 6.

McClintock, N. (2014). Radical, reformist, and garden-variety neoliberal: Coming to terms with urban agriculture's contradictions. *Local Environment, 19*(2), 147–171.

Mendes, W. (2008). Implementing social and environmental policies in cities: The case of food policy in Vancouver, Canada. *International Journal of Urban and Regional Research, 32*(4), 942–967.

Miedema, J. M., & Pigott, K. (2007). *A Healthy Community Food System Plan for Waterloo Region.* Waterloo, ON: Region of Waterloo Public Health.

Miraftab, F. (2006). Feminist praxis, citizenship and informal politics: Reflections on South Africa's anti-eviction campaign. *International Feminist Journal of Politics, 8*(2), 194–218.

Morgan, K. (2010). Local and green, global and fair: The ethical foodscape and the politics of care. *Environment and Planning A, 42*(8), 1852–1867.

Oates, L., & Matthews, N. (2009). *Local Food Procurement Policy and Implementation Plan – Update.* Toronto, ON: City of Toronto.

Petrini, C. (2005). *Slow Food Nation.* New York, NY: Slow Food Editore.

Psarikidou, K., & Szerszynski, B. (2012). Growing the social: Alternative agrofood networks and social sustainability in the urban ethical foodscape. *Sustainability: Science, Practice, & Policy, 8*(1), 30–39.

Renting, H., Schermer, M., & Rossi, A. (2012). Building food democracy: Exploring civic food networks and newly emerging forms of food citizenship. *International Journal of Sociology of Agriculture and Food, 19*(3), 289–307.

Rhoads, A., & Guenin, H. (2010). *Portland Plan Background Report: Food Systems.* Portland, OR: City of Portland, Bureau of Planning and Sustainability.

Roberts, W. (2010). Food Policy Encounters of a Third Kind: How the Toronto Food Policy Council Socializes for Sustain-Ability. In A. Blay-Palmer (Ed.), *Imagining Sustainable Food Systems: Theory and Practice* (pp. 173–200). Surrey-Burligton: Ashgate Publishing.

Rotmans, J., Kemp, R., & van Asselt, M. (2001). More evolution than revolution: Transition management in public policy. *Foresight, 3*(1), 15–31.

Sandercock, L. (1998). *Making the Invisible Visible: A Multicultural Planning History.* Berkeley, CA: University of California Press.

SFDPH. (2011). *Healthy and Sustainable Food Policy for Food Served at SFDPH Events, Programs, & Institutions (GAD2).* San Francisco, CA: City and County of San Francisco, Department of Public Health.

Stringer, Scott M. (2009). *Food in the Public Interest.* New York, NY: Office of the Manhattan Borough President.

Sustain & ESD. (2007). *Newquay Growth Area – Food Strategy.* Newquay, England: Duchy of Cornwall.

Toronto Public Health. (2010). *Cultivating Food Connections: Toward a Healthy and Sustainable Food System for Toronto.* Toronto, ON: City of Toronto.

Vallianatos, M., Gottlieb, R., & Haase, M. A. (2004). Farm-to-school: Strategies for urban health, combating sprawl, and establishing a community food systems approach. *Journal of Planning Education and Research, 23*(4), 414–423.

Vermeulen, P. (2007). Renewal of urban–rural relationships: The key role of food [PowerPoint slides]. Retrieved from www.ccre.org/doc/amsterdam_food_strategy_vermeulen.ppt

Vermeulen, P. (2012). De kunst van het verbinden van grote en kleine voedselsystemen – ervaringen uit Amsterdam. In *Toekomst van de Stad: Essays* (pp. 69–76). The Hague: Raad voor de leefomgeving en infrastructuur.

Viljoen, A., & Bohn, K. (2005). Continuous productive urban landscapes: Urban agriculture as an essential infrastructure. *Urban Agriculture Magazine, 15*, 34–36.

Welsh, J., & MacRae, R. (1998). Food citizenship and community food security: Lessons from Toronto, Canada. *Canadian Journal of Development Studies/Revue Canadienne D'études Du Développement, 19*(4), 237–255.

Wiskerke, J. S. C. (2009). On places lost and places regained: Reflections on the alternative food geography and sustainable regional development. *International Planning Studies, 14*(4), 369–387.

Wiskerke, J. S. C., & van der Ploeg, J. D. (Eds.). (2004). *Seeds of Transition: Essays on Novelty Production, Niches and Regimes in Agriculture.* Assen: Royal Van Gorcum.

Worrel, G. (2012, January). Food groups: LA expands its menu of food policies and choices. *Planning, 78*(1), 23–26.

6   The untapped potential of new urban development projects

> We have never seen food's true potential, because it is too big to see. But viewed laterally it emerges as something with phenomenal power to transform not just landscapes, but political structures, public spaces, social relationships, and cities.
>
> – Carolyn Steel, *Hungry City*

Large-scale urban development projects offer a rare opportunity to test different pathways to transition the relationship between cities, their regional foodsheds, and the food system at large. New urban areas can be conceived so that a high quality of living, healthy nutrition, and environmental sustainability are concurrently ensured through the design of public and private spaces and the social practices they encourage. In the absence of established criteria for the planning and design of urban food environments, pilot agri–urban development projects can help orient planning professionals and local government officials in the possible approaches to this end and their strengths and limitations.

This chapter reviews original proposals to integrate food systems thinking in new urban transformation projects developed over the past decade. In particular, it sheds light on the different mechanisms through which urban agriculture land uses have entered into municipal plans and business practices. An overarching theme examined is the role that municipalities, citizens, nongovernmental organizations, and entrepreneurs play in changing urban transformation projects and developing new competencies in urban food planning. Depending on the main agent of change, four broad typologies of initiatives are examined: community-, business-, university-, and government-driven. Scales of intervention range from a 12-hectare (30-acre) neighborhood project in Wisconsin, Madison, in the US to an over 4,000-hectare (9,880-acre) new urban district in the Amsterdam metropolitan region in the Netherlands (Table 6.1).

In a nutshell, the cases uncover pioneer efforts to normalize urban food planning through policy and planning practice and invite us to critically reflect on the major challenges and opportunities that discrete agri–urban districts display as a means for transitioning cities and the food system to sustainability. The chapter concludes with a summary of some of the key concepts addressed and a list of critical questions for further discussion.

Table 6.1 Overview of the agri-urban development projects examined

Case	Driver	Total Area (ha)	Urban Farming (ha)	Housing
Troy Gardens	Community	12.5	8	30 co-housing units
Agriburbia	Business	18.6	15.4	11 dwelling units
Ekosofia	Business	45	25	450 housing units
Agromere	University	250	180	2,300 households
Almere Oosterwold	University/ Government	4,363	1,730	15,000 housing units
Newquay	Government	2,100	67	3,750 new homes

Community-driven

Radically new ideas are oftentimes born out of conflict and in the face of seemingly intractable problems. Tensions between real-estate development and urban agriculture projects have long been resolved one-sidedly, with either developers or gardeners taking over. In addition, community gardens have typically been spared to development in instances when more than one project was involved – the historic survival of over 100 community gardens in New York City in 1990s under Mayor Giuliani's administration is one case in point. Yet, the story of Troy Gardens – a community garden in Madison, Wisconsin, which was revamped and expanded alongside a residential development project – shows that land-use conflicts need not always be a zero-sum game and that a third way of urbanization is possible.

Troy Gardens

The event that spurred community mobilization and led to the Troy Gardens project goes back to 1995, when the State of Wisconsin decided to open a 15-acre (6-ha) area for development in the community of Troy Drive, near the Mendota Mental Health Center in the city of Madison. Though undeveloped, the area was not underutilized. The open space was an integral part of everyday social life and recreational activities in the community, and, for over 15 years, Troy Drive residents had been taking care of the "Sheboygan garden" – a four-acre community garden on the site (Lezberg, 1997). The prospect of losing the landscape and the garden altogether was thus unacceptable, and a group of community members committed to find an alternative strategy to the traditional real estate development of the area was established.

A first step in the process was the decision to involve a large community organization – the Northside Planning Council (NPC), representing residents of 17 of Madison's Northside neighborhoods and with competency and influence in the planning process. Instead of seeking to freeze development, the team started planning an alternative strategy for the area, challenging dominant assumptions of what could be achieved. As the collaboration made progress, several other influential nonprofit organizations were engaged, among which the Madison Area Community Land Trust (MACLT) and the Urban Open Space Foundation (UOSF). The broader working party led to the institution of the "Troy Gardens Coalition," later joined by the University of Wisconsin. The coalition produced a concept plan for integrated land use, combining housing with open space and a wide range of agricultural uses, adopted by the City of Madison in 1998. As a result, the State removed the parcel from the list of land available for development and gave the coalition a 16-year lease, according to which the land could be used for community gardens and open space.

The lease was subsequently extended to 50 years and a permission to buy the area was granted. This permission proved critical for the implementation of the Troy Gardens plan. Supported by the City of Madison with a low-interest loan for community development, the MACLT purchased the property and acquired the full title to the land three years later. This fostered the expansion of the existing community gardens, the development of 30 units of mixed-income housing, and a new five-acre community farm. The farm was the first urban farm in Madison and serves the larger urban community through a community supported agriculture (CSA) scheme, onsite pick-your-own services, and a year-round sprout and wholesale herb business. Owners of the farm are committed to sustainable agriculture practices – planting, weeding, mulching, and harvesting are done by hand and the farm produce is certified organic since 2001 (Community Ground Works, 2012).

Educational activities make up an important part of the Troy Gardens complex as well. Through the Madison Farm Works project, the farm offers support to citizens interested in developing gardening and farming skills, while an online course summarizes lessons learned from the unique urban development process. Course topics range from neighborhood-based planning to community engagement, conservation-based affordable housing, and mixed-income community development. In addition, a community center provides a shared space where citizens involved in the project can convene. For its many accomplishments, in 2007 Troy Gardens received the "Livable Communities Award" by the American National Association of Home Builders (NAHB) and the American Association of Retired Persons (AARP).

Thanks to the strength of its partners and subsequent municipal and state support, the Troy Gardens Coalition successfully brought about an alternative outcome of residential development in Madison. Urban agriculture uses were preserved and advanced, alongside housing, as a viable social and economic enterprise. Yet, the ability of single episodes of innovation like this one to transition everyday city planning practices is often limited, and much remains to be done to institutionalize public deliberation about food-sensitive urban development models into planning and regulatory processes.

Business-driven

While community-driven projects like Troy Gardens are to be celebrated and encouraged, the time and organizational effort they require make them an unlikely blueprint for the large-scale normalization of agri-urban development. If productive landscapes are to become an ordinary feature of new housing projects, cost-effective and easy-to-replicate models will have to be devised as well. The private domain, particularly architecture and planning firms and new specialized startups, can help accelerate research and development to this end. With few exceptions, however, for-profit enterprises have been slow to take on this challenge so far. This part of the chapter sheds light on two lesser-known business-driven initiatives – Agriburbia by the TSR Group (today Agriburbia LCC) in Denver, Colorado, and a permaculture-based model by Ekosofia (renamed ELIA in 2013) in Amsterdam in the Netherlands. These experiences show how seemingly overlapping goals for the integration of urban agriculture into planning can yield radically different urban food planning approaches.

Agriburbia

Low-density suburban development has been commonplace in the US since the mid-twentieth century, but, over the past 20 years, urban planning and public health scholars have started seriously questioning its social and environmental sustainability (e.g., Frumkin, 2002; Gillham, 2002). Encroachment of development on prime agricultural land and the consolidation of sedentary lifestyles have had detrimental effects on both human and ecological health. Rather than dismissing the idea of suburbanization altogether, some planners have begun researching new ways to cope with its limitations. Notably, proponents of the new urbanism movement and its recent offspring – the agricultural urbanism movement – have sought innovative ways to reconcile suburban growth with the creation of vibrant self-reliant urban communities, promoting walking and cycling over driving, and "terroir" over placeless foodscapes. One concrete example of this new turn in the urban planning field is Agriburbia.

Agriburbia is an alternative model for suburban development conceived by the TSR Group, Inc., an urban planning and design firm established in 1997 in Golden, Colorado, by environmental planners and farmers Matthew "Quint" and Jennifer Redmond. In 2004, they purchased a 2-acre (0.8-ha) plot in suburban Denver, Colorado, and used it as a test field for different design strategies to embed healthy living and sustainable agriculture principles in residential development on the urban fringe. The outcome of this experimentation was Agriburbia, "a commercially viable mechanism for individuals and businesses to become more self-sufficient and create truly sustainable communities" (TSR Group, 2010). Since its inception in 2006, the concept of Agriburbia has kept gaining popularity, and by 2012 the TSR Group were commissioned 14 Agriburbia projects – ranging from 5 to 10,000 acres (2 to 4,045 ha) – in the states of Colorado, Hawaii, Virginia, North Carolina, Wisconsin, California, Michigan, and Nebraska. Today, they have a history of over 50 commissioned and realized projects across the US and a recent 1,000-acre (405-ha) project in Shanghai, China. The firm has now set the ambitious goal of creating employment opportunities for 30 million farmers nationwide.

The evolution of Agriburbia into a thriving urban food planning niche owes much to the grit and determination of its proponents but also the evolving broader socioeconomic and cultural context that they resolved to transform. The years when Agriburbia was conceived, the first panel on community and regional food systems planning convened at the 2005 annual conference of the American Planning Association (APA) in San Francisco (Born, Glosser, Kaufman, Olinger, & Pothukuchi, 2005) and heralded the beginning of a new conversation between local food systems advocates and US urban planners. This was also the time when food started gaining saliency at the municipal level of government in Global North cities and, as we saw in the previous chapter, dozens of city mayors started devising sustainable food system strategies in concert with their city planning departments or newly appointed food policy task forces. Yet, what enabled the TSR planning team to make the most of this gradually opening window of opportunity was the right mix of design, management, and leadership skills they deployed to develop an agri–urban development model that is both technically and financially viable. At the heart of TSR's urban food planning philosophy is a clear set of sustainability principles used to guide the implementation of Agriburbia (see Table 6.2).

To ensure that local food procurement and self-sufficiency principles could be executed in practice, Agriburbia planners developed a holistic food system planning methodology and community food security indicators. The planning process is based on the use of geographic information systems (GIS) and a GIS–based metabolic agronomic model. Two of the main indicators the model

Table 6.2 The principles of the Agriburbia model and their implementation

Agriburbia principles	Implementation objectives
Sustainable agricultural production	No loss of agricultural value or revenue
Locally grown food	Production of a significant portion (30% to 50%) of dietary requirements grown within or in the immediate surrounding area of the community
Conserves and promotes natural resources	Appropriate and efficient use of natural resources to provide housing, transportation, recreation and fresh food through creative, harmonious land planning and landscape architecture for the community
Self-sufficiency	Provide a commercially viable opportunity for enhanced self-sufficiency for community residents, tenants, and guests
Sustainable energy practices	Integrate solar and geothermal technology to provide sustainable energy sources for the community
Integrated financing	Incorporate established entities (e.g., metropolitan districts) to finance both traditional infrastructure (streets, water, sewer) and environmentally friendly agricultural infrastructure (drip irrigation)

Source: TSR Group webpage.

uses are the community food fraction (CFF) and the metabolic distance (MD). The CFF calculates the ratio between the calories produced and the calories required in the geographic region where the urban development project takes place, whereas the MD indicates the radius within which food can be procured through nonindustrial means (Shumate, 2012; TSR Group, 2009). Using these data, while planning for the integration of agricultural uses in new urban development projects, allows the firm to evaluate different scenarios and select the one that best optimizes yield and revenue per area unit.

Much like the innovative planned development unit of Troy Gardens in Madison, Wisconsin, that the chapter started with and the Dutch projects of Agromere and Almere Oosterwold, which we will see later on, the planners of Agriburbia also stress the importance of going beyond a generic understanding of urban agriculture and articulate its integration in terms of different scales, places, socioeconomic arrangements, and purposes. Three distinct typologies of agricultural land uses are thus envisioned in any newly planned Agriburbia community – civic farming, steward farming, and private farming. Civic farming takes place on commonly owned parcels and farming practices are carried out by professional farmers with the aim to sell the produce either for export or a cooperative food buying club scheme. Unlike civic farms, steward farms are privately owned and are envisioned as an integral part of the residential lots; the main distribution channel for the produce grown at steward farms are cooperative food buying clubs. Private farms instead are small-scale operations that are either directly managed by the property owner or by a professional hired by the owner and the produce is for personal consumption or small-scale trade.

Ideally, the implementation of Agriburbia would generate two full-time farming jobs for every 3 acres (1.2 ha) of developed land. In fact, the vision for a sustainable urban food system that Redmond and his team espouse is a food system in which farmers have regained their authority and centrality in the supply chain, there are robust local food infrastructures, and micro-farming generates decent jobs in farming and supplementary income for local residents. The strong emphasis on the economic sustainability of new suburban communities and urban agriculture land uses is one of the distinguishing features of Agriburbia's philosophy when compared to other local food system initiatives. As the TSR Group website states, "Agriburbia is an economic and cultural model" (TSR Group, 2010). The creation of new jobs and local economic activity through stronger community food systems is suggested as the key to turning agricultural land uses competitive when compared to traditionally "highest and best" uses of land like profitable residential and commercial developments. As Redmond underscores: "Everyone thinks the most efficient, intense use for land is always density. . . . There are more intensive uses for urban land" (Blevins, 2009). One of the strategies that TSR has advanced to tap into this overlooked potential of productive urban landscapes is the construction of large temporary developer-owned farms, which are integrated within the construction site of master-planned communities and are gradually phased out as residential lots are developed. This way, the land is economically productive since the very beginning of construction and continues to create jobs and incomes well after the residential lots are sold through the permanent civic, steward, and private farms.

Besides the planning model itself, the flexible organizational structure of the TSR company and the wide range of services they have been able to offer alongside the design of Agriburbia projects have played an equally key role to its success and progressive stabilization. The establishment of a spin-off company specialized in the design and implementation of agricultural infrastructures – TSR Agristruction (2009), today Agriburbia Build LLC, is one organizational innovation that increased TSR's financial resilience in the early stages of its operation. By diversifying the range of services offered, the team could support the integration of small-scale intensive urban agriculture landscapes through the transformation of vacant or underutilized parcels into high-quality soils and urban gardens and by helping garden owners to connect with professional farmers and local and regional markets to sell their produce. This broader specialization helped the company stay resilient even when the economic downturn of 2008 heavily hit the building sector and investors shied away from suburban development schemes in which Agriburbia was about to be implemented, such as the Platte River Village in Colorado and the Farmstead community in North Carolina (Lerner, 2011).

In addition, rather than focusing on a single scale of intervention, Agriburbia planners have been successful in identifying a set of different scales at which the concept could be tested – from small-scale edible landscaping (1 acre or more) to mid-size urban farms (up to 20 acres [8 ha]) and large-scale agri-urban development subdivisions (over 20 acres). While TSR has hitherto been engaged mostly in the realization of small- to medium-scale projects, few large-scale commissions are in an advanced stage of development. One of them is a 46-acre (18.6-ha) project within a large-scale 780-acre (315.6-ha) mixed-use development in the City of Brighton, Colorado, sited 20 minutes from downtown Denver. The new community called Adams Crossing is in the process of implementation by WoodHawk Development and is expected to host about 10,000 residential units. The mixed-use portion designed by Agriburbia planners consists of about 38 acres (15.4 ha) of biointensive agriculture lots attached to 11 low-rise residential dwellings (Figure 6.1). The plan for the area translates in practice the company's vision of urban agriculture as an urban and ecological infrastructure. Each residence is equipped with a customizable "farm kit," which consists of an outdoors construction with a 2,048-square-feet (190-square-meters) base and a 512-square-feet (48 square meters) indoors greenhouse and can be used as a brewery, winery, home office, or extra living space (AgriNETx, 2015).

Part of the community-oriented buildings included in the plan are a Nursery Stock, from where homeowners can pick the seeds and plants for their new dwellings; a Hops Farm, which can be coupled with a Micro-Brewery; and an Innovation Center which will work as a de facto community food hub and include a truck market, a full Culinary Institute kitchen with classroom

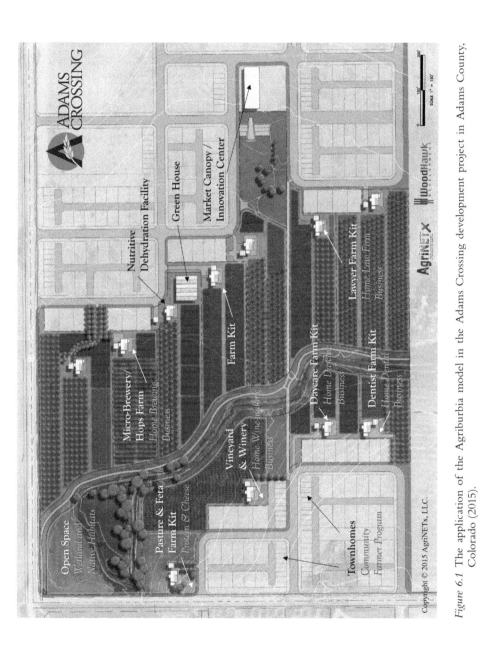

Figure 6.1 The application of the Agriburbia model in the Adams Crossing development project in Adams County, Colorado (2015).

Courtesy: © AgriNETx, LCC.

seating, walk-in refrigeration services, and a green roof with edible landscaping. All cultivation techniques used to grow food in the area will support the cultivation of produce that is entirely naturally grown. Instead of pesticides and herbicides, farmers will use tactics of smart placement and combination of plants to exploit their natural protective properties. Chemical fertilizers will be replaced by sustainable farming practices such as crop rotation and the use of local manure, compost, and companion plants encouraging each other's growth. Water will be preserved though drip irrigation and mulching techniques, while the use of fossil fuels will be limited by promoting hand planting and the use of biodiesel whenever possible. Among the annual crops that the community will grow are heirloom tomatoes, gourmet lettuce, beets, cucumbers, broccoli, and sweet potatoes.

In conclusion, Agriburbia offers a promising approach for translating the tenets of agricultural urbanism into a scalable and replicable model for agri-urban suburban development. Significant policy and regulatory barriers, however, still hinder the expansion and normalization of niche innovations as Agriburbia, thus local, state, and federal government officials have a key role to play in facilitating them. While new urban development projects cannot singlehandedly solve the structural causes of food system problems like poor access to healthy food options in low-income inner-city communities or the environmental impact of large-scale industrial farming operations, they do play an important role in challenging the dominant understanding that farming and urban development are two competing, irreconcilable goals and that the sustainability of one is inescapably jeopardized by the other.

Ekosofia / ELIA

By the time that low-density residential development was encroaching on vast portions of greenfields across North America over the past century, overseas, in the Netherlands, spatial planners were researching national strategies to cope with similar urbanization pressures. The famous Randstad-Green Heart principle of spatial organization (described in Chapter 2), one of the outcomes of these planning efforts, succeeded in containing development and became one of the symbols of Dutch spatial planning. Today, the Netherlands is one of the top three food exporters in the world and agricultural land continues to be highly valued. Yet, unmet housing demand is on the rise and the prospect of a third model of urbanization – able to reconcile housing with the preservation of open space – is being increasingly debated by Dutch planners. One budding entrepreneur-driven project in the Amsterdam metropolitan area, which seeks to address this conundrum, is Ekosofia (renamed to ELIA since 2013).

The project aims to provide a viable model for self-built ecological communities in modern city fringe areas and was ideated in 2005 by Amsterdam-based permaculturalist and designer Patrick van Uffelen. The name of the project, Ekosofia, stands for "wise place" – from the Greek words *oikos* (dwelling place) and *sophia* (wisdom). The project was inspired by principles of permaculture and biodynamic agriculture, which van Uffelen was experimenting with in a small-scale urban agriculture plot in the city. The Oxford Dictionary of English defines permaculture as "the development of agricultural ecosystems intended to be sustainable and self-sufficient," but permaculturalists like to think of permaculture as a cultural and ethical framework above all. The principles of permaculture-based development are to use and value diversity, produce no waste, make sure that each element performs multiple functions, use small and slow solutions, and value the marginal (Grubb, 2012).

In Ekosofia, van Uffelen tried to translate these permaculture principles into a workable and replicable model for urban development. The physical layout of the model represents a circular grid subdivided into four concentric functional zones: a central naturalistic area, an orchards area, a mixed-use area for housing and biodynamic agriculture, and an external area for leisure, public amenities (e.g., community spaces, restaurants, shops, schools, playgrounds, open-air theaters), and business activities (e.g., office buildings, artists' studios and workshops). The program was originally intended to guide the development of a pilot eco-community of between 50 and 150 residents, in which each household would have been responsible for the design of their residence and related permaculture area (Figure 6.2).

Figure 6.2 Model for the Ekosofia community envisioned by Patrick van Uffelen. Model view by Edward Smidt (2010).

Courtesy: © Patrick van Uffelen.

As the Ekosofia business plan was laid out, three different applications of the model were devised: small scale of around 0.10 ha (0.25 acres), intended for experimental gardens on vacant or derelict industrial land; mid-size of around 1 ha (2.5 acres), intended for urban farms with recreational activities on the urban fringe; and large scale, from 5 to over 5,000 ha (12 to over 12,000 acres), intended for the development of agri-urban neighborhoods and districts. In 2012, after a two-year-long participatory planning process, a plan for the large-scale application of Ekosofia was developed. The plan is for the development of a 40.5-ha (110-acre) area on the outskirts of Amsterdam and will comprise approximately 450 new dwellings. The goal of the group is to create a self-sufficient community where a variety of employment opportunities are available – from part-time to full-time occupations in landscape, housing, and business areas.

Besides monetary contribution, Ekosofia members must be willing to devote at least 7–14 hours per week to community activities and commit to sustainable food production and consumption practices. At present, there are about 50 participants in the project, collaborating through monthly workshops held in Amsterdam and seeking a proper site for the project realization. In Patrick van Uffelen's view, the best city planning environment for the implementation of Ekosofia is "one able to facilitate creativity and experimentation" (P. van Uffelen, personal communication, October 20, 2012). The neighboring municipality of Almere, which since 2013 embarked on a large-scale agri-urban development espousing a do-it-yourself-urbanism approach, has recently expressed interest in Ekosofia and may well provide the room for experimentation that the permaculturalist group is looking for.

Yet, Ekosofia is still a food planning niche in the making facing a number of technical and organizational challenges. Keeping the group committed, building credibility with local government, developing sound business plans, and reaching out to new members are some of the day-to-day tasks that the Ekosofia group has to effectively cope with. On the implementation end, the long-term self-sufficiency of the built community may also be challenging because, unlike Agriburbia's subdivisions we saw in the previous section, Ekosofia's urban agriculture land uses are not designed for intensive commercial gardening but for permaculture, and a sustained commitment to community activities and low-impact lifestyles by the future residents would be essential to the neighborhood operation. Additionally, if business interests are not there or suddenly change, the mixed-used self-sufficient community can easily turn into a residential-only suburb.

Notwithstanding their limitations, pilot agri-urban models like Ekosofia can be valuable experimental grounds for uncovering strengths and weaknesses of different approaches and helping food planners and decision-makers make more informed decisions on whether and how they can be replicated or scaled up.

University-driven

Almost concurrently with the Ekosofia experience, Almere – a Dutch town in the Amsterdam metropolitan area – was fostering the institutionalization of agri-urban development in a large-scale plan for its expansion. Almere is a "new town" inspired by the Garden City model of Ebenezer Howard (see Chapter 2) – an isolated case of its application in Dutch planning history – which was founded about 30 years ago. Despite the aspirations of the original plan, fast-paced residential development took over landscape planning and the design and regulation of the inner and periurban open spaces remained long unattended. In recent years, however, due to a growing demand for housing in the Amsterdam metropolitan area, the Dutch government decided to attribute to Almere a more strategic role in the region and double it in size and population (from 185,000 to 350,000 inhabitants). The local administration saw this as a key opportunity to rethink the city and address the unsolved gap between urban and landscape development.

Being surrounded by high-quality farmland and agricultural landscapes, the expansion of Almere started increasingly being seen – by researchers, civil society, and government – as a unique opportunity for agri-urban development experimentation. Two of the innovative proposals advanced are the Agromere research project, developed by Wageningen University scholars, and the subsequent "Almere Oosterwold" master plan, designed by the MVRDV architecture firm for the same area. Taken together, the projects illustrate how the coevolution of innovations in research, government, and spatial planning can bring about radically new approaches to urbanization and local food systems change.

Agromere

Agromere is a research project launched in 2005 by scholars from the Applied Plant Research Department of Wageningen University in response to the Dutch government's decision to expand Almere to the east. The new city district that will rise there will host up to 15,000 new dwellings and is part of a larger urban growth program for the creation of 60,000 new homes and 100,000 jobs in Almere over the next 30 years. The plan triggered the concern of scholars, since the development of the new district would lead to the urbanization of about 4,000 ha (9,880 acres) of prime agricultural land and displace about 50 farmers working in the area. The goal of the project was thus to propose an alternative urban development model that could effectively address this challenge. Hence the name of the project, "Agromere," implying that rural and urban are two not mutually exclusive pathways for the development of East Almere. The research team's interest in the topic was however not purely theoretical; they had the ambition to influence ongoing statutory planning processes and the final development strategy for the area.

Once the objective to present a viable agri-urban alternative for the new city district was set, the team had to decide how to approach its development. Scholars were in accord that the input for the design strategy should not come from academia alone but a much larger constituency of parties, either directly involved or affected by the project. After investing significant time and effort into the identification and engagement of potential partners, the group succeeded to build a large network of stakeholders including representatives of local farmers in the area, developers, the city councils of Almere and Zeewolde, the Province of Flevoland, environmental organizations, the board of small and medium-size businesses in Almere, and the Dutch Ministry of Agriculture.

To systematically solicit contributions and feedback from the participants in the network, the research team adopted two distinct approaches. The first drew on stakeholder management techniques documented in literature (Freeman, 1984), prescribing the practices of communicating, negotiating, contracting, managing relationships, and motivating, while the second one was a participatory framework specifically conceived for the project and comprising four action pillars: Describe, Explain, Explore, and Design (DEED).

The outcome of the collaboration was a shared urban development agenda advancing eight overarching Design Principles for Agromere (Table 6.3). The principles played a key role in clarifying and strengthening the expectations for the district as they were co-constructed by a wide group of contributors rather than just the group of Wageningen University experts. While this de facto community food planning blueprint recalls many of the principles of previously examined models – e.g., the attention to closed nutrient cycles of Ekosofia or the emphasis on financially viable local enterprises of Agriburbia – Agromere stands out for its framing of local food and sustainability. The sustainability of the community food system is defined neither by self-sufficiency nor through the assessment of local and regional foodsheds. The principle set by the stakeholders in the network was that half of the produce had to be exported for the global market and the remainder had to be distributed through local supermarkets (Jansma & Visser, 2011).

Table 6.3 The Agromere Design Principles

1	Nutrient cycles both within the farming systems and the urban systems have to be closed. Energy must be produced locally, resulting in a climate neutral or an energy-producing district.
2	For the calculation of the different farming systems, we assumed that 50% of the produced food and food products could be consumed in the district.
3	The district will not be an autarky for human food or animal feed.
4	Traditionally in any new district, a large part is reserved for public green areas and public services like schools, shopping malls, elderly care, etc. In the Agromere approach, the public area will be used for urban agriculture. Therefore, urban agriculture has to provide these facilities.
5	Housing and agriculture are integrated in this concept. Production and processing of food is therefore located directly next to the area's inhabitants, leading to the assumption that organic farming is more appropriate to Agromere.
6	Since the farms exchange material, the consequence of principle 6 is that all farming systems should be organic.
7	Farms are commercially healthy enterprises exploited by entrepreneurs.

Source: Jansma and Visser (2011).

The Agromere model sketches a compelling urban food planning agenda and offers a clear set of sustainability metrics for the design of local food system infrastructures. Unlike the case of Agriburbia, where localness of food procurement and self-sufficiency were key, for Agromere the leading parameters were average diet and daily food intake in the Netherlands. For researchers at Wageningen University, these data were useful in understanding the composition of demand and thereby identifying the most viable urban farming businesses for the new district. In particular, the analysis led to the development of four main urban farm typologies: farms with vegetables, fruits, chickens, and cereals (25 ha or 61.7 acres); greenhouses, with community services (6 ha, or 14.8 acres); arable farming with beef cattle (61 ha or 150.7 acres); and dairy and community services (88 ha, or 217.5 acres).

Importantly, the farms were designed to be not only viable but also competitive with respect to the mainstream agribusiness alternatives producing for the global market. For their multifunctionality and related extra income from services like energy production, elderly care, recreation, and education, the Agromere urban farm models were found to be more profitable than specialized ones of the same size. As Jan Eelco Jansma, a lead researcher in the project, explains:

> This new farm creates an enterprise not only in the farming part but also in the service part: not only selling the produce at a farmers market, but selling also services as teaching and education, connected to farming, . . . connected to tasteful and healthy food, to the season of the year. In cities, you don't have a lot of green spaces, fresh food is not always available, so this is an opportunity for farmers to extend their connections and, of course, to increase their incomes.
>
> (J. E. Jansma, personal communication, December 12, 2012)

What is more, the models were conceived considering farmers currently working in the area and how their farms could be possibly adapted to stay in business. Establishing urban agriculture as a viable land use in large-scale urban development, however, would require more than sound agronomic and economic studies. A cultural shift and the institutionalization of community food systems as part of everyday city planning is going to be as important. As we already saw with the case of the Amsterdam Food Strategy in Chapter 5, radical innovations alone are essential but not sufficient to change dominant urban planning regimes. Alignment of unconventional solutions with higher-order changes beyond the scope of innovation niches, such as political leadership and local government agendas, need to take place as well.

While in the case of Amsterdam an electoral shift stifled rather than accelerated the formation of innovation niches, Agromere managed to affect mainstream planning precisely because of the change in administration. Only a year after the project began, in 2006, a new city board was appointed. The new alderman for planning and urban development, Adri Duivesteijn, started off his mandate with the ambition to turn Almere into a progressive environment for urban planning. Consistently with his vision for urban transformation fostering sustainability, creativity, and direct citizen participation, Duivesteijn encouraged the development of the Almere Principles (Table 6.4). The Agromere model, which researchers presented to the administration, greatly resonated with the new municipal agenda and caught the attention of Duivesteijn.

Besides for its innovative design principles, Agromere managed to influence the Almere 2030 long-term planning strategy for several pragmatic reasons as well. In illustrating the rationale of the project, scholars underlined that integrating productive landscapes in the city's green spaces can result in lower management costs (Jansma & Visser, 2011), alleviating the burden of city budget for greenery maintenance. Transition theories scholars contend that if novel ideas are perceived as advantageous by the regime, second-order novelties are produced and a breakthrough in the trajectory of a sociotechnical transition takes place. Agromere succeeded in influencing the long-term development vision for the city and the master plan for the new agri-urban district Almere Oosterwold and prompted the establishment of the Development

Table 6.4 The Almere Principles for the growth and development of the city by 2030

The Almere Principles	Description
Cultivate diversity	To enrich the city, we acknowledge diversity as a defining characteristic of robust ecological, social, and economic systems. By appraising and stimulating diversity in all areas, we can ensure Almere will continue to grow and thrive as a city rich in variety.
Connect place and context	To connect the city, we will strengthen and enhance its identity. Based on its own strength and on mutual benefit, the city will maintain active relationships with its surrounding communities at large.
Combine city and nature	To give meaning to the city, we will consciously aim to bring about unique and lasting combinations of the urban and natural fabric and raise awareness of human interconnectedness with nature.
Anticipate change	To honor the evolution of the city, we will incorporate generous flexibility and adaptability in our plans and programs, in order to facilitate unpredictable opportunities for future generations.
Continue innovation	To advance the city, we will encourage improved processes, technologies, and infrastructures and we will support experimentation and the exchange of knowledge.
Design healthy systems	We will utilize "cradle to cradle" solutions, recognizing the interdependence, at all scales, of ecological, social, and economic health.
Empower people to make the city	Acknowledging citizens to be the driving force in creating, keeping, and sustaining the city, we facilitate them in pursuing their unique potential.

Source: RRAAM (2012).

Centre for Urban Agriculture – a new organizational space for urban agriculture innovations.

Thus, once a window of opportunity for innovation opens, the challenge is to build a robust framework for concerned action. A central dilemma for government now is thus how to maintain the energy of bottom-up efforts throughout the process, while providing the necessary guidance and stability to successfully implement the established urban development plan. What code of conduct needs to be in place so that the breadth and diversity of participation do not stifle progress, and what role conventional policy tools and plans can play in the process, were some of the key questions that many of the Agromere participants raised. The overall planning strategy pursued by the municipality of Almere and the ways that urban agriculture was integrated into the final Almere Oosterwold plan can provide some useful insights to this end.

From Agromere to Almere Oosterwold

Even though the Agromere research project ended in 2011, the concept continued to evolve as part of the formal planning process, and the scholars who initiated it took part in the development of the comprehensive plan Structuur Visie Almere 2.0 and the Almere Oosterwold plan. In the final version of the latter, almost half of the area (46%) was set aside for urban farming and the most frequent development plot typology comprised 61% of agricultural land uses. Productive landscapes were thus granted a principal rather than accessory role in the physical layout of the new urban district. Most importantly, Agromere had succeeded in changing not only the outcome of urban planning and design, but also the expectations of government for the role of urban farming in Almere. Ivonne de Nood, landscape architect and government official responsible for the Oosterwold plan in the municipality of Almere, explains some of the reasons for this change:

> We started from the question how we can grow not only by producing dwellings, but we wanted to do it really sustainable. So the question was: What is sustainable development for our city? . . . Urban farming is one of the initiatives born because we want a rural area, a rural development with less dwellings, we therefore made a strategy in which green developments and developments of urban agriculture combine with the development of dwellings and infrastructures.
>
> (I. de Nood, personal communication, November 25, 2012)

Besides the large portion dedicated to agriculture, another original feature of the Oosterwold plan is the diversity of urban farming activities envisioned. The implementation guidelines of the plan challenge the generic definition of "urban agriculture" and break it down in four distinct typologies of land uses: kitchen garden, allotment, urban farming, and agribusiness. The result is a hybrid farming space where micro- and large-scale operations coexist.

However, the fate of the farmers currently working in the area remains uncertain. Whether traditional businesses and farming in an entirely different fashion and for a global market can become part of the future economic activities of the area is one of the tough questions local administrators are currently faced with. Interviews with local farmers done by local government officials – a precedent in municipal planning practice – revealed that not all of them exclude the possibility to remain and maintain viable businesses. Around a quarter of them are willing to partner with the city, another quarter are not interested in changing their current practices, and the remaining half prefer to wait and see how the project develops and then decide whether to leave or join the project.

What makes the Almere Oosterwold plan a compelling urban food planning example, however, is not just the attentive integration of agriculture in urban development, but the way implementation is conceived. A major ambition of the local administration was to use the unprecedented opportunity for urban expansion, set by national planning policies, to transition Almere from the top-down planned "new town" in the 1970s, a "premeditated city" as local planners refer to it, to a "participatory city" built though bottom-up entrepreneurship and extensive civic participation. In his seminal work on planning and creativity, urban planning scholar Klaus R. Kunzmann (2011) suggests that, to allow original solutions to emerge, local governments need to overcome three key obstacles: established overregulation, gridlocked decision-making processes, and a lack of risk-taking bureaucrats. The ecosystem of rules that Almere's government set to guide planning and development throughout the subsequent 20 years – i.e., the Almere Principles, the structural vision for Almere 2.0, and the Almere Oosterwold district plan – were purposefully conceived to challenge institutional barriers to creativity and innovation.

Since the early stages of the planning process in 2007, Almere planners committed to two radical departures from conventional Dutch planning practice: the plan had to enable people to literally "make the city" and the final outcome had to emerge from the development process itself, not be fixed by a blueprint. Organic development – whereby dominant agents for urban transformation are prospective residents and time – was chosen as the overarching design framework for the Almere Oosterwold district. These tenets were later formalized in the Almere Principles released in 2008 and the Structural Vision for Almere 2.0 (Figure 6.3) conceived by the municipality of Almere and MVRDV, a globally renowned Dutch architecture office. The MVRDV plan envisioned a "do-it-yourself-urbanism" (DIYU) implementation approach, which greatly resonated with the local administration's ambition for a non-linear, bottom-up, organic development. But this meant also that planners would have to be prepared to aid the urbanization process without imposing its outcome:

> As government we will do only what's necessary. For example, the local infrastructures, we are not going to do them, but we can facilitate people

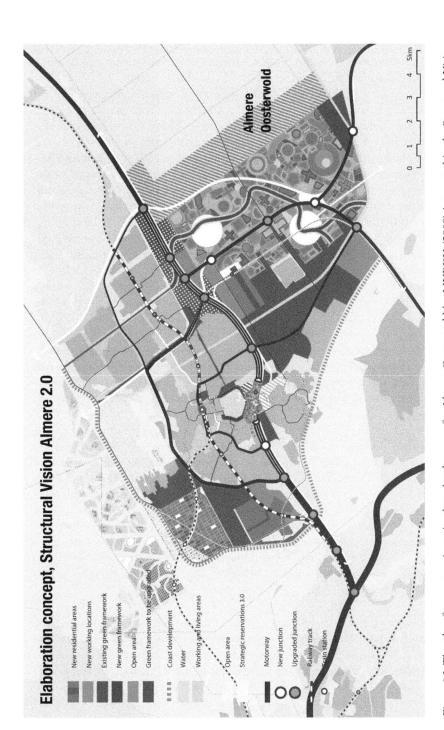

Figure 6.3 The plan for an organic agri-urban development for Almere Oosterwold by MVRDV (2009) integrated in the Structural Vision Almere 2.0 2030, Municipality of Almere.

Courtesy: © MVRDV.

to create them themselves. All the local infrastructures will be done through the initiative of citizens. . . . We make people responsible for their own part: you can build your own dwelling, but you have to make your own roads, you have to make the public green, you have to do some water-storage and the renewable energy facilities as well.

(I. de Nood, personal communication, November 25, 2012)

To provide a safe space for creativity and experimentation, however, planners felt that a shared rulebook for prospective residents and entrepreneurs in the area had to be in place. Thus, in collaboration with MVRDV, the municipality developed two levels of rules, one at the urban scale and a second at the scale of individual plots, to inspire and steer self-initiative, experimentation, and improvisation. Unlike common master-planning approaches, the spatial layout of the district will be shaped through plot typologies without fixing any locations in advance. Four typologies of agri-urban plots were defined: a standard plot to be developed on 60% of the total area, an agriculture plot (20% of the area), a core plot (5% of the area), and a landscape plot (15% of the area). Established proportions for the different land covers will ensure the distinct character of each plot. The standard plot typology, for instance, comprises 61% agriculture, 18% built, 13% landscape, 6% infrastructure, and 2% water land covers. Besides the general ratios of land uses for the area and the individual plots, no other limitations to the shape or size of the plots will be imposed. The size of the single plot will depend on the number of people that manage to pool resources together and cooperate, with the highest extension being determined by the overall percentage designated to each typology.

Two exceptional factors facilitated the advancement of this innovative agriculture-centered urbanization concept: land ownership and enlightened political leadership. The municipality of Almere owns the entire area earmarked for development, enjoying thereby a great leeway on decisions about its transformation. If this were not the case, restrictions from private real estate or higher-tier government policies would have easily hindered any attempt for deviation from established practice. The alderman for Spatial Planning and Housing in Almere – Adri Duivesteijn, strongly advocated for the ideas of organic planning and agri-urban development. The DIYU-based master plan for Oosterwold, proposed by MVRDV, thus ideally matched his vision for contemporary cities and their role in human life:

Modern cities are less and less a genuine product of their inhabitants, who seem to have become a mere derivative in a larger game. . . . The key question is therefore how, in the maelstrom of interests inevitably and inextricably linked with the city, to place the focus back to the people themselves. Can the city (again) be a place where people genuinely get the scope to give substance to their ideas, desires and fantasies?

(Duivesteijn, 2012)

Duivesteijn's sensitivity to the role of everyday people in shaping their own living environment, however, did not come from the political and design fads of the day. His understanding for what planning's purpose ought to be was deep-rooted in his personal experience and worldview. During the 1970s, he served as a community worker in Schilderswijk – a deprived city district in The Hague – and witnessed first-hand the jarring impacts of top-down urban renewal on communities there (Schilders, 2010). That experience left a lasting impression on him, and later on in his professional career he became determined to expand opportunities for civic engagement in city planning and enable people to shape directly decisions on urban design and development.

Even though "planned organic development" could sound as an oxymoron that no Dutch planner would give credence to, recent Almere history hints that this may not be the case. In fact, experimentation with bottom-up planning approaches has been taking place in different parts of the city since 2001. In Almere Buiten – one of the six centers of Almere, for example, 600 households were encouraged to design individually the layout of their house, while, in 2006, Duivesteijn launched the project Building-your-own-home-in-Almere, making Almere even more conducive to DIYU practices. In Almere-Poort, three different private and public–private commissioning mechanisms are now being tested as part of the project. For Almere Oosterwold, MVRDV partnered with the International New Town Institute of Almere (INTI) and created a simulation game, "Play Oosterwold!" to involve future landowners in the plan and regularly run at the permanent INTI exhibition "Making Almere" in Almere.

There are several institutional and operative challenges to the implementation of the Oosterwold vision, however. One institutional challenge for promoters of the Almere Oosterwold plan is effective communication across government departments and buy-in of the idea of urban agriculture as a centerpiece of urban development. To put it in transition theory perspective, at this point, system innovation greatly depends on second-order learning and change of deep-seated cognitive frames of all social groups involved – from government and citizens to researchers, industries, and investors. Provided that neither the form nor the deadline for completion of the district are known, the area could have an unfinished appearance for a long time or even remain incomplete. Development might moreover concentrate in a single plot typology – standard, agricultural, core, or landscape – and sporadic urbanization could lead to misshapen residual spaces and discontinuous infrastructure.

The great amount of uncertainty that organic planning comes with can impact the real estate market and thereby the financial viability of the plan's implementation. Marit Geluk, office coordinator at INTI, underscores that, in the absence of a fixed zoning and functional aggregation of land, the character of the surroundings of each estate would be virtually impossible to predict and, as a result, the price of land would be very hard to determine. This is no small challenge for the owner of the land, the municipality of Almere, who will have to find alternative ways to define the right market price of the different plots and cope with an unstable environment.

Despite the open questions on the future of Almere Oosterwold, the strategy for the area offers a rare transitional space for experimentation and remains a unique example of food-sensitive urban design in Europe and internationally. As de Nood points out, one of the major accomplishments of the initiative thus far is to "have designed all green areas to be productive and combined with the residential development" (I. de Nood, personal communication, November 25, 2012). While critical commentators may still dismiss the integration of urban agriculture in planning practice as wishful thinking, the Almere Oosterwold plan is well poised to make a breakthrough in this endeavor.

Government-driven

Despite the unprecedented wave of urban and regional food system strategies devised over the past decade, municipal governments have been hesitant to include local food infrastructure in new urban development plans. With few exceptions, regulatory frameworks directing the development of new urban areas have mostly remained unaffected. The 2011 plan for the Newquay Growth Area in the Duchy of Cornwall in the UK is one such exception. The case is relevant not only because it shows how food system elements can be incorporated into conventional master plans, but also because of the insights it provides into the dynamics of the inception of urban food planning as a practice in the public realm. Introducing sustainable food systems thinking in planning for urban growth entails more than adding a new land use in the plan. The Newquay experience suggests that for the dominant planning regime to be changed, innovation across multiple domains needs to take place – transforming business, civil society, public policy, and ordinary citizen practices.

The Newquay Growth Area

The Newquay Growth Area extends for about 2,100 ha (5,190 acres) at the east end of Newquay, a small town on the western coast of the Cornwall county peninsula. The area has been planned for development since 1991, but it was not until the early 2000s that formal planning began. The Duchy of Cornwall, one of the principal landowners of the area, was asked to support the plan by developing part of the housing and facilities needed. In 2001, the boundaries of the area were officially fixed through the Restormel Local Plan and, in 2004, the area was included in the Cornwall Structure Plan and the Council's Newquay Action Framework. One of the original features of the planning process that followed was the Enquiry by Design approach deployed as a means for early public engagement in the development of the area. The idea was put forward by The Prince's Foundation for the Built Environment and consisted of engaging all potential stakeholders, among which local authority representatives, residents, developers, landowners, and voluntary groups, in the collaborative creation of a shared vision for the Newquay Growth Area master plan. The community vision became the basis for the development of the formal master plan, later commissioned to Leon Krier, a renowned urbanist and already author of a plan for a neighboring town.

The Newquay Growth Area plan went through a long phase of public consultation, after which, in 2011, it was approved by the Cornwall Council as the principle framework that would guide development over the next 50 years. The total built-up area will be around 1,100 ha (2,718 acres) and is expected to host 3,750 new homes and an equal amount of jobs. Over 65 ha (160 acres) will be set apart for community food spaces and infrastructure, including 43 ha (106.2 acres) of orchards and 24 ha (59.3 acres) of allotment gardens. The inclusion of productive landscapes in the plan was not accidental but resulted from the unconventional planning approach that government officials decided to pursue. Unlike other urban development projects, the physical plan for the Newquay Growth Area is only a small part of a much larger comprehensive sustainability plan, in which food is given equal weight as energy, water, and transportation. Sustainable food system objectives are consistently addressed across all sections of the plan and thoroughly articulated in a separate food systems strategy.

In common planning practice, one can hardly expect to see allotments among the basic amenities required for new neighborhoods. The Newquay Growth Area Building Code, however, not only features allotments but also underscores the environmental and social benefits from their integration in the urban environment:

> Allotments can form an important part of healthy neighbourhoods and will be encouraged in the Newquay Growth Area, reducing the need for food to be transported long distances by road. Furthermore, allotments can play an important role in the wider community: for example, educating school children about gardening and food production and playing a role in the provision of therapy for the disabled and mentally ill.
>
> (ADAM Architecture, 2009, p. 20)

The code moreover encourages environmentally sound food consumption practices, such as responsible purchasing, organic food procurement through farmers markets and basket schemes, and sustainable food growing – all prescriptions entirely absent from previous building and planning regulations.

Apart from the involvement of one of UK's most influential nongovernmental organizations in the domain of sustainable food, Sustain, Newquay's progressive food planning vision was also the result of the great political saliency food had gained in the UK over the previous decade. The wave of social movements advocating for radical food system change, such as the sustainable food movement and the Transition Towns movement, played an important role in changing urban discourses on urban sustainability nationwide. The introduction to Newquay Growth Area's Food Strategy reflects that

> the Duchy of Cornwall considers food to be an essential component of a sustainable lifestyle and therefore effort should be made during the planning process to ensure that facilities are provided within the new development to make sustainable lifestyle choices easier for the inhabitants of Newquay.
> (Duchy of Cornwall & Restormel Borough Council, 2009, p. 29)

Another factor that positively influenced local administration's perception of urban agriculture uses was that allotments were already popular in neighboring municipalities and, perhaps most important, the Duchy of Cornwall had already advanced their integration in other development plans on its properties. Thus, the coevolution of a rising societal and political relevance of place-based sustainable food strategies and their alignment with the expectations of the chief developer of the area, the Duchy of Cornwall, codetermined the innovative outcome of the planning process. In 2012, a planning application for the development of 54 ha (133 acres) of the plan was submitted, featuring about 800 new homes of which 30% is affordable housing, a live–work quarter comprising 40 units, a 1 ha (1.5 acres) community orchard, a 420-pupils primary school, and other educational, commercial and recreational facilities. A center for training and apprenticeships in traditional trades, the Estate Yard, will be a centerpiece in the educational and economic activities of the new community.

By all measures, the Newquay experience is a forerunner in the introduction of sustainable food planning in the public realm and urban planning culture. Nevertheless, unlike the previously examined cases of Troy Gardens, Agriburbia, and Ekosofia, local food systems do not have a structuring role in the organization of residential development, nor is agriculture intended to provide economic revenue for the subsistence of residents. Rather, the emphasis is on the integration of small-scale community- and privately-owned productive landscapes and the reshaping of urban-rural linkages through institutional food procurement and individual food choices and purchasing practices.

Concluding remarks

The pace of urbanization in developed economies may be nothing compared to their Global South counterparts, but their contribution to the unsustainability of the global food system has outpaced the developing world long ago. Plans for new urban development in wealthy cities therefore constitute important entry points to radically rethink their relationship with the regional and global foodsheds that sustain them. Chapter 6 looked into some of the pilot proposals testing this underexplored grounds for city action. The cases suggested that while tensions between community food activities and residential development are arguably unavoidable, their outcome is not inevitable. Most important, the integration of local food systems in the design of new suburban communities can be a financially viable land use able to compete with, or temporarily replace, residential uses. In addition, the Dutch experiences showed that for regime change to occur, disruptive designs alone might not be enough and their alignment with progressive political leadership is essential. As in the other domains where endeavors to reconnect food and cities by design take place, agri-urban development projects are faced with a number of challenges. How they can avoid becoming subtle mechanisms for more farmland consumption (Ladner, 2011), or ensure that the new community food systems would benefit more than a restricted urban elite, are two critical concerns that beg further investigation.

Questions for further consideration

- Why do you think the Troy Gardens community succeeded in preventing mainstream development from taking over? To what extent is their experience replicable? How so?
- Is the integration of productive landscapes enough to preserve and/or increase the value of agricultural land and make it competitive with residential land uses? If so, why or why not?
- Skeptic observers contend that models for agri-urban development may increase the pace of farmland consumption, thus jeopardizing it as a valid alternative to traditional residential development approaches. Do you agree and, if so, how do you think this could be avoided?
- Why were researchers successful in influencing the mainstream planning process in Almere? Which were some of the innovative features of the Agromere Oosterwold agri-urban development?
- How did the Newquay Growth Area plan address sustainable food system goals? Why was urban agriculture considered a valuable neighborhood amenity?

References

ADAM Architecture. (2009). *Newquay Growth Area – Building Code* (2nd ed.). Newquay, England: Duchy of Cornwall.

AgriNETx. (2015). *WoodHawk Adams Crossing – Plan Concept.* Golden, CO: TSR Group.

Blevins, J. (2009, October 24). "Agriburbia" sprouts on Colorado's front range. *The Denver Post.* Retrieved from www.denverpost.com

Born, B., Glosser, D., Kaufman, J., Olinger, M., & Pothukuchi, K. (2005). Food System Planning White Paper. *Prepared for the American Planning Association's Legislative & Policy Committee.*

Community Ground Works. (2012). *A Brief History of Troy.* Retrieved from www.community groundworks.com

Duchy of Cornwall & Restormel Borough Council. (2009). *Newquay Growth Area –* *Sustainability Strategy* (2nd ed.). Newquay, England: Duchy of Cornwall.

Duivesteijn, A. (2012). Steering the City. In INTI (Ed.), *Making Almere: Who Makes the City?* (pp. 27–28). Almere: Tripiti.

Freeman, R. E. (1984). *Strategic Management: A Stakeholder Approach.* Boston, MA: Pitman Publishing.

Frumkin, H. (2002). Urban sprawl and public health. *Public Health Reports, 117*(June), 201–217.

Gillham, O. (2002). *The Limitless City: A Primer on the Urban Sprawl Debate.* Washington, DC: Island Press.

Grubb, A. (2012). Permaculture as a Permanent Culture. In P. de Roosden, A. Grubb, H. Wiskerke, & L. Sheppard (Eds.), *Food for the City – A Future for The Metropolis* (pp. 90–95). Rotterdam: NAi Publishers.

Jansma, J. E., & Visser, A. J. (2011). Agromere: Integrating urban agriculture in the development of the city of Almere. *Urban Agriculture Magazine, 25,* 28–31.

Kunzmann, K. R. (2011, July 27). *Creative Planning for a Slow Society.* Keynote presentation at the Alta Scuola Politecnica, Module on "The dynamics of creativity for a territory in stand-by." Sestriere, Italy.

Ladner, P. (2011). *The Urban Food Revolution: Changing the Way We Feed Cities.* Gabriola Island, BC: New Society Publishers.

Lerner, J. (2011). Eat your subdivision. *Landscape Architecture Magazine, 101*(2), 78–87.

Lezberg, S. (1997). Grow your own: Gardening coalition seeks to preserve urban gardening land. *The Wisconsin Foodshed, 1*(2), 1–4.

MVRDV. (2009). *Draft Structural Vision Almere 2.0.* Almere, The Netherlands: Municipality of Almere.

Rijk-regioprogramma Amsterdam - Almere - Markermeer (RRAAM). (2012). *Almere 2.0 Werkmaatschappij Almere Oosterwold - Almere Oosterwold: Land-Goed voor Initiatieven.* Almere, The Netherlands: Municipality of Almere.

Schilders, P. (2010). *The Organic City: Method or Metaphor? The Meaning of "Organic" in Architecture and Urban Planning.* Almere: INTI.

Shumate, N. C. (2012). *Success on the Ground: Case Studies of Urban Agriculture in a North American Context* (Master thesis). Retrieved from UWSpace at University of Waterloo (https://uwsapce.uwaterloo.ca/handle/100012/6819).

TSR Group. (2009). *Building Infrastructure for the Next Generation of Farming: Agriburbia* [PDF document]. Retrieved from www.oneprize.org/semifinalists.html

TSR Group. (2010). About Agriburbia. *Agriburbia.* Retrieved December 10, 2012, from http://www.agriburbia.com/about.html

7 New governance arenas for food policy and planning

Without . . . institutions mandated to engage governments in multi-departmental collaboration and engage citizens in deliberative democracy, sustainability efforts won't get out of the starting gate.

– Wayne Roberts, *Food Policy Encounters of a Third Kind*

As cities are beginning to see food as an urban system and part of the solution to a wide range of complex urban problems – from hunger and poverty to climate resiliency, public health, and waste management – a demand for new institutional spaces that could support the development and implementation of comprehensive urban food system projects, policies, and strategies has begun to manifest. While urban networks for an alternative food system governance started forming more than two decades ago through the work of nongovernmental groups, which in North America led to the development of the first food policy councils in the 1980s–1990s, their exponential diffusion during the past 10 years has not had a parallel within government structures yet. This is greatly due to the lack of a formal mandate for urban food policy in the public domain, but also to the insufficient clarity about the kind of institutional arrangements that are best suited to integrate this novel area of competency in existing government structures.

One still largely unsolved question is where urban food planning can take place. Food system issues, like most sustainable development issues, are complex, span across multiple sectoral spheres of municipal competency, and therefore lack a single jurisdictional home (Mendes, 2008). Yet the creation of a distinct institutional space and a collective of forerunners with the mandate to pursue sustainable food system goals is an essential step toward the stabilization of informal food planning practices in cities. In the food system, cities are still largely perceived as marginal agents of change exerting negligible, if any, pressure on established rules of conduct (e.g., world trade, localization practices, quality and type of produce). However, through the creation of new alliances among disenfranchised and powerful groups in the food system, as well as different food sectors and levels of government, cities can begin to challenge the asymmetries of power causing many of the system's current inefficiencies.

This chapter begins to chart this emerging terrain of research and practice by highlighting some of the seeds of transition toward the legitimation and development of urban food governance and planning competencies. After a brief introduction to the notion of governance arenas and their role in socio-technical transitions, we will examine some of the main drivers for the inception of novel loci for food governance at the city level, the variety of their organizational structures, and the emerging food policy "entrepreneurs" who, in the absence of formally accredited urban food planners, have managed to creatively advance urban food planning practices and sustainable food system goals in communities, government departments, and professional and academic circles.

Governance arenas and transition management

Our post-industrial cities and the sociotechnical systems that sustain them – from housing to energy, water, parks, and transportation – can no longer be governed in a top-down centralized fashion as they used to be throughout much of the early days of town and country planning (see also Chapter 2). Planning and public policy scholars have persistently pointed out that the progressive devolution of powers from central governments to the private sector, coupled with the growing complexity of social organization and the rise of the "network society" (Castells, 2002), have made single-handed government approaches to system change outdated and ineffective. Governance, through the creation of multiactor networks of market, government, and civil society agents, rather than government, has been recognized as the only viable way to account for a growing societal complexity and tackle urban development challenges. The arenas of governance (Healey, 2002, 2006) are the institutional sites where multiactor deliberation takes place and new strategies for collective action are forged. In the urban planning domain in particular, such arenas can provide space for citizen groups to voice their concerns about a policy issue, urban plan, or project that affects them and may be created to justify government intervention in the private sector (Healey, 2012).

Transitions to sustainability are inherently complex, not only for the high degree of sociotechnical diversity and their contested politics, but because we have yet to pin down both the problem and its potential solutions (Bulkeley, Castàn Broto, Hodson, & Marvin, 2011). The food system – which is a system of systems (e.g., agriculture, processing, distribution, consumption, and waste management) – is one particularly intractable domain when it comes to planning and sustainability transitions. As Hinrichs (2010, p. 17) points out, it is impossible to define once and for all what a sustainable food system entails; what matters is that we resolve to the recurrent and critical revision of our working definitions. Though food is gaining political saliency at the local scale, municipalities are still hesitant to provide a stable institutional space for such collective reflection and action. There is, however, an evolving eco-system of grassroots-driven arenas for an integrated urban food governance

(Wiskerke, 2009), which try to bring together representatives from government, market, and civil society institutions, and have so far been instrumental to the development of urban food policies, strategies, and projects.

While we are just beginning to map newly emerging arenas for urban food governance, gaining a better understanding of the extent they can be effective outposts for steering food systems transitions is key. Theories of sociotechnical transition, and the conceptual framework of transition management (Frantzeskaki, Loorbach, & Meadowcroft, 2012; Loorbach, 2010; Loorbach & Rotmans, 2006; Rotmans, Kemp, & van Asselt, 2001), can provide useful insights to this end. The transition management framework was developed about 15 years ago by Dutch transition scholars and offers a new governance approach to sustainable development. In a nutshell, transition management is about creating robust governance networks of forerunners who, through participatory and reflexive planning practices, work to collectively imagine transition pathways and long-term objectives and pool the steering capabilities necessary to incrementally transition a given sociotechnical system toward such objectives. The model draws on complexity theory and, in part, on existing transition frameworks like the multilevel perspective and strategic niche management (see Chapter 1).

The establishment of a "transition arena" represents the first of four steps in a transition management cycle (Loorbach, 2010), and it is instrumental to the development of coalitions, transition agendas, and targeted niche experiments and to the recursive monitoring and evaluation of transition management practices and their outcomes. A transition arena consists of small but open network of frontrunners and creative people, not necessarily experts, with an influential vision on the transition process. The purpose of a transition arena is to create a novel space for niche and regime actors to come together (Frantzeskaki et al., 2012) and engage in collaborative problem-setting and problem-solving practices.

Unlike traditional policy arenas, which tend to be sectoral, short-term (5–10 years), aimed at incremental improvements, and with a linear approach to knowledge development, transition arenas are multidomain, long-term oriented (25–50 years), aimed at system innovation, and engaged with learning-by-doing and doing-by-learning practices (van der Brugge, Rotmans, & Loorbach, 2005). The overall transition management cycle relies on the skillful performance of four sets of management practices: *strategic* (long-term and focused on a wholesale system change), *tactical* (medium-term and focused on institutional/ regime change in a subsystem), *operational* (short-term and focused on tangible change though projects), and *reflexive* (assessing both the transition management process and its impacts) practices (Loorbach, 2010).

Although the extent to which transition management tactics can be applied out of the Netherlands is yet to be seen, many of their tenets are reflected in the work and organizational structures of emerging networks for urban food governance. Acquiring a better understanding of what these groups do, what value they add to traditional food policy arenas, typically segmented in agriculture and food safety and nutrition, and what the main limitations and challenges they face are will be increasingly important as cities are developing an interest in food system transitions. Drawing on seminal investigations in the field and on theories of sociotechnical transition, the next section explores some of these emerging arenas for urban food governance and planning.

Food policy councils

According to Toronto-based urban food policy pioneer Wayne Roberts (2014), food policy councils are "likely the fastest-growing municipal government institution in the world." In fact, in North America their number has increased from just a handful in the late 1990s (Pothukuchi & Kaufman, 1999) to over 280 in 2015 (Figure 7.1, Center for a Livable Future, 2015). Most of them are still overwhelmingly concentrated in the US and Canada, but some are beginning to form in Western Europe (e.g., Bristol, Rotterdam, Amsterdam [in the making]) and Australia (Schiff, 2007, 2008) as well. Some of the oldest, best documented, and most celebrated food policy councils to date are the Knoxville/Knox County Food Policy Council (1982), the Toronto Food Policy Council (1991), the City of Hartford Advisory Commission on Food Policy (1991), the Connecticut Food Policy Council (1997), and the Vancouver Food Policy Council (2003). Food policy councils exist at the state, provincial/ county, and city level of government and can be housed in or outside government institutions, as well as in between government and civil society organizational structures.

Despite the increasing diffusion of local organizations regarded as food policy councils, there is no single definition of what a food policy council is or should be. Broadly viewed, a food policy council is a social innovation that fosters the creation of small yet diverse groups of committed food system experts, citizens, and government officials, part of both niche (e.g., community food initiatives, urban agriculture projects, CSAs) and regime (e.g., agribusiness, food retail, waste management) domains of the urban food system, with the aim to assess the current state of the system and develop recommendations on how to collaboratively tackle its complex issues. Food policy councils are also key to the inclusion of marginalized urban and rural populations whose problems and concerns would otherwise remain unacknowledged by mainstream policy and planning processes. System thinking, innovation, and out-of-the-box solutions developed through cross-sectoral and interdepartmental cooperation are at the heart of the food policy councils' mission-driven work and are the qualities that enable them to unmask the benefits of a more inclusive and environmentally sound local food system. An overview of the rationale, participants, and key activities of food policy councils is sketched in Figure 7.2.

Seen through the prism of transition management (Frantzeskaki et al., 2012; Loorbach, 2010; Loorbach & Rotmans, 2006), food policy councils can be regarded as governance arenas for food system transitions to sustainability. In fact, they are engaged in the advancement of a wide array of *strategic*

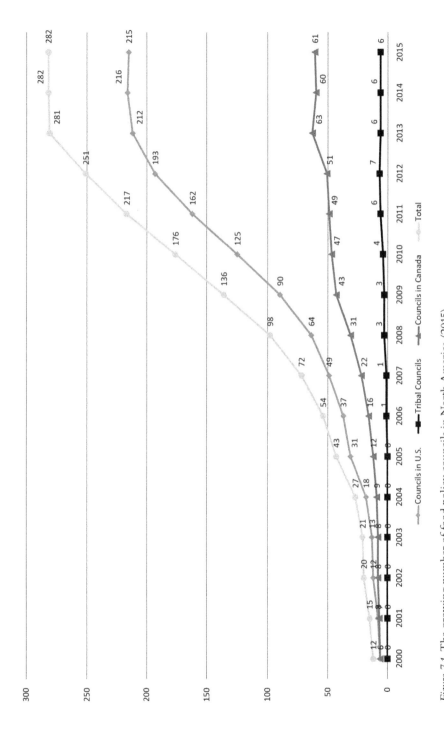

Figure 7.1 The growing number of food policy councils in North America (2015).

Courtesy: Center for a Livable Future, John Hopkins University.

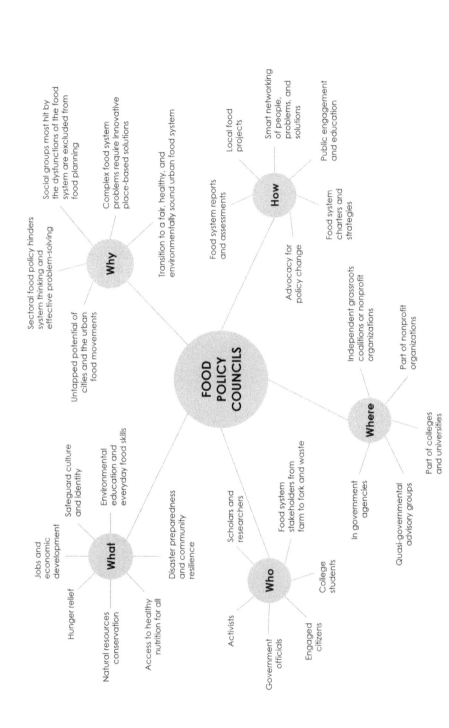

Figure 7.2 Sketch of the rationale and key characteristics of food policy councils.

Source: Own elaboration based on review of academic literature on the topic.

(e.g., problem framing of food system issues and visions for alternative food futures), *tactical* (e.g., developing cross-sectoral social networks and food system strategies and action plans), *operational* (e.g., supporting small-scale innovative food projects and community services), and *reflexive* (e.g., devising food system assessments and monitoring progress toward the implementation of food plans) practices, which ideally constitute what transition scholars call the "transition management cycle" (e.g., Loorbach, 2010). That is, the bundle of social practices that allows for long-term planning, innovative experimentation, and recursive adaptation of overarching visions and intervention strategies and brings about a wholesale societal transition.

Strategic practices

Rethinking the meaning and role of food in the city is what makes food policy councils a strategic site for the development and normalization of urban food planning. The rebranding of food as a solution rather than a problem (Roberts, 2014) constitutes a first step toward the advancement of food policy goals within the dominant urban policy regime. Showing how a food system perspective can enable existing city departments advance the work they already do, but better (Argenti, 2000, p. 3), is thus part of the preliminary research and visioning efforts that successful food policy council collectives commit to. This attitude is well encapsulated in the Toronto Food Policy Council's initiative for a primer on What Food Can Do for Toronto launched in view of the 2014 mayoral elections. Shifting the public perception of food activists from advocates to "problem-solvers" (Roberts, 2014) is one additional challenge that food policy councils seek to address though their work.

Food policy councils perform strategic practices also by making visible the connections between food issues and established "big" issues that mayors are already trying to cope with, like job creation, public health, hunger, air pollution, and waste management. The strong connection between food and public health is, for instance, what played a decisive role in the inception of the Toronto Food Policy Council (Blay-Palmer, 2009) in the Public Health Department of the City of Toronto, while the connection between food and social equity and a motion for a "just and sustainable" food system laid the groundwork for the inception of the Vancouver Food Policy Council and the normalization of food policy within Vancouver's Social Planning Department (Mendes, 2008).

Framing the role that city administrations can play in advancing sustainable food system goals is yet another practice of strategic relevance that food policy councils advance. One of the early Toronto local food policy action plans, The Growing Season (2001), devised by the Toronto Food Policy Council together with the Food and Hunger Action Committee (FHAC), for example, lays out four roles the city can play in transitioning the food system: a food security advocate, a coordinator of community-based food security initiatives, a supporter of food programs and projects, and an innovator in food security

(FHAC, 2002). In devising a food system assessment for the city of Bristol in the UK – "Who Feeds Bristol? Towards a Resilient Food Plan" – food systems planner Joy Carey (2011, p. 114) takes a similar approach and draws attention to the "positive food planning powers" that cities have to reshape the food system from growing and processing to distribution, consumption, and waste disposal infrastructures.

Challenging basic assumptions about what it means to plan for the urban food system is another set of strategic practices that typically experienced food policy councils engage with as well. In his field guide *Food for City Building*, Wayne Roberts (2014), who directed the Toronto Food Policy Council from 2000 to 2010, stresses the need to reframe modernist ideas of planning as a business of solving problems to planning as the more organic and complex practice of "issue management," as he puts it. This worldview is very much in line with the argument of transition management scholars that blueprints are of little use in the pursuit of complex sociotechnical transitions; rather than controlling, they suggest that steering and navigating are more useful concepts to guide purposeful action. In short, it is not about giving up planning and system change, but changing the way planning and system change are approached. Thus, food systems planning, which entails "the strategic integration of agriculture and food into the way that cities are designed, planned and managed" (Carey, 2011, p. 5), is not so much about designing new sectoral blueprints, but augmenting existing city-regional governance capacities and steering them in a way that they can contribute to urban and food system sustainability in tandem.

Tactical practices

The added value of food policy councils in spearheading urban food planning practices at the municipal level is often associated first and foremost with their distinct "tactical" capabilities, consisting in the ability to develop comprehensive food system strategies and action plans and set up robust cross-sectoral partnerships to ensure their implementation. Successful food policy councils can, in fact, play an important role in the development of a "strategic urban governance capacity," to use Patsy Healey's term (2002), to address complex food system issues in cities (Mendes, 2008). Such capacity, consisting both of legally binding provisions and participatory and inclusionary food systems planning and policymaking, is an essential precondition for the advancement of any endeavor toward an integrated model of urban food governance (Wiskerke, 2009). That is, a food governance bypassing, in innovative and place-based ways, traditional divisions between government, market, and civil society groups involved in food system change and breaching artificial public policy divisions due to departmental silos (e.g., public health, agriculture, economic development, retail, sanitation).

Besides leading the collaborative development of city and regional food system charters and plans – which can be viewed as transition agendas (Loorbach,

2010), food policy councils can also influence comprehensive urban and regional development plans. Three notable examples of this influence are the integration of local food system objectives in Toronto's comprehensive plan of 2002, facilitated by the Toronto Food Policy Council (Roberts, 2014; Wekerle, 2004), the integration of a local food section in Chicago's metropolitan sustainable development plan GO TO 2040, informed by the Chicago Food Policy Advisory Council (now Chicago Food Policy Action Council), and the adoption of a Planning Advice Note (PAN) in 2011 on how urban food growing can be integrated in new development projects, initiated by the Brighton and Hove Food Partnership in collaboration with Food Matters, lead nonprofit organization pioneering sustainable food projects in Brighton and Hove and across the UK. The integration of sustainable food system objectives in comprehensive city plans contribute to the development of a much-needed institutional framework, which budding food planners and grassroots innovators can refer to in legitimating their efforts and applying for public and private funding.

Social networking and the development of broad and deep collaborative networks – vital to the protection and maturing of niche experiments (Kemp, Rip, & Schot, 2001; Smith & Raven, 2012) – are a core tactical subset of practices that food policy councils do. In a recent report on Canadian food policy initiatives, Rod MacRae, the first chair of the Toronto Food Policy Council, and Kendal Donahue (2013, p. 26) stress the ability of food policy councils to "bring together people who don't normally spend time with each other" as the number one key for success of food policy councils. Roberts (2014), who succeeded MacRae in 2000, effectively synthesizes this idea in his definition of food policy councils as "bridge builders" involved in the business of "knitting, weaving, creating collaborative infrastructure, finding common ground, matchmaking, [and] setting up strange bedfellows."

The apt creation of new communities of practice around food, social equity, and green economy in the city enables food policy councils to see potential "win-win" solutions and connect seemingly distant problems. For instance, the development of new community food infrastructures, like community food hubs, can also be a strategy for repurposing old industrial buildings laying vacant and creating new jobs, alongside tackling food poverty; the creation of jobs for first-generation immigrants with experience in farming can also be a means to greening the city and catering to an unmet demand for ethnic foods. Oftentimes, these new connections are accompanied by changes in cities' existing policies and regulations, like amendments of zoning and building codes for urban agriculture uses or the introduction of new ones, like the adoption of new institutional procurement standards prioritizing sustainable food sources. As food systems planning scholar Branden Born (2012) underscores, food policy councils are strategically located to drive policy change, while positively influencing individual behavior.

The need for a coordinated approach to the management of large volumes of food transportation, catering, and waste, during the World Fair of 1982, while making sure that displaced inner-city residents have adequate access to food, was one of the triggers for the establishment of the very first municipal food policy council in Knoxville, Tennessee (Yeatman, 1994, p. 23). The realization that an interdepartmental municipal approach was the only way to effectively cope with hunger and community food access to safe and affordable food was similarly the driver for the institution of another pioneer food policy council in the US – the Hartford Advisory Commission on Food Policy in Hartford, Connecticut, in 1991. For its success in establishing a precedent-setting collaboration between multiple city departments – from education, through business development, to land use and transportation – on a single issue, the Commission's work has been regarded as one of the "best examples of food system planning to date" (Winne, 2004, p. 14).

Diverse and influential partnerships are indeed one of the essential ingredients of social innovation, which involves the collaborative development of "new ideas that meet unmet needs" (Mulgan, Tucker, Ali, & Sanders, 2008). The skillful knitting of partnerships in the urban food system also determines the very existence and stability of food policy councils as such. A seminal research on the role of partnerships in food policy councils in the US conducted by food system scholars at the Johns Hopkins Center for a Livable Future (Clayton, Frattaroli, Palmer, & Pollack, 2015) showed that, depending on the kind of alliances (e.g., including or not a food policy expert, a government official, a researcher), food policy councils can be more or less successful in developing and carrying out their policy agendas. According to this study, the nature of partnerships was found to have a key role in improving the visibility and legitimacy of food policy councils in the policy arena, helping them focus and prioritize their goals, as well as frame their work in a way that resonates with the needs of local administrations and food system stakeholders.

Among the partners and organizations that commonly sit on food policy councils are urban gardeners, regional farmers, city or county councilors or commissioners, policy experts, urban planners, just food activists, environmental organizations, anti-hunger organizations, grassroots coalitions for urban agriculture, representatives of national ministries of public health and agriculture, municipal departments of social services, university researchers and students, independent urban food retailers, mobile food vendors and corner store owners, restaurant associations, institutional caterers, chefs, artisanal food crafters, women's associations, and representatives of public schools and departments of education (Clancy, Hammer, & Lippoldt, 2008; Harper, Alkon, Shattuck, Holt-Giménez, & Lambrick, 2009). Yet, the creation of such wide-ranging and heterogeneous coalitions may not suffice or can even hinder the prospects of an inclusive and balanced collaboration. This may be due either to existing asymmetries of power between different sectors in the food system (e.g., small-scale farmers vs. corporate retail giants) or to barriers imposed by some of the organizations already in the partnership precluding the food policy council to access other partners in the community (Clayton et al., 2015, p. 10).

Operational practices

Food policy councils perform as de facto transition arenas also for the conducive role they play in the development of a great variety of food system novelties. Some of these are short-lived, but others evolve into successful niches providing alternative products and services to urban and rural communities. One example of urban food system novelty is The Stop Community Food Center in Toronto (e.g., Friedmann, 2007; Levkoe, 2011), which is a nonprofit organization uniquely blending emergency food, community food growing, and education and was awarded a C$100,000 grant through the Livegreen program of the City of Toronto. An example of institutional change that brought about the formation of a new niche for urban food growing – rooftop farming – is the integration of rooftop gardens in the municipal building code and greening incentives programs (Roberts, 2010). Though operating as a nongovernmental organization, the Oakland Food Policy Council also effectively affected regulations previously hindering the expansion of urban agriculture projects and, as a result of their "Right to Grow" initiative, urban farmers are now allowed to grow and sell their produce throughout the City of Oakland.

Another compelling example of how food policy councils can be conducive to urban agriculture initiatives is provided by the already-cited Brighton and Hove Food Partnership, which even though does not have "council" in its name has operated as a de facto food policy council in Brighton and Hove in the UK since 2005 (Stierand, 2012). Besides the local food strategy (*From Spade to Spoon*, released in 2003 and refreshed in 2009) which laid out a comprehensive framework for the promotion of local food in the city, the partnership has been able to provide financial support to community initiatives through a "Good food grants" scheme, facilitating the development of over 20 urban agriculture projects per year since 2006. Being able to attract substantial funding (£500,000) for a directly run citywide urban agriculture initiative called Harvest Brighton and Hove enabled them also to expand the conversion of vacant urban lots into gardens throughout the city and make gardening skills more ubiquitous.

Getting municipalities to comply with new standards of fair and sustainable food procurement is another important niche innovation that food policy councils help foster. This objective has been, for instance, an integral part of the work of the Chicago Food Policy Action Council (Good Food Purchasing Policy, passed in 2012 by the City) and the Los Angeles Food Policy Council, both independent advisory bodies to city administrations. The creation of certification companies that can hold institutional procurement practices to new quality standards (e.g., nutritional, environmental, labor) is another food system niche that food policy councils, through their networking capabilities, can help develop. This was the case of the Local Food Plus company launched in Toronto (Levkoe, 2011; Roberts, 2010) and funded through the Land Food People Foundation from 2005 through 2014. Hybridizing part of the urban food retail infrastructure through innovative startups like independently run mobile food carts businesses (e.g., Oakland Food Policy Council) or the revamping of existing neighborhood markets and corner stores (e.g., Los Angeles Food Policy Council) is also part of the operational practices that food policy councils engage with to transition the dominant food system regime.

Reflexive practices

A major hurdle to the integration of food system goals in established municipal practices and routines is the lack of data and basic knowledge about the food system and the way such practices already, albeit tacitly, affect it. Food policy councils can fill this gap by collecting and systematically analyzing ancillary data on the urban food system and the major trends, problems, emergent grassroots solutions, and opportunities for cities to take action. Most of these reports are the basis on which municipalities commission tactical policy tools to food policy councils, such as the elaboration of a food charter, an action plan, or a comprehensive food system strategy. The release of a number of seminal food system reports (e.g., *Food for Thought: A What We Heard Report*, 2000; *Planting the Seeds*, 2000) by the Food and Hunger Action Committee of the Toronto Food Policy Council led to the development of an action plan (*The Growing Season*) and the Toronto Food Charter in 2001. The implementation progress of the action plan was evaluated through an assessment report two years later (*Tending the Garden*, 2003). This ensemble of food system assessments and city-driven food policies fostered a new public understanding of why food matters and prepared the terrain for the development of the comprehensive Toronto food strategy *Growing Food Connections* in 2010, currently under review (City of Toronto, 2015).

While food policy councils play a vital role in helping cities see themselves through a food system lens and spur the development of new strategies for action, the other way around is also true. The Vancouver Food Policy Council for instance was established following the Food Action Plan prepared by a designated food policy task force of experts already involved in various food system related initiatives in the city. As in Toronto, a Food Charter was adopted only after the food policy council was in place. This was not the case for Bristol, where the adoption of a food charter by the municipality preceded the institution of the food policy council, which operates outside the municipal administration but had a leading role in the development of the Bristol Good Food Plan produced with the support of the City Council in 2013. No matter how food policies come into being, they fulfill strategic food system planning functions, and this systemic food system knowledge can help cities anticipate major threats or windows of opportunity for city-driven food system change. As Mark Winne (2004, p. 15), US pioneer of urban food policy and cofounder of the City of Hartford Food Policy Commission and the Connecticut Food Policy Council, puts it, thanks to the wide array of visioning, assessment, planning, and evaluation practices food policy councils have turned into "de facto food system planning agencies."

Challenges

Food policy councils are a budding novelty for urban food system governance, but like every niche innovation in its infancy, they are also fragile. As Wayne Roberts (2010, p. 175) warns, while all newborn food policy councils burn bright at first, later many burn out due to the lack of government support. In fact, this is often the source of other major challenges food policy councils struggle with, such as lack of adequate funding, staff, leadership, and partnership-wide commitment to the council's comprehensive agenda. Taken together, all these factors determine the strategic governance capacity that food policy councils, and local government authorities in general, have to advance food system change.

The organizational position (Dahlberg, 1994) of a food policy council – i.e., where a food policy council is sited vis-à-vis government institutions – plays an important role in its evolution and normalization in mainstream policy-making and budget distribution processes. Kenneth Dahlberg, who conducted one of the earliest studies of North American food policy councils, noted that both insider and outsider positions entail risks for the effectiveness and longevity of food policy councils and require thoughtful consideration. A position closer to government leaders and mayoral offices can enable a food policy council to gain access to information and resources vital to sustain and strategically orient its work; however, this support may quickly disappear due to electoral shifts and the appointment of new mayors no longer interested in food issues. Additionally, the objectives that a food policy council embedded in government tries to pursue may be politicized and refocused to a degree that no longer reflect the council's original vision and mission.

Conversely, an independent food policy council operating out of government institutions may enjoy a greater freedom in terms of agenda setting and project development, but without the support of government agencies can face major barriers to change of incumbent policies and institutional practices. Rebecca Schiff, who researched Australian and North American food policy councils, further stresses this point calling attention to the way food policy councils may be perceived by government if operating as a nongovernmental organization. If a food policy council works outside dominant political bureaucracies, Schiff (2007, p. 185) argues, it is easily "imagined as existing outside of politics and therefore may lack the power to influence these same institutions." That said, it would be misleading to assume that the credibility and political leverage of councils formed under the auspices of government institutions can be taken for granted. In an effort to update the seminal survey of US and Canadian food policy councils done by Dahlberg (1994), Clancy et al. (2008) examined eight government-sanctioned food policy councils and found that conveying the value of a food policy council and what it does is a key challenge even for those councils.

The trade-offs between a government and independent location of a food policy council confront us with a conundrum – a food policy council has to be close enough to government to be able to effectively affect incumbent policy tools and routines, while maintaining its independence, room for critical analysis, and diversity to spur innovation. Transition theorists call this phenomenon the "niche paradox" (Monaghan, 2009; Smith, 2006) – to influence the dominant sociotechnical regime a niche innovation needs to be somewhat compatible with the regime. Other scholars have termed this challenge the "paradox of embedded agency" (Battilana, Leca, & Boxenbaum, 2009) – social groups aiming at radical innovation but embedded in dominant institutions are part of the rules and structures they try to transform. In some cases, these niches can even end up reinforcing rather than reconfiguring the dominant regime (Schuitmaker, 2012). Yet evidence on the diverse organizational forms that food policy councils can assume suggests that this challenge may be not unsurmountable.

Several observers have noted that a "third" way of setting up a food policy council – so that it maintains strong connections both to decision-makers in government and to community members and other food system stakeholders – is possible (Clancy et al., 2008; Dahlberg, 1994; Harper et al., 2009; Schiff, 2008). These are commonly referred to as "hybrid" food policy councils. In their in-depth exploration of over 60 Canadian food policy initiatives, which include but are not limited to food policy councils, MacRae and Donahue (2013, pp. 9–10) provide a taxonomy of the different organizational arrangements blending government and civil society organizations emerged to date and point at two hybrid models in particular: with *direct links* to government (e.g., formally endorsed and being held accountable by government, having structural links to government bodies) and with *indirect links* to government (e.g., formally endorsed by government, but with weaker connections to government departments and resources such as funding and staff).

Food policy councils that fall into the first category are, for instance, the already-mentioned Toronto Food Policy Council, reporting to the City of Toronto Department of Public Health, and the Vancouver Food Policy Council, held accountable by the Social Planning Department. In the US, a hybrid of this kind is arguably the Philadelphia Food Policy Advisory Council part of the Mayor's Office of Sustainability, with ex-officio members from government departments, but with appointed members from nongovernmental organizations. An effective UK parallel to these models is the London Food Board, which was inspired by the Toronto Food Policy Council (Reynolds, 2009) and was created directly by the Mayor of London in 2004. The board is made of over 30 leading experts, directors, and entrepreneurs across London's food system – from health professionals to chefs, policy analysts, mainstream retailers, and urban food growers – and advises the mayor on food policy and planning issues. The group played a key role in the development of the London Food Strategy (2006) and Action and Implementation Plan (2007); it also contributed to the development of a comprehensive food procurement vision for the 2012 Olympic and Paralympic Games.

While MacRae and Donahue (2013) do not point at any specific examples of Canadian food policy councils of the second hybrid type, i.e., endorsed by government but with less direct links to its formal institutional structures and resources, likely American candidates in this category include The City of Hartford Advisory Commission on Food Policy, which was formally insti- tuted in 1991 to implement the recommendations of the Mayor's Task Force on Hunger, but is staffed through the Hartford Food System, a nonprofit orga- nization founded by food systems planning forerunner Mark Winne in 1978; the Los Angeles Food Policy Council, initiated by the then Los Angeles Mayor Villaraigosa in 2010, as part of the implementation of the "Good Food for All Agenda" regional food plan, housed at City Hall, but operating as an inde- pendent nonprofit organization (LAFPC, 2015); and the Detroit Food Policy Council, established by The Detroit City Council in 2009 with three coun- cilors appointed by the Mayor but also operating as an independent advisory body (Fox, 2010).

An original proposal for a potential hybrid food policy council in New York City, which has been at the forefront of the just and sustainable food move- ment but does not have a formal food policy council yet, has been put forward by The New York City Food Policy Center (2013). In a Background Memo on Food Policy Councils, the Center suggests that the Independent Budget Office (IBO) of the City of New York – a publicly funded agency, which how- ever maintains an independent view and critically assesses incumbent budget spending schemes in the city – can offer one such opportunity for integrat- ing urban food policy competencies within existing institutional structures. Alternatively, the notion of hybrid food policy councils can be used also to denote food policy organizations operating outside of government but linked to government through members from government agencies or one-off food planning episodes, like urban food charters or specific government grants and programs (e.g., Schiff, 2008). Independently from where one draws the line, a more nuanced image capturing the whole gamut of hybrid organizational models that have been experimented to date would enable us to better assess the specific challenges and opportunities that each model entails.

A greater distance from government may burden food policy councils with the daunting task of raising funds and relying on piecemeal grants from chari- table organizations, individuals, and foundations. This poses a number of chal- lenges to their work. First, it may take substantial time from their core work on food policy and advocacy and thus compromise the effectiveness of their efforts (Clancy et al., 2008). Second, if relying entirely on grants, the aggregate of the projects and programs carried out by a food policy council may not necessarily reflect a system-wide approach to food system change, but may be bent to single topics and areas of intervention. Third, the designation of a food policy council may hinder its ability to secure funding from private founda- tions since it can be viewed as the responsibility of government to support such councils. These barriers affect a disproportioned number of extant food policy councils because, as of 2015, only a small percentage (18%) of the over- all 282 food policy councils in North America are embedded in government and an even smaller percentage (12%) receive direct funding from government

(Center for a Livable Future, 2015). The corollary of funding challenges is exiguous staff. As of 2009, the overwhelming majority of food policy councils, about 90%, had no paid staff or relied just on one part-time employee (Harper et al., 2009). An appropriate indicator of success of food policy councils at this stage of their development as governance innovation may well therefore be their very capacity to remain into existence (Schiff, 2007).

Achieving a balanced representation of all sectors in the food system (i.e., production, processing, distribution, consumption, and waste management) and all domains of the so-called "societal pentagon" (Loorbach, 2010) (i.e., representatives of government, research centers, businesses, nongovernmental organizations, and intermediaries like consultant companies) is another uneasy challenge that food policy councils face. While all aim at providing an inclusive arena that can bring a wide variety of food system stakeholders together, some sectors like processing and waste management are still widely underrepresented (Harper et al., 2009) and, in general, "alternative" businesses are overrepresented (MacRae & Donahue, 2013). It is fair to say that emerging food-minded professionals and businesses in the domains of architecture, landscape architecture, and urban design and planning, which are beginning to reshape different parts of the physical infrastructure at the interface of cities and food (e.g., public markets, vegetable gardens, rooftop farms, green walls, food hubs, thematic guides and maps), are also rarely part of food policy councils as yet.

Individual interests and skills of food policy council members may constitute yet another challenge to achieving a balanced deliberation process. Some members may be more concerned with a single issue rather than a system-wide transition, while others may prefer to focus on the process rather than on actions (Clancy et al., 2008). Additionally, some of the council members may be at the table more to learn than to contribute, and, as a result, the actual skilled contributors can represent only a small group of the whole council (MacRae & Donahue, 2013). Disparate interests and levels of expertise are key to allow for diversity, but can also be the source of divisiveness and fragmentation, which puts the onus of effective and inclusive collaboration on leaders and facilitators in the council. In laying out the essential qualities that contributors in transitions arenas for sustainable development should possess, transitions theorist Derk Loorbach (2010, pp. 173–174) points at six basic skills: ability to think through complex problems at a high level of abstraction, readiness to cross the boundaries of one's own background or discipline, ability to effectively convey sustainable development visions in their own social circles, ability to exert some degree of influence on other networks, propensity to work with others, and having a mind open to research and innovation rather than sticking with ready-made solutions.

Loorbach, however, is quick to point out that transition arenas have nothing to do with large advisory committees made of multiple city agencies and nongovernmental organizations, but are ideally tight groups of 10–15 forerunners in their respective fields, including some representatives of government. Food policy councils, particularly of the hybrid type we saw, may be well positioned to perform as such transition arenas for system innovation, and the fact that the vast majority of them are still out of government structures can be seen as an underexplored opportunity rather than a limitation. Most of them comprise 12–14 people (Clancy et al., 2008) and do reflect the principle that selection of members in the arena is best done by the core group of forerunners that initiates the process, rather than by a single authority. Thus, the real challenge in front of the budding community of food policy council "entrepreneurs" could be turning some of their greatest limitations into an opportunity for innovation. Some food policy councils are already playing a strategic role in the nurturing and alignment of urban food system novelties and, taken together, still constitute an underused tool for food system transitions.

Government agencies and departments

While social innovations often tend to be associated with alliances forged outside of government institutions, they are not exclusive to the nongovernmental sphere. Social innovations can be driven by politics and government (Mulgan et al., 2007) as well. In the realm of urban food systems, local governments can initiate interdepartmental food teams, food policy task forces, and establish dedicated offices for food policy initiatives as new platforms for deliberation and cooperation to advance community food security and sustainable food system goals.

The Interdepartmental Food Team of the City of Seattle is one exemplary government-led institutional innovation that has gained international acclaim for its work on integrating food policy objectives into the mayoral agenda, while making sure that all city departments work toward their implementation. The Team is hosted at the Seattle's Office of Sustainability and the Environment but comprises lead members from a wide array of city departments – from Parks and Recreation, Public Utilities, Planning and Development, Sustainability, and Human Services to Economic Development, Public Health, and Civil Rights. Historically, the group formed after the adoption of a resolution for a city-wide Local Food Action Initiative adopted in 2008 sponsored by the chair of the Environment, Emergency Planning and Utilities Committee of the City Council. Along with the variety of food initiatives and projects that the Interdepartmental Food Team spearheaded since its inception (e.g., alternatives to commercial food packaging disposal, growing food in planting strips, youth and low-income individuals meal programs), two comprehensive food planning efforts stand out: The City of Seattle Food Action Plan released in 2012 and a topical report on how to integrate food policy into the city's comprehensive planning practices commissioned to the Puget Sound Regional Council, also released in 2012 (PSR Council, 2012).

Convening a strong task force on food policy and sustainable community and regional food systems can also be an effective tactic to start developing food governance capacities. This was the case for cities like New York – where the FoodWorks task force gathered experts with over 15 years of experience in the field and led to the development of the city's first comprehensive food system plan in 2010. In Vancouver, in 2003, a food policy task force developed the first Action Plan on just and sustainable food in the city and recommended the establishment of a food policy council embedded in government. In Los Angeles, in 2010, a food policy task force devised a regional food system plan, The Good Food for All Agenda, and led to the establishment of a food policy council connected to but operating externally of government. In San Francisco, a food security task force outlived a subsequently established food policy council by the mayor. While the council disbanded about a year after its inception (Fox, 2010), the Food Security Task Force, hosted at the Department of Public Health and instituted by the San Francisco Board of Supervisors in 2005, continued to be a central arena for the advancement of food issues in the municipality (e.g., through the development of a strategic food security plan, food security assessments, and a hunger-free city resolution).

A designated mayoral office for food policy initiatives is another approach that cities are taking to institutionalize local food policy. Examples of such offices are the New York City Office of the Food Policy Coordinator (now Office of the Director of Food Policy), which was established in 2007 and pioneered the city's Green Carts program, thanks to which a thousand new mobile vendors of fruits and vegetables were introduced in underserved neighborhoods throughout the city, and the Boston Mayor's Office of Food Initiatives established in 2010 to provide a shared space where representatives of the different city departments and the Boston Food Council, instituted by the mayor in 2008, and its partners could join forces to work toward the implementation of the Mayoral Food Directives. The Directives focused on ensuring access to healthy food for all, the expansion of opportunities for urban agriculture, the promotion of the local food economy through financing of food businesses in the city, and the facilitation of public–private partnerships to advance these goals.

City planning departments may be another option for providing cross-sectoral urban food policy issues with a jurisdictional home. Instances of cities that have begun to integrate food policy initiatives through their planning departments are Baltimore, with the Mayoral Food Policy Initiative operating through the City Planning Department; Portland, where the Bureau of Planning and Sustainability oversees a Sustainable Food Program; and Amsterdam, where the Department of Physical Planning (DRO) has advanced the city's first comprehensive food systems strategy. The case of the Baltimore Food Policy Initiative in particular blends several institutional arrangements we already came across: it started off by means of a food policy task force convened by the mayor, the recommendations of the group led to the establishment of a permanent position for a Food Policy Director, and the Food Policy Initiative team operates as an interdepartmental unit with members across planning, public health, sustainability, and economic development departments. This unique mix of governance arrangements enabled the initiative to effectively influence the *Baltimore Sustainability Plan* and set the goal for Baltimore to become a "leader in sustainable, local food systems" in the city's long-term planning agenda (Baltimore Office of Sustainability, 2009, p. 72).

On the whole, however, these episodes of purposeful integration of food planning practices in municipal institutions remain more the exception than the rule, and the bulk of food policy-oriented work continues to be carried outside of government. Nearly 20 years after pioneer food planning scholars Pothukuchi and Kaufman (2000) surveyed US planners in 1997–1998 and found that food was virtually nonexistent as a policy focus in the planning domain, a 2014 survey by Samina Raja, a distinguished food systems planning scholar in the US, reconfirmed their findings. At present, still few planners and local government officials consider the food system as a priority in their work. The reason for this, argues Raja (2015), is easily that there is still no "department of food," hence a formal mandate for governments and planners to engage with food system issues.

In an earlier paper on the roles that municipal institutions can play in advancing food systems planning, Pothukuchi and Kaufman (1999) provided useful insights into what a department of food could look like. A municipal department of food, in their view, can be strategic in fulfilling at least five food systems planning roles: regularly devise market analyses of the food system to facilitate market operations; advise the general public and the business community on potential shocks in the food economy that may impair urban food access; delineate and periodically review the responsibilities of local government in food policy; carry out the development of a strategic long-term (10–20 years) community food security plan; and track progress on the implementation of city food policies and plans to advise on future actions.

Other proposals for a more robust integration of urban food policy in government are the Community Food Security Coalition's recommendation for a Foodshed Authority to be established by the Seattle City Council (Fisher & Roberts, 2011, p. 16), which would enable the city to treat food as a public utility, like water and electricity, and expand its opportunities to protect the regional foodshed through local laws and regulations, and the thought-provoking Manifesto for a "London Food Parliament" by UK architect C.J. Lim outlined in his book *Food City* (2014). The food parliament is a fictional legislative authority overseeing food issues in London and its region which, in Lim's view, would facilitate the transition of food from a mere sustenance to the primary social capital used to reshape the urban economy, space, and society.

Intercity food policy networks

Alongside food policy councils and food policy initiatives embedded in government, the gradual activation of the local level of food policy is being heralded also by the formation of novel supralocal networks of cities willing to be more effective at advancing food system goals in the public interest. Examples for such alliances formed at the national level are the Sustainable Food Cities network in the UK established in 2011 and the Food Policy Task Force of the United States Conference of Mayors established in 2012.

The creation of the Sustainable Food Cities network was spearheaded by Tom Andrews, Associate Director at the Soil Association, a lead organic food certifier and a nonprofit sustainable food organization in the UK. A major driver for the establishment of the network was the paucity of shared metrics and indicators that could help cities measure progress toward the implementation of their food policies, programs, and comprehensive strategies. The formation of the network was facilitated through a national survey with the goal to identify and connect cities that had already adopted, or were in the process of adopting, a sustainable food systems charter, strategy, or action plan.

The United States Conference of Mayors is a nongovernmental organization whose overarching aim is to provide US mayors of cities with 30,000 inhabitants or more with research, training, and technical support to meet shared complex challenges as hunger, homelessness, unemployment, and brownfields redevelopment, among others. It was originally established through a municipal assistance bill passed in 1932 in the wake of the Great Depression. The Food Policy Task Force of the Conference set a precedent because it framed food policy issues as an important urban matter in need of a strong mayoral leadership next to traditional task forces on work, education, and defense. The task force was first chaired by the mayor of the City of Boston and was instituted to serve as a knowledge exchange platform for US mayors at the forefront of advancing urban food policies – e.g., by promoting initiatives to tackle obesity, improve access to healthy and affordable food for underserved urban communities, or setting specific food supply standards to privilege local food businesses and farmers. One of the core activities of the task force is to gather information on innovative food programs across the United States, highlight best practices, and consider how the US Farm Bill can support the development of healthy and resilient urban food environments.

The power of the "public plate" and school food procurement practices in particular (Morgan, 2008; Morgan & Sonnino, 2008; Sonnino, 2009) represent a largely underused lever for systemic food system change that cities are just beginning to consider. One promising intercity coalition, formed out of the will to transition the dominant US school food system and bring about public health and environmental well-being in tandem, is The Urban School Food Alliance. The Alliance was created in 2012 by school food professionals from the six largest school districts in the US – New York, Los Angeles, Chicago, Miami, Dallas, and Orlando – and has the potential to redirect over $550 million to fair and environmentally sound food sources per year. Together, the six cities oversee the school food supply of more than 4,500 schools, which equals 2.9 million meals per day. Considering that large European cities like Milan in Italy oversee the procurement of about 80,000 meals in public schools per day, which is already a considerable lever that can have tangible impact on the city-regional foodshed (Porro, Corsi, Scudo, & Spigarolo, 2014), the US Alliance is a giant by all standards. Some of its accomplishments to date include the adoption of an antibiotic-free standard for chicken products in 2014 and the substitution of all polystyrene trays with compostable plates in 2015.

Turning from the national to the international scale, the Community Food Security Coalition is an example of an influential nongovernmental alliance of alliances that had played a pivotal role in propelling community-based food policy initiatives, among which are food policy councils, for over 16 years (1994–2012) across the US and Canada. Globally oriented urban food policy networks driven by sustainable food systems and urban agriculture scholars and research centers, like the International Council for Local Environmental Initiatives (ICLEI), the Resource Centres on Urban Agriculture and Food Security (RUAF), the International Urban Food Network (IUFN), the International Development Research Centre (IDRC), and the Food and Agriculture Organization of the United Nations (FAO) – and joint programs like the City Region Food Systems between RUAF and FAO started in 2015 – are also an important and growing slice of the social and knowledge infrastructure that can help cities develop essential governance capacities to effectively steer food system transitions. The Milan Urban Food Policy Pact, which was signed by 117 cities in occasion of the 2015 Universal Exhibition "Feeding the Planet, Energy for Life," constitutes a major milestone toward the normalization of food policy and planning as an urban matter.

Concluding remarks

This chapter was about one of the most dynamic domains of the urban food planning "movement" – the emerging arenas for food policy and planning at the local level. The notion of "transition arenas," part of the transition management framework in theories of sociotechnical transitions, was used to advance the proposition that, despite their instability and limitations, these emerging institutional spaces can – and some already are – serve as platforms for the development and implementation of urban food system innovations. Lack of adequate funding, dwindling staff, unreliable government and stakeholder buy-in, and tensions between quick and measurable results and an inclusive, system-wide planning approach to food issues are key challenges that many of these budding organizations, particularly nongovernmental food policy councils, face. Yet, for most cities they are the only resource and chance to "see" themselves through a food system lens and begin to recover the governance capacities needed to purposefully influence the urban food system, improving the quality of urban life, economic vitality in their local foodsheds, and the ecosystems integrity.

We saw, however, that food policy councils and local food partnerships are not the only emerging arena for food policy and planning in cities. Some municipal agencies and departments are also beginning to promote a wide variety of city-regional food system initiatives through food policy task forces, interdepartmental food teams, offices for food policy coordinators, and city planning departments. National and international alliances of cities already addressing the challenge to effectively integrate food in the remit of their institutional competencies are also emerging and helping expand the opportunities for knowledge exchange and a stronger local leadership in the field. A greater social networkedness between urban food policy champions can enable the strategic connection of disparate emergent niche innovations and challenge current asymmetries of power between niche and regime actors in the system. We are already witnessing the fast-paced replication of many of the local food initiatives across cities and nations and the creation of denser social infrastructures for collaboration that will arguably help the initiatives that prosper outnumber those that die out.

Much like in all processes of innovation in their early stages of development, the learning curve in the organizational department of urban food planning is still pretty steep, and there is much to be learned from both novelties that thrive and those that disband. In addition, urban food planning scholarship would benefit from comparative research improving our understanding of how other urban policy foci like transportation, public health, land use, and many others have morphed into established city council committees and subcommittees with the ability to promote new legislation and hold stakeholders in the respective systems accountable. Graduating to skillful navigators of this take-off phase in the transition of food – from an exclusive purview of market and civil society entrepreneurs to an institutionalized competency of municipal governments – requires also from us to begin to systematically uncover what food-related work existing city agencies are already doing and how their work directly or indirectly affects the pursuit of fair, environmentally sound, and healthy urban food systems. This is an important interdisciplinary task, which many of the emerging food governance arenas are ideally positioned to advance.

Questions for further consideration

- In what ways can cities, as jurisdictions, make room for urban food policy and planning?
- What is an urban food governance network? And a transition arena? Who, do you think, should be part of an urban governance arena for food system transitions and why?
- Which are some of the major strengths and limitations of food policy councils? Are they indispensable for recovering the local level of food policy? Why?
- Why, do you think, is there no municipal department of food yet? What could be the value of such authority? Would it enable or stifle emergent niches for food system innovation? How so?

References

Argenti, O. (2000). Food for the Cities: Food Supply and Distribution Policies to Reduce Urban Food Security (Food into Cities Publication, DT/43–00E). Rome: Food and Agriculture Organization of the United Nations (FAO).

Baltimore Office of Sustainability. (2009). *The Baltimore Sustainability Plan*. Baltimore, MD: Author.

Battilana, J., Leca, B., & Boxenbaum, E. (2009). How actors change institutions: Towards a theory of institutional entrepreneurship. *The Academy of Management Annals, 3*(1), 65–107.

Blay-Palmer, A. (2009). The Canadian pioneer: The genesis of urban food policy in Toronto. *International Planning Studies, 14*(4), 401–416.

Born, B. (2012). Food Access and Food Policy: Local Examples from Seattle. In *Washington State Food and Nutrition Council Podcasts*. Podcast Retrieved from http://www.pccnatural markets.com/podcasts/wsfnc/wsfnc_branden_born.htm

Bulkeley, H., Castàn Broto, V., Hodson, M., & Marvin, S. (2011). Introduction. In H. Bulkeley, V. Castàn Broto, M. Hodson, & S. Marvin (Eds.), *Cities and Low Carbon Transitions* (pp. 1–10). New York-Abingdon: Routledge.

Carey, J. (2011). "Who Feeds Bristol? Towards a Resilient Food Plan." Retrieved from www.bristol.gov.uk/whofeedsbristol

Castells, M. (2002). Local and global: Cities in the network society. *Tijdschrift Voor Economische En Sociale Geografie, 93*(5), 548–558.

Center for a Livable Future. (2015). Food Policy Council Directory, 2015 Update. [PowerPoint slides]. Retrieved November 12, 2015, from https://assets.jhsph.edu/clf/mod_clfResource/doc/FPC_Trends_Slides_2015_10_28.pdf

City of Toronto. (2015). Toronto Food Strategy Webpage. Retrieved December 15, 2015, from http://www1.toronto.ca/wps/portal/contentonly?vgnextoid=75ab044e17e32410VgnVCM10000071d60f89RCRD

Clancy, K., Hammer, J., & Lippoldt, D. (2008). Food Policy Councils: Past, Present, Future. In C. C. Hinrich & T. A. Lyson (Eds.), *Remaking the North American Food System Strategies for Sustainability* (pp. 121–143). Lincoln, NE: University of Nebraska Press.

Clayton, M. L., Frattaroli, S., Palmer, A., & Pollack, K. M. (2015). The role of partnerships in U.S. food policy council policy activities. *Plos One, 10*(4), 1–14.

Dahlberg, K. A. (1994). Food Policy Councils: The Experience of Five Cities and One County. Paper presented at the Joint Meeting of the Agriculture Food and Human Values Society and the Association for the Study of Food and Society. Tucson, AZ. Retrieved from http://unix.cc.wmich.edu/~dahlberg/F4.pdf

Fisher, A., & Roberts, S. (2011). *Community Food Security Coalition: Recommendations for Food Systems Policy in Seattle*. Community Food Security Coalition.

Food and Hunger Action Committee. (2000). *Planting the Seeds: Phase 1 Report*. Toronto, ON: City of Toronto.

Food and Hunger Action Committee. (2001). *The Growing Season: Phase 2 Report*. Toronto, ON: City of Toronto.

Food and Hunger Action Committee. (2002). *Progress Report on "The Growing Season: The Phase II Report of the FHAC."* Retrieved from www.toronto.ca/legdocs/2002/agendas/council/cc020618/cms6rpt/cl010.pdf

Food and Hunger Action Committee. (2003). *Tending the Garden: Final Report*. Toronto, ON: City of Toronto.

Fox, C. (2010). *Food Policy Councils: Innovations in Democratic Governance for Equitable Food System*. Retrieved from https://goodfoodlosangeles.files.wordpress.com/2011/01/fpc_final_dist-5-indd.pdf

Frantzeskaki, N., Loorbach, D., & Meadowcroft, J. (2012). Governing societal transitions to sustainability. *International Journal of Sustainable Development, 15*(1/2), 19–36.

Friedmann, H. (2007). Scaling up: Bringing public institutions and food service corporations into the project for a local, sustainable food system in Ontario. *Agriculture and Human Values, 24*(3), 389–398.

Harper, A., Alkon, A., Shattuck, A., Holt-Giménez, E., & Lambrick, F. (2009). *Food Policy Councils: Lessons Learned*. Development Report No. 21. Oakland, CA: Food First.

Healey, P. (2002). On creating the "city" as a collective resource. *Urban Studies, 39*(10), 1777–1792.

Healey, P. (2006). Transforming governance: Challenges of institutional adaptation and a new politics of space. *European Planning Studies, 14*(3), 299–320.

Healey, P. (2012). Re-enchanting democracy as a mode of governance. *Critical Policy Studies, 6*(1), 19–39.

Hinrichs, C. C. (2010). Conceptualizing and Creating Sustainable Food Systems: How Interdisciplinarity Can Help. In A. Blay-Palmer (Ed.), *Imaging Sustainable Food Systems: Theory and Practice* (pp. 17–36). Farnham-Burlington: Ashgate Publishing.

Kemp, R., Rip, A., & Schot, J. (2001). Constructing Transition Paths Through the Management of Niches. In R. Garud & P. Karnøe (Eds.), *Path Dependence and Creation* (pp. 269–299). Mahwah, NJ: Lawrence Erlbaum Associates.

LAFPC. (2015). Los Angelis Food Policy Council Webpage. Retrieved from http://good foodla.org/about/

Levkoe, C. Z. (2011). Towards a transformative food politics. *Local Environment, 16*(7), 687–705.

Lim, C.J.(2014). *Food City*. New York, NY: Routledge.

Loorbach, D. (2010). Transition management for sustainable development: A prescriptive, complexity-based governance framework. *Governance, 23*(1), 161–183.

Loorbach, D., & Rotmans, J. (2006). Managing Transitions for Sustainable Development. In X. Olsthoorn & A. J. Wieczorek (Eds.), *Understanding Industrial Transformation: Views from Different Disciplines* (pp. 187–206). Dordrecht: Springer.

MacRae, R., & Donahue, K. (2013). Municipal Food Policy Entrepreneurs: A Preliminary Analysis of How Canadian Cities and Regional Districts are Involved in Food System Change. Retrieved from http://tfpc.to/wordpress/wp-content/uploads/2013/05/Report-May30-FINAL.pdf

Mendes, W. (2008). Implementing social and environmental policies in cities: The case of food policy in Vancouver, Canada. *International Journal of Urban and Regional Research, 32*(4), 942–967.

Monaghan, A. (2009). Conceptual niche management of grassroots innovation for sustainability: The case of body disposal practices in the UK. *Technological Forecasting and Social Change, 76*(8), 1026–1043.

Morgan, K. (2008). Greening the realm: Sustainable food chains and the public plate. *Regional Studies, 42*(9), 1237–1250.

Morgan, K., & Sonnino, R. (2008). *The School Food Revolution: Public Food and the Challenge of Sustainable Development*. London: Earthscan.

Mulgan, G., Tucker, S., Ali, R., & Sanders, B. (2007). *Social Innovation: What It Is, Why It Matters and How It Can Be Accelerated*. Oxford Said Business School. Basingstoke, UK: The Basingstoke Press.

Porro, A., Corsi, S., Scudo, G., & Spigarolo, R. (2014). The contribution of Bioregione research project to the development of local sustainable agri-food systems. *Scienze Del Territorio, 2*, 319–326.

Pothukuchi, K., & Kaufman, J. L. (1999). Placing the food system on the urban agenda: The role of municipal institutions in food systems planning. *Agriculture and Human Values, 16*(2), 213–224.

Pothukuchi, K., & Kaufman, J. L. (2000). The Food System. *Journal of the American Planning Association, 66*(2), 113–124.

Raja, S. (2015, April 3). Why all cities should have a Department of Food. *The Conversation.* Retrieved from http://theconversation.com/why-all-cities-should-have-a-department-of-food-39462

Reynolds, B. (2009). Feeding a world city: The London food strategy. *International Planning Studies, 14*(4), 417–424.

Roberts, W. (2010). Food Policy Encounters of a Third Kind: How the Toronto Food Policy Council Socializes for Sustain-Ability. In A. Blay-Palmer (Ed.), *Imagining Sustainable Food Systems: Theory and Practice* (pp. 173–200). Surrey-Burligton: Ashgate Publishing.

Roberts, W. (2014). *Food for City Building: A Field Guide for Planners, Actionists & Entrepreneurs.* Toronto: Hypenotic Inc.

Rotmans, J., Kemp, R., & van Asselt, M. (2001). More evolution than revolution: Transition management in public policy. *Foresight, 3*(1), 15–31.

Schiff, R. (2007). *Food Policy Councils: An Examination of Organisational Structure, Process, and Contribution to Alternative Food Movements* (Doctoral dissertation). Retrieved from Murdoch University Research Repository (http://researchrepository.murdoch.edu.au/id/eprint/293).

Schiff, R. (2008). The role of food policy councils in developing sustainable food systems. *Journal of Hunger & Environmental Nutrition, 3*(2–3), 206–228.

Schuitmaker, T. J. (2012). Identifying and unravelling persistent problems. *Technological Forecasting and Social Change, 79*(6), 1021–1031.

Smith, A. (2006). Green niches in sustainable development: The case of organic food in the United Kingdom. *Environment and Planning C: Government and Policy, 24*(3), 439–458.

Smith, A., & Raven, R. (2012). What is protective space? Reconsidering niches in transitions to sustainability. *Research Policy, 41*(6), 1025–1036.

Sonnino, R. (2009). Quality food, public procurement, and sustainable development: The school meal revolution in Rome. *Environment and Planning A, 41*(2), 425–440.

Stierand, P. (2012). Food Policy Councils: Recovering the Local Level in Food policy. In J.S.C. Wiskerke & A. Viljoen (Eds.), *Sustainable Food Planning: Evolving Theory and Practice* (pp. 67–79). Wageningen: Wageningen Academic Publishers.

van der Brugge, R., Rotmans, J., & Loorbach, D. (2005). The transition in Dutch water management. *Regional Environmental Change, 5*(4), 164–176.

Wekerle, G. R. (2004). Food justice movements: Policy, planning, and networks. *Journal of Planning Education and Research, 23*(4), 378–386.

Winne, M. (2004). Food system planning: Setting the community's table. *Progressive Planning, 158,* 13–15.

Wiskerke, J. S. C. (2009). On places lost and places regained: Reflections on the alternative food geography and sustainable regional development. *International Planning Studies, 14*(4), 369–387.

Yeatman, H. (1994). Food Policy Councils in North America – Observations and Insights. World Health Organization. Retrieved from https://www.uow.edu.au/content/groups/public/@web/@health/documents/doc/uow025389.pdf

8 A journey that has just begun

Planning for community food systems is an issue that has just begun to surface. . . .
To date, planners have paid little attention to this big hole in the planning field. I'm
convinced that they should do more.

– Jerome L. Kaufman, *Viewpoint*

With Chapter 7, which introduced us to the progressive inception of new
spaces for food systems governance at the local scale, we came a full circle
in our exploration of urban food planning novelties taking shape in some
of the wealthiest cities on the planet. Now it is time to look back and take
stock of what we learned from all those instances we hopefully referred to
as "seeds of transition" along the way. What the multiple episodes of conceptual, analytical, design, and organizational experimentation can tell us
about the kind of practice urban food planning has evolved into, more than
a decade after planners first called attention to it, and what this means for the
upcoming generations of urban food planning scholars, public administrators,
design professionals, and activists, are the two major questions this final chapter attempts to answer. At this point, the great dynamism of the field – with
initiatives quickly assembled, reassembled, and dismantled each year – defies
any attempt for a definitive assessment, yet, we can still appreciate its emergent features and use them as pointers for future action. For one last time, we
will put on our transition theories spectacles to spot the budding assemblages
of like-minded urban food planning practices and sketch a tentative hypoth-
esis of where capacity-building efforts will be most needed to fast-forward its
normalization.

A niche in the making

Our global journey in the realm of urban food planning has surely left us
with many open questions and uncertainties, but if there is one thing we can
be certain about, it is that the food system is no more a "stranger" to mayors
and planners in post-industrial cities. Of course, we are still far from Carolyn
Steel's ideal for Sitopia – a place and time in which cities and their relation to

people and the environment are seen through a food lens and food is used as a design tool for crafting more sustainable cities. Yet, the growing bundle of different research, public policy, and design practices around food in the city, and their increasing overlap and alignment, suggests that the niche of urban food planning – as a practice and a field of practices – is in the making.

Mayoral food system plans, amendments to building and zoning codes for urban agriculture, statutory and community food policy councils, research grants for community food system assessments and projects, university courses on food systems in urban planning and design schools, and models for food-sensitive housing and urban development projects put forward by private professionals and real estate developers are all part of the patchwork of budding novelties working to hybridize the dominant food system. On the evolutionary scale of sociotechnical transitions (e.g., Rotmans, Kemp, & van Asselt, 2001; van der Ploeg et al., 2004), this positions urban food planning slightly ahead of the start line and in a development phase in which disparate novelties are starting to network around a shared idea. No dominant design has emerged as yet, but the critical mass and diversity of solutions being tested on the ground has begun to influence the regime on the margins.

According to the multilevel perspective framework on transitions (e.g., Geels, 2002), for a niche to transition to the next phase in its evolutionary development and get closer to opportunities to structurally affect the incumbent regime, a process of further alignment and consolidation of emergent solutions is needed. One way to construe what this means for urban food planning as a niche for social innovation is to look at the stage of advancement of each subset of practices that comprise it. For the purpose of our analysis, throughout the six central chapters of the book, we broadly distinguished between four kinds of urban food planning novelties: *conceptual* – pertaining to new understandings and ideas about why and how the linkages connecting food and cities should be rewired; *analytical* – pertaining to new research tools, analytical skills, and metrics leading to new representations of the incumbent relationships between cities and the food system; *design* – using a broad-brush term to signify all future-oriented projects, policies, or plans for intervention aimed at transitioning from the status quo; and *organizational* – comprising all new spaces and forms of social cooperation being developed to advance new understandings about the system and the problems and opportunities at stake, devise collaborative intervention strategies, and gather the needed resources for their implementation.

This distinction of course is artificial and, in reality, in order to be carried out each single practice relies on all four dimensions. Yet, when thinking about urban food planning as a bundle of different practices which, in the aggregate, determine its overall advancement as a distinct domain of practice, this distinction can be helpful. Depending on how well each part of the quartet is doing and how well synergies between them are forged, we can have a more or less stable niche for innovation able to appear more or less convincing to social groups in the dominant sociotechnical regime. How robust each of

these subdomains is has important repercussions not only for the normalization of the niche via its progressive acceptance by the regime, but also on
the prospective expansion or contraction of the community of practitioners
involved. A messy and inconclusive niche – which is fine and even necessary
for the first stages of niche formation – could, in the long run, make pioneer
practitioners defect and potential newcomers shy away.

Conceptual

A key value of grassroots innovations or social niches (Kirwan, Ilbery, Maye, &
Carey, 2013; Seyfang & Smith, 2007; Smith & Seyfang, 2013) is their ability
to develop new ideas about how and why routine ways of doing things should
change. In the realm of urban food planning, this translates into new visions
of the dominant routines governing how cities relate to food and the role of
cities in challenging such routines. Emergent redefinitions of cities, food, and
the remit of expert and mundane practices involved in their administration are
some of the markers of the city-driven reconceptualization of the food system
underway (Figure 8.1).

Examples of new concepts redefining what the city is through the lens
of food worth recalling are Sitopia by British architect Carolyn Steel (2009),
Agropolitana by Italian urban planning scholar Viviana Ferrario (Ferrario,
2009, 2011), Agriburbia by US food systems planners Quint and Jennifer Redmond (TSR Group, 2010), Sustainable Food City by Sustainable Food Cities
coalition based in the UK (ca. 2012), slow food city or Cittaslow introduced
in 1999 by Paolo Saturnini who was inspired by Carlo Petrini, leader of the
Slow Food movement, and "food city" by British architect and urban scholar
CJ Lim (2014). Examples of new concepts redefining what the food system is
through an urban lens are the notion of food as an urban system as important
as other urban systems like housing, energy, and transportation (Pothukuchi &
Kaufman, 2000), of food as urban infrastructure (e.g., Portland Plan 2010;
Vancouver Greenest City Plan 2020), and of local food infrastructure (e.g.,
community gardens, farmers markets, compost centers) as an urban amenity
as relevant as religious centers, schools, and greenery (e.g., the Almere Oosterwold plan). Concepts relinking cities to the nonurban geography of food, like
the notion of the urban foodshed (N. Cohen, 2009, 2011; Getz, 1991) – meaning
the aggregate of places through which a given urban population is fed – are
also playing a critical role in changing entrenched perceptions about food and
its relation to the city.

The development of new narratives about food in the public domain is
another key layer of the reconceptualization of food in the city we came across
repeatedly throughout the book. Mayors, borough presidents, city council
speakers, and other influential decision-makers at the local scale have started
reframing food not only as an urban system, but also as a public good and
part of the responsibilities of local government. The skeptics might easily
dismiss these emergent discourses as pure rhetoric with little impact on the

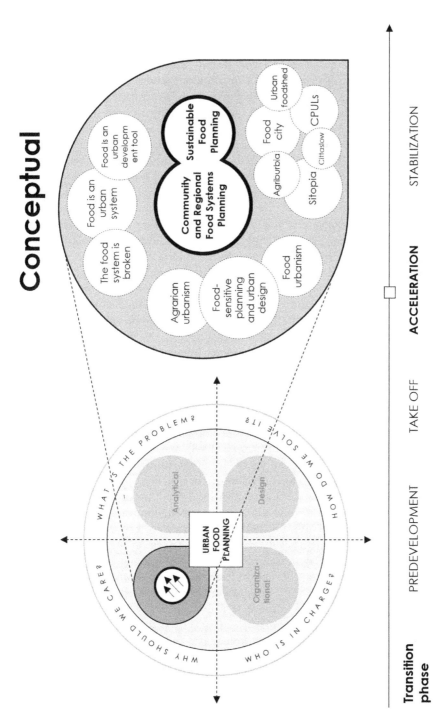

Figure 8.1 A snapshot of emerging novelties in the bundle of conceptual urban food planning practices.

Source: The author.

business-as-usual state of the system, but these discourses are starting to affect the list of priorities on the mayoral agenda and make room for food, be it as an entry point for addressing structural challenges such as poverty and social inequality or coping with the obesity "epidemic" and its soaring healthcare and social costs; matters which mayors deeply care about and cannot simply shy away from. The first mayoral forum on food, which took place in New York City in 2013 and confronted mayoral candidates with the topic, is one case in point. Equally significant is the narrative, emergent from the dozens of urban food system strategies released to date, that cities need not merely take a backseat as passive observers, but are poised to "lead the way" (e.g., Toronto Food Strategy, Los Angelis Regional Good Food Plan, New York FoodWorks Plan, London Food Strategy) in transitioning their food systems to a model less dependent on fossil fuels, deforestation, underpaid labor, chemical inputs, and scarce fresh water resources.

One last important piece of the puzzle is the inception of new ideas about the integration of food system competencies in technical disciplines and professions hitherto exclusively concerned with the built environment – such as urban planning, urban design, and architecture. Instances of these novel conceptual frameworks, seeking the reconciliation between sustainable city and food system goals, are community and regional food systems planning (Samina Raja, Born, & Kozlowski Russell, 2008), sustainable food planning (Viljoen & Wiskerke, 2012), urban food planning (Morgan, 2009, 2013), food urbanism (Verzone, 2012; Verzone, Bertschinger, Huang, Dumondel, & Woods, 2011), agrarian urbanism (Duany & DPZ, 2012), agricultural urbanism (de la Salle & Holland, 2010; Mullinix et al., 2008), agriurbanisme (Vidal, 2009, 2014; Vidal & Fleury, 2008), and food-sensitive planning and urban design (Donovan, Larsen, & McWhinnie, 2011). Other observers are putting the emphasis on the notion of food as a tool for urban development more broadly (e.g., Miazzo & Minkjan, 2013; Stierand, 2008), therefore suggesting its relevance for all existing ramifications of the urban planning field and related professions. New discourses for the relevance of urban planning provisions in enabling or hindering the development of local food infrastructures put forward by just and sustainable food advocates (e.g., Neighbourhoods Green et al., 2014; Sustain, 2011, 2014; Winne, 2008) have also started gaining prominence, further increasing the premises for the institutionalization of the notion that planners have a role to play in transitioning the food system.

In sum, the value of new concepts in fostering societal transitions cannot be overstated. This tenet has also been increasingly acknowledged in transition theories literature, often suspected of a mismatch between its intentions to treat the societal and technological dimensions of transitions on equal footing and the reality, whereby the latter have enjoyed the largest share of scholarly attention. This gap has puzzled some transition scholars arguing that, in thinking of managing transitions to sustainability, it is key to recognize that technology is only a means to the "real" end-goal of transitions, not the end per se (Hegger, van Vliet, & van Vliet, 2007). In fact, the relevance of this omission is even more pronounced in cases of grassroots social innovations in which technology is only subsidiary to the development of sustainable development solutions. Conceptual niche management (Hegger et al., 2007; Monaghan, 2009) is one novel transition management approach that builds on the strategic niche management framework (Kemp, Schot, & Hoogma, 1998) but specializes in shepherding specifically concept-driven experiments of sustainable development. Being a social niche in the making, urban food planning can arguably benefit from similar approaches to further strengthen the core concepts that drive it and envision meaningful pathways for their consolidation.

Analytical

Agrifood systems have a distinct spatial dimension that constitutes them at multiple geographical scales – from cities to regions to global food webs. World cities (Sassen, 1994; P. Taylor, Derudder, Saey, & Witlox, 2007), but really all Western cities, have lost touch with the chain of places that bring about the production of modern food from seed to table to soil and energy again. If cities are to drive food system transitions, this knowledge gap must be closed. One of the tasks in front of urban food planning as a niche for city-driven food system innovations, therefore, is to recover the knowledge of what the urban food system is and what problems and opportunities – technical, social, economic, and political – there are to transition it to a regime of greater public and ecological health (Lang, Barling, & Caraher, 2009). This requires not only the ability to demarcate urban food planning's subject matter, but also to creatively use available research tools, expertise, and resources and be prepared to develop new ones if needed. That is why for the urban food planning niche to prosper, developing a robust bundle of analytical capabilities is essential. While the domain of novel practices trying to meet this need is still very amorphous and dynamic, it is possible to discern some alignments and shared approaches taking shape. Four main clusters of assessment practices have started forming so far – valuations of current and prospective potential for city and regional food production and procurement, assessments of urban food retail distribution and community food access, reviews of incumbent urban policies and regulations affecting the food system, and community food assessments and comprehensive food system reports seeking to portray the city-regional food system in its entirety, encompassing the production, processing, distribution, consumption, and disposal practices that compose it at the local scale (Figure 8.2).

The question of the extent to which local and regional productive land, farms, and gardens can contribute to feeding the city has gained prominence among university researchers, citizen scientists, and private-practice professionals. Emergent ways to address it span from graphic simulations visualizing the spatial equivalent of big cities' diets (e.g., Maas, Hackhauf, Haikola, Kalmeijer, & Salij, 2009) to detailed geospatial analysis of the potential for supplementing city's food supply with produce from its own backyards (Ackerman et al., 2014; Colasanti & Hamm, 2010; Grewal & Grewal, 2012; Kremer &

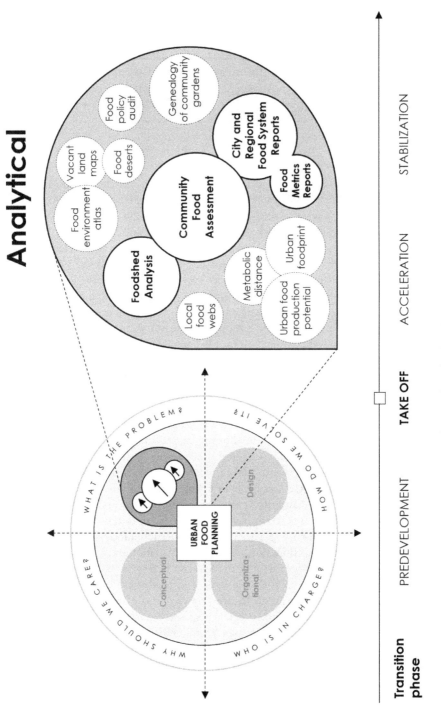

Analytical

Transition phase   PREDEVELOPMENT   TAKE OFF   ACCELERATION   STABILIZATION

Figure 8.2 A snapshot of emerging novelties in the bundle of analytical urban food planning practices.

Source: The author.

DeLiberty, 2011; MacRae et al., 2010; McClintock, Cooper, & Khandeshi, 2013). Different mapping techniques to assess the distribution, extent, and current use of urban vacant land have also been an important focus for both academic (Kremer, Hamstead, & McPhearson, 2013; Mendes, Balmer, Kaethler, & Rhoads, 2008; J. R. Taylor & Lovell, 2012) and community-based (Segal, 2015) research teams. Urban foodshed analysis (Kloppenburg, Hendrickson, & Stevenson, 1996) is one other prominent subset of assessments that has begun to consolidate as a separate branch of local food system analysis and has hitherto been carried out by using a wide range of spatial scales as the unit of analysis: an urban region (Darrot, 2012; Hopkins, Thurstain-Goodwin, & Fairlie, 2009; Lister, 2007; Martin et al., 2012; Thompson, Harper, & Kraus, 2008), a group of urban regions (Kurita, Yokohari, & Bolthoise, 2008; Urban Design Lab, 2011), a state (Peters, Bills, Lembo, Wilkins, & Fick, 2009, 2011; Peters, Bills, Wilkins, & Fick, 2008), or an entire country (Johansson, 2008; Urban Design Lab, 2010).

At the urban scale, new food system metrics, like the metabolic distance indicator developed by the TSR Group in Denver, Colorado, are being deployed not only for assessing extant and potential urban-rural linkages, but as a design tool for the development of new urban communities with integrated local food infrastructures and reduced ecological footprint. Other studies have also begun to map and spatialize the variety of emergent urban-rural linkages in densely urbanized urban regions, visualizing their diverse distribution networks, new places of exchange, and ubiquitous communities of practitioners (Coviello, Graglia, & Villa, 2009; Porro, Corsi, Scudo, & Spigarolo, 2014). Attentive agroeconomic analyses of the viable typologies of urban farms for the development of a localized layer of the urban food system have been relatively rare, but have also begun to emerge (e.g., Jansma & Visser, 2011). From an institutional standpoint, the majority of research has been advanced by single research units; however, more recently international research collectives advancing collaborative projects on the topic have also begun to come together (e.g., FOODMETERS 2012–2015, Urban Agriculture Europe 2011–2016), particularly in the context of European Union financing programs. One notable effort to map local food webs nationwide that has been advanced so far is the UK initiative Mapping Local Food Webs funded through the Campaign to Protect Rural England; the local food webs of some 20 towns have been mapped since 2008 and a mapping toolkit for current and prospective participants was released in 2012.

New representations of the urban food retail system and related geographies of access to healthy and affordable food options is another growing cluster of experimental research practices in the domain of urban food planning. The concept of mapping urban "food deserts" (Wrigley, Warm, & Margetts, 2003) has gained popularity particularly in the UK and North America, and scholars are now increasingly using geospatial data (Eckert & Shetty, 2011), also in combination with direct observation (LeClair & Aksan, 2014), to pursue it. Geographic information systems (GIS) have also been used to represent changes in the geography of chain food stores over time, migrating from inner-city areas to the suburbs (Larsen & Gilliland, 2008), and the kinds of food outlets available specifically around schools (Frank et al., 2006). Urban planning scholars have also drawn attention to the limitations of the food desert concept as an analytical prism to assess the urban food environment and have put forward valuation approaches that take into account the contribution of small grocery stores, not just supermarkets, to community food security (Raja, Ma, & Yadav, 2008; Short, Guthman, & Raskin, 2007). Studies of the impact of farmers markets on food access and food prices at the neighborhood level (Larsen & Gilliland, 2009) constitute a further novelty in the cluster of urban food systems research practices.

The emergence of sociospatial analyses of local food retail at the national scale have begun to surface and make an important addition to the set of analytical tools urban food planners can use in their research. By using nationwide available county-level data on food retail in the US, researchers have revealed the existence of "rural food deserts" (Blanchard & Matthews, 2007), thus debunking the myth that access to fresh, healthy, and affordable food is exclusively an urban issue. Using social media data, particularly geolocated tweets, to assess the prevalence of healthy and unhealthy food outlets is one innovative research approach recently experimented with by scholars in the US (Widener & Li, 2014), which could provide helpful ancillary findings impossible to capture as rapidly and cost-effectively otherwise. The online Food Environment Atlas developed by the Economic Research Service (ERS) of the United States Department of Agriculture (USDA) and released in 2014 is a singular novelty in the arsenal of analytical tools that could help planners engage with the food system at the local level and contains county-level data on a variety of local food system elements – from farmers markets to fast food outlets and recipients of federal food subsidies.

Studies taking a more holistic approach to community food security and the social, economic, and environmental sustainability of the city-regional food system more broadly constitute a third bundle of analytical practices, which pioneer food system planners and enlightened local administrators have put forward in the past decade and a half. Among these, the community food assessment is one tool that has been developed with the support of urban planning scholars (Pothukuchi, 2004; Pothukuchi, Joseph, Burton, & Fisher, 2002) and federal government officials (B. Cohen, Andrews, & Kantor, 2002) in the US to aid a wide range of social groups – from nongovernmental organizations to local government officials and businesses – in assessing access to healthy, fresh, and affordable food at the community level. Without a doubt, municipal and regional food system reports make up another significant group of the assessment endeavors that have taken a comprehensive approach to evaluating the state of the art of local agrifood systems. Many of these are part of food system plans and strategies and inform future-oriented goals and objectives to tackle major challenges stemming from the current conditions. Next to food security, farmland decline, energy consumption, and unsustainable food waste management are additional major issues analyzed and quantified through available data at the national, regional, and the urban scale. Community food activists, advocacy planners, and government agencies have used such reports to make visible the multiplicity of grassroots food system innovations that had taken place within and around their cities. A limited number of these reports have been supplemented by a section on food system indicators (e.g., Vancouver Regional Food Systems Strategy, 2011) or a stand-alone food metrics report (e.g., New York 2012, 2014; London 2011, 2012, 2013, 2014), outlining relevant indicators that could help not only represent the current state of the city-regional food system but monitor its transformation, or the lack thereof, as a result of government and community interventions.

Getting a grip on the urban food system, however, entails not only becoming familiar with the geography of its functional components – from field to landfill, but also the policies and regulations (Pothukuchi & Kaufman, 2000) that shape it across different levels of government, including the urban one. Research practices and analytical frameworks to this end are still in their infancy, but some original experiences have begun to emerge. Among these is the food policy audit tool (O'Brien & Cobb, 2012) developed by environmental planning scholars at the University of Virginia in the US to inquire about the presence or absence of policies vis-à-vis different spheres of food system and the online Planning Food Cities toolkit (Sustain, 2014), developed by one of the leading NGOs for sustainable food in the UK, Sustain, to help citizens and community food activists navigate the urban planning system and use the opportunities it provides to advance community food growing initiatives.

Last but not least, transversal historical accounts of a single city's food system and the evolution of the town–country relationships that have shaped its physical space, economy, and society over time (e.g., Steel, 2009) represent a key yet still largely underrepresented part of the budding novelties in the analytical domain of the urban food planning niche in the making. Retrospective analyses of the genesis of community agriculture practices (Drake & Lawson, 2014) or the practice of food system planning itself (Donofrio, 2007; Vitiello & Brinkley, 2014) are equally rare research approaches to the development of new knowledge about present-day urban food system geographies and how they came about. As transition theory literature suggests, cumulative knowledge of past sociotechnical transitions, or the efforts to engender them, is essential to the development of analytical tools that could help us make sense of past experiences of system innovation but also refine our tactics and strategies to steer sustainability-oriented ones in the future.

The above-summarized landscape of novelties suggests that, while no dominant research design to examine city and regional food production potential, community food security, or the performance of the entire food system against social equity and environmental indicators has emerged as yet, some alignments are already in the making. Second-order novelties like the introduction of local food production and farmland protection indicators in sustainable building certification systems, such as LEED for neighborhood development

(US Green Building Council, 2014) or the comprehensive review and valuation of existing local food system assessment techniques (Freedgood, Pierce-Quiñonez, & Meter, 2011), represent further markers of the growing maturity of this domain of urban food planning practices and can constitute promising steps toward the development of a more stable and credible urban food planning niche.

Notwithstanding the significant progresses made in crafting the analytical toolbox of community and regional food systems planners, several assessment challenges beg for further investigation. Making visible the merits of alternative food networks to the improvement of public health, social equity, and the integrity of cultural and ecosystem services is one area of research that would greatly benefit the advancement of urban food planning as a field of scholarly practice. So far, groundbreaking practices to this end have been developed particularly in the domain of urban agriculture, with interdisciplinary teams of scholars, nonprofit groups, and citizens scientists working together to put the physical and informational infrastructure in place and show the annual yields of urban gardens in the city (Farming Concrete, 2015; Gittleman, Jordan, & Brelsford, 2012) and also their broad ecological, community empowerment, and physical and mental health benefits (N. Cohen, Reynolds, & Sanghvi, 2012). Making further progress along these lines of research would be essential, as would extending them to gauge the benefits of new urban food procurement practices more broadly, encompassing community-supported vegetables and fish purchasing schemes as well as farmers markets and innovative food recovery and recycling initiatives.

A further point of contention that will have to be settled as we refine our analytical tools and food system lenses is the way notions of "local" food and food systems are established. At this time, geographers have made it clear that ideas of place and space are not the mere result of objective physical boundaries but, above all, are socially constructed. How these processes of social co-construction unfold and which forms of localness contribute to sustainability transitions better compared to others is a puzzle that merits a place in future investigations. In addition, to date, still a minority of assessments have shed light on the potential synergies between global and regional food system logistics and transportation (van der Schans, 2010) and how a meaningful interface between them can be designed. This is a field in which novelties are greatly wanted given that such synergies would play a key role in informing strategic niche innovations aimed at reconfiguring the dominant agrifood system regime.

Lastly, much of the narrative that propelled original research and practice in representing neighborhoods, cities, regions, and even nations through a food lens has been in line with the old saying that "you cannot manage what you cannot measure." While this tenet has its well-founded merits, the risk is that we eventually manage *only* what we can measure. As it happens, many of the benefits of urban food growing practices, like the generation of social–ecological knowledge and its contribution to urban resiliency (Barthel,

Parker, & Ernstson, 2015; Barthel, Folke, & Colding, 2010), are hard to quantify and take a multidisciplinary approach to pin down in a rigorous and
replicable fashion. Finding creative ways to render both the measurable and
nonmeasurable benefits of local food infrastructures would be key as the
urban food planning niche strives to get the attention of regime actors and
bring about systemic change. Universities and research centers focusing on
public health and sustainability research are uniquely positioned to make a
contribution to this end and use their resources to develop strategic research
partnerships with community organizations, small businesses, and government agencies.

Design

At the heart of sociotechnical transitions is the development of new technologies and forms of social collaboration able to overhaul dominant sociotechnical arrangements with adverse effects on people and the environment. While
urban food planning is predominantly a niche for social and not technological
innovation and thus concerned with remaking the linkages between cities and
food through expert and mundane social practices, it also involves the development of a wide range of physical infrastructures that could facilitate the normalization of such practices at the system level. To refer to the entire bundle of
emergent social practices aimed at transforming the local food system, through
material and nonmaterial interventions, in this book we used the broad notion
of design. The analysis of emblematic novelties in this domain of urban food
planning revealed the formation of three large groups of future-oriented activities that have been put forward through social and political mobilization at the
city scale: site- and institution-specific projects; comprehensive food system
plans and strategies; and sectoral regulations, policies, and funding programs
(Figure 8.3).

   Within the realm of local food system projects, to date, urban planners,
designers, architects, and sustainable food activists have begun to redesign a
wide range of elements of the urban food environment by creatively integrating edible landscapes in open spaces, buildings, and new residential complexes.
Edible front yards, community gardens, urban and periurban allotments, commercial and recreational agricultural parks, and continuous productive landscapes corridors are some of the conversions of open spaces into local food
infrastructures underway. Buildings are also being reimagined: the rooftops
of existing ones are now increasingly deemed as an untapped opportunity for
the integration of rooftop farms and greenhouses in the built environment,
while experimental designs for skyscraper farms, local food hubs, and housing units equipped with facilities for intensive food production are testing the
grounds for a more substantial relocalization of urban food supply. Models for
the development of new agri-urban communities in suburban and exurban
settings are yet another bourgeoning strand in the project-oriented domain of
urban food planning novelties. Lastly, efforts to rethink the role of historical

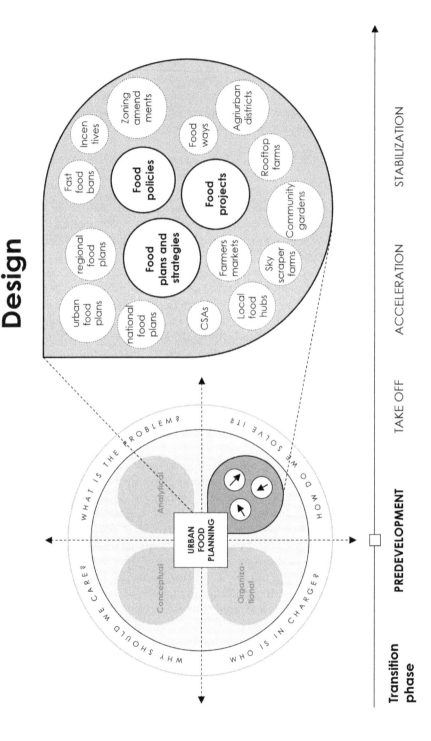

Figure 8.3 A snapshot of emerging novelties in the bundle of design-oriented urban food planning practices.

Source: The author.

farming estates in metropolitan regions by repurposing them for agri-tourism and educational centers for sustainable farming practices is one further sphere of design and social innovation emerging in post-industrial urban regions.

A second budding group of city-driven efforts to rethink the dominant food system regime is represented by city, regional, and national food system plans and strategies, which had often been heralded by the release of a local food charter. Over 90 such plans have been devised in the Global North in the past 15 years, some by community groups, an increasing number by government agencies, and a small but rapidly growing group through the joint collaboration of universities, community groups, and representatives of local government. The approach to food system transformation that such documents reveal puts the emphasis on the need to first describe the system through the already available quantitative and qualitative data that government agencies at different levels gather, identify ways in which the public sector already affects the urban and regional food system, acknowledge the host of nongovernmental initiatives that have emerged to tackle some of its gravest shortcomings, and uncover opportunities and restrictions for governments to further expand and enable civil-society and business-driven innovations. The analysis of the latter is typically translated in a comprehensive framework of goals, objectives, and, to a lesser extent, specific targets and performance metrics, together defining the current and desired state of the urban food system and demarcating the role for local governments in the transition.

The form that such local food strategies have taken so far is either of stand-alone plans, devised by purposefully established task forces of experts and practitioners in different segments of local food system (e.g., agriculture, processing, retail, consumption, waste management), or as subsections and cross-cutting topics in comprehensive long-term sustainability plans, devised by dedicated mayoral offices for sustainability. Instances of stand-alone urban agriculture plans (e.g., Minneapolis, Baltimore, Toronto) have only recently begun to surface and constitute a further marker of the evolution of this domain of pioneer urban food planning practices. The precedent-setting international Urban Food Policy Pact, signed by 117 cities in Milan, Italy, in 2015, provided an important networking opportunity that could positively affect the stabilization and replication of food system policies and plans put forward by local administrations.

While cities have limited regulatory and financial power over the agribusiness, processing, and transportation rings in the food chain, they do enjoy some leeway in making decisions about urban land use and institutional food procurement practices. Indeed, along with system-wide reports and strategies, generally lacking a legally binding status, cities have begun to explore the interstices for purposeful food system change at the local scale by developing new, or amending existing, local laws, mayoral directives, and sectoral policies and programs. Some of the most widespread novelties in this respect in North America have been the amendment of city zoning codes and ordinances to legalize urban agriculture uses in urban areas and, in some cases, establish new rules to permit small animal husbandry and beekeeping practices. Removal of building code restrictions for the integration of rooftop farms on top of existing industrial buildings and incentives for their integration in new buildings have been an important addition to the arsenal of concrete interventions that cities can advance to enable emergent urban food system innovations.

Another group of policy-centered food planning novelties pertains to the urban food retail infrastructure shaping individual and institutional food purchasing practices. Creating zoning and financial incentives aimed at attracting fresh food retailers to underserved urban communities, where residents have limited financial means and are disproportionately affected by diet-related diseases like obesity and diabetes, is one of the innovative attempts to alter market-driven anomalies in the urban food environment. Bans on fast food chains in school districts represent an additional city regulatory strategy to cope with the clustering of abundant unhealthy food options near the most vulnerable of urban populations. Next to enabling and restrictive regulations tackling inefficiencies in conventional food retail, direct investments in more inclusive alternative food market venues like farmers markets and street fruit and vegetable carts have also emerged as one of the interstices for city-driven food system change that wealthy cities have begun to exploit. Finally, an emergent group of urban food policy novelties that are not spatial in nature but have important implications for city and regional productive landscapes are the introduction of institutional procurement standards privileging local and seasonal produce and pilot organic food recycling initiatives aimed at testing opportunities for instituting a citywide organic waste collection and composing system.

Overall, the design department of the urban food planning niche, so to speak, has grown into a particularly dynamic environment where novelties are multiplying both quantitatively and qualitatively, through the tentative probing of different tactics and solutions. Alignments are still hard to grasp, but replication of promising models is in progress on different fronts of urban food system change – from local food growing to retail and waste prevention and disposal. The overwhelming majority of cities are still getting a grip on what the urban food system consists of, what the major problems are, and what cities' role in fixing it could be. A small cohort of frontrunners, however, are also beginning to reflect on what has worked so far and why, thereby engaging in critical learning practices. As strategic niche management scholars point out, learning, along with developing realistic expectations and robust social networks, is one of the essential transition management practices that distinguishes successful from inconsequential niches for innovation.

Learning from design experiments is key not just for the sake of improving the outcome of a specific project or policy, but also for identifying the areas of intervention where new analytical capabilities are most needed. For the moment, however, only a handful of urban and regional food plans have been supplemented by a detailed system of progress metrics and performance indicators and many have deferred their development to food policy councils yet to be established or subsequent phases in the policymaking process. For comprehensive food system plans, which are inherently long-term in scope, this is a perilous omission. The general lack of legally binding provisions that can ensure that such plans would be followed through by multiple administrations and endure political shifts has also put them jeopardy in many instances. In addition, not engaging mainstream players like supermarkets and institutional catering companies in the system, having little clarity on how other interested government departments would collaborate toward the execution of such comprehensive food system plans, and typically being granted only limited staff and budgets have often clashed with their ambitious goals and expectations.

On the other hand, independently from their actual implementation, pioneer local food system plans have changed many of the entrenched Global North narratives about food as a perfectly working system in no need of public intervention. They have inspired other municipalities to take the lead and start thinking about creative ways in which cities can make the food system work in the public interest, improving the well-being of people, in cities and in rural communities, and the environment, from vacant lots to entire watersheds. Accelerating imitation and replication processes have manifested also in the domain of project-oriented novelties. Nonprofit and commercial rooftop farms, as well as greenhouses atop public housing projects and supermarkets, are some of the design hybrids that have proved successful enough to be transplanted to new sites run by the same organizations or to entirely new institutional settings. The locational patterns of some of the elite fresh food retailers, like Wholefoods, are also being reconsidered to include less affluent neighborhoods. The same goes for urban farmers markets networks, which in many North American cities are now stretching to reach underserved communities on the margins of the mainstream food system, thus catering to a share of the urban population that goes beyond the popular core of upper-class locavores.

Some of the major hurdles still stifling the progress of urban agriculture innovations, and thus hampering the overall stability of the niche, are precarious land tenure arrangements and insufficient recognition of such practices and their benefits to urban sustainability in mainstream urban planning and decision-making processes. Rezoning that affects community access to fresh food outlets is also rarely the subject of formal public deliberations. Excessive regulation and normative restrictions at multiple levels are instead the major concerns voiced by advocates and planners of innovative agri-urban developments, trying to put their bold visions for new urban communities designed through the lens of food into practice.

While regulations are often changed by precedent-setting disruptive practices, like seeding a green roof or slaughtering a chicken in the street, equally promising tactics that have proved critical in securing funding for urban food growing and small-scale regional farming are reframing the role that such projects can play in contributing to the implementation of mainstream policy objectives (e.g., public health; flood protection; air, water, and soil quality; and education) and forging smart linkages between typically compartmentalized problems (e.g., community food security and rural development). The development of broad coalitions between governmental and nongovernmental, or quasi-governmental, partners is vital, but getting the attention of top leaders at the national level of government is equally decisive, as the endorsement of urban gardening by First Lady Michelle Obama in the US and Queen Elizabeth II in the UK have proven.

Indeed, to effectively mature and stabilize, nascent niches necessitate the protection and support of social networks that are both broad and deep, that is, with the capacity to exert large-scale influence through few strategic decisions. Yet, at the same time, to secure this financial and institutional support for a sufficiently prolonged period, niche actors need to continue to deliver convincing results and find compelling ways to illustrate the merits of their unconventional solutions. On the other hand, to make the urban food planning niche more convincing and robust, institutions, in and outside of government, will have to find ways to learn from these pilot experiments and put ancillary physical, financial, and informational infrastructures in place to provide a safe space for further experimentation.

Organizational

Devising a local food system plan or strategy, or any intervention aimed at producing a systemic food system change for that matter, warrants a markedly interdisciplinary, cross-sectoral intellectual effort. Institutional spaces that can be conducive to emergent policymaking practices and productively engage food system experts, elected officials, and community members in the process are therefore pivotal for the advancement of any form of urban food planning endeavor. In addition, while university food system planning courses and dedicated planning curricula are still in their initial stages of development, it is key to establish who the interim food system planners are and what technical and analytical skills they consider vital for effectively getting food system policy and planning work done. When thinking of sustainability transitions, we are often tempted to think in terms of innovative projects, yet the organizational scaffolding that makes such innovations possible is as important. Making the effort to look back and take stock of the myriad of novel organizational spaces and the experience of pioneer food system planning practitioners, who have propelled food policy at the local scale in the past few decades, is therefore essential and is the kind of learning practice that would enable urban food planning, as a niche for social innovation, to get a better grip on what is needed for its stabilization and help it transition to a position in which regime change is within reach.

What emerged from the exploration of this domain of urban food planning is the striking diffusion of one specific organizational innovation, the food policy council, across North America and now in the workings in different cities across Western Europe and Australia. While the extent of diffusion of food policy councils may, at first sight, suggest that they have emerged as some sort of dominant design to follow in the creation of new food governance spaces at the local scale, the reality is that there is no single model for the successful food policy council to follow as yet. Food policy councils greatly vary in their institutional affiliation, scale, funding sources, and focus. They can be entirely part of nongovernmental groups, be sited within government departments, or work through hybrid organizational arrangements between governmental and nongovernmental institutions. Food policy councils can moreover operate at the city, county, state, or regional levels of government and receive support either from private philanthropic organizations or from government agencies. In terms of their organizational and decision-making structure, some food policy councils can have specialized subcommittees, while others can work as one single research and development unit. Food policy councils also greatly vary in their primary focus and missions – some, for instance, focus on direct actions to tackle community and regional food insecurity, while others opt for research and advocacy as a means for policy change.

Besides the food policy council, which in some instances can be disguised as a food board, office of the food policy director, or a food partnership, a wide array of other forms of institutional cooperation around food system change have also begun to assemble (Figure 8.4). Municipal interdepartmental teams working on food system issues from different sectoral planning perspectives (e.g., the Seattle IDT) are one original novelty in this respect and so are the burgeoning intercity coalitions being formed at national and international scales (e.g., the Food Policy Task Force of the US Conference of Mayors, the Sustainable Food Cities Network in the UK, the International Urban Food Network in France, the coalition of cities signees of the Milan Urban Food Policy Pact). Interdisciplinary groups of urban food systems scholars and practitioners hosted within professional and scholarly planning associations (e.g., the Food Interest Group of the American Planning Association, the Sustainable Food Planning group of the Association of European Schools of Planning) also constitute a key novelty in the mosaic of new political spaces for urban food planning that have emerged at the local level.

While community and regional planners may seem distant from grassroots food system innovations, those of them becoming part of these emergent food policy networks and organizations have been playing an important role in normalizing the understanding that food is an urban matter and is part of the responsibilities of local administrations, who in any case have always affected local and regional food systems with their decisions. Some of them have been important mentors in the establishment of new food policy councils (e.g., Kevin Morgan for the Bristol Food Policy Council and Arnold van der Valk for the emerging Amsterdam Food Policy Council) and substantial contributors to the advancement of existing ones (e.g., Kameshwari Pothukuchi for the Detroit Food Policy Council, Martin Bailkey for the Madison Food Policy Council, Branden Born for the Puget Sound Regional Food Policy Council, Wendy Mendes for the Vancouver Food Policy Council).

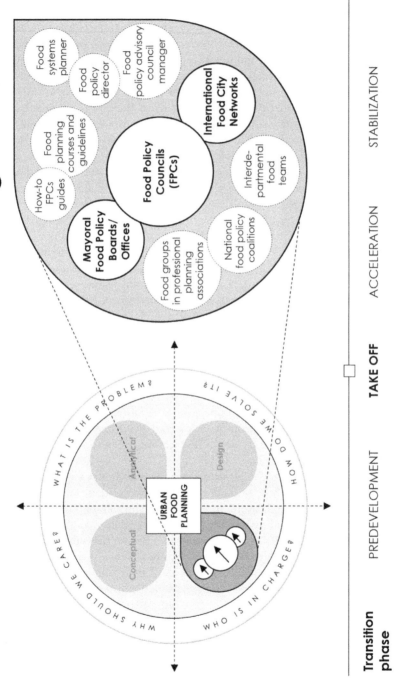

Organizational

- Food systems planner
- Food policy director
- Food policy advisory council manager
- How-to FPCs guides
- Food planning courses and guidelines
- **Mayoral Food Policy Boards / Offices**
- **Food Policy Councils (FPCs)**
- **International Food City Networks**
- Food groups in professional planning associations
- National food policy coalitions
- Inter-departmental food teams

WHAT IS THE PROBLEM?

HOW DO WE SOLVE IT?

Analytical

Design

URBAN FOOD PLANNING

Conceptual

WHY SHOULD WE CARE?

WHO IS IN CHARGE?

Transition phase	PREDEVELOPMENT	TAKE OFF	ACCELERATION	STABILIZATION

Figure 8.4 A snapshot of emerging novelties in the bundle of organizational urban food planning practices.

Source: The author.

Others have been instrumental to the launching of path-breaking munici-pal and community food system initiatives such as farmers markets (e.g., Barry Benepe, who initiated the Greenmarkets in New York City), community food system assessments (e.g., Robert Gottlieb and his students from UCLA's Graduate School of Architecture and Urban Planning in Los Angeles), urban food strategies (e.g., Pim Vermeulen who spearheaded the Amsterdam Food Strategy), and innovative urban food growing projects (e.g., the late professor Jerome Kaufman who was mentor of Will Allen in the predevelopment stages of his award-winning urban agriculture startup Growing Power in Milwau-kee, Wisconsin). Recent surveys in the US (Raja, 2015), however, have con-firmed that, for the time being, these experiences are still positive outliers in an urban planning regime largely unconcerned with food system issues. As isolated as these novelties may be, they point to a key untapped organizational resource for the budding niche of urban food planning – planners, with their holistic perspective and analytical and communicative skills, are uniquely positioned to ignite large-scale food system change through strategic small-scale actions.

As urban food planning continues to evolve as a domain of local food sys-tems research, activism, and transformation, providing credible justifications for the existence and expansion of institutional spaces where urban food plan-ning practices can actually be carried out will continue to be decisive. A major challenge is the impossibility to assess their efficacy with respect to their stated goals since the majority have been around for just few years; in fact, one could say that they are successful just by managing to stay in existence. The overwhelming majority are located outside of government agencies and, not-withstanding the greater independence and critical liberty this position grants them, it also puts them in a very precarious position. An additional challenge is the paucity of research able to demonstrate the value they add to providing a more democratic alternative to mainstream decision-making processes about the local food system. As with any other form of organization, a food policy council per se may not necessarily be a guaranty for a more inclusive and par-ticipatory urban food planning practice.

Yet, from the vantage point of sociotechnical transitions, these experimental food planning offices – no matter whether in or outside government, stand-alone or interdepartmental – are vital incubation rooms for local food system innovations, in which unforeseen combinations between problems and solu-tions are discovered and unconventional solutions tested. The recent emer-gence of second-generation practices, as the annual monitoring of the network of existing food policy councils (Center for a Livable Future, 2015; Harper, Alkon, Shattuck, Holt-Giménez, & Lambrick, 2009; Scherb, Palmer, Frat-taroli, & Pollack, 2012) and the release of how-to guidelines (e.g., Burgan & Winne, 2012) to aid the development of prospective ones, testify their growing recognition and appeal at a time when no municipal department of food exists as yet, though coordinating figures like director of food policy (e.g., New York City, Baltimore, Boston), director of food systems (e.g., San Francisco), food policy advisor (e.g., Seattle), food policy advisory council manager (e.g., Phila-delphia) and food access planner (e.g., Baltimore) are already being appointed to oversee many of the responsibilities that an urban department of food would have had to take on.

Finally, who the food systems planners are is still a matter of dispute. Observ-ers are divided between all-encompassing definitions and the need to put a robust educational system in place to prepare the next generation of experts in the field. Some pioneering food system planners, "under cover" in various city departments, feel that the label could limit the scope of their work, while others emphasize that there is no need to go to a planning school to be a food systems planner (FIG, 2015). Thanks to the host of new institutional interstices for urban food policy and design practices in government, university, and businesses, the idea of serving as a food systems planner is however turning from an exotic oddity to a plausible job opportunity. Independently from their formal training or affiliation, strengthening food systems planners' working knowledge of the system – from family farmers struggling to stay in business to urbanites coping with poor access to healthy and affordable food options – is one of the basic prerequisites to transition urban food planning from a quirky niche to routine practice.

What's the plan for urban food planning?

The purposeful transition of complex sociotechnical systems like the food sys-tem involves transitioning both the social practices and physical infrastructures that constitute them and, thus, requires the concerted effort of providers, inter-mediaries, regulators, and end users in the system to pursue it. Transition man-agement scholars emphasize the importance of visioning practices to achieve a dynamic consensus on such long-term goals, whereby the different social groups having interest in the transition co-create a shared "basket of images" of the desired future state of the system and work backwards to achieve it through the development of strategic niches for innovation (Loorbach & Rot-mans, 2006). So what is the shared basket of images, or "the plan," we have for urban food planning as an interdisciplinary, sustainability-oriented field of theory and practice?

To evolve into a credible problem solver in the eyes of both grassroots inno-vators and the dominant regime, urban food planning is in need of more robust conceptual, analytical, design, and organizational capabilities and a clearer vision for the course of its transition from a niche to a ubiquitous prac-tice. Each practitioner in the bundle of urban food planning practices possesses distinct strengths and competitive advantages to advance the sustainable food system agenda. Beginning to map and recognize such strengths, alongside the obvious limitations of working in a niche, is a task in need of timely research. This final section of the book sketches the contours of such map by highlight-ing some of the unique practices that scholars, government officials, private sector practitioners, and activists have already engaged or are in the process of engaging with, thereby advancing the urban food planning agenda from their own position of strength. Of course, these affiliations are only indicative and a single person can be part of more than one group of practitioners.

Scholars

Scholars in the fields of planning and geography, and in the social, design, and environmental sciences more broadly, can greatly contribute to the development of compelling representations of the urban food system as a distinct space for research, design, and public policy and make visible socioecological interdependencies hitherto concealed by the schism between urban and rural development disciplines. Researchers versed in geospatial analysis techniques could help create more inclusive repositories of urban and regional food system data, making visible, for instance, the way public health, environmental, economic, and demographic features are distributed across city-regions and overlap in space and time to create thriving or dysfunctional urban food environments. Social scientists in the fields of technology and sustainability transitions can, for example, take a historiographic approach to represent the food system and uncover the way past sociotechnical transitions have unfolded and conditioned the development of a distinct food system regime and patterns of urban development in a particular urban region.

Scientists apt in case study, ethnographic, or action research methods can help unmask the multiple ways in which local administrations are already shaping the urban, periurban and rural tracts of the agrifood system. Agroecologists, geospatial analysts, and urban planners can partner to assess different scenarios for the partial re-regionalization of the urban foodshed – both in terms of local food procurement and organic waste recycling – and expose the merits, limits, and overall trade-offs that each one entails. Transportation planning experts can help map current and prospective food distribution networks in the region and advise meaningful ways to augment existing infrastructure to accommodate local food hubs and processing facilities, while taking into consideration the communities disproportionately affected by urban food traffic and related air pollution. Compiling robust sets of metrics and indicators that can help policymakers and the general public grasp the benefits of urban agriculture and its related practices, like environmental education, community empowerment, and composting, is an area of research to which scholars from a wide array of disciplinary backgrounds can contribute to advancing. Creating permanent systems and structures for the gathering and updating of the related data – similar to the observatories for farmland consumption or, more recently, for the activity of North American food policy councils for instance – is another compartment of the urban food planning toolbox that universities and their research centers can help develop.

As food is gaining political saliency in the city, local administrations are increasingly pondering whether a food policy council is a good way to jumpstart their food policy work, and, if so, what kind of food policy council would be most appropriate to establish or join. There is a growing need for research in this area, and experts in the field of organizational studies can be resourceful allies to food systems scholars in filling the knowledge gap and increase learning capacity of the niche. Scholars working and teaching in the fields of design – from architecture and interior design to landscape architecture and urbanism – can advance seminal research in urban food planning by investigating the different ways in which local food infrastructure can be physically integrated into the built environment. There are technical, financial, and regulatory challenges that need to be overcome, and engaging in specific community-centered pilot projects is key to begin to creatively tackle them. In addition, constructive criticism on which attributes any "localized" component, or set of relationships, of the food system ought to have, in order to be environmentally sound and equitable is an important contribution that academics are well suited to provide.

Finally, as we already saw, action-oriented scholarship can be conducive to the development of different grassroots novelties in the organizational dimension of the urban food system. Providing mentorship to municipal food policy taskforces, community-based food partnerships, and student coalitions for sustainable food on campus (e.g., the Real Food Challenge in the US) is an important role that faculty members in North American and Western European universities have already begun to play. Even more important, scholars have a decisive role to play as educators of the next generation of food systems planners. Considering ways in which a food system perspective can be integrated into existing university courses in urban planning and related disciplines or be the central topic of new ones is an essential first step. There are already surveys of food system planning courses offered in universities across the US, shared online by the budding community of urban food planning academics. Scholars in different countries can build on these emerging knowledge-exchange platforms and replicate or expand them to share experience on course design and pedagogy approaches that could help faculty in different parts of the world develop engaging seminars, lectures, and design studios on the topic.

Government officials

While one of the principle sources of power of niche actors, compared to actors in mainstream sociotechnical regimes, are their networking capabilities (Grin, 2010), enlightened government officials, sympathetic with or even part of niche innovations on the margins of the regime, enjoy some dispositional powers as well and therefore have the ability to change at least part of the rules of the game. This puts them into a strategic position to identify and remove regulatory barriers that stifle grassroots innovations and entrepreneurship in the urban food system, with the caveat that these changes need to be politically desirable. In fact, one of the key tasks in front of government officials willing to pioneer sustainable food system goals through public policy is to develop a credible argument about why planning for the food system should be the responsibility of local government.

Evidence provided by nongovernmental organizations and scholarly research is surely helpful to this end, but equally important are the internal links to existing government programs and objectives that elected officials can make to justify support for alternative urban food infrastructure. Municipal plans for sustainable development, affordable housing, green infrastructure, transportation, and climate resiliency and environmental protection are all potential entry points for engaging with food systems planning in the public domain. Making connections to overarching sustainability frameworks as the United Nations' Sustainable Development Goals or the Milan Urban Food Policy Pact, and the commitments made by cities in it constitutes an additional opportunity to frame food system issues as an obvious and necessary area of policymaking at the local level.

Government officials in municipal land-use planning, economic development, and public health departments can play a key role in enabling emergent novelties in the urban food system by revising legislation and improving the available services and information to those involved. Providing citywide data about vacant lots, quality of the soil, ways to procure tools and materials (seeds, soil, water, construction materials), finance programs for the conversion of vacant land and flat roofs into urban gardens, and consider legislation that could secure perpetual land tenure for urban and periurban gardeners and farmers are just a handful of the ways in which local governments can begin to engage with the urban food system. Reconsidering the way new urban development and buildings projects are regulated and enabling them to incorporate local food infrastructures in a holistic fashion throughout the design process is an additional critical area of intervention to which city planners and other government officials can positively contribute.

Urban agriculture is not the only way local governments can normalize the notion of fresh food sources as an urban amenity. They can use their land use competencies and deploy zoning incentives in underserved areas to confront so-called "supermarket urbanism" and the uneven distribution of chain stores across the city. They can also use their food procurement budgets to redirect significant portions of food supply and connect to urban and regional food producers. Besides the advancement of targeted policies, incentives, and grant programs, considering how a food systems perspective can be built into current planning processes and institutionalized review procedures (e.g., environmental quality review, land use review) can be a considerable step forward in the stabilization of food planning competencies at the municipal level of public policy.

The effective development of urban food governance and planning capacities within government institutions is tightly related to the availability of stable spaces for cross-sectoral and interdepartmental collaboration. In advocating for the development of formal or informal groups of this kind, government officials can provide much-needed room for testing food system planning processes in the statutory domain. Such collaborative spaces and collectives can be the prelude to the development of comprehensive food system reports and strategies or the spearheading of focused pilot projects – from rooftop farming in public housing, to farmers markets incentives for citizens with limited financial means, to composting. Perhaps, even more important, they can incite mayors to devise administration-wide directives laying out the specific roles and responsibilities that each city agency and department has in advancing urban food system goals.

Private sector practitioners

Practitioners in the private sector – from product and urban designers to entrepreneurs setting up new farming, community supported agriculture, or food waste prevention and recycling startups – represent a growing share of the innovators working to transition the urban food system to a more hybrid and place-based regime. These professionals can play a vital role in prototyping and testing new city-food and urban-rural relationships through the redesign of the everyday places and services people use at work, in their leisure time, while commuting, or at home. The work of this group of unconventional design and social businesses can uncover new opportunities to close disrupted organic cycles and reshape urban metabolism through the objects and tools we use to interact with or get rid of organic matter in the city. Their successful and failed experiments can point at what projects work where and why and provide clues into what it would take to scale them up or replicate them elsewhere.

Examples of specific areas of intervention include providing technical support for the redesign of vacant lots, rooftops, and front yards into urban farms and gardens; the creative restoration of old urban food markets and a reintroduction of their original function; the repurposing of old industrial buildings for kitchen incubators that serve as nurseries for creative urban food startups; and the design of new regional food processing facilities and food hubs that could help network and centralize the distribution of produce from independent small-scale farms. The connection of different isolated elements of the emergent public local food infrastructure – community gardens, community farms, community supported agriculture drop-off sites, farmers markets, and community-based compost processing facilities – through continuous productive landscapes corridors throughout the city and from the city to the countryside is yet another design challenge that could substantially increase the social and ecological connectivity of the emergent urban layer of the food system.

Apart from advancing original technical solutions to the integration of local food infrastructure into existing and newly built urban areas, private sector practitioners, particularly those who have chosen this as the primary area of their activity, can provide important insights into the business and organizational models necessary to make it financially viable. In cities, some entrepreneurs have already come up with sophisticated management schemes, whereby design services at different scales are offered next to implementation, farming, maintenance, and short supply distribution services, thus providing multiple options for income to the company. In regions, small-scale organic farmers who have decided to diversify their operations and include agri-tourism, educational activities for schools and adults, pick-your-own operations, and direct sale services can equally provide invaluable first-hand knowledge to other farmers considering to reorient their business and inform government programs, at the regional and national level, on the most effective ways to facilitate this specific kind of multifunctional agricultural enterprises.

Activists

Just as food advocates and environmentalists have been at the forefront of local food systems change for over four decades, their work had in fact laid the groundwork for the emergent engagement of urban planners, architects, designers, and other traditionally urban-oriented professions, with the food system and its challenges. While historically separated, even antagonistic, these two movements are now beginning to come together under the auspices of a shared urban food planning and policy agenda. Sustainable food advocates in nongovernmental organizations working at the frontier of this nascent, more inclusive urban movement are in a unique position to make strategic linkages between the solutions of problems that governments tend to deal with in a compartmentalized manner.

By working outside of the sectoral scaffolding of statutory planning processes, civil society collectives – like sustainable food partnerships, food policy councils, and community food security coalitions – have proved that they and their members can play a key role in creating new organizational and political spaces where the different parties of the city-regional food system can come together to design shared strategies and tackle seemingly unrelated challenges in tandem – those seeking to alleviate hunger collaborate with commercial food establishments throwing away uneaten meals or unpurchased produce, those having an expertise in green roof development partner with owners of flat-roofed buildings, and those running community-centered composting, farmers markets, and kitchen incubators reach out to unemployed youth and women. In fact, a great value that people working in these emergent political spaces have for advancing the seeds of transition of urban food planning is their rewiring of small but strategic segments of the urban foodshed. Notwithstanding their limited resources and staff, the collaborative spaces that urban food activists create and maintain serve as social networking hubs resulting not only in greater opportunities for innovation, but also the alignment and stabilization of extant novelties.

Advancing qualitative and quantitative data collection and community food mapping projects is another strategic role that just and sustainable food activists play and which is essential in restoring cities' capabilities to see themselves through a food system lens. In a way, these new spaces for urban food governance serve as Geddesian "Outlook Towers" engaging the public to observe the places they inhabit and take for granted through a new, coevolutionary perspective and become themselves citizen scientists, making visible the major dysfunctions and emergent grassroots solutions in their communities. But it is not just data collection and analytical practices that civil society organizations have an important role to play in. They can offer innovative educational programs and help form the next generation of urban food entrepreneurs, farmers, farmers market managers, and master composters. In addition, based on their firsthand experience, they can devise pragmatic how-to guidelines for setting up a variety of urban food system novelties – from food policy councils to youth farmers markets, school farms, and community composting operations – and thus further support the replication of and dissemination of lessons learned to the broader community of practitioners in their country and abroad.

Besides through their outstanding networking, civic engagement, and action-oriented tutoring record, local food activists, with their often disruptive practices – from unregulated food growing projects on rooftops and parking lots to slaughtering a chicken on the sidewalk – are in the unique position to set precedents, shake the dominant sociotechnical regime, and possibly bring about change in urban laws and regulations that play a non-negligible role in shaping the city food system. Thought-provoking and even shocking art installations in public spaces can also have an influential effect on public perception and start challenging entrenched understandings and conventions. The caveat of disruptive practices is that they work as niches for innovation as long as they are not an expression of a purely destructive (rather than constructive) criticism of the dominant system. It is not the not-in-my-backyard, reactionary attitude that helps transitions progress, but the fact that niche actors believe and act like they are part of the solution.

Concluding remarks

One of the biggest challenges in trying to grasp a transition process in its early stages of development is that the speed of change is such that by the time one takes a snapshot of a fragment of the system, the entire landscape has already changed – some novelties have died out, others have moved on, and new ones have emerged. This can be frustrating for the investigator, let alone the planner or the policymaker, seeking to legitimize their research, long-term plans, or policy proposals. Yet, as Martin Bailkey – pioneer food systems planner based in Madison, Wisconsin – recently put it (Campbell, 2015), not being able to keep up with the pace of innovation is "a good challenge to have." Throughout this book, we navigated the vastly heterogeneous and amorphous domain of urban food planning novelties and tried to construe it through the lens of transition theories. What emerged from the partial mosaic we pieced together along the way is a niche of innovative practices still oscillating between the predevelopment and the take-off phases along the transition pathway. This is indicative of an instability due to the differential advancement of its different subdomains of practice and a need of further alignment and coordination of ongoing efforts to justify, represent, and re-envision the city as a locus for food system transitions.

This last chapter highlighted some of the strategic roles that different food system makers can play to facilitate the normalization of urban food planning practices. These, of course, were just hints without any pretention of comprehensiveness or ambition to provide any definitive prescriptions. To craft a robust research and practice agenda – or a cohesive plan for urban food planning as we referred to it in this chapter – requires a concerted effort and deliberation between the different interest groups and practitioners making up the family of budding food system planners and the leveraging of intellectual and organizational powers of the institutional networks they are part of. The signing of the Milan Urban Food Policy Pact was an important step in the right direction, but there are many more left to make. There is already a soft organizational infrastructure in place made of annual conferences, academic journals, university courses, working groups in professional associations, and a small cohort of government-based food policy councils, which are all providing a fertile terrain for expanding the niche and moving it to the next stage of transition. Yet, to do so, a more vigorous specialization and production of a generalized knowledge that goes beyond the contingent lessons learned from single practices (Geels & Deuten, 2006) is needed.

In this book, we looked at emergent urban food planning novelties in cities in the Global North, or developed economies more broadly, but there is much to be learned from cities in emerging economies as well and the host of creative shortcuts in the mainstream food system they have been successful in making. Pilot projects of the Food and Agriculture Organization of the United Nations (FAO), the Resource Centres on Urban Agriculture and Food Security (RUAF), and the International Council for Local Environmental Initiatives (ICLEI) are already beginning to create important bridges for knowledge exchange. Such opportunities need to be expanded alongside in-depth research in industrialized nations, and it is imperative that we acknowledge that the normalization of urban food planning is a global journey, not a single city's destination. Looking back to the advancements made over the past two decades, there are many reasons to be optimistic, but a lot of work has yet to be done. We will often have to make the road as we go and many uncertainties lie ahead, but one thing is certain – the journey is going to be full of opportunities to create a better urban future and truly nourishing urban food systems, and it is a journey that has just begun.

References

Ackerman, K., Conard, M., Culligan, P., Plunz, R., Sutto, M. P., & Whittinghill, L. (2014). Sustainable food systems for future cities: The potential of urban agriculture. *Economic and Social Review, 45*(2), 189–206.

Barthel, S., Folke, C., & Colding, J. (2010). Social–ecological memory in urban gardens – Retaining the capacity for management of ecosystem services. *Global Environmental Change, 20*(2), 255–265.

Barthel, S., Parker, J., & Ernstson, H. (2015). Food and green space in cities: A resilience lens on gardens and urban environmental movements. *Urban Studies, 52*(7), 1321–1338.

Blanchard, T. C., & Matthews, T. L. (2007). Retail Concentration, Food Deserts, and Food-Disadvantaged Communities in Rural America. In C. C. Hinrichs & T. A. Lyson (Eds.), *Remaking the North American Food System: Strategies for Sustainability (Our Sustainable Future)*. Lincoln, NE: University of Nebraska Press, 201–215.

Burgan, M., & Winne, M. (2012). *Doing Food Policy Councils Right: A Guide to Development and Action.* Retrieved from www.markwinne.com/wp-content/uploads/2012/09/FPC-manual.pdf

Campbell, M. C. (2015). Faces of Food Systems Planning: Martin Bailkey. Retrieved December 7, 2015, from https://apafig.wordpress.com/category/interview/page/2/

Center for a Livable Future. (2015). Food Policy Council Directory, 2015 Update. [PowerPoint slides]. Retrieved November 12, 2015, from https://assets.jhsph.edu/clf/mod_clfResource/doc/FPC_Trends_Slides_2015_10_28.pdf

Cohen, B., Andrews, M., & Kantor, L. S. (2002). *Community Food Security Assessment Toolkit.* Washington, DC: USDA Economic Research Service.

Cohen, N. (2009). Designing the sustainable foodshed: A cross-disciplinary undergraduate environmental studies course. *Innovative Higher Education, 35*(1), 51–60.

Cohen, N. (2011). How great cities are fed revisited: Ten municipal policies to support the New York City foodshed. *Fordham Environmental Law Review, 22*(3), 691–710.

Cohen, N., Reynolds, K., & Sanghvi, R. (2012). *Five Borough Farm: Seeding the Future of Urban Agriculture in New York City.* New York: Design Trust for Public Space.

Colasanti, K., & Hamm, M. (2010). Assessing the local food supply capacity of Detroit, Michigan. *Journal of Agriculture, Food Systems, and Community Development, 1*(2), 41–58.

Coviello, F., Graglia, A., & Villa, D. (2009). *Produrre e Scambiare Valore Territoriale.* (G. Ferraresi, Ed.). Firenze: Alinea.

Darrot, C. (2012). *Rennes Ville Vivriere: Scenarios of Food Autonomy for Rennes Metropole (France)* [PDF document]. Retreived from www.reseaurural.fr/files/catherine_darrot_rennes_metropole_ville_vivriere_0.pdf

de la Salle, J., & Holland, M. (2010). *Agricultural Urbanism: Handbook for Building Sustainable Food & Agricultural Systems in 21st Century Cities.* Winnipeg: Green Frigate Books.

Donofrio, G. A. (2007). Feeding the city. *Gastronomica, 7*(4), 30–41.

Donovan, J., Larsen, K., & McWhinnie, J. (2011). *Food-Sensitive Planning and Urban Design: A Conceptual Framework for Achieving a Sustainable and Healthy Food System.* Melbourne: National Heart Foundation of Australia.

Drake, L., & Lawson, L. J. (2014). Validating verdancy or vacancy? The relationship of community gardens and vacant lands in the U.S. *Cities, 40*, 133–142.

Duany, A., & DPZ. (2012). *Garden Cities: Theory & Practice of Agrarian Urbanism* (2nd ed.). London: The Prince's Foundation for the Built Environment.

Eckert, J., & Shetty, S. (2011). Food systems, planning and quantifying access: Using GIS to plan for food retail. *Applied Geography, 31*(4), 1216–1223.

Farming Concrete. (2015). Data Collection Toolkit. Retrieved September 23, 2015, from https://farmingconcrete.org/toolkit/

Ferrario, V. (2009). Agropolitana. Dispersed City and Agricultural Spaces in Veneto Region (Italy). In L. Qu, C. Yang, X. Hui, & D. Sepúlveda (Eds.), *The 4th International Conference of the International Forum on Urbanism (IFoU)* (pp. 637–646). Amsterdam-Delft: IFoU.

Ferrario, V. (2011). Governare i territori della dispersione. Il ruolo dello spazio agrario. In A. Migliaccio & M. Mininni (Eds.), *XIV Conferenza SIU Abitare l'Italia. Territori, Economie, Diseguaglianze – Atelier 4 Sostenibilità Ambientale*. Rome, Italy: Planum.

Food Interest Group (FIG). (2015). *Faces of Food Systems Planning*. Retrieved from https:// apafig.wordpress.com/

Frank, L., Glanz, K., Mccarron, M., Sallis, J., Saelens, B., & Chapman, J. (2006). The spatial distribution of food outlet type and quality around schools in differing built environment and demographic contexts. *Berkeley Planning Journal, 19*, 79–95.

Freedgood, J., Pierce-Quiñonez, M., & Meter, K. (2011). Emerging assessment tools to inform food system planning. *Journal of Agriculture, Food Systems, and Community Development, 2*(1), 83–104.

Geels, F. W. (2002). Technological transitions as evolutionary reconfiguration processes: A multi-level perspective and a case-study. *Research Policy, 31*(8–9), 1257–1274.

Geels, F. W., & Deuten, J. J. (2006). Local and global dynamics in technological development: A socio-cognitive perspective on knowledge flows and lessons from reinforced concrete. *Science and Public Policy, 33*(4), 265–275.

Getz, A. (1991). Urban foodsheds. *Permaculture Activist, 7*(3), 26–27.

Gittleman, M., Jordan, K., & Brelsford, E. (2012). Using citizen science to quantify community garden crop yields. *Cities and the Environment (CATE), 5*(1), 1–14.

Grewal, S. S., & Grewal, P. S. (2012). Can cities become self-reliant in food? *Cities, 29*(1), 1–11.

Grin, J. (2010). Modernization as Multilevel Dynamics: Lessons from Dutch Agriculture. In J. Grin, J. Rotmans, & J. Schot (Eds.), *Transitions to Sustainable Development: New Directions in the Study of Long Term Transformative Change* (pp. 285–314). New York-Abingdon: Routledge.

Harper, A., Alkon, A., Shattuck, A., Holt-Giménez, E., & Lambrick, F. (2009). *Food Policy Councils: Lessons Learned*. Development Report No. 21. Oakland, CA: Food First.

Hegger, D. L., Van Vliet, J., & Van Vliet, B. J. (2007). Niche management and its contribution to regime change: The case of innovation in sanitation. *Technology Analysis & Strategic Management, 19*(6), 729–746.

Hopkins, R., Thurstain-Goodwin, M., & Fairlie, S. (2009). Can Totnes and District feed itself? Exploring the practicalities of food relocalisation. Retrieved from transitionculture.org/wp-content/uploads/cantotnesfeeditself1.pdf.

Jansma, J. E., & Visser, A. J. (2011). Agromere: Integrating urban agriculture in the development of the city of Almere. *Urban Agriculture Magazine, 25*, 28–31.

Johansson, S. (2008). The Swedish Foodshed: Re-imagining Our Support Area. In C. Farnworth, J. Jiggins, & E. V. Thomas (Eds.), *Creating Food Futures: Trade, Ethics and the Environment* (pp. 55–78). Hampshire: Gower Publishing, Ltd.

Kemp, R., Schot, J., & Hoogma, R. (1998). Regime shifts to sustainability through processes of niche formation: The approach of strategic niche management. *Technology Analysis & Strategic Management, 10*(2), 175–195.

Kirwan, J., Ilbery, B., Maye, D., & Carey, J. (2013). Grassroots social innovations and food localisation: An investigation of the local food programme in England. *Global Environmental Change, 23*(5), 830–837.

Kloppenburg, J., Hendrickson, J., & Stevenson, G. W. (1996). Coming in to the foodshed. *Agriculture and Human Values, 13*(3), 33–42.

Kremer, P., & DeLiberty, T. L. (2011). Local food practices and growing potential: Mapping the case of Philadelphia. *Applied Geography, 31*(4), 1252–1261.

Kremer, P., Hamstead, Z. A., & McPhearson, T. (2013). A social–ecological assessment of vacant lots in New York City. *Landscape and Urban Planning, 120*, 218–233.

Kurita, H., Yokohari, M., & Bolthoise, J. (2008). The potential of intra-regional supply and demand of agricultural products in an urban fringe area: A case study of the Kanto Plain, Japan. *Geografisk Tidsskrift-Danish Journal of, 109*(2), 147–159.

Lang, T., Barling, D., & Caraher, M. (2009). *Food Policy.* Oxford: Oxford University Press.

Larsen, K., & Gilliland, J. (2008). Mapping the evolution of "food deserts" in a Canadian city: Supermarket accessibility in London, Ontario, 1961–2005. *International Journal of Health Geographics, 7*(1), 16.

Larsen, K., & Gilliland, J. (2009). A farmers' market in a food desert: Evaluating impacts on the price and availability of healthy food. *Health & Place, 15*(4), 1158–62.

LeClair, M. S., & Aksan, A.-M. (2014). Redefining the food desert: Combining GIS with direct observation to measure food access. *Agriculture and Human Values, 31*(4), 537–547.

Lim, CJ. (2014). *Food City.* New York, NY: Routledge.

Lister, N. M. (2007). Placing food: Toronto's edible landscape. *FOOD, 47*(3), 150–185.

Loorbach, D., & Rotmans, J. (2006). Managing Transitions for Sustainable Development. In X. Olsthoorn & A. J. Wieczorek (Eds.), *Understanding Industrial Transformation: Views from Different Disciplines* (pp. 187–206). Dordrecht: Springer.

Maas, W., Hackhauf, U., Haikola, P., Kalmeijer, B., & Salij, T. (2009). *Food Print Manhattan.* Rotterdam: The Why Factory.

MacRae, R., Gallant, E., Patel, S., Michalak, M., Bunch, M., & Schaffner, S. (2010). Could Toronto provide 10% of its fresh vegetable requirements from within its own boundaries? Matching consumption requirements with growing spaces. *Journal of Agriculture, Food Systems, and Community Development, 1*(2), 105–127.

Martin, S., Doherty-Chapman, K., Wise, R., Foust, S., Sullivan, R., Seavert, C., & Scolnik, E. (2012). Growing a Sustainable Portland Metropolitan Foodshed. Report produced for the Western Sustainable Agriculture Research and Education, Project SW-143.

McClintock, N., Cooper, J., & Khandeshi, S. (2013). Assessing the potential contribution of vacant land to urban vegetable production and consumption in Oakland, California. *Landscape and Urban Planning, 111,* 46–58.

Mendes, W., Balmer, K., Kaethler, T., & Rhoads, A. (2008). Using land inventories to plan for urban agriculture: Experiences from Portland and Vancouver. *Journal of the American Planning Association, 74*(4), 435–449.

Miazzo, F., & Minkjan, M. (Eds.). (2013). *Farming the City: Food as a Tool for Today's Urbanization.* Amsterdam: Valiz/Trancity.

Monaghan, A. (2009). Conceptual niche management of grassroots innovation for sustainability: The case of body disposal practices in the UK. *Technological Forecasting and Social Change, 76*(8), 1026–1043.

Morgan, K. (2009). Feeding the city: The challenge of urban food planning. *International Planning Studies, 14*(4), 341–348.

Morgan, K. (2013). The rise of urban food planning. *International Planning Studies, 18*(1), 1–4.

Mullinix, K., Henderson, D., Holland, M., De Salle, J., Porter, E., & Fleming, P. (2008). Agricultural Urbanism and Municipal Supported Agriculture: A New Food System Path for Sustainable Cities. Proceedings from the *2008 Surrey Regional Economic Summit* (pp. 1–12), Surrey, BC: Kwantlen Polytechnic University.

Neighbourhoods Green, Capital Growth, & Planning Aid for London. (2014). *Edible Estates: A Good Practice Guide to Food Growing for Social Landlords.* London: National Housing Federation.

O'Brien, J., & Cobb, T. D. (2012). The food policy audit: A new tool for community food system planning. *Journal of Agriculture, Food Systems, and Community Development, 2*(3), 177–192.

Peters, C. J., Bills, N. L., Lembo, A. J., Wilkins, J. L., & Fick, G. W. (2009). Mapping potential foodsheds in New York state: A spatial model for evaluating the capacity to localize food production. *Renewable Agriculture and Food Systems, 24*(1), 72.

Peters, C. J., Bills, N. L., Lembo, A. J., Wilkins, J. L., & Fick, G. W. (2011). Mapping potential foodsheds in New York state by food group: An approach for prioritizing which foods to grow locally. *Renewable Agriculture and Food Systems, 27*(2), 125–137.

Peters, C. J., Bills, N. L., Wilkins, J. L., & Fick, G. W. (2008). Foodshed analysis and its relevance to sustainability. *Renewable Agriculture and Food Systems, 24*(1), 1–7.

Porro, A., Corsi, S., Scudo, G., & Spigarolo, R. (2014). The contribution of Bioregione research project to the development of local sustainable agri-food systems. *Scienze Del Territorio, 2*, 319–326.

Pothukuchi, K. (2004). Community food assessment: A first step in planning for community food security. *Journal of Planning Education and Research, 23*(4), 356–377.

Pothukuchi, K., Joseph, H., Burton, H., & Fisher, A. (2002). *What's Cooking in Your Food System? A Guide to Community Food Assessment.* Venice, CA: Community Food Security Coalition.

Pothukuchi, K., & Kaufman, J. L. (2000). The food system: A stranger to the planning field. *Journal of the American Planning Association, 66*(2), 113–124.

Raja, S. (2015, April 3). Why all cities should have a Department of Food. *The Conversation.* Boston, MA. Retrieved from http://theconversation.com/why-all-cities-should-have-a-department-of-food-39462

Raja, S., Born, B., & Kozlowski Russell, J. (2008). *A Planners Guide to Community and Regional Food Planning.* Chicago: American Planning Association.

Raja, S., Ma, C., & Yadav, P. (2008). Beyond food deserts: Measuring and mapping racial disparities in neighborhood food environments. *Journal of Planning Education and Research, 27*(4), 469–482.

Rotmans, J., Kemp, R., & van Asselt, M. (2001). More evolution than revolution: Transition management in public policy. *Foresight, 3*(1), 15–31.

Sassen, S. (1994). *Cities in a World Economy.* Thousand Oaks, CA-London-New Delhi: Pine Forge Press.

Scherb, A., Palmer, A., Frattaroli, S., & Pollack, K. (2012). Exploring food system policy: A survey of food policy councils in the United States. *Journal of Agriculture, Food Systems, and Community Development, 2*(4), 3–14.

Segal, P. Z. (2015). From open data to open space: Translating public information into collective action. *Cities and the Environment, 8*(2), 1–9.

Seyfang, G., & Smith, A. (2007). Grassroots innovations for sustainable development: Towards a new research and policy agenda. *Environmental Politics, 16*(4), 584–603.

Short, A., Guthman, J., & Raskin, S. (2007). Food deserts, oases, or mirages?: Small markets and community food security in the San Francisco Bay Area. *Journal of Planning Education and Research, 26*(3), 352–364.

Smith, A., & Seyfang, G. (2013). Constructing grassroots innovations for sustainability. *Global Environmental Change, 23*(5), 827–829.

Steel, C. (2009). *Hungry City: How Food Shapes Our Lives.* London: Random House.

Stierand, P. (2008). *Food and the City: The Relevance of the Food System for Urban Development* (original title in German, *Stadt und Lebensmittel: Die Bedeutung des Ernährungssystems für die Stadtentwicklung*) (Doctoral dissertation). Retrieved from Eldorado Database, Technical University of Dortmund (http://hdl.handle.net/2003/25789).

Sustain. (2011). *Good Planning for Good Food: Using Planning Policy for Local and Sustainable Food.* London: Author.

Sustain. (2014). *Planning Sustainable Cities for Community Food Growing: A Guide to Using Planning Policy to Meet Strategic Objectives Through Community Food Growing.* London: Author.

Taylor, J. R., & Lovell, S. T. (2012). Mapping public and private spaces of urban agriculture in Chicago through the analysis of high-resolution aerial images in Google Earth. *Landscape and Urban Planning, 108*(1), 57–70.

Taylor, P., Derudder, B., Saey, P., & Witlox, F. (Eds.). (2007). *Cities in Globalization: Practices, Policies and Theories.* London-New York: Routledge.

Thompson, E. J., Harper, A. M., & Kraus, S. (2008). *Think Globally – Eat Locally: San Francisco Foodshed Assessment.* San Francisco, CA: American Farmland Trust.

TSR Group. (2010). Agriburbia. Retrieved August 15, 2015, from http://www.agriburbia.com/concept.html

Urban Design Lab. (2010). National Integrated Regional Foodshed Model. Retrieved October 12, 2015, from http://urbandesignlab.columbia.edu/projects/food-and-the-urban-environment/national-integrated-regional-foodshed-model/

Urban Design Lab. (2011). NYC Regional Foodshed Initiative. Retrieved October 12, 2015, from http://urbandesignlab.columbia.edu/projects/food-and-the-urban-environment/nyc-regional-food-shed-initiative/

US Green Building Council. (2014). *LEED v4 for Neighborhood Development.* Washington, DC: Author.

van der Ploeg, J. D., Bouma, J., Rip, A., Rijkenberg, F. H. J., Ventura, F., & Wiskerke, J. S. C. (2004). On Regimes, Novelties, Niches and Co-Production. In J. S. C. Wiskerke & J. D. van der Ploeg (Eds.), *Seeds of Transition. Essays on Novelty Production, Niches and Regimes in Agriculture* (pp. 1–30). Assen: Royal Van Gorcum.

van der Schans, J. W. (2010). Urban agriculture in the Netherlands. *Urban Agriculture Magazine, 24*, 40–43.

Verzone, C. (2012). The Food Urbanism Initiative. In A. Viljoen & J. S. C. Wiskerke (Eds.), *Sustainable Food Planning: Evolving Theory and Practice* (pp. 517–531). Wageningen: Wageningen Academic Publishers.

Verzone, C., Bertschinger, L., Huang, J., Dumondel, M., & Woods, C. (2011). Food Urbanism Initiative. Retrieved November 15, 2015, from http://www.foodurbanism.org

Vidal, R. (2009). L'agriurbanisme: Une nouvelle approche professionnelle pour reconstruire les relations entre la ville et l'agriculture. *Innovations Agronomiques, 5*(Mai), 97–106.

Vidal, R. (2014). *L'Agriurbanisme: En 40 pages.* Toulouse: Uppr Editions.

Vidal, R., & Fleury, A. (2008). Agriculture in Urban Planning in Ile-De-France. Retrieved from http://www.agroterritori.org/ficha.php?doc=396&cid=1

Viljoen, A., & Wiskerke, J. S. C. (Eds.). (2012). *Sustainable Food Planning: Evolving Theory and Practice.* Wageningen: Wageningen Academic Publishers.

Vitiello, D., & Brinkley, C. (2014). The hidden history of food system planning. *Journal of Planning History, 13*(2), 91–112.

Widener, M. J., & Li, W. (2014). Using geolocated Twitter data to monitor the prevalence of healthy and unhealthy food references across the US. *Applied Geography, 54*, 189–197.

Winne, M. (2008). *Closing the Food Gap: Resetting the Table in the Land of Plenty.* Boston, MA: Beacon Press.

Wrigley, N., Warm, D., & Margetts, B. (2003). Deprivation, diet, and food-retail access: Findings from the leeds "food deserts" study. *Environment and Planning A, 35*(1), 151–188.

Index

Bold numbers in index refer to tables or figures.

 Taylor & Francis eBooks

Helping you to choose the right eBooks for your Library

Add Routledge titles to your library's digital collection today. Taylor and Francis ebooks contains over 50,000 titles in the Humanities, Social Sciences, Behavioural Sciences, Built Environment and Law.

Choose from a range of subject packages or create your own!

Benefits for you

- » Free MARC records
- » COUNTER-compliant usage statistics
- » Flexible purchase and pricing options
- » All titles DRM-free.

 REQUEST YOUR FREE INSTITUTIONAL TRIAL TODAY

Free Trials Available
We offer free trials to qualifying academic, corporate and government customers.

Benefits for your user

- » Off-site, anytime access via Athens or referring URL
- » Print or copy pages or chapters
- » Full content search
- » Bookmark, highlight and annotate text
- » Access to thousands of pages of quality research at the click of a button.

eCollections – Choose from over 30 subject eCollections, including:

Archaeology	Language Learning
Architecture	Law
Asian Studies	Literature
Business & Management	Media & Communication
Classical Studies	Middle East Studies
Construction	Music
Creative & Media Arts	Philosophy
Criminology & Criminal Justice	Planning
Economics	Politics
Education	Psychology & Mental Health
Energy	Religion
Engineering	Security
English Language & Linguistics	Social Work
Environment & Sustainability	Sociology
Geography	Sport
Health Studies	Theatre & Performance
History	Tourism, Hospitality & Events

For more information, pricing enquiries or to order a free trial, please contact your local sales team:
www.tandfebooks.com/page/sales

 **Routledge** Taylor & Francis Group | The home of Routledge books

www.tandfebooks.com